Asymmetric Cryptography

SCIENCES

Computer Science
Field Directors – Valérie Berthé and Jean-Charles Pomerol

Cryptography, Data Security, Subject Head – Damien Vergnaud

Asymmetric Cryptography

Primitives and Protocols

Coordinated by
David Pointcheval

WILEY

First published 2022 in Great Britain and the United States by ISTE Ltd and John Wiley & Sons, Inc.

ISTE Ltd
27-37 St George's Road
London SW19 4EU
UK

www.iste.co.uk

John Wiley & Sons, Inc.
111 River Street
Hoboken, NJ 07030
USA

www.wiley.com

Library of Congress Control Number: 2022941485

British Library Cataloguing-in-Publication Data
A CIP record for this book is available from the British Library
ISBN 978-1-78945-096-5

ERC code:
PE6 Computer Science and Informatics
  PE6_5 Cryptology, security, privacy, quantum cryptography

Contents

Foreword xi
David POINTCHEVAL

Chapter 1. Public-Key Encryption and Security Notions 1
Nuttapong ATTRAPADUNG and Takahiro MATSUDA

  1.1. Basic definitions for PKE 2
    1.1.1. Basic notation 2
    1.1.2. Public-key encryption 2
    1.1.3. IND-CPA and IND-CCA security 2
    1.1.4. Other basic security notions and relations 4
  1.2. Basic PKE schemes 5
    1.2.1. Game-based proofs 5
    1.2.2. ElGamal encryption 6
    1.2.3. Simplified CS encryption 8
    1.2.4. Cramer–Shoup encryption 11
    1.2.5. Other specific PKE schemes 14
  1.3. Generic constructions for IND-CCA secure PKE 16
    1.3.1. Hybrid encryption 17
    1.3.2. Naor–Yung construction and extensions 19
    1.3.3. Fujisaki-Okamoto and other transforms in the RO model 21
    1.3.4. Other generic constructions for IND-CCA secure PKE 23
  1.4. Advanced topics 25
    1.4.1. Intermediate notions related to CCA 25
    1.4.2. IND-CCA security in multi-user setting and tight security 26
    1.4.3. Key-dependent message security 28
    1.4.4. More topics on PKE 30
  1.5. References 31

Chapter 2. Signatures and Security Notions   47
Marc FISCHLIN

2.1. Signature schemes   47
2.1.1. Definition   47
2.1.2. Examples of practical schemes   49
2.2. Unforgeability   51
2.2.1. Discussion   51
2.2.2. Existential unforgeability under chosen-message attacks   53
2.2.3. Unforgeability of practical schemes   54
2.3. Strong unforgeability   56
2.3.1. Discussion   56
2.3.2. Strong existential unforgeability under chosen-message attacks . .   57
2.3.3. Strong unforgeability of practical schemes   58
2.3.4. Building strongly unforgeable schemes   59
2.4. Summary   60
2.5. References   60

Chapter 3. Zero-Knowledge Proofs   63
Ivan VISCONTI

3.1. Introduction   63
3.2. Notation   64
3.3. Classical zero-knowledge proofs   64
3.3.1. Zero knowledge   65
3.4. How to build a zero-knowledge proof system   68
3.4.1. ZK proofs for all $\mathcal{NP}$ 70
3.4.2. Round complexity   71
3.5. Relaxed security in proof systems   72
3.5.1. Honest-verifier ZK   72
3.5.2. Witness hiding/indistinguishability   73
3.5.3. Σ-Protocols   74
3.6. Non-black-box zero knowledge   75
3.7. Advanced notions   75
3.7.1. Publicly verifiable zero knowledge   76
3.7.2. Concurrent ZK and more   77
3.7.3. ZK with stateless players   78
3.7.4. Delayed-input proof systems   79
3.8. Conclusion   80
3.9. References   80

Chapter 4. Secure Multiparty Computation 85
Yehuda LINDELL

4.1. Introduction 85
    4.1.1. A note on terminology 87
4.2. Security of MPC 87
    4.2.1. The definitional paradigm 87
    4.2.2. Additional definitional parameters 89
    4.2.3. Adversarial power 89
    4.2.4. Modular sequential and concurrent composition 91
    4.2.5. Important definitional implications 92
    4.2.6. The ideal model and using MPC in practice 92
    4.2.7. Any inputs are allowed 92
    4.2.8. MPC secures the process, but not the output 92
4.3. Feasibility of MPC 93
4.4. Techniques 94
    4.4.1. Shamir secret sharing 94
    4.4.2. Honest-majority MPC with secret sharing 95
    4.4.3. Private set intersection 97
    4.4.4. Threshold cryptography 99
    4.4.5. Dishonest-majority MPC 100
    4.4.6. Efficient and practical MPC 100
4.5. MPC use cases 101
    4.5.1. Boston wage gap (Lapets et al. 2018) 101
    4.5.2. Advertising conversion (Ion et al. 2017) 101
    4.5.3. MPC for cryptographic key protection (Unbound Security;
    Sepior; Curv) 101
    4.5.4. Government collaboration (Sharemind) 102
    4.5.5. Privacy-preserving analytics (Duality) 102
4.6. Discussion 102
4.7. References 103

Chapter 5. Pairing-Based Cryptography 107
Olivier BLAZY

5.1. Introduction 108
    5.1.1. Notations 108
    5.1.2. Generalities 108
5.2. One small step for man, one giant leap for cryptography 109
    5.2.1. Opening Pandora's box, demystifying the magic 110
    5.2.2. A new world of assumptions 112
5.3. A new world of cryptographic protocols at your fingertips 116
    5.3.1. Identity-based encryption made easy 117

5.3.2. Efficient deterministic compact signature 118
5.4. References 119

Chapter 6. Broadcast Encryption and Traitor Tracing 121
Duong HIEU PHAN

6.1. Introduction 121
6.2. Security notions for broadcast encryption and TT 123
6.3. Overview of broadcast encryption and TT 125
6.4. Tree-based methods 129
6.5. Code-based TT 132
6.6. Algebraic schemes 135
6.7. Lattice-based approach with post-quantum security 142
6.8. References 143

Chapter 7. Attribute-Based Encryption 151
Romain GAY

7.1. Introduction 151
7.2. Pairing groups 152
7.2.1. Cyclic groups 152
7.2.2. Pairing groups 152
7.3. Predicate encodings 153
7.3.1. Definition 153
7.3.2. Constructions 154
7.4. Attribute-based encryption 156
7.4.1. Definition 156
7.4.2. A modular construction 158
7.5. References 165

Chapter 8. Advanced Signatures 167
Olivier SANDERS

8.1. Introduction 167
8.2. Some constructions 169
8.2.1. The case of scalar messages 169
8.2.2. The case of non-scalar messages 171
8.3. Applications 173
8.3.1. Anonymous credentials 173
8.3.2. Group signatures 176
8.3.3. Direct anonymous attestations 180
8.4. References 184

Chapter 9. Key Exchange 187
Colin BOYD

9.1. Key exchange fundamentals 187
   9.1.1. Key exchange parties 188
   9.1.2. Key exchange messages 189
   9.1.3. Key derivation functions 189
9.2. Unauthenticated key exchange 191
   9.2.1. Formal definitions and security models 191
   9.2.2. Constructions and examples 192
9.3. Authenticated key exchange 194
   9.3.1. Non-interactive key exchange 195
   9.3.2. AKE security models 196
   9.3.3. Constructions and examples 200
9.4. Conclusion 206
9.5. References 207

Chapter 10. Password Authenticated Key Exchange: Protocols and Security Models 213
Stanislaw JARECKI

10.1. Introduction 213
10.2. First PAKE: EKE 215
10.3. Game-based model of PAKE security 218
   10.3.1. The BPR security model 218
   10.3.2. Implicit versus explicit authentication 221
   10.3.3. Limitations of the BPR model 221
   10.3.4. EKE instantiated with Diffie–Hellman KE 223
   10.3.5. Implementing ideal cipher on arbitrary groups 224
10.4. Simulation-based model of PAKE security 225
   10.4.1. The BMP security model 225
   10.4.2. Advantages of BMP definition: arbitrary passwords,
tight security 229
   10.4.3. EKE using RO-derived one-time pad encryption 230
   10.4.4. BMP model for PAKE with explicit authentication
(PAKE-EA) 231
10.5. Universally composable model of PAKE security 232
10.6. PAKE protocols in the standard model 236
10.7. PAKE efficiency optimizations 239
10.8. Asymmetric PAKE: PAKE for the client-server setting 242
10.9. Threshold PAKE 244
10.10. References 246

Chapter 11. Verifiable Computation and Succinct Arguments for NP 257
Dario FIORE

11.1. Introduction 257
11.1.1. Background 258
11.2. Preliminaries 259
11.3. Verifiable computation 260
11.4. Constructing VC 261
11.4.1. VC for circuits in three steps 261
11.4.2. Succinct non-interactive arguments for non-deterministic computation 263
11.4.3. Verifiable computation from SNARG 264
11.5. A modular construction of SNARGs 264
11.5.1. Algebraic non-interactive linear proofs 265
11.5.2. Bilinear groups 267
11.5.3. SNARGs from algebraic NILPs with degree-2 verifiers using bilinear groups 269
11.6. Constructing algebraic NILPs for arithmetic circuits 271
11.6.1. Arithmetic circuits 271
11.6.2. Quadratic arithmetic programs 271
11.6.3. Algebraic NILP for QAPs 274
11.7. Conclusion 279
11.8. References 279

List of Authors 283

Index 285

Foreword

David POINTCHEVAL
CNRS, ENS/PSL, Inria, Paris, France

With the seminal paper by Diffie and Hellman (1976), and the introduction to *public-key cryptography*, a very broad area of research has emerged. Public-key cryptography includes not only the asymmetric variants of encryption and authentication, i.e. public-key encryption and signature schemes, but also many other innovative and impressively powerful tools.

This book aims at presenting the main cryptographic primitives that have been proposed within the last 40 years, with chapters written by famous cryptographers, who are all specialists in the specific domains, with several publications in the main international venues on cryptography. I am very honored they all accepted my invitation to participate and make this book as complete as possible.

This book starts with a presentation of the main primitives of public key cryptography, namely *public-key encryption* and *signatures*, including definitions and security models. This chapter also gives the flavor of the meaning of provable security, explaining what it means when one claims a cryptographic scheme to be secure. In the second chapter we present *zero-knowledge proofs*. This is a quite magical tool that is thereafter used as a building block in many other protocols. Zero-knowledge proofs allow to convince a verifier of the validity of any true statement, without revealing any additional information. In the same vein, *secure multiparty computation* allows two or more players with private inputs to compute the output of a well-defined function on these joint inputs, without revealing anything else than this intended output.

After they were initially used for attacking the discrete logarithm problem on elliptic curves, pairings have extensively been applied to construct new primitives, primarily to propose new types of encryption and signature schemes. Consequently, we first make a general introduction to *pairing-based cryptography*, and then we present advanced cryptographic schemes for confidentiality and authentication, which satisfy additional properties. The first such scheme we present is *broadcast encryption*, which improves on usual encryption by targeting multiple recipients when sending private information. One could of course give the same decryption key to many users, but if one wants to dynamically change the target set, different personal decryption keys are required. With *traitor tracing*, it is then possible to trace traitors who reveal their decryption keys to non-legitimate users. *Attribute-based encryption* is a generalization of broadcast encryption, where the target set can be specified by a policy and attributes. It is then possible to describe the target set in a fine-grained manner, for each new ciphertexts. *Advanced signatures* add anonymity properties to signature and authentication. Thanks to pairings, it is indeed possible to efficiently authenticate to a service without revealing much about personal data.

Besides encryption and signatures schemes, *key exchange* is a major tool in real life, as it allows two or more players to agree on a common session key, which can be used to establish a secure communication channel. While it looks like a simple and well-defined task, key exchange protocols are intricate, with many various security notions to consider. There are also several ways to authenticate the users: either by signing the messages or by showing the capability of decryption. The use of a pre-shared symmetric key is also possible. However, the most practical and challenging authentication setting is when the parties hold a *short* pre-shared symmetric key. The latter common information is called a *password*, and to address this setting we consider *password-authenticated key exchange*.

With the massive outsourcing of storage and computation, *verifiable computation* became a very active domain, where one wants to have strong guarantees on the output of the outsourced computation. Of course, the goal is to be able to verify computation in a much more efficient way than performing the computation itself, hence the development of *succinct non-interactive arguments* (SNARGs).

The various chapters give a broad overview of some recent advances in public-key cryptography. This is definitely not exhaustive, and each presentation is the author's point of view of the field. There are some general descriptions, or sometimes more focused examples to illustrate the purpose. They are appropriate for a large audience to discover or learn more about public-key cryptography.

1

Public-Key Encryption and Security Notions

Nuttapong Attrapadung and Takahiro Matsuda
*National Institute of Advanced Industrial Science
and Technology (AIST), Tokyo, Japan*

Public-key encryption (PKE) allows a sender to use a receiver's public key to encrypt a message under it and send it to the receiver, who possesses the corresponding secret key. There has been a tremendous amount of research on PKE since the first introduction of the concept by Diffie and Hellman (1976). One of the main goals would be to devise efficient PKE schemes that are provably secure in strong security notions using weak and reasonable computational assumptions. This chapter aims to provide some basic knowledge on PKE and its security notions and survey important results in this field.

We begin the chapter by centering around the security notion called indistinguishability against chosen-ciphertext attacks (IND-CCA), which is widely accepted as the de facto standard notion for PKE. In the first part, we study in detail the Cramer–Shoup (CS) PKE (Cramer and Shoup 1998), which is the first practical IND-CCA secure PKE under a reasonable assumption. This part may also serve as introductory material for a popular method to prove security, namely, using the game-based approach. In the second part, we provide a survey on specific and generic constructions for IND-CCA secure PKE. In the last part, we briefly cover some advanced recent research topics for PKE, such as tight security, key-dependent-message (KDM) security, and so on.

Asymmetric Cryptography,
coordinated by David Pointcheval. © ISTE Ltd. 2022.

1.1. Basic definitions for PKE

1.1.1. *Basic notation*

For $n \in \mathbb{N}$, we define $[n] := \{1, \ldots, n\}$. For a discrete finite set S, $|S|$ denotes its size and $x \leftarrow_{\mathrm{R}} S$ denotes choosing an element x uniformly at random from S. For strings x and y, $|x|$ denotes the bit-length of x and $x\|y$ denotes their concatenation.

For a (probabilistic) algorithm or a function A, $y \leftarrow_{\mathrm{R}} \mathsf{A}(x)$ denotes assigning to y the output of A on input x, and if we need to specify a randomness r used in A, we denote $y \leftarrow \mathsf{A}(x; r)$ (in which case the computation of A is understood as deterministic on input x and r). If $\mathcal{O}(\cdot)$ denotes a function or an algorithm, then "$\mathsf{A}^{\mathcal{O}(\cdot)}$" means that A has oracle access to $\mathcal{O}(\cdot)$, which upon given an input x returns $\mathcal{O}(x)$ to A (but A cannot see the internal description/calculation of $\mathcal{O}$). λ always denotes a security parameter. PPT stands for *probabilistic polynomial time*. A function $f(\lambda)$ is said to be *negligible* if $f(\lambda)$ tends to 0 faster than λ^{-c} for any constant $c > 0$.

1.1.2. *Public-key encryption*

A PKE scheme consists of the three PPT algorithms $(\mathsf{KG}, \mathsf{Enc}, \mathsf{Dec})$ with the following syntax:

Key Generation:	**Encryption:**	**Decryption:**
$(pk, sk) \leftarrow_{\mathrm{R}} \mathsf{KG}(1^{\lambda})$	$c \leftarrow_{\mathrm{R}} \mathsf{Enc}(pk, m)$	m (or $\perp$) $\leftarrow \mathsf{Dec}(sk, c)$

where Dec is a deterministic algorithm, (pk, sk) is a public/secret key pair and c is a ciphertext of a plaintext m under pk. We typically allow Dec to output the special symbol $\perp$ (which is distinguished from any element of the plaintext space) indicating that c is invalid.

We say that a PKE scheme is *correct* if for all $\lambda \in \mathbb{N}$, (pk, sk) output by $\mathsf{KG}(1^{\lambda})$, and m, we have $\mathsf{Dec}(sk, \mathsf{Enc}(pk, m)) = m$.

Historically, the concept of PKE was first introduced by the seminal work by Diffie and Hellman (1976), and the first feasible construction was proposed by Rivest et al. (1978) known as the RSA encryption scheme. Earlier proposed PKE systems such as RSA consider schemes with deterministic encryption algorithms (or, deterministic PKE, a.k.a. a trapdoor function [TDF]). Goldwasser and Micali (1982) were the first to treat PKE with a probabilistic encryption algorithm.

1.1.3. *IND-CPA and IND-CCA security*

Here, we review the two central basic security notions for PKE: indistinguishability against chosen-plaintext attacks (*IND-CPA security*) and *IND-CCA security*.

We first review their formal definitions. For a PKE scheme $\Pi = (\text{KG}, \text{Enc}, \text{Dec})$ and an adversary $\mathcal{A} = (\mathcal{A}_1, \mathcal{A}_2)$, consider the IND-CPA experiment $\text{Expt}_{\Pi,\mathcal{A}}^{\text{indcpa}}(\lambda)$ and IND-CCA experiment $\text{Expt}_{\Pi,\mathcal{A}}^{\text{indcca}}(\lambda)$ as described in Figure 1.1. In both the experiments, st denotes an arbitrary internal state information passed from $\mathcal{A}_1$ to $\mathcal{A}_2$, and it is required that $|m_0| = |m_1|$. Furthermore, in the IND-CCA experiment, $\mathcal{A}_2$ is not allowed to submit the challenge ciphertext c^* to the decryption oracle $\text{Dec}(sk, \cdot)$.

DEFINITION 1.1.– *We say that a PKE scheme Π is* IND-CCA *secure if for any PPT adversary $\mathcal{A}$, its IND-CCA advantage* $\text{Adv}_{\Pi,\mathcal{A}}^{\text{indcca}}(\lambda) := |\Pr[\text{Expt}_{\Pi,\mathcal{A}}^{\text{indcca}}(\lambda) = 1] - 1/2|$ *is negligible.* IND-CPA *security of a PKE scheme is defined analogously using the* IND-CPA *experiment* $\text{Expt}_{\Pi,\mathcal{A}}^{\text{indcpa}}(\lambda)$ *and* IND-CPA *advantage* $\text{Adv}_{\Pi,\mathcal{A}}^{\text{indcpa}}(\lambda) := |\Pr[\text{Expt}_{\Pi,\mathcal{A}}^{\text{indcpa}}(\lambda) = 1] - 1/2|.$

$$\text{Expt}_{\Pi,\mathcal{A}}^{\text{indcpa}}(\lambda):$$
$$(pk, sk) \leftarrow_R \text{KG}(1^\lambda)$$
$$(m_0, m_1, \text{st}) \leftarrow_R \mathcal{A}_1(pk) \quad {}^{(\dagger)}$$
$$b \leftarrow_R \{0,1\}$$
$$c^* \leftarrow_R \text{Enc}(pk, m_b)$$
$$b' \leftarrow_R \mathcal{A}_2(c^*, \text{st})$$
$$\text{Return } (b' \stackrel{?}{=} b).$$

$$\text{Expt}_{\Pi,\mathcal{A}}^{\text{indcca}}(\lambda):$$
$$(pk, sk) \leftarrow_R \text{KG}(1^\lambda)$$
$$(m_0, m_1, \text{st}) \leftarrow_R \mathcal{A}_1^{\text{Dec}(sk, \cdot)}(pk) \quad {}^{(\dagger)}$$
$$b \leftarrow_R \{0,1\}$$
$$c^* \leftarrow_R \text{Enc}(pk, m_b)$$
$$b' \leftarrow_R \mathcal{A}_2^{\text{Dec}(sk, \cdot)}(c^*, \text{st}) \quad {}^{(\ddagger)}$$
$$\text{Return } (b' \stackrel{?}{=} b).$$

Figure 1.1. *The IND-CPA experiment (left) and the IND-CCA experiment (right) for PKE.* [†] *It is required that $|m_0| = |m_1|$.* [‡] *$\mathcal{A}_2$ is disallowed to submit c^* to $\text{Dec}(sk, \cdot)$*

The names IND-CPA and IND-CCA, and more generally the notation combining the security goal (IND) and the attack model (CPA/CCA), were introduced by Bellare et al. (1998), and the notation has been frequently adopted for other types of security notions. IND-CPA security is the very first formal definition for PKE introduced by Goldwasser and Micali (1982). They also gave another formal definition of security for PKE called *semantic security*, using the notion of a simulator. (A security notion defined using a simulator is often called a simulation-based security definition.) Roughly speaking, semantic security captures the intuition that a ciphertext does not leak any partial information on the encrypted plaintext except for its length (against an adversary passively observing the ciphertext). This notion aimed at formalizing the computational variant of the security notion for an encryption scheme called *perfect secrecy* considered by Shannon (1949). Goldwasser and Micali (1982) showed that IND-CPA security and semantic security are equivalent. It is easy to see that IND-CPA security cannot be achieved by a PKE scheme of which the encryption algorithm is deterministic.

The notion of security against chosen-ciphertext attacks was first formalized by Naor and Yung (1990), whose definition captures the so-called *IND-CCA1 security*, where an adversary's decryption query after receiving the challenge ciphertext is not allowed. (This type of attack is also called a *non-adaptive* chosen-ciphertext attack.) Chosen-ciphertext attack that take into account an adversary's decryption queries after receiving the challenge ciphertext were first considered (Rackoff and Simon 1992). (This type of attack is called an *adaptive* chosen-ciphertext attack.) The formal definition of IND-CCA security we reviewed above is the one most widely used nowadays. IND-CCA security is sometimes called IND-CCA2 security to make it explicit that it takes care of adaptive chosen-ciphertext attacks.

In contrast to IND-CPA security, IND-CCA security captures security against "active" adversaries that have access to the decryption oracle. However, it might not be obvious from its definition why we should care about this security notion. The practical importance of IND-CCA security was first widely recognized by the famous attack on the PKE scheme PKCS#1v1.5 by Bleichenbacher (1998). His attack recovers a plaintext from a ciphertext by accessing an oracle that on input a ciphertext returns whether the queried ciphertext is in a valid form (according to the decryption algorithm). This attack is ineffective if a PKE scheme is IND-CCA secure. In response to Bleichenbacher's attack, PKCS#1 was updated and adopted the RSA-OAEP scheme (Bellare and Rogaway 1995) that was proven to be IND-CCA secure (in the random oracle model). Besides, IND-CCA security has been shown to imply many useful and important security notions for PKE (in terms of both practical and theoretical viewpoints), such as non-malleability (Dolev et al. 1991), as explained in the next section. Therefore, IND-CCA security is nowadays considered one of the golden standard security notions for PKE that should be achieved by ones used in practice.

1.1.4. *Other basic security notions and relations*

Here, we review two other basic security notions for PKE that are as basic as IND-CPA and IND-CCA security. (We do not give formal definitions, and thus interested readers are referred to the original or related papers.) We also describe some more security notions in section 1.4.

1.1.4.1. *One-wayness*

One-wayness is a security notion that captures the intuition that given a ciphertext c encrypting a randomly chosen plaintext m, one cannot entirely recover m. It might sound sufficiently strong as a security notion for PKE. When formalized, however, it does not guarantee that no partial information on m is leaked from c. Moreover, this security notion is not suitable for PKE schemes that encrypt messages that do not have much entropy (say, a single bit). Like indistinguishability security notions, we can consider this notion under the CPA and CCA settings. For PKE schemes (with a sufficiently large plaintext space), IND-CPA (respectively, IND-CCA) security implies one-wayness under CPA (respectively, CCA).

1.1.4.2. Non-malleability

Non-malleability is a security notion that captures the intuition that given a ciphertext c encrypting some plaintext m, one cannot come up with a ciphertext c' that can be decrypted to a plaintext m' that is "meaningfully related" to m (e.g. $m' = m + 1$). This type of security is, for example, necessary for PKE used in a sealed-bit auction. Non-malleability was first introduced by Dolev et al. (1991), who gave a simulation-based formalization. Later, several other formalizations for non-malleability were proposed (Bellare et al. 1998; Bellare and Sahai 1999, 2006; Pass et al. 2007). Non-malleability would sound like a security notion for integrity rather than confidentiality. However, in any of the above formalizations, non-malleability under CPA implies IND-CPA security.

Bellare et al. (1998) and Dolev et al. (2000) (the journal version of Dolev et al. (1991)) showed that IND-CCA security and one form of non-malleability under chosen-ciphertext attacks are equivalent, supporting the importance of IND-CCA security. Bellare and Sahai (1999) showed the equivalence among several forms of non-malleability, namely, a simulation-based one capturing the spirit of Dolev et al. (1991), the comparison-based one introduced in Bellare et al. (1998), and an indistinguishability-based one that uses the notion of a "parallel decryption query" (introduced also in Bellare and Sahai (1999)). Bellare and Sahai (2006) (the updated full version of Bellare and Sahai (1999)) and Pass et al. (2007) clarified some subtleties of the treatment of invalid ciphertexts (decrypting to the invalid symbol $\perp$) in the formalizations of non-malleability for PKE. In particular, the latter work showed that for PKE schemes of which the decryption algorithm may return $\perp$, simulation-based non-malleability is strictly stronger than indistinguishability-based one.

1.2. Basic PKE schemes

We describe some basic PKE schemes and prove their security. We will focus on PKE schemes that are based on related problems associated with discrete logarithms, namely, the ElGamal PKE and the CS PKE, of which its IND-CPA and IND-CCA security, respectively, rely on the hardness of the Decisional Diffie–Hellman (DDH) problem. To understand the rationale in their designs (of the Crame-Shoup PKE, in particular), we follow the approach in Katz (2004), which gradually modifies the ElGamal PKE via an intermediate scheme and finally obtain the CS PKE. We will conclude the section by providing a brief survey on other families of specific PKE schemes.

1.2.1. Game-based proofs

Another purpose of the following sections is to demonstrate how we prove the security of complex schemes using the *game-based* approach (e.g. Shoup 2004;

Bellare and Rogaway 2006), or also called *hybrid arguments*. In this approach, we normally define a sequence of games where the first is the real attack game defined by the security notion (e.g. IND-CCA game) that we want to prove and the last is the attack game that is trivially secure (the adversary's advantage is zero). We then prove that the difference of the adversary's advantages between the adjacent games is negligible. When combining all of them, we can thus conclude that the advantage in the original game is close to negligible. A main benefit of doing this is that we can focus on an assumption that the scheme relies on *one at a time* (note that a complex scheme rather relies on many assumptions or ingredients), and analyzing such a change based on one assumption/ingredient should be simple. As a preliminary, we state one useful lemma:

LEMMA 1.1 (Difference Lemma (Shoup 2004)).– *Let A, B, F be events defined in some probability distribution, and suppose that $A \wedge \neg F = B \wedge \neg F$. Then we have $|\Pr[A] - \Pr[B]| \leq \Pr[F]$.*

1.2.2. *ElGamal encryption*

The ElGamal scheme (ElGamal 1984) is one of the most well-known PKE schemes. Its IND-CPA security relies on the hardness of the DDH problem.

We start by defining a group generator. A group generator $\mathcal{G}$ is a PPT algorithm that, on input 1^λ, outputs a description of a cyclic group $\mathbb{G}$, its order q, which is a prime with bit length λ, and a random generator g.

DEFINITION 1.2.– *Let $(\mathbb{G}, q, g) \leftarrow_R \mathcal{G}(1^\lambda)$. The DDH advantage for an algorithm $\mathcal{D}$ is defined as*

$$\mathsf{Adv}_{\mathcal{G},\mathcal{D}}^{\mathsf{ddh}}(\lambda) := |\Pr[\alpha, \beta, \gamma \leftarrow_R \mathbb{Z}_q : \mathcal{D}(\mathbb{G}, q, g, g^\alpha, g^\beta, g^\gamma) = 1]$$
$$- \Pr[\alpha, \beta \leftarrow_R \mathbb{Z}_q : \mathcal{D}(\mathbb{G}, q, g, g^\alpha, g^\beta, g^{\alpha\beta}) = 1]|.$$

We say that the DDH assumption holds for $\mathcal{G}$ if for all PPT algorithms $\mathcal{D}$, its DDH advantage is negligible.

The ElGamal scheme for $\mathcal{G}$ can be described in Figure 1.2. Its plaintext space is $\mathbb{G}$. The correctness follows from $c_2/c_1^x = h^y \cdot m/(g^y)^x = m$.

THEOREM 1.1.– *Suppose the DDH assumption holds for $\mathcal{G}$. Then the ElGamal scheme for $\mathcal{G}$ is IND-CPA secure.*

PROOF.– Let $\mathcal{A}$ be any PPT adversary that attacks the IND-CPA security of the ElGamal scheme. We consider a sequence of games. Let S_i be the event that $\mathfrak{b} = \mathfrak{b}'$ in Game i.

$\text{KG}(1^\lambda):$	$\text{Enc}(pk, m):$	$\text{Dec}(sk, C):$
$(\mathbb{G}, q, g) \leftarrow_{\text{R}} \mathcal{G}(1^\lambda)$	$r \leftarrow_{\text{R}} \mathbb{Z}_q$	Parse $(u, w) \leftarrow C.$
$x \leftarrow_{\text{R}} \mathbb{Z}_q$	$u := g^r$	$m \leftarrow w/u^x$
$h := g^x$	$w := h^r \cdot m$	Return $m.$
$pk := (\mathbb{G}, q, g, h)$	Return $C := (u, w).$	
$sk := x$		
Return $(pk, sk).$		

Figure 1.2. *The ElGamal encryption*

Game 0. This is exactly the IND-CPA game instantiated by the ElGamal scheme with the adversary $\mathcal{A}$. By definition, we have $\text{Adv}^{\text{indcpa}}_{\text{ElGamal},\mathcal{A}}(\lambda) = |\Pr[S_0] - 1/2|$.

Game 1. We now make a change to Game 0 by instead computing $w = g^z \cdot m_b$ for a random $z \leftarrow_{\text{R}} \mathbb{Z}_q$.

More precisely, we can write the two games algorithmically as follows, where we highlight the change in gray.

Game 0 :	*Game 1* :
$(\mathbb{G}, q, g) \leftarrow_{\text{R}} \mathcal{G}(1^\lambda)$	$(\mathbb{G}, q, g) \leftarrow_{\text{R}} \mathcal{G}(1^\lambda)$
$x \leftarrow_{\text{R}} \mathbb{Z}_q$	$x \leftarrow_{\text{R}} \mathbb{Z}_q$
$(m_0, m_1, \text{st}) \leftarrow_{\text{R}} \mathcal{A}_1(\mathbb{G}, q, g, g^x)$	$(m_0, m_1, \text{st}) \leftarrow_{\text{R}} \mathcal{A}_1(\mathbb{G}, q, g, g^x)$
$b \leftarrow_{\text{R}} \{0,1\}, \quad r \leftarrow_{\text{R}} \mathbb{Z}_q$	$b \leftarrow_{\text{R}} \{0,1\}, \quad r \leftarrow_{\text{R}} \mathbb{Z}_q, \quad z \leftarrow_{\text{R}} \mathbb{Z}_q$
$u := g^r, \quad w := g^{xr} \cdot m_b$	$u := g^r, \quad w := g^z \cdot m_b$
$b' \leftarrow_{\text{R}} \mathcal{A}_2(u, w, \text{st})$	$b' \leftarrow_{\text{R}} \mathcal{A}_2(u, w, \text{st})$

Figure 1.3. *Sequence of games for the security proof of the ElGamal scheme*

CLAIM 1.1.– $|\Pr[S_0] - \Pr[S_1]| = \text{Adv}^{\text{ddh}}_{\mathcal{G},\mathcal{D}}(\lambda)$ *for some PPT algorithm* $\mathcal{D}$.

To prove this claim, we construct $\mathcal{D}$ as follows. Recall that $\mathcal{D}$ is given $(\mathbb{G}, q, g, g^\alpha, g^\beta, g^\gamma)$ as its input, and tries to guess if $\gamma = \alpha\beta$ or γ is random.

Algorithm $\mathcal{D}(\mathbb{G}, q, g, g^\alpha, g^\beta, g^\gamma):$
$(m_0, m_1, \text{st}) \leftarrow_{\text{R}} \mathcal{A}_1(\mathbb{G}, q, g, g^\alpha), \quad b \leftarrow_{\text{R}} \{0,1\}, \quad w := g^\gamma \cdot m_b$
$b' \leftarrow_{\text{R}} \mathcal{A}_2(g^\beta, w, \text{st}).$ If $b = b'$ then output 1, else output 0.

Intuitively, the algorithm $\mathcal{D}$ interpolates between Games 0 and 1 with $x = \alpha, r = \beta, z = \gamma$. If $\gamma = \alpha\beta$, then $\mathcal{D}$ effectively simulates Game 0. If γ is random, then $\mathcal{D}$ effectively simulates Game 1. Note that $\mathcal{D}$ outputs 1 only when $b = b'$ holds. Hence, its advantage is exactly $|\Pr[S_0] - \Pr[S_1]|$.

CLAIM 1.2.– $\Pr[S_1] = 1/2$.

This claim follows from the fact that in Game 1, the element g^z functions as a one-time pad that completely hides m_b.

Combining the two claims, we see that $|\Pr[S_0] - 1/2| = \mathsf{Adv}^{\mathsf{ddh}}_{\mathcal{G},\mathcal{D}}(\lambda)$, which is negligible under the DDH assumption. This concludes the proof of the theorem. $\Box$

1.2.3. *Simplified CS encryption*

We next describe the simplified CS (or the Cramer–Shoup-"lite") scheme. This scheme is an intermediate scheme toward the CCA security; it can be shown to achieve IND-CCA1 (non-adaptive CCA) security. It can be viewed as a modification from ElGamal mainly in two ways: now it uses two generators and it requires a validity check at decryption. We define $(\mathbb{G}, q, g_1, g_2) \leftarrow_{\mathsf{R}} \mathcal{G}'(1^\lambda)$ as $(\mathbb{G}, q, g_1) \leftarrow_{\mathsf{R}} \mathcal{G}(1^\lambda)$, then choose $\ell \leftarrow_{\mathsf{R}} \mathbb{Z}_q$ and set $g_2 := g_1^\ell$. Throughout this chapter, we fix ℓ to always denote $\log_{g_1} g_2$. The scheme is as follows.

KG(1^λ):	Enc(pk, m):	Dec(sk, C):
$(\mathbb{G}, q, g_1, g_2) \leftarrow_{\mathsf{R}} \mathcal{G}'(1^\lambda)$	$r \leftarrow_{\mathsf{R}} \mathbb{Z}_q$	Parse $(u, v, w, e) \leftarrow C$.
$x, y, a, b \leftarrow_{\mathsf{R}} \mathbb{Z}_q$	$u := g_1^r$	If $u^a v^b \neq e$
$h := g_1^x g_2^y$	$v := g_2^r$	$\quad m \leftarrow \perp$
$c := g_1^a g_2^b$	$w := h^r \cdot m$	Else
$pk := (\mathbb{G}, q, g_1, g_2, h, c)$	$e := c^r$	$\quad m \leftarrow w/(u^x v^y)$
$sk := (x, y, a, b)$	Return $C := (u, v, w, e)$.	Return m.
Return (pk, sk).		

Figure 1.4. *The Simplified Cramer-Shoup encryption*

As for correctness, for a ciphertext $C := (u, v, w, e)$ that is constructed honestly as in Enc, we can see that it passes the validity check as $u^a v^b = g_1^{ra} g_2^{rb} = (g_1^a g_2^b)^r = c^r = e$. Moreover, it is clear that $h^r = u^x v^y$, and hence decryption will correctly yield the message m.

We briefly describe some intuitions. First, the use of two generators allows multiple possible pairs of secret keys (x, y) under one fixed public key constrained by g_1, g_2, h. This allows our algorithm $\mathcal{D}$ to simulate the decryption oracle while also be able to embed the DDH problem instance. Second, the validity check is crucial for rejecting "illegal" ciphertexts queried to the decryption oracle in the proof. If not rejected, such illegal ciphertexts would potentially give more information on a secret key pair (x, y) to the adversary (claim 1.6). Moreover, the validity check is also designed so that illegal ciphertexts will be rejected with all but negligible probability (claim 1.5).

Game 0 :

$(\mathbb{G}, q, g_1, g_2) \leftarrow_R \mathcal{G}'(1^\lambda)$

$x, y, a, b \leftarrow_R \mathbb{Z}_q, \; sk := (x, y, a, b)$

$h := g_1^x g_2^y, \quad c := g_1^a g_2^b$

$pk := (\mathbb{G}, q, g_1, g_2, h, c)$

$(m_0, m_1, \mathsf{st}) \leftarrow_R \mathcal{A}_1^{\mathsf{Dec}(sk, \cdot)}(pk)$

$\mathsf{b} \leftarrow_R \{0, 1\}, \quad r \leftarrow_R \mathbb{Z}_q$

$u := g_1^r, \quad v := g_2^r$

$w := g_1^{xr} g_2^{yr} \cdot m_\mathsf{b}, \quad e := g_1^{ar} g_2^{br}$

$\mathsf{b}' \leftarrow_R \mathcal{A}_2(u, v, w, e, \mathsf{st})$

Game 1 :

$(\mathbb{G}, q, g_1, g_2) \leftarrow_R \mathcal{G}'(1^\lambda)$

$x, y, a, b \leftarrow_R \mathbb{Z}_q, \; sk := (x, y, a, b)$

$h := g_1^x g_2^y, \quad c := g_1^a g_2^b$

$pk := (\mathbb{G}, q, g_1, g_2, h, c)$

$(m_0, m_1, \mathsf{st}) \leftarrow_R \mathcal{A}_1^{\mathsf{Dec}(sk, \cdot)}(pk)$

$\mathsf{b} \leftarrow_R \{0, 1\}, \quad r, \boxed{r'} \leftarrow_R \mathbb{Z}_q$

$u := g_1^r, \quad \boxed{v := g_2^{r'}}$

$\boxed{w := g_1^{xr} g_2^{yr'} \cdot m_\mathsf{b}}, \quad \boxed{e := g_1^{ar} g_2^{br'}}$

$\mathsf{b}' \leftarrow_R \mathcal{A}_2(u, v, w, e, \mathsf{st})$

Figure 1.5. *Game 0 and 1 for the security proof of the SimpCS scheme*

THEOREM 1.2.– *Suppose the DDH assumption holds for $\mathcal{G}$. Then the simplified CS scheme for $\mathcal{G}$ is IND-CCA1 secure.*

PROOF.– Let $\mathcal{A}$ be any PPT adversary that attacks the IND-CCA1 security of this scheme. We use the following games. Let S_i be the event that $\mathsf{b} = \mathsf{b}'$ in Game i.

Game 0. This game is exactly the IND-CCA1 game instantiated by the SimpCS scheme with the adversary $\mathcal{A}$. By definition, $\mathsf{Adv}^{\mathsf{indcca1}}_{\mathsf{SimpCS}, \mathcal{A}}(\lambda) = |\Pr[S_0] - 1/2|$.

Game 1. We now make a change to Game 0 by instead computing the challenge ciphertext with $u = g_1^r, v = g_2^{r'}, w = g_1^{xr} g_2^{yr'} \cdot m_\mathsf{b}$, and $e = g_1^{ar} g_2^{br'}$, for random $r, r' \leftarrow_R \mathbb{Z}_q$.

Game 2. This is exactly Game 1 except that we pick $\ell \leftarrow_R \mathbb{Z}_q^*$ and $r' \leftarrow_R \mathbb{Z}_q \setminus \{r\}$, to set $g_2 := g_1^\ell$ and $v := g_2^{r'}$ In particular, we have $\ell \neq 0$ and $r \neq r'$.

Game 3. This is exactly Game 2 with the exception that the decryption oracle now also rejects (meaning returns $\bot$ for) any decryption query $C_i = (u_i, v_i, w_i, e_i)$ such that $\log_{g_1} u_i \neq \log_{g_2} v_i$ (we call such C_i an *illegal* ciphertext) and $u_i^a v_i^b = e_i$ (which means it passes the validity check in Dec). Note that i refers to the ith query.

CLAIM 1.3.– $|\Pr[S_0] - \Pr[S_1]| = \mathsf{Adv}^{\mathsf{ddh}}_{\mathcal{G}, \mathcal{D}}(\lambda)$ *for some PPT algorithm $\mathcal{D}$.*

We prove this by constructing a PPT algorithm $\mathcal{D}$ that attacks the DDH problem as follows.

Algorithm $\mathcal{D}(\mathbb{G}, q, g, g^\alpha, g^\beta, g^\gamma)$:

$x, y, a, b \leftarrow_R \mathbb{Z}_q, \; sk := (x, y, a, b)$

$(m_0, m_1, \mathsf{st}) \leftarrow_R \mathcal{A}_1^{\mathsf{Dec}(sk, \cdot)}(\mathbb{G}, q, g, g^\alpha, g^{x+\alpha y}, g^{a+\alpha b})$

$\mathsf{b} \leftarrow_R \{0, 1\}, \quad w := g^{\beta x + \gamma y} \cdot m_\mathsf{b}, \quad e := g^{\beta a + \gamma b}$

$\mathsf{b}' \leftarrow_R \mathcal{A}_2(g^\beta, g^\gamma, w, e, \mathsf{st})$. If $\mathsf{b} = \mathsf{b}'$ then output 1, else output 0.

Now we can see that $\mathcal{D}$ interpolates between Games 0 and 1 with $g_1 = g, g_2 = g^\alpha, u = g^\beta, v = g^\gamma$. If $\gamma = \alpha\beta$, then $\mathcal{D}$ simulates Game 0. If γ is random, then $\mathcal{D}$ simulates Game 1. Therefore, its advantage is exactly $|\Pr[S_0] - \Pr[S_1]|$, and hence the claim.

CLAIM 1.4.– $|\Pr[S_1] - \Pr[S_2]|$ *is negligible.*

From the difference lemma, we have that $|\Pr[S_1] - \Pr[S_2]| \leq \Pr[E]$, where E is the event that $\ell = 0$ or $r = r'$ where $\ell, r' \leftarrow_R \mathbb{Z}_q$, and observe that E occurs with negligible probability since q is exponential.

CLAIM 1.5.– $|\Pr[S_2] - \Pr[S_3]|$ *is negligible.*

Since this claim is information-theoretic, we will prove that the statement holds even if $\mathcal{A}$ is an all-powerful adversary, who may possibly be able to compute, for example, the discrete logarithms. To prove the claim, we let F be the event that the adversary $\mathcal{A}$ queries at least one illegal ciphertext that passes the validity check. From our definition of F, we have $S_2 \wedge \neg F = S_3 \wedge \neg F$. Hence, from the difference lemma, we have $|\Pr[S_2] - \Pr[S_3]| \leq \Pr[F]$. Now we derive the maximum bound for $\Pr[F]$. Recall $\ell = \log_{g_1} g_2$. For each query $C_i = (u_i, v_i, w_i, e_i)$, we denote $r_i = \log_{g_1} u_i$, $r_i' = \log_{g_2} v_i$ and $z_i = \log_{g_1} e_i$. The validity check equality in Dec, namely, $u_i^a v_i^b = e_i$, is equivalent to $r_i a + r_i' \ell b = z_i$. Therefore, $\mathcal{A}$ can make its first query to be illegal while also pass the validity check by guessing $(r_1, r_1', z_1) \in \mathbb{Z}_q^3$ with $r_1 \neq r_1'$ such that $r_1 a + r_1' \ell b = z_1$. Now we observe that the information $\mathcal{A}$ knows about a, b is only from the public key, namely, $c = g_1^a g_2^b$, and for an all-powerful adversary it may thus know $\log_{g_1} c = a + \ell b$. But since $r_1 \neq r_1'$, we have that $r_1 a + r_1' \ell b$ is linearly independent of $a + \ell b$, and hence it can only guess z_1 correctly with probability $1/q$.

For the ith query, $\mathcal{A}$ can make it to be illegal by guessing similarly, but now it has more information on a, b from previous illegal queries that did not pass the check. More precisely, for an illegal query $C_j = (u_j, v_j, w_j, e_j)$ that is rejected, where $j < i$, $\mathcal{A}$ learns that $r_j a + r_j' \ell b \neq z_j$. This eliminates one possibility of (a, b) from q possible pairs constrained to its knowledge of $a + \ell b$. There are at most $i - 1$ such queries before the ith query. Hence, $\mathcal{A}$ can guess z_i correctly with probability at most $1/(q - (i - 1))$. Let k be the total number of queries. From the union bound, we have that $\Pr[F]$ is at most $k/(q - k + 1)$. Since k is polynomial and q is exponential in λ, this amount is negligible.

CLAIM 1.6.– $\Pr[S_3] = 1/2$.

To prove this claim, it is sufficient to prove that the exponent of the message mask term is uniformly random given all the known exponents in the view of $\mathcal{A}$ in Game 3. This is equivalent to prove that $xr + \ell yr'$ is uniformly random given the knowledge of $\ell, x + \ell y$ (from pk), r, r' (from the challenge ciphertext) and some from answers to its decryption queries. Without the latter, this holds since $xr + \ell yr'$ is linearly independent of $x + \ell y$ since $r \neq r'$ and $\ell \neq 0$. We then argue further that even given answers to its decryption queries, there is no additional information on x, y. Now, since in Game 3, we reject all the illegal queries that pass the validity check, the remaining queries do not pass the check or are not illegal queries. In the first case, the check does not involve x, y (hence no information on them). In the latter case, we have $r_i = r'_i$ and $\mathcal{A}$ learns $\log_{g_1} m_i = z_i - r_i x - \ell r_i y$. But this is linearly dependent on $x + \ell y$. Hence, $\mathcal{A}$ has no additional information on x, y.

Combining all the differences, we have

$$\left| \Pr[S_0] - 1/2 \right| \leq \left| \Pr[S_0] - \Pr[S_1] \right| + \left| \Pr[S_1] - \Pr[S_2] \right| + \left| \Pr[S_2] - \Pr[S_3] \right|.$$

This is negligible due to the above claims and the DDH assumption. $\square$

We note that the proof of claim 1.5 fails if we extend the security game to the case of full IND-CCA (not only IND-CCA1). Intuitively, this is because the adversary obtains further information on a, b from the challenge ciphertext.

1.2.4. *Cramer–Shoup encryption*

We now describe the full-fledged CS encryption ((Cramer and Shoup 1998), (Cramer and Shoup 2003)) in the figure below. This scheme is important since it is the first efficient IND-CCA secure scheme in the standard model (not relying on idealized structures such as random oracles).

The CS scheme will use one more ingredient: a collision-resistant hash function family.[1] We briefly recall its definition: it is a family $\mathcal{H}$ of hash functions for which it is hard for an adversary to obtain $H \leftarrow_R \mathcal{H}$, and choose inputs x, y such that $x \neq y$ but $H(x) = H(y)$.

The correctness is analog to the simplified scheme. In particular, for a ciphertext $C := (u, v, w, e)$ constructed honestly as in Enc, we can see that it passes the check as $u^{a+ta'} v^{b+tb'} = g_1^{ar+ta'r} g_2^{br+tb'r} = (g_1^a g_2^b)^r (g_1^{ta'} g_2^{tb'})^r = c^r d^{tr} = e$.

THEOREM 1.3.– *Suppose the DDH assumption holds for $\mathcal{G}$. Then the CS scheme for $\mathcal{G}$ is IND-CCA secure.*

PROOF.– Let $\mathcal{A}$ be any PPT adversary that attacks the IND-CCA security of the CS scheme. We use the following games. Let S_i be the event that $b = b'$ in Game i. Denote the challenge ciphertext as $C^* = (u^*, v^*, w^*, e^*)$ and the ith ciphertext query as $C_i = (u_i, v_i, w_i, e_i)$.

---

[1] A weaker primitive called a universal one-way family of hash functions (Naor and Yung 1989) (or also alternatively called target-collision resistant hash) can also be used. However, here we opted to use collision-resistant hash function for simplicity.

$KG(1^\lambda)$:	$Enc(pk, m)$:	$Dec(sk, C)$:
$(\mathbb{G}, q, g_1, g_2) \leftarrow_R \mathcal{G}'(1^\lambda)$	$r \leftarrow_R \mathbb{Z}_q$	Parse $(u, v, w, e) \leftarrow C$.
$H \leftarrow_R \mathcal{H}$	$u := g_1^r$	$t := H(u, v, w)$
$x, y, a, b, a', b' \leftarrow_R \mathbb{Z}_q$	$v := g_2^r$	If $u^{a+ta'} v^{b+tb'} \neq e$
$h := g_1^x g_2^y$	$w := h^r \cdot m$	$\quad m \leftarrow \perp$
$c := g_1^a g_2^b$	$t := H(u, v, w)$	Else
$d := g_1^{a'} g_2^{b'}$	$e := (cd^t)^r$	$\quad m \leftarrow w/(u^x v^y)$
$pk := (H, \mathbb{G}, q, g_1, g_2, h, c, d)$	Return $C := (u, v, w, e)$.	Return m.
$sk := (x, y, a, b, a', b')$		
Return (pk, sk).		

Figure 1.6. *The Cramer-Shoup encryption*

Game 0. Let this game be exactly the IND-CCA game instantiated by the CS scheme with the adversary $\mathcal{A}$. By definition, we have $\mathsf{Adv}_{CS,\mathcal{A}}^{\mathsf{indcca}}(\lambda) = |\Pr[S_0] - 1/2|$.

Game 1. This is exactly Game 0 with the exception that the decryption oracle now also rejects any post-challenge decryption query $C_i = (u_i, v_i, w_i, e_i)$ such that $(u_i, v_i, w_i) = (u^*, v^*, w^*)$ but $e_i \neq e^*$.

Game 2. We now make a change to Game 1 by instead computing the challenge ciphertext with $u^* = g_1^r, v^* = g_2^{r'}, w^* = g_1^{xr} g_2^{yr'} \cdot m_b$, and $e^* = g_1^{ar+ta'r} g_2^{br'+tb'r'}$, for random $r, r' \leftarrow_R \mathbb{Z}_q$.

Game 3. This is exactly Game 2 except that $\ell \neq 0$ and $r \neq r'$.

Game 4. This is exactly Game 3 with the exception that the decryption oracle now also rejects any query $C_i = (u_i, v_i, w_i, e_i)$ such that

$$(u_i, v_i, w_i) \neq (u^*, v^*, w^*) \text{ but } H(u_i, v_i, w_i) = H(u^*, v^*, w^*) \quad\quad [1.1]$$

Game 5. This is exactly Game 4 with the exception that the decryption oracle now also rejects query $C_i = (u_i, v_i, w_i, e_i)$ such that $\log_{g_1} u_i \neq \log_{g_2} v_i$ (i.e. C_i is an illegal ciphertext) and was not rejected in Game 3.

CLAIM 1.7.– $\Pr[S_0] = \Pr[S_1]$.

The change from Games 0 to 1 is only conceptual (no real change). Indeed, it is straightforward to see that the query such that $(u_i, v_i, w_i) = (u^*, v^*, w^*)$ but $e_i \neq e^*$ is always rejected.

CLAIM 1.8.– $|\Pr[S_1] - \Pr[S_2]| = \text{Adv}^{\text{ddh}}_{\mathcal{G},\mathcal{D}}(\lambda)$ *for some PPT algorithm* $\mathcal{D}$.

The above claim can be proved in almost the same manner as claim 1.3 and is omitted here.

CLAIM 1.9.– $|\Pr[S_2] - \Pr[S_3]|$ *is negligible.*

The above is exactly the same as claim 1.4.

CLAIM 1.10.– $|\Pr[S_3] - \Pr[S_4]|$ *is negligible, assuming that* $\mathcal{H}$ *is a collision-resistant hash family.*

Suppose the exception event in Game 4 occurs. Then, this means that we have found a collision of H as exactly described in relation [1.1]. This should happen with negligible probability due to the security of $\mathcal{H}$. Using the difference lemma, we can conclude the claim.

CLAIM 1.11.– $|\Pr[S_4] - \Pr[S_5]|$ *is negligible.*

To prove this claim, we let F be the event that the adversary $\mathcal{A}$ queries at least one illegal ciphertext that is not rejected in Game 4. As before, it is sufficient to derive an information-theoretic bound for $\Pr[F]$ since $|\Pr[S_1] - \Pr[S_2]| \leq \Pr[F]$. Recall that $\mathcal{A}$ is not allowed to query $(u_i, v_i, w_i, e_i) = (u^*, v^*, w^*, e^*)$. This property, together with the conditions for rejection up to Game 4, we have that a query for F to occur must conform $H(u_i, v_i, w_i) \neq H(u^*, v^*, w^*)$. Let $t_i = H(u_i, v_i, w_i)$ and $t = H(u^*, v^*, w^*)$ (hence $t_i \neq t'$). Let $\ell = \log_{g_1} g_2$. For each query $C_i = (u_i, v_i, w_i, e_i)$, we denote $r_i = \log_{g_1} u_i$, $r'_i = \log_{g_2} v_i$ and $z_i = \log_{g_1} e_i$. The validity check equality in Dec, namely, $u_i^{a+t_i a'} v_i^{b+t_i b'} = e_i$, is equivalent to $r_i(a + t_i a') + r'_i \ell(b + t_i b') = z_i$. For simplicity, we first assume w.l.o.g. that $\mathcal{A}$ does not query before the challenge. Therefore, $\mathcal{A}$ can make its first (post-challenge) query to be illegal while also not to be rejected in Game 4 by guessing $(r_1, r'_1, z_1) \in \mathbb{Z}_q^3$ with $r_1 \neq r'_1$ such that

$$r_1(a + t_1 a') + r'_1 \ell(b + t_1 b') = z_1.$$

Now we observe that the information $\mathcal{A}$ possibly knows about a, b, a', b' consists of

$$a + \ell b, \quad a' + \ell b' \qquad \text{(from } pk)$$

$$r(a + ta') + r'\ell(b + tb') \qquad \text{(from } e^* \text{ in the challenge ciphertext).}$$

Also recall that $\ell \neq 0$ and $r \neq r'$. We argue that the probability of guessing z_1 correctly is $1/q$. This holds since the expression of z_1 is linearly independent from $a + \ell b, a' + \ell b'$, and $r(a + ta') + r'\ell(b + tb')$ exactly when $r \neq r'$ and $r_1 \neq r'_1$ and $t_1 \neq t'$. This can be confirmed by forming the system of equations over the variable vector (a, a', b, b') and obtaining the coefficient matrix as

$$\begin{pmatrix} r_1 & r_1 t_1 & r_1' \ell & r_1' \ell t_1 \\ 1 & 0 & \ell & 0 \\ 0 & 1 & 0 & \ell \\ r & rt' & r'\ell & r'\ell t' \end{pmatrix},$$

and seeing that its determinant is $\ell^2 (r - r')(r_1 - r_1')(t' - t_1) \neq 0$.

Next, to deal with the case where $\mathcal{A}$ does query before the challenge and the case for multiple illegal queries, we proceed similarly as in the proof of claim 1.5 (when we considered the ith query there). From this, we can conclude that $\Pr[F]$ is negligible.

CLAIM 1.12.– $\Pr[S_5] = 1/2$.

The above claim can be proved in exactly the same manner as claim 1.6.

Combining all the claims we have that $|\Pr[S_0] - 1/2|$ is negligible under the DDH assumption and the security of $\mathcal{H}$, as desired. $\qquad\square$

1.2.5. *Other specific PKE schemes*

We list some important PKE schemes in the literature, together with their security, assumptions and some features. Note that the list here is by no means exhaustive.

1.2.5.1. *PKE based on problems related to factoring*

– RSA (Rivest et al. 1978): One-wayness secure under the RSA assumption.

– Rabin (Rabin 1979): One-wayness secure under the hardness of factoring.

– Goldwasser-Micali (Goldwasser and Micali 1982): The first proven IND-CPA secure PKE, under the quadratic residuosity (QR) assumption. Similar to the RSA assumption (and DCR below), the QR assumption is related to, but not known to follow from, the hardness of factoring.

– Blum–Goldwasser (Blum and Goldwasser 1984): IND-CPA secure under the hardness of factoring.

– Paillier (Paillier 1999): IND-CPA secure under the decisional composite residuosity (DCR) assumption. It is one of most well-known PKE that features the additive homomorphic property. Damgård and Jurik (2001) proposed an extended scheme of which the plaintext space is larger, under the same assumption. Antecedents to the Paillier scheme include schemes by Benaloh (1994), Naccache and Stern (1998) and Okamoto and Uchiyama (1998).

– Cramer–Shoup (2002) (Cramer and Shoup 2002): IND-CCA secure PKE schemes, one under the DCR assumption and another under the QR assumption. In fact, they provide a framework based on the so-called hash-proof systems (HPSs), which generalizes (and also captures) the original DDH-based Cramer–Shoup (1998) scheme (Cramer and Shoup 1998).

– Hofheinz–Kiltz (2009) (Hofheinz and Kiltz 2009): The first practical IND-CCA secure PKE under the hardness of factoring.

– Cramer–Hofheinz–Kiltz (Cramer et al. 2010): An IND-CCA secure PKE scheme under the RSA assumption. They also provide at least another scheme (see below).

1.2.5.2. *PKE based on problems related to discrete logarithm*

– ElGamal (ElGamal 1984) and Cramer–Shoup (1998) (Cramer and Shoup 1998). We described them in details above.

– Kurosawa–Desmedt (Kurosawa and Desmedt 2004): IND-CCA secure based on the DDH assumption, a target-collision-resistant hash and an authenticated symmetric-key encryption (SKE). This scheme improves the efficiency of the Cramer–Shoup PKE; notably the ciphertext size is reduced by one group element. As of writing, this scheme remains one of the most efficient IND-CCA secure PKE schemes based on the DDH assumption (at least in terms of the ciphertext size). It can be viewed as hybrid encryption (see section 1.3.1).

– Boyen–Mei–Waters (Boyen et al. 2005): IND-CCA secure under the decisional bilinear Diffie–Hellman (DBDH) assumption (Boneh and Franklin 2001). This scheme has the most compact ciphertexts among all these efficient PKE schemes, but relies on a stronger tool, bilinear pairing.

– Hofheinz–Kiltz (Hofheinz and Kiltz 2007) and Shacham (Shacham 2007): IND-CCA secure under the k-Decision Linear (k-DLin) assumption, for any positive integer k. We note that 1-Dlin assumption is the DDH assumption itself, and $(k + 1)$-DLin is strictly weaker than k-Dlin. On the other hand, in these schemes, the sizes of keys and ciphertexts are linear in k.

– Cash–Kiltz–Shoup (Cash et al. 2008), Hanaoka–Kurosawa (Hanaoka and Kurosawa 2008), Haralambiev et al. (Haralambiev et al. 2010) and Cramer–Hofheinz–Kiltz (Cramer et al. 2010): IND-CCA secure PKE schemes under the computational Diffie–Hellman (CDH) assumption. Note that CDH is strictly weaker than DDH. Moreover, these direct constructions are more efficient than the generic hard-core predicate approach (Goldreich and Levin 1989) to construct PKE based on hardness of search problems like CDH.

1.2.5.3. *PKE based on problems related to lattices (and more)*

– Regev (Regev 2005): The first IND-CPA secure PKE under the learning-with-error (LWE) assumption.

– Peikert and Waters (Peikert and Waters 2008): The first IND-CCA secure PKE under the LWE assumption. A direct construction that improves efficiency is given by Micciancio and Peikert (2012).

There are also PKE schemes related to other mathematical structures such as error-correcting codes, isogenies, multivariate polynomials and so on. Lattice-based schemes and these latter schemes are in the field of post-quantum cryptography, covered by another book in the series.   .

1.2.5.4. *PKE in the random oracle model*

Up to now, we have described and listed only PKE schemes in the *standard model*. Another popular approach that usually yields very efficient IND-CCA secure PKE is to construct a scheme in the *random oracle model* (RO) (Bellare and Rogaway 1993). Random oracle is a uniformly random function that is provided in the form of oracle. In the RO model, hash functions used in the scheme are replaced by random oracles in the security proof. On the downside, the random-oracle model approach is only heuristic and is not sound in general (e.g. (Canetti et al. 1998)). An example of PKE in the RO model is the RSA-OAEP scheme (Bellare and Rogaway 1995), which is shown to be IND-CCA secure in the RO model under the RSA assumption (Fujisaki et al. 2001). Another example is the so-called DHIES scheme (Abdalla et al. 2001) of which the IND-CCA security in the RO model can be reduced to the so-called gap-DH assumption (Okamoto and Pointcheval 2001a), which says that the CDH assumption holds even if an adversary has access to the oracle solving the DDH problem. Yet another scheme that is worth mentioning is a variant of ElGamal called Twin ElGamal (Cash et al. 2008), which is IND-CCA secure in the RO model under the CDH assumption, and enjoys very compact ciphertexts like the original ElGamal PKE. In fact, DHIES and Twin ElGamal have the structure of hybrid encryption (see section 1.3.1).

Furthermore, we also have more "generic" constructions that can generically transform a base scheme (which typically satisfies some weak form of security such as IND-CPA or one-wayness under CPA) into one achieving IND-CCA security in the RO model. (In fact, RSA-OAEP is of this kind, obtained from the OAEP transform applied to the RSA encryption scheme.) We touch on them in section 1.3.3.

1.3. Generic constructions for IND-CCA secure PKE

The previous section describes some *specific* PKE schemes based on concrete mathematical assumptions. This section describes *generic* IND-CCA secure PKE constructions that are based on generic cryptographic primitives.

1.3.1. *Hybrid encryption*

Usually, computation for public-key cryptography is orders-of-magnitude heavier and slower than that for symmetric-key cryptography. *Hybrid encryption* is a practical technique to enjoy the functionality of PKE and the efficiency of SKE as much as possible. Specifically, to encrypt a (long) message, we only encrypt a random, fixed-length "session" key K by a PKE scheme, and the actual message to be sent is encrypted by an SKE using the key K. Cramer and Shoup (2003) introduced a modern treatment and formalization for hybrid encryption (also known as the KEM/DEM framework), where the process of encrypting a random session-key K is formalized as a dedicated primitive called *key encapsulation mechanism (KEM)*.[2]

In this section, we review the modern treatment of hybrid encryption. Specifically, we recall the formalizations of KEM and SKE, and then review the construction of hybrid encryption and related results in the literature.

A KEM consists of the three PPT algorithms $(\mathsf{KKG}, \mathsf{Encap}, \mathsf{Decap})$ with the following syntax:

Key Generation:	**Encapsulation:**	**Decapsulation:**
$(pk, sk) \leftarrow_{\mathrm{R}} \mathsf{KKG}(1^\lambda)$	$(c, K) \leftarrow_{\mathrm{R}} \mathsf{Encap}(pk)$	$K \text{ (or } \perp) \leftarrow \mathsf{Decap}(sk, c)$

where Decap is a deterministic algorithm, (pk, sk) is a public/secret key pair and c is a ciphertext of a session-key K under pk. As in PKE, Decap is allowed to output the special invalid symbol $\perp$.

For a KEM, IND-CCA security and IND-CPA security are defined in a very similar manner to those for PKE. The only essential difference is that in the security experiments for a KEM, instead of choosing two challenge plaintexts, an adversary is given the challenge ciphertext c^* and either a real session-key K^* (generated together with c^*) or a completely random session-key K' and is tasked to distinguish the two cases.

An SKE scheme (also called DEM in the context of hybrid encryption) consists of the two PPT algorithms (E, D) with the following syntax:

Encryption:	**Decryption:**
$c \leftarrow_{\mathrm{R}} \mathsf{E}(K, m)$	$m \text{ (or } \perp) \leftarrow \mathsf{D}(K, c)$

where D is a deterministic algorithm, K denotes a key and c denotes a ciphertext of a plaintext m under K. As in PKE and KEM, D is allowed to output the special invalid

---

2 Correspondingly, the process of encrypting an actual message is called *data encapsulation mechanism (DEM)*, but since its functionality is equivalent to SKE, we will mainly use SKE.

symbol $\perp$. In this syntax, the length of the key K decides the security parameter. In general, an SKE scheme may also have a dedicated key generation algorithm, but here we do not consider such a syntax for simplicity.

When considering the security of SKE in general, we will need to consider an adversary that also has access to an encryption oracle since, unlike the PKE case, an adversary cannot generate a ciphertext by itself. On the other hand, for SKE in the context of hybrid encryption here, we will only require "one-time" encryption since hybrid encryption will only perform single encryption under a single session key, which is fresh per each encryption. Now recall that the security notions of PKE already provide one encryption in the form of challenge ciphertext c^* (see Figure 1.1). Therefore, security notions for "one-time" SKE can thus be defined precisely as the security notions for PKE with the only exception that the public key pk given as an input to an adversary becomes null. We refer to the security notions for SKE derived from IND-CCA (respectively, IND-CPA) security for PKE with this interpretation as *IND-OT-CCA security* (respectively, *IND-OT security*) where OT stands for "one-time encryption".

It may be worth mentioning that constructing IND-OT and IND-OT-CCA secure SKE schemes is somewhat straightforward. The so-called "pseudorandom-one-time pad" scheme (i.e. a one-time pad scheme where we define its key as the output of a pseudorandom generator with a random input) is an example of IND-OT secure SKE. Similarly, any strong pseudorandom permutation (Luby and Rackoff 1988) can be viewed as an IND-OT-CCA secure SKE scheme, where we encrypt a message by inputting it to the permutation. Note that, theoretically, such a permutation can be constructed from any one-way function (Håstad et al. 1999; Luby and Rackoff 1988). From these two examples, we have that both IND-OT-CCA and IND-OT secure SKE can be achieved by encryption schemes of which the encryption algorithm is deterministic and the ciphertext overhead (i.e. the difference between the size of the ciphertext and the size of the plaintext to be encrypted) is zero.

Given a KEM $(\mathsf{KKG}, \mathsf{Encap}, \mathsf{Decap})$ and an SKE scheme (E, D), the hybrid encryption construction of a PKE scheme $(\mathsf{KG}, \mathsf{Enc}, \mathsf{Dec})$ is as described in Figure 1.7.

$\mathsf{KG}(1^\lambda)$:	$\mathsf{Enc}(pk, m)$:	$\mathsf{Dec}(sk, C)$:
$(pk, sk) \leftarrow_R \mathsf{KKG}(1^\lambda)$	$(c, K) \leftarrow_R \mathsf{Encap}(pk)$	Parse $(c, c') \leftarrow C$.
Return (pk, sk).	$c' \leftarrow_R \mathsf{E}(K, m)$	$K \leftarrow \mathsf{Decap}(sk, c)$
	Return $C := (c, c')$.	If $K = \perp$ then return $\perp$.
		$m \leftarrow \mathsf{D}(K, c')$
		Return m.

Figure 1.7. *Hybrid encryption: Construction of PKE from KEM and SKE*

Cramer and Shoup (2003) showed that if the underlying KEM is IND-CCA secure and the underlying SKE scheme is IND-OT-CCA secure, then the hybrid encryption construction is an IND-CCA secure PKE scheme. Furthermore, Herranz et al. (2010) investigated the relation between the security notions achieved by the hybrid encryption construction and those of the underlying KEM/SKE scheme. In particular, they showed that if the underlying KEM is IND-CCA1 secure (respectively, IND-CPA) and the underlying SKE scheme is IND-OT secure, then the hybrid encryption construction is IND-CCA1 (respectively, IND-CPA) secure. Hofheinz and Kiltz (2007) showed yet another result for hybrid encryption: If the underlying KEM is secure in the sense of *constrained CCA security* (which is a security notion strictly weaker than IND-CCA security), and the underlying SKE scheme is secure in the sense of (one-time) authenticated encryption (Bellare and Namprempre 2000) (considering IND-OT security and one-time authenticity at the same time), then the hybrid encryption construction still achieves IND-CCA security. We note that an SKE scheme that achieves both IND-OT security and one-time authenticity simultaneously automatically achieves IND-OT-CCA security; therefore, the requirement of being secure in the sense of one-time authenticated encryption is stronger than IND-OT-CCA security.

Abe et al. (2005) showed another hybrid encryption paradigm different from the one explained above, called the Tag-KEM/DEM framework. This framework defines a new primitive called tag-KEM. Its syntax differs from a normal KEM described above by allowing feedback input from the SKE/DEM part when generating a KEM-ciphertext. One of the merits of this framework is that the underlying SKE scheme can just be IND-OT secure, while constructing a tag-KEM is typically more difficult than constructing an ordinary KEM.

These results on hybrid encryption allow us to focus on the designs of appropriate KEMs when designing an IND-CCA secure PKE scheme.

1.3.2. *Naor–Yung construction and extensions*

We describe a classic method by Naor and Yung (1990) to construct IND-CCA1 secure PKE from an IND-CPA scheme and a *non-interactive zero-knowledge* (NIZK) proof system (Blum et al. 1988). In this construction, the plaintext is encrypted twice under independent keys and randomnesses, and then NIZK is used in order to prove that both ciphertexts encrypt the same plaintext. The intuition is that if the adversary can somehow obtain two ciphertexts that independently encrypt the same plaintext, then essentially it must already know the plaintext. Therefore, the decryption oracle should be useless to the adversary.

We first briefly recapitulate the concept of NP languages and the syntax of NIZK for such languages. More details on zero-knowledge proofs can be found in Chapter 3.

A language is a set of binary strings, say $L \subset \{0,1\}^*$. A language L is in the class called NP if there exists a deterministic polynomial-time Turing machine M such that $x \in L$ if and only if there exists a *witness* w of length polynomial in the length of x such that $M(x, w) = 1$.

$\mathsf{KG}'(1^\lambda)$:	$\mathsf{Enc}'(pk', m)$:	$\mathsf{Dec}'(sk', C)$:
$(pk_1, sk_1) \leftarrow_\mathsf{R} \mathsf{KG}(1^\lambda)$	$w_1, w_2 \leftarrow_\mathsf{R} \{0,1\}^\ell$	Parse $(c_1, c_2, \pi) \leftarrow C$.
$(pk_2, sk_2) \leftarrow_\mathsf{R} \mathsf{KG}(1^\lambda)$	$c_1 \leftarrow \mathsf{Enc}(pk_1, m; w_1)$	$x := (pk_1, pk_2, c_1, c_2)$
$r \leftarrow_\mathsf{R} \mathsf{CRSGen}(1^\lambda)$	$c_2 \leftarrow \mathsf{Enc}(pk_2, m; w_2)$	If $\mathsf{V}(r, x, \pi) = 0$
$pk' := (pk_1, pk_2, r)$	$x := (pk_1, pk_2, c_1, c_2)$	Return $\bot$.
$sk' := (sk_1, pk')$	$w := (m, w_1, w_2)$	Else
Return (pk', sk').	$\pi \leftarrow_\mathsf{R} \mathsf{P}(r, x, w)$	Return $\mathsf{Dec}(sk_1, c_1)$.
	Return $C := (c_1, c_2, \pi)$.	

Figure 1.8. *Naor-Yung construction*

An NIZK proof system for an NP language L in the *common random string* (CRS) model consists of the three algorithms $(\mathsf{CRSGen}, \mathsf{P}, \mathsf{V})$ with the following syntax:

CRS Generation: **Proving:**   **Verification:**
$r \leftarrow_\mathsf{R} \mathsf{CRSGen}(1^\lambda)$ $\pi \leftarrow_\mathsf{R} \mathsf{P}(r, x, w)$ $b \leftarrow \mathsf{V}(r, x, \pi)$

where V is a deterministic algorithm, r denotes a CRS, x and w denote a statement and its corresponding witness in the language L and $b \in \{0,1\}$ represents whether V accepts ($b = 1$) or not ($b = 0$). NIZK should satisfy *completeness* (meaning that if $x \in L$, then in the above process, the verifier V will always accept), *soundness* (meaning that if $x \notin L$, then even all-powerful prover P' cannot output a proof π' that V accepts) and *zero-knowledge* (intuitively, meaning that V should not "learn" anything beyond b). NIZK for any NP language can be constructed, for example, from the hardness of factoring (Feige et al. 1990, 1999), bilinear pairings (Groth et al. 2006b, 2012), and lattices (Peikert and Shiehian 2019). (As of writing, the theory on NIZK is still rapidly developing. Interested readers are referred to recent papers (Canetti et al. 2019; Couteau et al. 2020; Kitagawa et al. 2020).

The Naor-Yung PKE construction is shown in Figure 1.8, where we construct a new PKE scheme $(\mathsf{KG}', \mathsf{Enc}', \mathsf{Dec}')$ based on a PKE scheme $(\mathsf{KG}, \mathsf{Enc}, \mathsf{Dec})$ such that the randomness space of Enc is $\{0,1\}^\ell$ for some polynomial $\ell = \ell(\lambda)$, and an NIZK system in the CRS model $(\mathsf{CRSGen}, \mathsf{P}, \mathsf{V})$ for the NP language L defined by

$$L := \left\{ (pk_1, pk_2, c_1, c_2) \mid \exists (m, w_1, w_2) : \begin{array}{l} c_1 = \mathsf{Enc}(pk_1, m; w_1) \\ \wedge\, c_2 = \mathsf{Enc}(pk_2, m; w_2) \end{array} \right\}.$$

Naor and Yung (1990) showed that if the underlying PKE scheme is IND-CPA and the underlying NIZK is *adaptively secure* (sound and zero-knowledge), then the resulting PKE scheme is *IND-CCA1* secure. Dolev et al. (1991) extended the Naor–Yung construction and achieved the first feasibility result for *full-fledge IND-CCA* secure PKE (as opposed to IND-CCA1). Sahai (1999) showed that the Naor–Yung construction as-is can be proved IND-CCA secure if the underlying NIZK system satisfies a stronger form of soundness called *one-time simulation soundness*. Subsequent works (De Santis et al. 2001; Lindell 2003) showed improved and simplified constructions.

1.3.2.1. Connection to the Cramer–Shoup PKE

It is worth mentioning that the Cramer–Shoup PKE Cramer and Shoup (1998, 2003) can be seen as being inspired by the Naor–Yung paradigm. First, the Cramer–Shoup scheme can be viewed loosely as encryption of a message under multiple possible secret keys. This is similar to the Naor–Yung paradigm, which utilizes two secret keys. Second, the validity check in the Cramer–Shoup PKE has a similar functionality as verifying the NIZK proof that the ciphertext is "well-formed". Moreover, as mentioned earlier in section 1.2.5, Cramer and Shoup (2002) provided a generalization of their scheme based on HPSs. HPS can be viewed as a special type of NIZK proof system for a specific class of NP languages called subset membership problems (of which, a problem such as the one related to DDH is a particular instance). We briefly survey further results based on HPS in section 1.3.4.

1.3.3. Fujisaki–Okamoto and other transforms in the RO model

We next describe one of the most popular and versatile generic transformations for achieving IND-CCA secure PKE in the RO model, called the Fujisaki-Okamoto (FO) transform.

Let (KG, Enc, Dec) be a PKE scheme such that its plaintext space is $\{0, 1\}^\lambda$ and the randomness space of Enc is $\{0, 1\}^\ell$ for some polynomial $\ell = \ell(\lambda)$. Let (E, D) be an SKE scheme. Let $H : \{0, 1\}^* \rightarrow \{0, 1\}^\ell$ and $G : \{0, 1\}^\lambda \rightarrow \{0, 1\}^\lambda$ be hash functions (which will be modeled as random oracles). Given these ingredients, the PKE scheme $\Pi_{FO} = (KG_{FO}, Enc_{FO}, Dec_{FO})$ constructed from the FO transform is described in Figure 1.9. The plaintext space of Π_{FO} is the same as that of the underlying SKE scheme.

Fujisaki and Okamoto (2013) showed that if the underlying PKE scheme satisfies one-wayness under CPA and a natural property that the min-entropy of the output of the encryption algorithm $Enc(pk, \cdot)$ (when its randomness is chosen randomly) is sufficiently high for any pk generated by KG (which is usually satisfied by most PKE schemes by default), and the underlying SKE scheme is IND-OT secure, then the resulting PKE scheme Π_{FO} is IND-CCA secure in the RO model where H and G are modeled as random oracles.

$KG_{FO}(1^\lambda)$:	$Enc_{FO}(pk, m)$:	$Dec_{FO}(sk, C)$:
$(pk, sk) \leftarrow_R KG(1^\lambda)$	$s \leftarrow_R \{0, 1\}^\lambda$	Parse $(c, c') \leftarrow C$.
Return (pk, sk).	$K \leftarrow G(s)$	$s \leftarrow Dec(sk, c)$
	$c' \leftarrow_R E(K, m)$	If $s = \perp$ then return $\perp$.
	$R \leftarrow H(s, c')$	$R \leftarrow H(s, c')$
	$c \leftarrow Enc(pk, s; R)$	If $Enc(pk, s; R) \neq c$ then return $\perp$.
	Return $C := (c, c')$.	$K \leftarrow G(s)$
		Return $m := D(K, c')$.

Figure 1.9. *The Fujisaki-Okamoto transform*

We remark that the FO transform shown in this section is from Fujisaki and Okamoto (2013), which fixes a minor bug in the conference version (Fujisaki and Okamoto 1999b). We also note that Fujisaki and Okamoto proposed another transform (Fujisaki and Okamoto 1999) that converts any IND-CPA secure PKE scheme (with the same requirement of the min-entropy on Enc) into an IND-CCA secure PKE scheme in the RO model. Okamoto and Pointcheval (2001b) and Coron et al. (2002a) proposed variants of the FO transform, called REACT and GEM, respectively, which are simpler than the FO transform but require the underlying PKE scheme to satisfy a somewhat non-standard security notion called one-wayness under plaintext-checking attacks (PCA) (where an adversary is given access to the oracle that on input a ciphertext c and a plaintext m tells the adversary whether c decrypts to m). Dent (2003) proposed a KEM-variant of the FO transform. Hofheinz et al. (2017) gave a modular security analysis on the FO transform.

There are other generic conversions in the RO model that are applicable to TDFs or trapdoor permutations (TDPs). Bellare and Rogaway (1993) in the very first paper introducing the RO model proposed a transformation that transforms any one-way TDF into an IND-CCA secure PKE scheme in the RO model. One of the most famous and important generic transforms in the RO model is the OAEP (Optimal Asymmetric Encryption Padding) transform proposed by Bellare and Rogaway (1995), which converts any TDP that satisfies a stronger form of one-wayness called partial-domain one-wayness (Shoup 2001a; Fujisaki et al. 2001), into an IND-CCA secure PKE scheme in the RO model. The RSA-OAEP scheme (the OAEP applied to the RSA encryption scheme) is standardized in PKCS#1v.2.1. In the literature, several variants of OAEP have been considered, which include OAEP+ (Shoup 2001a), OAEP++ (Kobara and Imai 2002), SAEP and SAEP+ (Boneh 2001), and so on (Coron et al. 2002b; Komano and Ohta 2003; Phan and Pointcheval 2003; Dodis et al. 2004; Phan and Pointcheval 2004; Abe et al. 2008).

Since the public competition for post-quantum cryptography organized by NIST[3] started in 2016, the FO transforms and variants have regained renowned attention due to the versatility. In particular, several recent works (Targhi and Unruh 2016; Hofheinz et al. 2017; Saito et al. 2018; Jiang et al. 2018, 2019a,b; Ambainis et al. 2019; Bindel et al. 2019; Kuchta et al. 2020) have analyzed the IND-CCA security of FO transforms and variants in the *quantum* RO model (Boneh et al. 2011) in which superposition of hash queries by an adversary is taken into account.

1.3.4. *Other generic constructions for IND-CCA secure PKE*

One major line of research on PKE is to clarify what generic assumption is sufficient for constructing IND-CCA secure PKE, and in particular whether its existence is implied by an IND-CPA secure one. Here, we give a survey on the results in this line of research (other than the NIZK-based constructions that we have explained above).

1.3.4.1. *Transformations from ID-based encryption and tag-based encryption*

Canetti et al. (2004) showed how to transform an identity-based encryption scheme (Shamir 1984; Boneh and Franklin 2001), which is a special class of PKE, into an IND-CCA secure PKE scheme, using a one-time secure signature scheme. Boneh and Katz (2005) proposed a variant of this transformation that is potentially more efficient than the one by Canetti et al. (2004) using lighter primitives than a one-time signature scheme. Kiltz (2006) showed that these transformations are applicable to a tag-based encryption scheme (a.k.a. PKE with labels), which is generally a weaker primitive than identity-based encryption.

1.3.4.2. *Constructions based on TDFs and related primitives*

Peikert and Waters (2008) showed how to construct an IND-CCA secure PKE scheme from a trapdoor function with a special property, called a lossy TDF, which can in turn be constructed from homomorphic encryption with some natural property (Hemenway and Ostrovsky 2012), lossy (probabilistic) encryption (introduced by Bellare et al. (2009)) which can encrypt messages longer than its encryption-randomness (Hemenway and Ostrovsky 2013), or a primitive called trapdoor hash (Döttling et al. 2019). Subsequent works showed that TDFs with weaker security/functionality properties are sufficient for obtaining IND-CCA secure PKE schemes (Rosen and Segev 2009; Kiltz et al. 2010; Wee 2010; Yamakawa et al. 2016). Finally, in a very recent work, Hohenberger et al. (2020) showed how to construct an IND-CCA secure PKE scheme from any TDF that achieves only standard one-wayness.

---

3 Available at: https://csrc.nist.gov/projects/post-quantum-cryptography.

1.3.4.3. *Further constructions from (variants of) hash proof systems*

As mentioned earlier, Cramer and Shoup (2002) introduced a notion called HPS and provided a framework to construct IND-CCA secure PKE based on HPS. Wee (2010) introduced another framework for constructing IND-CCA secure PKE schemes based on the hardness of computational (search-type) problems rather than decisional (indistinguishability-type) problems, called (all-but-one) *extractable HPSs*, which was further extended in Matsuda and Hanaoka (2013) to capture a wider class of constructions. The framework of extractable HPSs can capture many efficient IND-CCA secure PKE schemes that are not instances of the framework of (ordinary) HPS, such as those by Boyen et al. (2005); Cash et al. (2008); Hanaoka and Kurosawa (2008); Hofheinz and Kiltz (2009); Haralambiev et al. (2010).

1.3.4.4. *Constructions via KDM security*

A series of works (Matsuda and Hanaoka 2015b; Hajiabadi and Kapron 2015; Kitagawa et al. 2019a; Kitagawa and Matsuda 2020) showed how to construct an IND-CCA secure PKE scheme from an encryption scheme satisfying various forms of key-dependent message security, which we will discuss in section 1.4.3. In particular, the latest work by Kitagawa and Matsuda (2020) showed that an IND-CCA secure PKE scheme can be constructed from an IND-CPA secure PKE scheme and a bit-SKE scheme satisfying a very weak form of KDM security called circular security.

1.3.4.5. *Constructions from cryptographic obfuscation*

Sahai and Waters (2014) showed, among other things, how to construct an IND-CCA secure PKE scheme from a general-purpose cryptographic obfuscator (Barak et al. 2001; Garg et al. 2013) satisfying indistinguishability-type security notion, so-called indistinguishability obfuscation. Matsuda and Hanaoka (2014a) showed how to construct an IND-CCA secure PKE scheme based on a point-function-obfuscator.

1.3.4.6. *Other constructions relying on additional tools/assumptions*

Matsuda and Hanaoka (2014b) showed another construction from an IND-CPA secure PKE scheme and a hash family satisfying one of the universal computational extractors (UCE) assumptions (Bellare et al. 2013) that tries to formalize some aspects of security properties achieved by a random oracle in the standard model. Koppula and Waters (2019) showed how to construct an IND-CCA secure PKE scheme based on the combination of an IND-CPA secure PKE scheme and a pseudorandom generator (PRG) satisfying a special security property, called a hinting PRG. Dachman-Soled (2014) and Matsuda and Hanaoka (2016) showed how to construct an IND-CCA secure PKE scheme from a PKE scheme that satisfies (weak) simulatability and the (standard model) plaintext awareness under the multiple keys setting (Bellare and Palacio 2004; Myers et al. 2012).

1.4. Advanced topics

1.4.1. *Intermediate notions related to CCA*

This section briefly describes some security notions that are present between IND-CPA and IND-CCA security.

1.4.1.1. *Replayable CCA security*

In some situations, the security property achieved by IND-CCA security could be too strong or strict. For example, no encryption scheme that allows rerandomization of a ciphertext or a homomorphic property can achieve IND-CCA security. *Replayable CCA security*, introduced by Canetti et al. (2003), is a security notion that tries to relax the strictness of IND-CCA security and yet capture sufficiently strong security required in practical applications. It is defined by using an IND-CCA-like security experiment in which when an adversary makes a decryption query c after given the challenge ciphertext; if c decrypts to one of the challenge plaintexts m_0 or m_1 (chosen by the adversary at the challenge), the adversary is only informed of this fact and is not given the actual decryption result. Security notions with a very similar flavor were introduced with a similar motivation: benign non-malleability (Shoup 2001b) and generalized CCA security (An et al. 2002).

The definition of replayable CCA security might sound somewhat artificial. However, it turns out that in the context of viewing a public key encryption scheme as a tool (or a resource) for establishing/constructing a confidential channel, replayable CCA security is the right security notion in the sense that a PKE scheme satisfying this security notion is sufficient for the purpose. For the details and the discussions on the variants and subtleties on this security notion, see Canetti et al. (2003); Coretti et al. (2013); Badertscher et al. (2021). It is also worth mentioning that, unlike IND-CCA security, replayable CCA security can be achieved by a PKE scheme supporting rerandomizability and/or a homomorphic property (Prabhakaran and Rosulek 2007, 2008).

1.4.1.2. *Detectable CCA security*

Hohenberger et al. (2012) introduced a security notion similar to RCCA security, called *detactable CCA* security, where there is a binary relation R over two ciphertexts (specific to a scheme), and the decryption oracle does not answer to a query c satisfying $R(c^*, c) = 1$, where c^* denotes the challenge ciphertext. Note that CCA (respectively, CPA) security can be considered a special case of this notion where $R(c^*, c) = 1$ iff $c^* = c$ (respectively, $R(c^*, c) = 1$ for all c^*, c). Hohenberger et al. (2012) showed that if some scheme satisfies detectable CCA security with respect to a relation R satisfying a requirement called unpreditabability (which says that if c^* is not given, coming up with a ciphertext c satisfying $R(c^*, c) = 1$ is hard), then it can be generically transformed to a PKE scheme satisfying IND-CCA security. Hohenberger et al. (2012) used this notion to give a simpler solution to the problem of constructing an IND-CCA secure multi-bit PKE scheme from an IND-CCA secure bit-PKE scheme (without using additional building blocks), which had been solved by Myers and Shelat (2009). An interested reader is also referred to Matsuda and Hanaoka (2015a), which further studied detectable CCA security and showed an even simpler one-bit-to-multi-bit transformation for IND-CCA secure PKE.

1.4.1.3. *More notions related to CCA*

Other (somewhat minor) security notions that are present between IND-CPA and IND-CCA include the following. *Bounded CCA security* (Cramer et al. 2007) and its variants (Matsuda and Matsuura 2011; Myers et al. 2012) where the number of the adversary's decryption queries is a priori bounded (and the number may be hardwired into the scheme itself); *self-destruct CCA security* (Coretti et al. 2015, 2016), where once an adversary's decryption query results in $\perp$, then the decryption oracle will "self-destruct" and will not answer any future decryption queries from the adversary. One motivation why these intermediate notions have been considered is to study a security notion that can be achieved by a PKE scheme that is constructed solely from an IND-CPA security notion. As mentioned earlier, whether an IND-CCA secure PKE scheme can be constructed solely from an IND-CPA secure one is a major open problem on PKE, and interestingly, the security notions mentioned above (in some parameter settings) can be achieved by PKE schemes constructed solely from an IND-CPA secure one.

1.4.2. *IND-CCA security in multi-user setting and tight security*

The standard definition of IND-CCA security deals with a single key pair and a single challenge ciphertext, and hence seems to capture only the scenario in which there is only a single user sending a single encrypted message. It might be a priori not clear whether IND-CCA security guarantees sufficiently strong security in a situation where there are multiple users sending multiple encrypted messages.

Bellare et al. (2000) formalized a version of IND-CCA security for PKE in which there are multiple users and multiple challenge ciphertexts. Here, we call it *multi-user/challenge IND-CCA security*, and quickly recall the definition. For a PKE scheme $\Pi = (\mathsf{KG}, \mathsf{Enc}, \mathsf{Dec})$, $n \in \mathbb{N}$, and an adversary $\mathcal{A}$, the n-user/multi-challenge IND-CCA experiment is defined as in Figure 1.10. We say that Π is multi-user/challenge IND-CCA secure if for any PPT adversary $\mathcal{A}$ and any polynomial $n = n(\lambda)$, the advantage function $\mathsf{Adv}_{\Pi,\mathcal{A},n}^{m-indcca}(\lambda) := |\Pr[\mathsf{Expt}_{\Pi,\mathcal{A},n}^{m-indcca}(\lambda) = 1] - 1/2|$ is negligible.

Bellare et al. (2000) showed that if a PKE scheme is IND-CCA secure, then it is automatically multi-user/multi-challenge IND-CCA secure. More specifically, they showed that for any PKE scheme Π, if there exists an adversary $\mathcal{A}$ in the n-user/multi-challenge IND-CCA experiment that makes q encryption queries to $\mathcal{O}_{enc}$, there exists another adversary $\mathcal{B}$ (with similar running time to $\mathcal{A}$) that attacks the (single-user/challenge) IND-CCA experiment so that we have

$$\mathsf{Adv}_{\Pi,\mathcal{A},n}^{m-indcca}(\lambda) \leq n \cdot q \cdot \mathsf{Adv}_{\Pi,\mathcal{B}}^{indcca}(\lambda).$$

$\mathsf{Expt}_{\Pi,\mathcal{A},n}^{m-indcca}(\lambda):$
  $L_{enc} \leftarrow \emptyset$
  $\forall i \in [n]:$
  $(pk_i, sk_i) \leftarrow_R KG(1^\lambda)$
  $\mathfrak{b} \leftarrow_R \{0,1\}$
  $\mathfrak{b}' \leftarrow_R \mathcal{A}^{\mathcal{O}_{enc}(\cdot,\cdot,\cdot),\mathcal{O}_{dec}(\cdot,\cdot)}((pk_i)_{i \in [n]})$
  Return $(\mathfrak{b}' \overset{?}{=} \mathfrak{b})$.

$\mathcal{O}_{enc}(j, m_0, m_1) : // j \in [n]$
  If $|m_0| \neq |m_1|$
    then return $\perp$.
  $c \leftarrow_R Enc(pk_j, m_\mathfrak{b})$
  $L_{enc} \leftarrow L_{enc} \cup \{(j, c)\}$
  Return c.

$\mathcal{O}_{dec}(j, c) : // j \in [n]$
  If $(j, c) \in L_{enc}$
    then return $\perp$.
  Return $Dec(sk_j, c)$.

Figure 1.10. *The multi-user/multi-challenge IND-CCA experiment for PKE*

Although this result gives us an *asymptotic* guarantee (any PPT adversary attacking the multi-user/challenge IND-CCA security has only negligible advantage), its guarantee is not satisfactory if we consider more *concrete* security guarantee: Even if $\mathsf{Adv}_{\Pi,\mathcal{B}}^{indcca}$ is sufficiently small (say, 2^{-128}), $\mathsf{Adv}_{\Pi,\mathcal{A},n}^{m-indcca}$ may not be bounded by a small-enough value depending on the values n and q. Let us see this using simple examples. Suppose $n = 2^{32}$ and $q = 2^{40}$ (say, each of half the world population sends a single encrypted message per day in 1 year), and suppose we have a "secure" PKE scheme Π that can be assumed to achieve $\mathsf{Adv}_{\Pi,\mathcal{B}}^{indcca} \leq 2^{-128}$ for any adversary $\mathcal{B}$ whose running time is much larger than $n \cdot q$. Then, the result of Bellare et al. (2000) only guarantees that $\mathsf{Adv}_{\Pi,\mathcal{A},n}^{m-indcca} \leq 2^{-48}$ for an adversary $\mathcal{A}$ whose running time is similar to that of $\mathcal{B}$. Alternatively, if we would like to have the guarantee $\mathsf{Adv}_{\Pi,\mathcal{A},n}^{m-indcca} \leq 2^{-128}$, the PKE scheme Π needs to satisfy $\mathsf{Adv}_{\Pi,\mathcal{B}}^{indcca} \leq 2^{-200}$.

In general, to prove that a PKE scheme Π is IND-CCA secure in the n-user setting against an adversary $\mathcal{A}$ making q_{enc} encryption queries and q_{dec} decryption queries based on the hardness of some problem P, we construct another adversary (reduction algorithm) $\mathcal{B}$ whose running time is similar to $\mathcal{A}$ and that satisfies

$$\mathsf{Adv}_{\Pi,\mathcal{A},n}^{m-indcca}(\lambda) \leq F_{loss}(n, q_{enc}, q_{dec}, \lambda) \cdot \mathsf{Adv}_{\mathcal{B}}^{P}(\lambda) + F'(n, q_{enc}, q_{dec}) \cdot \epsilon(\lambda),$$

where F_{loss} and F' are polynomials, $\mathsf{Adv}_{\mathcal{B}}^{P}(\lambda)$ denotes the advantage of $\mathcal{B}$ in solving the problem P, and $\epsilon(\lambda)$ is a negligible function in λ independent of n, q_{enc}, q_{dec}, $\mathcal{A}$

and $\mathcal{B}$.[4] F_{loss} denotes the *security loss* of the reduction. In the literature, a security reduction for proving the multi-user/challenge IND-CCA security of a PKE scheme based on the hardness of a problem P is said to be *tight* if F_{loss} is just a constant, independent of n, q_{enc}, q_{dec} and λ. In this case, the PKE scheme is also said to be *tightly secure* (based on P).[5] The case F_{loss} is polynomial of small degree in λ (and independent of n, q_{enc} and q_{dec} or dependent only logarithmically on them) is called almost-tight (or sometimes also just called tight).

Bellare et al. (2000) proved the multi-user/challenge IND-CCA security of the Cramer–Shoup scheme (Cramer and Shoup 1998) based on the DDH assumption with the security loss depending only on the number of encryption queries (and independent of the number of users and decryption queries). It was more than a decade later that the first tightly secure PKE scheme based on a well-known and -studied assumption was shown by Hofheinz and Jager (2012). Their scheme is based on the Naor–Yung paradigm, and its security is based on the DLin assumption in bilinear groups. It is however inefficient as the public key and ciphertext consist of several hundreds of group elements. Since the work by Hofheinz and Jager (2012), there have been a number of works that construct a tightly secure PKE scheme based on that assumption: Abe et al. (2013); Hofheinz et al. (2015); Libert et al. (2015); Attrapadung et al. (2015); Gong et al. (2016); Hofheinz (2016); Gay et al. (2016); Hofheinz (2017); Gay et al. (2017); Han et al. (2019) (among which all but the first one are with only almost tight reductions). Notably, the DDH-based (almost) tightly secure scheme of Gay et al. (2017) has similar efficiency to the practical (non-tight) DDH-based schemes of Cramer and Shoup (1998); Kurosawa and Desmedt (2004).

1.4.3. *Key-dependent message security*

In the standard security notions for PKE, it is implicitly assumed that messages to be encrypted are not dependent on a secret key (except that they can be dependent on the corresponding public key). However, there are some applications in which we would like to (or have to) encrypt messages that are dependent on a secret key, for example, hard-disc encryption (Boneh et al. 2008), anonymous credentials (Camenisch and Lysyanskaya 2002) and fully homomorphic encryption (Gentry 2009).

---

4 Strictly speaking, if we are interested only in an asymptotic security guarantee, it is sufficient that $\mathsf{Adv}_{\mathcal{B}}^{\mathsf{P}}(\lambda)$ in the right-hand side is replaced with $(\mathsf{Adv}_{\mathcal{B}}^{\mathsf{P}}(\lambda))^c$ for some positive constant $c \leq 1$, and the running time of $\mathcal{B}$ can be a polynomial of $\mathcal{A}$'s running time. Such more general cases go the opposite way to the tightness of reductions.

5 Note that a PKE scheme is always tightly secure based on the assumption that "the scheme is multi-user/challenge IND-CCA secure". Hence, tight security makes sense only when the underlying assumption (problem) P is a well-studied one in the literature, such as DDH.

Key-dependent message (KDM) security is a security notion that guarantees confidentiality even if encrypted messages are dependent on a secret key. KDM security was first introduced and formalized by Black et al. (2003) for SKE. A limited form of KDM security (called *circular security*) was introduced and studied independently by Camenisch and Lysyanskaya (2002). The standard formalization of KDM security for PKE was given by Boneh et al. (2008). KDM security is parameterized by a function class $\mathcal{F}$ that expresses the dependence of a message on a secret key, and the more expressive $\mathcal{F}$ is, the stronger KDM security becomes. Informally, KDM security with respect to $\mathcal{F}$ (we call this $\mathcal{F}$-KDM security) guarantees that a ciphertext encrypting $f(sk)$ for any $f \in \mathcal{F}$ is indistinguishable from one encrypting some fixed message of length $|f(sk)|$. Like the standard indistinguishability security notions, KDM security can also be considered in the CPA and CCA settings, which are, respectively, denoted by KDM-CPA and KDM-CCA. One might wonder whether standard indistinguishability security notions imply KDM security. Unfortunately, a series of works (Acar et al. 2010; Cash et al. 2012; Rothblum 2013; Marcedone and Orlandi 2014; Koppula et al. 2015; Bishop et al. 2015; Goyal et al. 2017c,b,a) showed that under a standard cryptographic assumption (e.g. the LWE assumption), there is a PKE scheme that is IND-CPA secure but is not circular secure. Furthermore, Hajiabadi and Kapron (2017) showed that it is impossible to construct a circular-secure bit-encryption scheme based only on an IND-CPA secure PKE scheme in the sense of "black-box" constructions (Reingold et al. 2004; Baecher et al. 2013).

In the RO model, KDM-CPA/CCA secure PKE schemes are relatively easy to achieve. In particular, the RSA-OAEP scheme (Bellare and Rogaway 1995), (a slight variant of) the hybrid encryption construction and the FO-transformed PKE scheme (Fujisaki and Okamoto 2013) are shown to be KDM-CCA secure in the RO model with respect to all efficiently computable functions in Backes et al. (2008), Davies and Stam (2014) and Kitagawa et al. (2016), respectively. In the standard model, KDM-CPA secure PKE schemes with respect to specific (simple) class of functions were constructed in, for example, Boneh et al. (2008); Applebaum et al. (2009); Brakerski and Goldwasser (2010); Brakerski et al. (2011); Malkin et al. (2011); Döttling (2015); Hajiabadi et al. (2016); Wee (2016); Brakerski et al. (2018); Lai et al. (2021), and KDM-CPA secure PKE schemes with respect to any functions (computable by poly-sized circuits) were constructed in, for example, Barak et al. (2010); Applebaum (2011); Bellare et al. (2012b); Marcedone et al. (2016). KDM-CCA secure PKE schemes with respect to specific class of functions were constructed in, for example, Galindo et al. (2012); Hofheinz (2013); Han et al. (2016); Kitagawa and Tanaka (2018); Libert and Qian (2019); Kitagawa et al. (2019b). KDM-CCA secure PKE schemes with respect to any functions (computable by poly-sized circuits) can be achieved via the methods for "enhancing" KDM security: enhancing from KDM security with respect to simpler functions to that with respect to wider/more complex functions (Applebaum 2011; Kitagawa and Matsuda

2019, 2020), and enhancing from KDM-CPA to KDM-CCA (e.g. Camenisch et al. 2009; Kitagawa and Matsuda 2019, 2020).

1.4.4. *More topics on PKE*

1.4.4.1. *Fully homomorphic encryption*

Homomorphic encryption allows computation on ciphertexts while preserving the security of the scheme. For example, in additive homomorphic PKE, one can obtain $\mathsf{Enc}(pk, m_1 + m_2)$ from $\mathsf{Enc}(pk, m_1)$ and $\mathsf{Enc}(pk, m_2)$. Examples of additive homomorphic PKE include Goldwasser and Micali (1982) and Paillier (1999), while those of multiplicative homomorphic PKE include RSA and ElGamal PKE. These earlier works allow either one type of operations, a limited number of operations (e.g. Boneh et al. 2005), or confined to a set of specific operations (e.g. Sander et al. 1999; Ishai and Paskin 2007). Gentry (2009) proposed the first fully homomorphic PKE, which allows unlimited numbers of both modular additions and multiplications, and thus arbitrary arithmetic circuit computations. We refer to a survey on this topic by Acar et al. (2019).

1.4.4.2. *Leakage-resilient security*

Typical security notions like IND-CCA require the secret key sk to be kept completely private. However, in real-world applications, this requirement might not be perfectly fulfilled due to side-channel attacks or malware and so on. *Leakage-resilient* security is a notion that allows the adversary to adaptively learn information about the secret key sk, subjected only to the constraint that the total amount of the information leaked is bounded by some parameter. Such a notion in the PKE setting was initiated by Akavia et al. (2009). We refer to Alwen et al. (2010) and Kalai and Reyzin (2019) for surveys on this topic.

1.4.4.3. *Adaptive security and security against selective-opening attacks*

Selective-opening (SO) security considers attack scenarios in multi-user settings where the adversary can adaptively corrupt some users and learn (i.e. "open") all the information of corrupted users including randomness, while the security concerns those ciphertexts created by or sent to uncorrupted users (depending on the flavor of SO security, namely, sender security and receiver security, respectively). This attack scenario first arose in the context of adaptively secure multi-party computation (Canetti et al. 1996), where the adversary can corrupt some encrypted channels. SO security can be considered for both the sender corruption case and the receiver corruption case.

Bellare et al. (2009) are the first to formalize selective-opening security for sender (sender SO security, for short), who gave simulation-based and indistinguishability-based definitions. The case of receiver corruption (receiver SO security) was formalized and studied by Bellare et al. (2012a); Hazay et al. (2015). A series of works (Bellare et al. 2009, 2012a; Böhl et al. 2012; Hofheinz and Rupp 2014; Hazay et al. 2015; Hofheinz et al. 2016b) showed that a standard security notion such as IND-CPA (or even IND-CCA) does not imply sender or receiver SO security. Note that hybrid arguments do not help to bridge standard notions to the multi-user setting considered here, since in this case, in particular, the randomness is required to be opened (and standard notions do not allow so). (The work of Fuchsbauer et al. (2016), on the other hand, showed that IND-CPA security implies SO security under a certain condition on the corruption.) Sender SO secure PKE schemes were constructed in many works (Bellare et al. 2009; Fehr et al. 2010; Hemenway et al. 2011; Hofheinz 2012; Huang et al. 2013; Liu and Paterson 2015; Heuer et al. 2015; Hofheinz et al. 2016a; Heuer and Poettering 2016; Hoang et al. 2016; Libert et al. 2017; Lyu et al. 2018). Receiver SO secure PKE schemes were constructed in, for example, Hazay et al. (2015); Jia et al. (2016, 2017); Hara et al. (2018); Huang et al. (2019); Yang et al. (2020).

1.5. References

Abdalla, M., Bellare, M., Rogaway, P. (2001). The oracle Diffie–Hellman assumptions and an analysis of DHIES. In *CT-RSA 2001*, vol. 2020 of *LNCS*, Naccache, D. (ed.). Springer, Heidelberg.

Abe, M., Gennaro, R., Kurosawa, K., Shoup, V. (2005). Tag-KEM/DEM: A new framework for hybrid encryption and a new analysis of Kurosawa-Desmedt KEM. In *EUROCRYPT 2005*, vol. 3494 of *LNCS*, Cramer, R. (ed.). Springer, Heidelberg.

Abe, M., Kiltz, E., Okamoto, T. (2008). Chosen ciphertext security with optimal ciphertext overhead. In *ASIACRYPT 2008*, vol. 5350 of *LNCS*, Pieprzyk, J. (ed.). Springer, Heidelberg.

Abe, M., David, B., Kohlweiss, M., Nishimaki, R., Ohkubo, M. (2013). Tagged one-time signatures: Tight security and optimal tag size. In *PKC 2013*, vol. 7778 of *LNCS*, Kurosawa, K., Hanaoka, G. (eds). Springer, Heidelberg.

Acar, T., Belenkiy, M., Bellare, M., Cash, D. (2010). Cryptographic agility and its relation to circular encryption. In *EUROCRYPT 2010*, vol. 6110 of *LNCS*, Gilbert, H. (ed.). Springer, Heidelberg.

Acar, A., Aksu, H., Uluagac, A.S., Conti, M. (2019). A survey on homomorphic encryption schemes: Theory and implementation. *ACM Computing Surveys*, 51(4), 79, 1–35 [Online]. Available at: https://doi.org/10.1145/3214303.

Akavia, A., Goldwasser, S., Vaikuntanathan, V. (2009), Simultaneous hardcore bits and cryptography against memory attacks. In *TCC 2009*, vol. 5444 of *LNCS*, Reingold, O. (ed.). Springer, Heidelberg.

Alwen, J., Dodis, Y., Wichs, D. (2010). Survey: Leakage resilience and the bounded retrieval model. In *ICITS 09*, vol. 5973 of *LNCS*, Kurosawa, K. (ed.). Springer, Heidelberg.

Ambainis, A., Hamburg, M., Unruh, D. (2019). Quantum security proofs using semi-classical oracles. In *CRYPTO 2019, Part II*, vol. 11693 of *LNCS*, Boldyreva, A., Micciancio, D. (eds). Springer, Heidelberg.

An, J.H., Dodis, Y., Rabin, T. (2002). On the security of joint signature and encryption. In *EUROCRYPT 2002*, vol. 2332 of *LNCS*, Knudsen, L.R. (ed.). Springer, Heidelberg.

Applebaum, B. (2011). Key-dependent message security: Generic amplification and completeness. In *EUROCRYPT 2011*, vol. 6632 of *LNCS*, Paterson, K.G. (ed.). Springer, Heidelberg.

Applebaum, B., Cash, D., Peikert, C., Sahai, A. (2009). Fast cryptographic primitives and circular-secure encryption based on hard learning problems. In *CRYPTO 2009*, vol. 5677 of *LNCS*, Halevi, S. (ed.). Springer, Heidelberg.

Attrapadung, N., Hanaoka, G., Yamada, S. (2015). A framework for identity-based encryption with almost tight security. In *ASIACRYPT 2015, Part I*, vol. 9452 of *LNCS*, Iwata, T., Cheon, J.H. (eds). Springer, Heidelberg.

Backes, M., Dürmuth, M., Unruh, D. (2008). OAEP is secure under key-dependent messages. In *ASIACRYPT 2008*, vol. 5350 of *LNCS*, Pieprzyk, J. (ed.). Springer, Heidelberg.

Badertscher, C., Maurer, U., Portmann, C., Rito, G. (2021). Revisiting (R)CCA security and replay protection. In *PKC 2021, Part II*, vol. 12711 of *LNCS*, Garay, J. (ed.). Springer, Heidelberg.

Baecher, P., Brzuska, C., Fischlin, M. (2013). Notions of black-box reductions, revisited. In *ASIACRYPT 2013, Part I*, vol. 8269 of *LNCS*, Sako, K., Sarkar, P. (eds). Springer, Heidelberg.

Barak, B., Goldreich, O., Impagliazzo, R., Rudich, S., Sahai, A., Vadhan, S.P., Yang, K. (2001). On the (im)possibility of obfuscating programs. In *CRYPTO 2001*, vol. 2139 of *LNCS*, Kilian, J. (ed.). Springer, Heidelberg.

Barak, B., Haitner, I., Hofheinz, D., Ishai, Y. (2010). Bounded key-dependent message security. In *EUROCRYPT 2010*, vol. 6110 of *LNCS*, Gilbert, H. (ed.). Springer, Heidelberg, 423–444.

Bellare, M. and Namprempre, C. (2000). Authenticated encryption: Relations among notions and analysis of the generic composition paradigm. In *ASIACRYPT 2000*, vol. 1976 of *LNCS*, Okamoto, T. (ed.). Springer, Heidelberg.

Bellare, M. and Palacio, A. (2004). Towards plaintext-aware public-key encryption without random oracles. In *ASIACRYPT 2004*, vol. 3329 of *LNCS*, Lee, P.J. (ed.). Springer, Heidelberg.

Bellare, M. and Rogaway, P. (1993). Random oracles are practical: A paradigm for designing efficient protocols. In *ACM CCS 93*, Denning, D.E., Pyle, R., Ganesan, R., Sandhu, R.S., Ashby, V. (eds). ACM Press.

Bellare, M. and Rogaway, P. (1995). Optimal asymmetric encryption. In *EUROCRYPT'94*, vol. 950 of *LNCS*, Santis, A.D. (ed.). Springer, Heidelberg.

Bellare, M. and Rogaway, P. (2006). The security of triple encryption and a framework for code-based game-playing proofs. In *EUROCRYPT 2006*, vol. 4004 of *LNCS*, Vaudenay, S. (ed.). Springer, Heidelberg.

Bellare, M. and Sahai, A. (1999). Non-malleable encryption: Equivalence between two notions, and an indistinguishability-based characterization. In *CRYPTO'99*, vol. 1666 of *LNCS*, Wiener, M.J. (ed.). Springer, Heidelberg.

Bellare, M. and Sahai, A. (2006). Non-malleable encryption: Equivalence between two notions, and an indistinguishability-based characterization. Cryptology ePrint Archive, Report 2006/228 [Online]. Available at: https://eprint.iacr.org/2006/228.

Bellare, M., Desai, A., Pointcheval, D., Rogaway, P. (1998). Relations among notions of security for public-key encryption schemes. In *CRYPTO'98*, vol. 1462 of *LNCS*, Krawczyk, H. (ed.). Springer, Heidelberg.

Bellare, M., Boldyreva, A., Micali, S. (2000). Public-key encryption in a multi-user setting: Security proofs and improvements. In *EUROCRYPT 2000*, vol. 1807 of *LNCS*, Preneel, B. (ed.). Springer, Heidelberg.

Bellare, M., Hofheinz, D., Yilek, S. (2009). Possibility and impossibility results for encryption and commitment secure under selective opening. In *EUROCRYPT 2009*, vol. 5479 of *LNCS*, Joux, A. (ed.). Springer, Heidelberg.

Bellare, M., Dowsley, R., Waters, B., Yilek, S. (2012a). Standard security does not imply security against selective-opening. In *EUROCRYPT 2012*, vol. 7237 of *LNCS*, Pointcheval, D., Johansson, T. (eds). Springer, Heidelberg.

Bellare, M., Hoang, V.T., Rogaway, P. (2012b). Foundations of garbled circuits. In *ACM CCS 2012*, Yu, T., Danezis, G., Gligor, V.D. (eds). *CCS '12: Proceedings of the 2012 ACM Conference on Computer and Communications Security*, 784–796 [Online]. Available at: https://doi.org/10.1145/2382196.2382279.

Bellare, M., Hoang, V.T., Keelveedhi, S. (2013). Instantiating random oracles via UCEs. In *CRYPTO 2013, Part II*, vol. 8043 of *LNCS*, Canetti, R., Garay, J.A. (eds). Springer, Heidelberg.

Benaloh, J. (1994). Dense probabilistic encryption. *Proceedings of the Workshop on Selected Areas of Cryptography*, 120–128.

Bindel, N., Hamburg, M., Hövelmanns, K., Hülsing, A., Persichetti, E. (2019). Tighter proofs of CCA security in the quantum random oracle model. In *TCC 2019, Part II*, vol. 11892 of *LNCS*, Hofheinz, D., Rosen, A. (eds). Springer, Heidelberg.

Bishop, A., Hohenberger, S., Waters, B. (2015). New circular security counterexamples from decision linear and learning with errors. In *ASIACRYPT 2015, Part II*, vol. 9453 of *LNCS*, Iwata, T., Cheon, J.H. (eds). Springer, Heidelberg.

Black, J., Rogaway, P., Shrimpton, T. (2003). Encryption-scheme security in the presence of key-dependent messages. In *SAC 2002*, vol. 2595 of *LNCS*, Nyberg, K., Heys, H.M. (eds). Springer, Heidelberg.

Bleichenbacher, D. (1998). Chosen ciphertext attacks against protocols based on the RSA encryption standard PKCS #1. In *CRYPTO'98*, vol. 1462 of *LNCS*, Krawczyk, H. (ed.). Springer, Heidelberg.

Blum, M. and Goldwasser, S. (1984). An efficient probabilistic public-key encryption scheme which hides all partial information. In *CRYPTO'84*, vol. 196 of *LNCS*, Blakley, G.R., Chaum, D. (eds). Springer, Heidelberg.

Blum, M., Feldman, P., Micali, S. (1988). Non-interactive zero-knowledge and its applications (extended abstract). In *20th ACM STOC*. ACM Press.

Böhl, F., Hofheinz, D., Kraschewski, D. (2012). On definitions of selective opening security. In *PKC 2012*, vol. 7293 of *LNCS*, Fischlin, M., Buchmann, J., Manulis, M. (eds). Springer, Heidelberg.

Boneh, D. (2001). Simplified OAEP for the RSA and Rabin functions. In *CRYPTO 2001*, vol. 2139 of *LNCS*, Kilian, J. (ed.). Springer, Heidelberg.

Boneh, D. and Franklin, M.K. (2001). Identity-based encryption from the Weil pairing. In *CRYPTO 2001*, vol. 2139 of *LNCS*, Kilian, J. (ed.). Springer, Heidelberg.

Boneh, D. and Katz, J. (2005). Improved efficiency for CCA-secure cryptosystems built using identity-based encryption. In *CT-RSA 2005*, vol. 3376 of *LNCS*, Menezes, A. (ed.). Springer, Heidelberg.

Boneh, D., Goh, E.-J., Nissim, K. (2005). Evaluating 2-DNF formulas on ciphertexts. In *TCC 2005*, vol. 3378 of *LNCS*, Kilian, J. (ed.). Springer, Heidelberg.

Boneh, D., Halevi, S., Hamburg, M., Ostrovsky, R. (2008). Circular-secure encryption from decision Diffie–Hellman. In *CRYPTO 2008*, vol. 5157 of *LNCS*, Wagner, D. (ed.). Springer, Heidelberg.

Boneh, D., Dagdelen, Ö., Fischlin, M., Lehmann, A., Schaffner, C., Zhandry, M. (2011). Random oracles in a quantum world. In *ASIACRYPT 2011*, vol. 7073 of *LNCS*, Lee, D.H., Wang, X. (eds). Springer, Heidelberg.

Boyen, X., Mei, Q., Waters, B. (2005). Direct chosen ciphertext security from identity-based techniques. In *ACM CCS 2005*, Atluri, V., Meadows, C., Juels, A. (eds). ACM Press.

Brakerski, Z. and Goldwasser, S. (2010). Circular and leakage resilient public-key encryption under subgroup indistinguishability (or: Quadratic residuosity strikes back). In *CRYPTO 2010*, vol. 6223 of *LNCS*, Rabin, T. (ed.). Springer, Heidelberg.

Brakerski, Z., Goldwasser, S., Kalai, Y.T. (2011). Black-box circular-secure encryption beyond affine functions. In *TCC 2011*, vol. 6597 of *LNCS*, Ishai, Y. (ed.). Springer, Heidelberg.

Brakerski, Z., Lombardi, A., Segev, G., Vaikuntanathan, V. (2018). Anonymous IBE, leakage resilience and circular security from new assumptions. In *EUROCRYPT 2018, Part I*, vol. 10820 of *LNCS*, Nielsen, J.B., Rijmen, V. (eds). Springer, Heidelberg.

Camenisch, J. and Lysyanskaya, A. (2002). Dynamic accumulators and application to efficient revocation of anonymous credentials. In *CRYPTO 2002*, vol. 2442 of *LNCS*, Yung, M. (ed.). Springer, Heidelberg.

Camenisch, J., Chandran, N., Shoup, V. (2009). A public key encryption scheme secure against key dependent chosen plaintext and adaptive chosen ciphertext attacks. In *EUROCRYPT 2009*, vol. 5479 of *LNCS*, Joux, A. (ed.). Springer, Heidelberg.

Canetti, R., Feige, U., Goldreich, O., Naor, M. (1996). Adaptively secure multi-party computation. In *28th ACM STOC*. ACM Press.

Canetti, R., Goldreich, O., Halevi, S. (1998). The random oracle methodology, revisited (preliminary version). In *30th ACM STOC*. ACM Press.

Canetti, R., Krawczyk, H., Nielsen, J.B. (2003). Relaxing chosen-ciphertext security. In *CRYPTO 2003*, vol. 2729 of *LNCS*, Boneh, D. (ed.). Springer, Heidelberg.

Canetti, R., Halevi, S., Katz, J. (2004). Chosen-ciphertext security from identity-based encryption. In *EUROCRYPT 2004*, vol. 3027 of *LNCS*, Cachin, C., Camenisch, J. (eds). Springer, Heidelberg.

Canetti, R., Chen, Y., Holmgren, J., Lombardi, A., Rothblum, G.N., Rothblum, R.D., Wichs, D. (2019). Fiat–Shamir: From practice to theory. In *51st ACM STOC*, Charikar, M., Cohen, E. (eds). ACM Press.

Cash, D., Kiltz, E., Shoup, V. (2008). The twin Diffie–Hellman problem and applications. In *EUROCRYPT 2008*, vol. 4965 of *LNCS*, Smart, N.P. (ed.). Springer, Heidelberg.

Cash, D., Green, M., Hohenberger, S. (2012). New definitions and separations for circular security. In *PKC 2012*, vol. 7293 of *LNCS*, Fischlin, M., Buchmann, J., Manulis, M. (eds). Springer, Heidelberg.

Coretti, S., Maurer, U., Tackmann, B. (2013). Constructing confidential channels from authenticated channels – Public-key encryption revisited. In *ASIACRYPT 2013, Part I*, vol. 8269 of *LNCS*, Sako, K., Sarkar, P. (eds). Springer, Heidelberg.

Coretti, S., Maurer, U., Tackmann, B., Venturi, D. (2015). From single-bit to multi-bit public-key encryption via non-malleable codes. In *TCC 2015, Part I*, vol. 9014 of *LNCS*, Dodis, Y., Nielsen, J.B. (eds). Springer, Heidelberg.

Coretti, S., Dodis, Y., Tackmann, B., Venturi, D. (2016). Non-malleable encryption: Simpler, shorter, stronger. In *TCC 2016-A, Part I*, vol. 9562 of *LNCS*, Kushilevitz, E., Malkin, T. (eds). Springer, Heidelberg.

Coron, J.-S., Handschuh, H., Joye, M., Paillier, P., Pointcheval, D., Tymen, C. (2002a). GEM: A generic chosen-ciphertext secure encryption method. In *CT-RSA 2002*, vol. 2271 of *LNCS*, Preneel, B. (ed.). Springer, Heidelberg.

Coron, J.-S., Joye, M., Naccache, D., Paillier, P. (2002b). Universal padding schemes for RSA. In *CRYPTO 2002*, vol. 2442 of *LNCS*, Yung, M. (ed.). Springer, Heidelberg.

Couteau, G., Katsumata, S., Ursu, B. (2020). Non-interactive zero-knowledge in pairing-free groups from weaker assumptions. In *EUROCRYPT 2020, Part III*, vol. 12107 of *LNCS*, Canteaut, A., Ishai, Y. (eds). Springer, Heidelberg.

Cramer, R. and Shoup, V. (1998). A practical public key cryptosystem provably secure against adaptive chosen ciphertext attack. In *CRYPTO'98*, vol. 1462 of *LNCS*, Krawczyk, H. (ed.). Springer, Heidelberg.

Cramer, R. and Shoup, V. (2002). Universal hash proofs and a paradigm for adaptive chosen ciphertext secure public-key encryption. In *EUROCRYPT 2002*, vol. 2332 of *LNCS*, Knudsen, L.R. (ed.). Springer, Heidelberg.

Cramer, R. and Shoup, V. (2003). Design and analysis of practical public-key encryption schemes secure against adaptive chosen ciphertext attack. *SIAM Journal on Computing*, 33(1), 167–226.

Cramer, R., Hanaoka, G., Hofheinz, D., Imai, H., Kiltz, E., Pass, R., Shelat, A., Vaikuntanathan, V. (2007). Bounded CCA2-secure encryption. In *ASIACRYPT 2007*, vol. 4833 of *LNCS*, Kurosawa, K. (ed.). Springer, Heidelberg.

Cramer, R., Hofheinz, D., Kiltz, E. (2010). A twist on the Naor-Yung paradigm and its application to efficient CCA-secure encryption from hard search problems. In *TCC 2010*, vol. 5978 of *LNCS*, Micciancio, D. (ed.). Springer, Heidelberg.

Dachman-Soled, D. (2014). A black-box construction of a CCA2 encryption scheme from a plaintext aware (sPA1) encryption scheme. In *PKC 2014*, vol. 8383 of *LNCS*, Krawczyk, H. (ed.). Springer, Heidelberg.

Damgård, I. and Jurik, M. (2001). A generalisation, a simplification and some applications of Paillier's probabilistic public-key system. In *PKC 2001*, vol. 1992 of *LNCS*, Kim, K. (ed.). Springer, Heidelberg.

Davies, G.T. and Stam, M. (2014). KDM security in the hybrid framework. In *CT-RSA 2014*, vol. 8366 of *LNCS*, Benaloh, J. (ed.). Springer, Heidelberg.

De Santis, A., Di Crescenzo, G., Ostrovsky, R., Persiano, G., Sahai, A. (2001). Robust non-interactive zero knowledge. In *CRYPTO 2001*, vol. 2139 of *LNCS*, Kilian, J. (ed.). Springer, Heidelberg.

Dent, A.W. (2003). A designer's guide to KEMs. In *9th IMA International Conference on Cryptography and Coding*, vol. 2898 of *LNCS*, Paterson, K.G. (ed.). Springer, Heidelberg.

Diffie, W. and Hellman, M.E. (1976). New directions in cryptography. *IEEE Transactions on Information Theory*. 22(6), 644–654.

Dodis, Y., Freedman, M.J., Jarecki, S., Walfish, S. (2004). Versatile padding schemes for joint signature and encryption. In *ACM CCS 2004*, Atluri, V., Pfitzmann, B., McDaniel, P. (eds). ACM Press.

Dolev, D., Dwork, C., Naor, M. (1991). Non-malleable cryptography (extended abstract). In *23rd ACM STOC*. ACM Press.

Dolev, D., Dwork, C., Naor, M. (2000). Nonmalleable cryptography. *SIAM Journal on Computing*, 30(2), 391–437.

Döttling, N. (2015). Low noise LPN: KDM secure public key encryption and sample amplification. In *PKC 2015*, vol. 9020 of *LNCS*, Katz, J. (ed.). Springer, Heidelberg.

Döttling, N., Garg, S., Ishai, Y., Malavolta, G., Mour, T., Ostrovsky, R. (2019). Trapdoor hash functions and their applications. In *CRYPTO 2019, Part III*, vol. 11694 of *LNCS*, Boldyreva, A., Micciancio, D. (eds). Springer, Heidelberg.

ElGamal, T. (1984). A public key cryptosystem and a signature scheme based on discrete logarithms. In *CRYPTO'84*, vol. 196 of *LNCS*, Blakley, G.R., Chaum, D. (eds). Springer, Heidelberg.

Fehr, S., Hofheinz, D., Kiltz, E., Wee, H. (2010). Encryption schemes secure against chosen-ciphertext selective opening attacks. In *EUROCRYPT 2010*, vol. 6110 of *LNCS*, Gilbert, H. (ed.). Springer, Heidelberg.

Feige, U., Lapidot, D., Shamir, A. (1990). Multiple non-interactive zero knowledge proofs based on a single random string (extended abstract). In *31st FOCS*. IEEE Computer Society Press.

Feige, U., Lapidot, D., Shamir, A. (1999). Multiple noninteractive zero knowledge proofs under general assumptions. *SIAM Journal on Computing*, 29(1), 1–28.

Fuchsbauer, G., Heuer, F., Kiltz, E., Pietrzak, K. (2016). Standard security does imply security against selective opening for Markov distributions. In *TCC 2016-A, Part I*, vol. 9562 of *LNCS*, Kushilevitz, E., Malkin, T. (eds). Springer, Heidelberg.

Fujisaki, E. and Okamoto, T. (1999a). How to enhance the security of public-key encryption at minimum cost. In *PKC'99*, vol. 1560 of *LNCS*, Imai, H., Zheng, Y. (eds). Springer, Heidelberg.

Fujisaki, E. and Okamoto, T. (1999b). Secure integration of asymmetric and symmetric encryption schemes. In *CRYPTO'99*, vol. 1666 of *LNCS*, Wiener, M.J. (ed.). Springer, Heidelberg.

Fujisaki, E. and Okamoto, T. (2013). Secure integration of asymmetric and symmetric encryption schemes. *Journal of Cryptology*, 26(1), 80–101.

Fujisaki, E., Okamoto, T., Pointcheval, D., Stern, J. (2001). RSA-OAEP is secure under the RSA assumption. In *CRYPTO 2001*, vol. 2139 of *LNCS*, Kilian, J. (ed.). Springer, Heidelberg.

Galindo, D., Herranz, J., Villar, J.L. (2012). Identity-based encryption with master key-dependent message security and leakage-resilience. In *ESORICS 2012*, vol. 7459 of *LNCS*, Foresti, S., Yung, M., Martinelli, F. (eds). Springer, Heidelberg.

Garg, S., Gentry, C., Halevi, S., Raykova, M., Sahai, A., Waters, B. (2013). Candidate indistinguishability obfuscation and functional encryption for all circuits. In *54th FOCS*. IEEE Computer Society Press.

Gay, R., Hofheinz, D., Kiltz, E., Wee, H. (2016). Tightly CCA-secure encryption without pairings. In *EUROCRYPT 2016, Part I*, vol. 9665 of *LNCS*, Fischlin, M., Coron, J.-S. (eds). Springer, Heidelberg.

Gay, R., Hofheinz, D., Kohl, L. (2017). Kurosawa-desmedt meets tight security. In *CRYPTO 2017, Part III*, vol. 10403 of *LNCS*, Katz, J., Shacham, H. (eds). Springer, Heidelberg.

Gentry, C. (2009). Fully homomorphic encryption using ideal lattices. In *41st ACM STOC*, Mitzenmacher, M. (ed.). ACM Press.

Goldreich, O. and Levin, L.A. (1989). A hard-core predicate for all one-way functions. In *21st ACM STOC*. ACM Press.

Goldwasser, S. and Micali, S. (1982). Probabilistic encryption and how to play mental poker keeping secret all partial information. In *14th ACM STOC*. ACM Press.

Gong, J., Chen, J., Dong, X., Cao, Z., Tang, S. (2016). Extended nested dual system groups, revisited. In *PKC 2016, Part I*, vol. 9614 of *LNCS*, Cheng, C.-M., Chung, K.-M., Persiano, G., Yang, B.-Y. (eds). Springer, Heidelberg.

Goyal, R., Koppula, V., Waters, B. (2017a). Lockable obfuscation. In *58th FOCS*, Umans, C. (ed.). IEEE Computer Society Press.

Goyal, R., Koppula, V., Waters, B. (2017b). Separating IND-CPA and circular security for unbounded length key cycles. In *PKC 2017, Part I*, vol. 10174 of *LNCS*, Fehr, S. (ed.). Springer, Heidelberg.

Goyal, R., Koppula, V., Waters, B. (2017c). Separating semantic and circular security for symmetric-key bit encryption from the learning with errors assumption. In *EUROCRYPT 2017, Part II*, vol. 10211 of *LNCS*, Coron, J.-S., Nielsen, J.B. (eds). Springer, Heidelberg.

Groth, J., Ostrovsky, R., Sahai, A. (2006). Perfect non-interactive zero knowledge for NP. In *EUROCRYPT 2006*, vol. 4004 of *LNCS*, Vaudenay, S. (ed.). Springer, Heidelberg.

Groth, J., Ostrovsky, R., Sahai, A. (2012). New techniques for noninteractive zero-knowledge. *J. ACM*, 59(3), 11:1–11:35.

Hajiabadi, M. and Kapron, B.M. (2015). Reproducible circularly-secure bit encryption: Applications and realizations. In *CRYPTO 2015, Part I*, vol. 9215 of *LNCS*, Gennaro, R., Robshaw, M.J.B. (eds). Springer, Heidelberg.

Hajiabadi, M. and Kapron, B.M. (2017). Toward fine-grained blackbox separations between semantic and circular-security notions. In *EUROCRYPT 2017, Part II*, vol. 10211 of *LNCS*, Coron, J.-S., Nielsen, J.B. (eds). Springer, Heidelberg.

Hajiabadi, M., Kapron, B.M., Srinivasan, V. (2016). On generic constructions of circularly-secure, leakage-resilient public-key encryption schemes. In *PKC 2016, Part II*, vol. 9615 of *LNCS*, Cheng, C.-M., Chung, K.-M., Persiano, G., Yang, B.-Y. (eds). Springer, Heidelberg.

Han, S., Liu, S., Lyu, L. (2016). Efficient KDM-CCA secure public-key encryption for polynomial functions. In *ASIACRYPT 2016, Part II*, vol. 10032 of *LNCS*, Cheon, J.H., Takagi, T. (eds). Springer, Heidelberg.

Han, S., Liu, S., Lyu, L., Gu, D. (2019). Tight leakage-resilient CCA-security from quasi-adaptive hash proof system. In *CRYPTO 2019, Part II*, vol. 11693 of *LNCS*, Boldyreva, A., Micciancio, D. (eds). Springer, Heidelberg.

Hanaoka, G. and Kurosawa, K. (2008). Efficient chosen ciphertext secure public key encryption under the computational Diffie–Hellman assumption. In *ASIACRYPT 2008*, vol. 5350 of *LNCS*, Pieprzyk, J. (ed.). Springer, Heidelberg.

Hara, K., Kitagawa, F., Matsuda, T., Hanaoka, G., Tanaka, K. (2018). Simulation-based receiver selective opening CCA secure PKE from standard computational assumptions. In *SCN 18*, vol. 11035 of *LNCS*, Catalano, D., De Prisco, R. (eds). Springer, Heidelberg.

Haralambiev, K., Jager, T., Kiltz, E., Shoup, V. (2010). Simple and efficient public-key encryption from computational Diffie–Hellman in the standard model. In *PKC 2010*, vol. 6056 of *LNCS*, Nguyen, P.Q., Pointcheval, D. (eds). Springer, Heidelberg.

Håstad, J., Impagliazzo, R., Levin, L.A., Luby, M. (1999). A pseudorandom generator from any one-way function. *SIAM Journal on Computing*, 28(4), 1364–1396.

Hazay, C., Patra, A., Warinschi, B. (2015). Selective opening security for receivers. In *ASIACRYPT 2015, Part I*, vol. 9452 of *LNCS*, Iwata, T., Cheon, J.H. (eds). Springer, Heidelberg.

Hemenway, B. and Ostrovsky, R. (2012). On homomorphic encryption and chosen-ciphertext security. In *PKC 2012*, vol. 7293 of *LNCS*, Fischlin, M., Buchmann, J., Manulis, M. (eds). Springer, Heidelberg.

Hemenway, B. and Ostrovsky, R. (2013). Building lossy trapdoor functions from lossy encryption. In *ASIACRYPT 2013, Part II*, vol. 8270 of *LNCS*, Sako, K., Sarkar, P. (eds). Springer, Heidelberg.

Hemenway, B., Libert, B., Ostrovsky, R., Vergnaud, D. (2011). Lossy encryption: Constructions from general assumptions and efficient selective opening chosen ciphertext security. In *ASIACRYPT 2011*, vol. 7073 of *LNCS*, Lee, D.H., Wang, X. (eds). Springer, Heidelberg.

Herranz, J., Hofheinz, D., Kiltz, E. (2010). Some (in)sufficient conditions for secure hybrid encryption. *Information and Computation*, 208(11), 1243–1257.

Heuer, F. and Poettering, B. (2016). Selective opening security from simulatable data encapsulation. In *ASIACRYPT 2016, Part II*, vol. 10032 of *LNCS*, Cheon, J.H., Takagi, T. (eds). Springer, Heidelberg.

Heuer, F., Jager, T., Kiltz, E., Schäge, S. (2015). On the selective opening security of practical public-key encryption schemes. In *PKC 2015*, vol. 9020 of *LNCS*, Katz, J. (ed.). Springer, Heidelberg.

Hoang, V.T., Katz, J., O'Neill, A., Zaheri, M. (2016). Selective-opening security in the presence of randomness failures. In *ASIACRYPT 2016, Part II*, vol. 10032 of *LNCS*, Cheon, J.H., Takagi, T. (eds). Springer, Heidelberg.

Hofheinz, D. (2012). All-but-many lossy trapdoor functions. In *EUROCRYPT 2012*, vol. 7237 of *LNCS*, Pointcheval, D., Johansson, T. (eds). Springer, Heidelberg.

Hofheinz, D. (2013). Circular chosen-ciphertext security with compact ciphertexts. In *EUROCRYPT 2013*, vol. 7881 of *LNCS*, Johansson, T., Nguyen, P.Q. (eds). Springer, Heidelberg.

Hofheinz, D. (2016). Algebraic partitioning: Fully compact and (almost) tightly secure cryptography, In *TCC 2016-A, Part I*, vol. 9562 of *LNCS*, Kushilevitz, E., Malkin, T. (eds). Springer, Heidelberg.

Hofheinz, D. (2017). Adaptive partitioning. In *EUROCRYPT 2017, Part III*, vol. 10212 of *LNCS*, Coron, J.-S., Nielsen, J.B. (eds). Springer, Heidelberg.

Hofheinz, D. and Jager, T. (2012). Tightly secure signatures and public-key encryption. In *CRYPTO 2012*, vol. 7417 of *LNCS*, Safavi-Naini, R., Canetti, R. (eds). Springer, Heidelberg.

Hofheinz, D. and Kiltz, E. (2007). Secure hybrid encryption from weakened key encapsulation, In *CRYPTO 2007*, vol. 4622 of *LNCS*, Menezes, A. (ed.). Springer, Heidelberg.

Hofheinz, D. and Kiltz, E. (2009). Practical chosen ciphertext secure encryption from factoring. In *EUROCRYPT 2009*, vol. 5479 of *LNCS*, Joux, A. (ed.). Springer, Heidelberg.

Hofheinz, D. and Rupp, A. (2014). Standard versus selective opening security: Separation and equivalence results. In *TCC 2014*, vol. 8349 of *LNCS*, Lindell, Y. (ed.). Springer, Heidelberg.

Hofheinz, D., Koch, J., Striecks, C. (2015). Identity-based encryption with (almost) tight security in the multi-instance, multi-ciphertext setting. In *PKC 2015*, vol. 9020 of *LNCS*, Katz, J. (ed.). Springer, Heidelberg.

Hofheinz, D., Jager, T., Rupp, A. (2016a). Public-key encryption with simulation-based selective-opening security and compact ciphertexts. In *TCC 2016-B, Part II*, vol. 9986 of *LNCS*, Hirt, M., Smith, A.D. (eds). Springer, Heidelberg.

Hofheinz, D., Rao, V., Wichs, D. (2016b). Standard security does not imply indistinguishability under selective opening. In *TCC 2016-B, Part II*, vol. 9986 of *LNCS*, Hirt, M., Smith, A.D. (eds). Springer, Heidelberg.

Hofheinz, D., Hövelmanns, K., Kiltz, E. (2017). A modular analysis of the Fujisaki-Okamoto transformation. In *TCC 2017*, vol. 10677 of *LNCS*, Part I, Kalai, Y., Reyzin, L. (eds). Springer, Heidelberg.

Hohenberger, S., Lewko, A.B., Waters, B. (2012). Detecting dangerous queries: A new approach for chosen ciphertext security. In *EUROCRYPT 2012*, vol. 7237 of *LNCS*, Pointcheval, D., Johansson, T. (eds). Springer, Heidelberg.

Hohenberger, S., Koppula, V., Waters, B. (2020). Chosen ciphertext security from injective trapdoor functions. In *CRYPTO 2020, Part I*, vol. 12170 of *LNCS*, Micciancio, D., Ristenpart, T. (eds). Springer, Heidelberg.

Huang, Z., Liu, S., Qin, B. (2013). Sender-equivocable encryption schemes secure against chosen-ciphertext attacks revisited. In *PKC 2013*, vol. 7778 of *LNCS*, Kurosawa, K., Hanaoka, G. (eds). Springer, Heidelberg.

Huang, Z., Lai, J., Chen, W., Au, M.H., Peng, Z., Li, J. (2019). Simulation-based selective opening security for receivers under chosen-ciphertext attacks. *Designs, Codes and Cryptography*, 87(6), 1345–1371.

Ishai, Y. and Paskin, A. (2007). Evaluating branching programs on encrypted data. In *TCC 2007*, vol. 4392 of *LNCS*, Vadhan, S.P. (ed.). Springer, Heidelberg.

Jia, D., Lu, X., Li, B. (2016). Receiver selective opening security from indistinguishability obfuscation. In *INDOCRYPT 2016*, vol. 10095 of *LNCS*, Dunkelman, O., Sanadhya, S.K. (eds). Springer, Heidelberg.

Jia, D., Lu, X., Li, B. (2017). Constructions secure against receiver selective opening and chosen ciphertext attacks. In *CT-RSA 2017*, vol. 10159 of *LNCS*, Handschuh, H. (ed.). Springer, Heidelberg.

Jiang, H., Zhang, Z., Chen, L., Wang, H., Ma, Z. (2018). IND-CCA-secure key encapsulation mechanism in the quantum random oracle model, revisited. In *CRYPTO 2018, Part III*, vol. 10993 of *LNCS*, Shacham, H., Boldyreva, A. (eds). Springer, Heidelberg.

Jiang, H., Zhang, Z., Ma, Z. (2019a). Key encapsulation mechanism with explicit rejection in the quantum random oracle model. In *PKC 2019, Part II*, vol. 11443 of *LNCS*, Lin, D., Sako, K. (eds). Springer, Heidelberg.

Jiang, H., Zhang, Z., Ma, Z. (2019b). Tighter security proofs for generic key encapsulation mechanism in the quantum random oracle model. In *Post-Quantum Cryptography – 10th International Conference, PQCrypto 2019*, Ding, J., Steinwandt, R. (eds). Springer, Heidelberg.

Kalai, Y.T. and Reyzin, L. (2019). *A Survey of Leakage-Resilient Cryptography*. Association for Computing Machinery, New York.

Katz, J. (2004). Scribed lecture notes [Online]. Available at: https://www.cs.umd.edu/jkatz/gradcrypto2/scribes.html.

Kiltz, E. (2006). Chosen-ciphertext security from tag-based encryption. In *TCC 2006*, vol. 3876 of *LNCS*, Halevi, S., Rabin, T. (eds). Springer, Heidelberg.

Kiltz, E., Mohassel, P., O'Neill, A. (2010). Adaptive trapdoor functions and chosen-ciphertext security. In *EUROCRYPT 2010*, vol. 6110 of *LNCS*, Gilbert, H. (ed.). Springer, Heidelberg.

Kitagawa, F. and Matsuda, T. (2019). CPA-to-CCA transformation for KDM security. In *TCC 2019, Part II*, vol. 11892 of *LNCS*, Hofheinz, D., Rosen, A. (eds). Springer, Heidelberg.

Kitagawa, F. and Matsuda, T. (2020). Circular security is complete for KDM security. In *ASIACRYPT 2020, Part I*, vol. 12491 of *LNCS*, Moriai, S., Wang, H. (eds). Springer, Heidelberg.

Kitagawa, F. and Tanaka, K. (2018). A framework for achieving KDM-CCA secure public-key encryption. In *ASIACRYPT 2018, Part II*, vol. 11273 of *LNCS*, Peyrin, T., Galbraith, S. (eds). Springer, Heidelberg.

Kitagawa, F., Matsuda, T., Hanaoka, G., Tanaka, K. (2016). On the key dependent message security of the Fujisaki-Okamoto constructions. In *PKC 2016, Part I*, vol. 9614 of *LNCS*, Cheng, C.-M., Chung, K.-M., Persiano, G., Yang, B.-Y. (eds). Springer, Heidelberg.

Kitagawa, F., Matsuda, T., Tanaka, K. (2019a). CCA security and trapdoor functions via key-dependent-message security. In *CRYPTO 2019, Part III*, vol. 11694 of *LNCS*, Boldyreva, A., Micciancio, D. (eds). Springer, Heidelberg.

Kitagawa, F., Matsuda, T., Tanaka, K. (2019b). Simple and efficient KDM-CCA secure public key encryption. In *ASIACRYPT 2019, Part III*, vol. 11923 of *LNCS*, Galbraith, S.D., Moriai, S. (eds). Springer, Heidelberg.

Kitagawa, F., Matsuda, T., Yamakawa, T. (2020). NIZK from SNARG. In *TCC 2020, Part I*, vol. 12550 of *LNCS*, Pass, R., Pietrzak, K. (eds). Springer, Heidelberg.

Kobara, K. and Imai, H. (2002). OAEP++ : A very simple way to apply OAEP to deterministic OW-CPA primitives. Cryptology ePrint Archive, Report 2002/130 [Online]. Available at: https://eprint.iacr.org/2002/130.

Komano, Y. and Ohta, K. (2003). Efficient universal padding techniques for multiplicative trapdoor one-way permutation. In *CRYPTO 2003*, vol. 2729 of *LNCS*, Boneh, D. (ed.). Springer, Heidelberg.

Koppula, V. and Waters, B. (2019). Realizing chosen ciphertext security generically in attribute-based encryption and predicate encryption. In *CRYPTO 2019, Part II*, vol. 11693 of *LNCS*, Boldyreva, A., Micciancio, D. (eds). Springer, Heidelberg.

Koppula, V., Ramchen, K., Waters, B. (2015). Separations in circular security for arbitrary length key cycles. In *TCC 2015, Part II*, vol. 9015 of *LNCS*, Dodis, Y., Nielsen, J.B. (eds). Springer, Heidelberg.

Kuchta, V., Sakzad, A., Stehlé, D., Steinfeld, R., Sun, S. (2020). Measure-rewind-measure: Tighter quantum random oracle model proofs for one-way to hiding and CCA security. In *EUROCRYPT 2020, Part III*, vol. 12107 of *LNCS*, Canteaut, A., Ishai, Y. (eds). Springer, Heidelberg.

Kurosawa, K. and Desmedt, Y. (2004). A new paradigm of hybrid encryption scheme. In *CRYPTO 2004*, vol. 3152 of *LNCS*, Franklin, M. (ed.). Springer, Heidelberg.

Lai, Q., Liu, F.-H., Wang, Z. (2021). Rate-1 key-dependent message security via reusable homomorphic extractor against correlated-source attacks. In *PKC 2021, Part I*, vol. 12710 of *LNCS*, Garay, J. (ed.). Springer, Heidelberg.

Libert, B. and Qian, C. (2019). Lossy algebraic filters with short tags. In *PKC 2019, Part I*, vol. 11442 of *LNCS*, Lin, D., Sako, K. (eds). Springer, Heidelberg.

Libert, B., Peters, T., Joye, M., Yung, M. (2015). Compactly hiding linear spans – Tightly secure constant-size simulation-sound QA-NIZK proofs and applications. In *ASIACRYPT 2015, Part I*, vol. 9452 of *LNCS*, Iwata, T., Cheon, J.H. (eds). Springer, Heidelberg.

Libert, B., Sakzad, A., Stehlé, D., Steinfeld, R. (2017). All-but-many lossy trapdoor functions and selective opening chosen-ciphertext security from LWE. In *CRYPTO 2017, Part III*, vol. 10403 of *LNCS*, Katz, J., Shacham, H. (eds). Springer, Heidelberg.

Lindell, Y. (2003). A simpler construction of cca2-secure public-key encryption under general assumptions. In *EUROCRYPT 2003*, vol. 2656 of *LNCS*, Biham, E. (ed.). Springer, Heidelberg.

Liu, S. and Paterson, K.G. (2015). Simulation-based selective opening CCA security for PKE from key encapsulation mechanisms. In *PKC 2015*, vol. 9020 of *LNCS*, Katz, J. (ed.). Springer, Heidelberg.

Luby, M. and Rackoff, C. (1988). How to construct pseudorandom permutations from pseudorandom functions. *SIAM Journal on Computing*, 17(2), 373–386 [Online]. Available at: doi:10.1137/0217022.

Lyu, L., Liu, S., Han, S., Gu, D. (2018). Tightly SIM-SO-CCA secure public key encryption from standard assumptions. In *PKC 2018, Part I*, vol. 10769 of *LNCS*, Abdalla, M., Dahab, R. (eds). Springer, Heidelberg.

Malkin, T., Teranishi, I., Yung, M. (2011). Efficient circuit-size independent public key encryption with KDM security. In *EUROCRYPT 2011*, vol. 6632 of *LNCS*, Paterson, K.G. (ed.). Springer, Heidelberg.

Marcedone, A. and Orlandi, C. (2014). Obfuscation $\Rightarrow$ (IND-CPA security $\not\Rightarrow$ circular security). In *SCN 14*, vol. 8642 of *LNCS*, Abdalla, M., Prisco, R.D. (eds). Springer, Heidelberg.

Marcedone, A., Pass, R., Ahelat, A. (2016). Bounded KDM security from iO and OWF. In *SCN 16*, vol. 9841 of *LNCS*, Zikas, V., De Prisco, R. (eds). Springer, Heidelberg.

Matsuda, T. and Hanaoka, G. (2013). Key encapsulation mechanisms from extractable hash proof systems, revisited. In *PKC 2013*, vol. 7778 of *LNCS*, Kurosawa, K., Hanaoka, G. (eds). Springer, Heidelberg.

Matsuda, T. and Hanaoka, G. (2014a). Chosen ciphertext security via point obfuscation. In *TCC 2014*, vol. 8349 of *LNCS*, Lindell, Y. (ed.). Springer, Heidelberg.

Matsuda, T. and Hanaoka, G. (2014b). Chosen ciphertext security via UCE. In *PKC 2014*, vol. 8383 of *LNCS*, Krawczyk, H. (ed.). Springer, Heidelberg.

Matsuda, T. and Hanaoka, G. (2015a). An asymptotically optimal method for converting bit encryption to multi-bit encryption. In *ASIACRYPT 2015, Part I*, vol. 9452 of *LNCS*, Iwata, T., Cheon, J.H. (eds). Springer, Heidelberg.

Matsuda, T. and Hanaoka, G. (2015b). Constructing and understanding chosen ciphertext security via puncturable key encapsulation mechanisms. In *TCC 2015, Part I*, vol. 9014 of *LNCS*, Dodis, Y., Nielsen, J.B. (eds). Springer, Heidelberg.

Matsuda, T. and Hanaoka, G. (2016). Trading plaintext-awareness for simulatability to achieve chosen ciphertext security. In *PKC 2016, Part I*, vol. 9614 of *LNCS*, Cheng, C.-M., Chung, K.-M., Persiano, G., Yang, B.-Y. (eds). Springer, Heidelberg.

Matsuda, T. and Matsuura, K. (2011). Parallel decryption queries in bounded chosen ciphertext attacks. In *PKC 2011*, vol. 6571 of *LNCS*, Catalano, D., Fazio, N., Gennaro, R., Nicolosi, A. (eds). Springer, Heidelberg.

Micciancio, D. and Peikert, C. (2012). Trapdoors for lattices: Simpler, tighter, faster, smaller. In *EUROCRYPT 2012*, vol. 7237 of *LNCS*, Pointcheval, D., Johansson, T. (eds). Springer, Heidelberg.

Myers, S. and Shelat, A. (2009). Bit encryption is complete. In *50th FOCS*. IEEE Computer Society Press.

Myers, S., Sergi, M., Shelat, A. (2012). Blackbox construction of a more than non-malleable CCA1 encryption scheme from plaintext awareness. In *SCN 12*, vol. 7485 of *LNCS*, Visconti, I., Prisco, R.D. (eds). Springer, Heidelberg.

Naccache, D. and Stern, J. (1998). A new public key cryptosystem based on higher residues. In *ACM CCS 98*, Gong, L., Reiter, M.K. (eds). ACM Press.

Naor, M. and Yung, M. (1989). Universal one-way hash functions and their cryptographic applications. In *21st ACM STOC*. ACM Press.

Naor, M. and Yung, M. (1990). Public-key cryptosystems provably secure against chosen ciphertext attacks. In *22nd ACM STOC*. ACM Press.

Okamoto, T. and Pointcheval, D. (2001a). The gap-problems: A new class of problems for the security of cryptographic schemes. In *PKC 2001*, vol. 1992 of *LNCS*, Kim, K. (ed.). Springer, Heidelberg.

Okamoto, T. and Pointcheval, D. (2001b). REACT: Rapid enhanced-security asymmetric cryptosystem transform. In *CT-RSA 2001*, vol. 2020 of *LNCS*, Naccache, D. (ed.). Springer, Heidelberg.

Okamoto, T. and Uchiyama, S. (1998). A new public-key cryptosystem as secure as factoring. In *EUROCRYPT'98*, vol. 1403 of *LNCS*, Nyberg, K. (ed.). Springer, Heidelberg.

Paillier, P. (1999). Public-key cryptosystems based on composite degree residuosity classes. In *EUROCRYPT'99*, vol. 1592 of *LNCS*, Stern, J. (ed.). Springer, Heidelberg.

Pass, R., Shelat, A., Vaikuntanathan, V. (2007). Relations among notions of non-malleability for encryption. In *ASIACRYPT 2007*, vol. 4833 of *LNCS*, Kurosawa, K. (ed.). Springer, Heidelberg.

Peikert, C. and Shiehian, S. (2019). Noninteractive zero knowledge for NP from (plain) learning with errors. In *CRYPTO 2019, Part I*, vol. 11692 of *LNCS*, Boldyreva, A., Micciancio, D. (eds). Springer, Heidelberg.

Peikert, C. and Waters, B. (2008). Lossy trapdoor functions and their applications. In *40th ACM STOC*, Ladner, R.E., Dwork, C. (eds). ACM Press.

Phan, D.H. and Pointcheval, D. (2003). Chosen-ciphertext security without redundancy. In *ASIACRYPT 2003*, vol. 2894 of *LNCS*, Laih, C.-S. (ed.). Springer, Heidelberg.

Phan, D.H. and Pointcheval, D. (2004). OAEP 3-round: A generic and secure asymmetric encryption padding. In *ASIACRYPT 2004*, vol. 3329 of *LNCS*, Lee, P.J. (ed.). Springer, Heidelberg.

Prabhakaran, M. and Rosulek, M. (2007). Rerandomizable RCCA encryption. In *CRYPTO 2007*, vol. 4622 of *LNCS*, Menezes, A. (ed.). Springer, Heidelberg.

Prabhakaran, M. and Rosulek, M. (2008). Homomorphic encryption with CCA security. In *ICALP 2008, Part II*, vol. 5126 of *LNCS*, Aceto, L., Damgård, I., Goldberg, L.A., Halldórsson, M.M., Ingólfsdóttir, A., Walukiewicz, I. (eds). Springer, Heidelberg.

Rabin, M. (1979). Digitalized signatures and public-key functions as intractable as factorization. Paper, MIT Laboratory for Computer Science, Cambridge, MA.

Rackoff, C. and Simon, D.R. (1992). Non-interactive zero-knowledge proof of knowledge and chosen ciphertext attack. In *CRYPTO'91*, vol. 576 of *LNCS*, Feigenbaum, J. (ed.). Springer, Heidelberg.

Regev, O. (2005). On lattices, learning with errors, random linear codes, and cryptography. In *37th ACM STOC*, Gabow, H.N., Fagin, R. (eds). ACM Press.

Reingold, O., Trevisan, L., Vadhan, S.P. (2004). Notions of reducibility between cryptographic primitives. In *TCC 2004*, vol. 2951 of *LNCS*, Naor, M. (ed.). Springer, Heidelberg.

Rivest, R.L., Shamir, A., Adleman, L.M. (1978). A method for obtaining digital signatures and public-key cryptosystems. *Communications of the Association for Computing Machinery*, 21(2), 120–126.

Rosen, A. and Segev, G. (2009). Chosen-ciphertext security via correlated products. In *TCC 2009*, vol. 5444 of *LNCS*, Reingold, O. (ed.). Springer, Heidelberg.

Rothblum, R. (2013). On the circular security of bit-encryption. In *TCC 2013*, vol. 7785 of *LNCS*, Sahai, A. (ed.). Springer, Heidelberg.

Sahai, A. (1999). Non-malleable non-interactive zero knowledge and adaptive chosen-ciphertext security. In *40th FOCS*. IEEE Computer Society Press.

Sahai, A. and Waters, B. (2014). How to use indistinguishability obfuscation: Deniable encryption, and more. In *46th ACM STOC*, Shmoys, D.B. (ed.). ACM Press.

Saito, T., Xagawa, K., Yamakawa, T. (2018). Tightly-secure key-encapsulation mechanism in the quantum random oracle model. In *EUROCRYPT 2018, Part III*, vol. 10822 of *LNCS*, Nielsen, J.B., Rijmen, V. (eds). Springer, Heidelberg.

Sander, T., Young, A., Yung, M. (1999). Non-interactive cryptocomputing for NC1. In *40th FOCS*. IEEE Computer Society Press.

Shacham, H. (2007). A cramer-shoup encryption scheme from the linear assumption and from progressively weaker linear variants. Cryptology ePrint Archive, Report 2007/074 [Online]. Available at: https://eprint.iacr.org/2007/074.

Shamir, A. (1984). Identity-based cryptosystems and signature schemes. In *CRYPTO'84*, vol. 196 of *LNCS*, Blakley, G.R., Chaum, D. (eds). Springer, Heidelberg.

Shannon, C.E. (1949). Communication theory of secrecy systems. *Bell Systems Technical Journal*, 28(4), 656–715.

Shoup, V. (2001a). OAEP reconsidered. In *CRYPTO 2001*, vol. 2139 of *LNCS*, Kilian, J. (ed.). Springer, Heidelberg.

Shoup, V. (2001b). A proposal for an ISO standard for public key encryption. Cryptology ePrint Archive, Report 2001/112 [Online]. Available at: https://eprint.iacr.org/2001/112.

Shoup, V. (2004). Sequences of games: A tool for taming complexity in security proofs. Cryptology ePrint Archive, Report 2004/332 [Online]. Available at: https://eprint.iacr.org/2004/332.

Targhi, E.E. and Unruh, D. (2016). Post-quantum security of the Fujisaki-Okamoto and OAEP transforms. In *TCC 2016-B, Part II*, vol. 9986 of *LNCS*, Hirt, M., Smith, A.D. (eds). Springer, Heidelberg.

Wee, H. (2010). Efficient chosen-ciphertext security via extractable hash proofs. In *CRYPTO 2010*, vol. 6223 of *LNCS*, Rabin, T. (ed.). Springer, Heidelberg.

Wee, H. (2016). KDM-security via homomorphic smooth projective hashing. In *PKC 2016, Part II*, vol. 9615 of *LNCS*, Cheng, C.-M., Chung, K.-M., Persiano, G., Yang, B.-Y. (eds). Springer, Heidelberg.

Yamakawa, T., Yamada, S., Hanaoka, G., Kunihiro, N. (2016). Adversary-dependent lossy trapdoor function from hardness of factoring semi-smooth RSA subgroup moduli. In *CRYPTO 2016, Part II*, vol. 9815 of *LNCS*, Robshaw, M., Katz, J. (eds). Springer, Heidelberg.

Yang, R., Lai, J., Huang, Z., Au, M.H., Xu, Q., Susilo, W. (2020). Possibility and impossibility results for receiver selective opening secure PKE in the multi-challenge setting. In *ASIACRYPT 2020, Part I*, vol. 12491 of *LNCS*, Moriai, S., Wang, H. (eds). Springer, Heidelberg.

2

Signatures and Security Notions

Marc FISCHLIN

Technische Universität Darmstadt, Germany

We introduce the notion of digital signature schemes and discuss some example schemes used in practice. We then discuss basic security properties of signature schemes, especially unforgeability and strong unforgeability under chosen-message attacks.

2.1. Signature schemes

In this section, we describe the interfaces of a digital signature scheme, and the minimal functional requirement that genuine signatures generated by the signer can be verified as correct. We then discuss two classical examples of such signature schemes.

2.1.1. *Definition*

As with handwritten signatures, we expect a digital signature σ to tie the content of a message m from some space $\mathcal{M}$ of admissible messages to the signer. The signer is identified by a public key pk, which may be certified and thus attached to an identity. Since we expect only the signer to be able to create such signatures, the signer holds a matching secret key sk, generated together with pk via some KGen algorithm. Signing with the secret key sk is carried out by the Sig algorithm of the scheme, and verification under the public key pk is done via the Vf algorithm.

With the above interfaces, the three algorithms, KGen, Sig, and Vf, are not "connected" yet. This is done via the correctness property, mentioning that signatures

Asymmetric Cryptography,
coordinated by David POINTCHEVAL. © ISTE Ltd. 2022.

generated by algorithm Sig under keys generated by KGen are identified as correct by the verification algorithm Vf. Note that this is in principle trivial to achieve by letting Vf accept any signature. But we will later require that it is hard to find such valid signatures without knowledge of the secret key, that is, this unforgeability notion and the correctness requirement can be seen as opponents in this regard.

DEFINITION 2.1 (Signature Scheme).– *A digital signature scheme* S $=$ (S.KGen, S.Sig, S.Vf) *consists of three probabilistic polynomial-time algorithms such that*

– Key Generation: The key generation algorithm on input of the security parameter 1^λ *in unary outputs a pair of secret and public key,* (sk, pk) $\leftarrow_\$$ S.KGen(1^λ). *We assume that each key allows to recover* 1^λ *efficiently, and that the security parameter determines a message space* $\mathcal{M}_\lambda \subseteq \{0, 1\}^*$.

– Signing: The signing algorithm receives as input the secret key sk and a message $m \in \mathcal{M}_\lambda$, *and outputs a signature,* $\sigma \leftarrow_\$$ S.Sig(sk, m).

– Verification: The verification algorithm receives as input the public key pk, a message $m \in \mathcal{M}_\lambda$, *and a potential signature* σ, *and outputs a decision bit,* $d \leftarrow_\$$ S.Vf(pk, m, σ).

Correctness says that, with overwhelming probability (as a function in λ*), for any message* $m \in \mathcal{M}_\lambda$ *we have* $d = 1$ *for* $(sk, pk) \leftarrow_\$$ S.KGen(1^λ), $\sigma \leftarrow_\$$ S.Sig(sk, m) *and* $d \leftarrow_\$$ S.Vf(pk, m, σ). *If correctness holds with probability 1, then we say that the scheme is perfectly correct.*

We have defined signature schemes with respect to probabilistic verification algorithms. In all known schemes verification is deterministic, and if the signing algorithm outputs a signature, then the (deterministic) verifier also accepts this signature. Still, some practical signature schemes today, notably some lattice-based schemes like Dilithium (Bai et al. 2020), may fail to create a valid signature in a single execution, and thus iterate if this happens. In this case, the algorithm may theoretically run forever, or one needs to abort after some iterations, causing usually a negligible error in the signature generation process. For practical purposes, this probability is irrelevant, though.

We note that, in theory, it is easy to fix negligible correctness errors for deterministic verifiers, without violating unforgeability. For this, the signer first verifies the signature σ before outputting it, and instead outputs the signing key sk if verification fails. The verification algorithm then also accepts the secret key as a signature for any message m, such that any error in the signing process is cured. Here, we assume that one can check that sk is a valid signing key to pk. The latter is easy to achieve if sk includes the randomness used to generate the key pair by executing KGen. But let us stress again that this solution is only of theoretical interest.

2.1.2. *Examples of practical schemes*

In this section, we present two of the most widely deployed signature schemes in practice. We discuss their security properties after having presented the security notions in the following sections.

2.1.2.1. *Digital signature algorithm*

The digital signature algorithm (DSA) has been proposed by the National Institute of Standards and Technology (NIST), first as the only signature algorithm in the digital signature standard (National Institute of Standards and Technology 1994) in 1994. The algorithm uses a group $\mathbf{G}$ and works in a sub group of $\mathbf{G}$ of prime order q generated by an element $g \in \mathbf{G}$. We write $\langle g \rangle$ for this cyclic group generated by g. Initially, NIST has only suggested to use a group $\mathbf{G} = \mathbb{Z}_p^*$ for prime p between 512 bits and 1024 bits, and q to be of order 2^{160}. The latest version of the DSS standard (National Institute of Standards and Technology 2013) allows other choices of $(1024, 160)$, $(2048, 224)$, $(2048, 256)$ or $(3072, 256)$ bits for (p, q), and also includes an elliptic curve version called ECDSA. We first adopt here the multiplicative form over $\mathbb{Z}_p^*$ for describing the algorithm and discuss the changes to ECDSA afterwards.

For signing messages m, the DSA deploys a function H to hash messages to a short string. This string is subsequently embedded into $\mathbb{Z}_q$ by a standard string-to-integer conversion, requiring that the output of the hash algorithm is sufficiently short. We simply assume here that $\mathsf{H}(m)$ is a value from $\mathbb{Z}_q$. NIST recommends to use any secure hash algorithm specified as a secure hash algorithm in National Institute of Standards and Technology (2015). Since the latest version of the hash standard proposes different algorithms with varying output lengths, larger hash outputs possibly need to be truncated.

CONSTRUCTION 2.2 (Digital Signature Algorithm).– *The* DSA *over group* $\langle g \rangle \subseteq \mathbb{Z}_p^*$ *of prime order q, and with hash function* H, *consists of the following algorithms:*

– *Key Generation: For the given group, the key generation algorithm picks* $sk \leftarrow_\$$ $\mathbb{Z}_q$ *randomly, sets* $pk \leftarrow g^{sk} \bmod p$ *and outputs* (sk, pk) *as the key pair.*

– *Signing: To sign a message* $m \in \{0, 1\}^*$, *the signer picks a random* $k \leftarrow_\$ \mathbb{Z}_q^*$ *and computes*

$$r \leftarrow (g^k \bmod p) \bmod q, \qquad s \leftarrow k^{-1} \cdot (\mathsf{H}(m) + sk \cdot r) \bmod q,$$

where k^{-1} *is the inverse to k over* $\mathbb{Z}_q$. *It outputs* $\sigma \leftarrow (r, s)$ *as the signature for m. If* $r = 0$ *or* $s = 0$, *then the signer shall restart the signature process.*

– *Verification: On input* pk, m *and* $\sigma = (r, s)$ *the verifier checks that r and s are in* $\mathbb{Z}_q^*$, *that is,* $0 < r, s < q$, *then computes*

$$w \leftarrow s^{-1} \bmod q, \qquad u_1 \leftarrow \mathsf{H}(m) \cdot w \bmod q, \qquad u_2 \leftarrow rw \bmod q,$$

and checks that $r = (g^{u_1} \cdot pk^{u_2} \bmod p) \bmod q$. *If and only if all tests succeed, the verifier outputs* 1, *and* 0 *otherwise.*

For correctness, we note that for a well-formed signature $\sigma = (r, s)$ for message m under key pk, we have

$$w = s^{-1} = k \cdot (\mathsf{H}(m) + sk \cdot r)^{-1} \bmod q$$

such that

$$g^{u_1} \cdot pk^{u_2} = g^{\mathsf{H}(m) \cdot s^{-1}} \cdot g^{sk \cdot r \cdot s^{-1}} = g^{(\mathsf{H}(m) + sk \cdot r) \cdot s^{-1}} = g^k \bmod p.$$

It follows that taking this value modulo q yields the value r and the verifier accepts the signature.

The elliptic curve version, called ECDSA, operates on special groups (also of prime order q) where group elements consist of pairs of an x-coordinate and y-coordinate. The elliptic curve also provides a group operation, usually called addition instead of multiplication. As such, the generator consists of a pair $g = (g_x, g_y)$ and we can interpret the step g^k as the k-fold addition of (g_x, g_y) over the curve.

Note that we can leave the scalar operations in $\mathbb{Z}_q$ from the original DSA unchanged, but only need to adapt the operations $\bmod p$, specifically the computation of $r \leftarrow (g^k \bmod p) \bmod q$ in the signing step, and the verification of $r = (g^{u_1} \cdot pk^{u_2} \bmod p) \bmod q$ when checking a signature. In the elliptic curve case, we cannot simply compute g^k and then reduce it to $\bmod q$, because the group element consists of pairs of coordinates. The ECDSA standard instead lets r be the x-coordinate of g^k, and the verifier checks that the x-coordinate of the computed group element matches the given r.

2.1.2.2. *Schnorr signature scheme*

The Schnorr signature scheme (Schnorr 1990, 1991) is a discrete logarithm-based variant of the Fiat–Shamir paradigm (Fiat and Shamir 1987) to turn identification schemes into signature schemes. It thus follows the commitment–challenge–response paradigm where the challenge in the non-interactive signature scheme is computed by a hash function H applied to the initial commitment and the message. As in the DSA case, the range of the hash function can again be embedded into $\mathbb{Z}_q$ for a prime q, denoting the group order of $\langle g \rangle$ of a generator g. Indeed, the security proof of Schnorr incited the use of a prime order q. For the presentation, we again assume that the group generated by g lies in $\mathbb{Z}_p^*$. There is also an elliptic curve variant, which is a straightforward adaption to the operations over the elliptic curve.

CONSTRUCTION 2.3 (Schnorr Signature Scheme).– *The Schnorr signature scheme* Schnorr *over group* $\langle g \rangle \subseteq \mathbb{Z}_p^*$ *of prime order q and with hash function* H *consists of the following algorithms:*

Key Generation: For the given group, the key generation algorithm picks sk ←$ $\mathbb{Z}_q$ randomly, sets pk ← g^{sk} mod p and outputs (sk, pk) as the key pair.

Signing: To sign a message m ∈ {0,1}*, the signer picks a random r ←$ $\mathbb{Z}_q$ and computes

$$R \leftarrow g^r \bmod p, \qquad c \leftarrow \mathsf{H}(R, m), \qquad y \leftarrow r + c \cdot sk \bmod q,$$

and outputs σ ← (c, y) as the signature for m.

Verification: On input pk, m and σ = (c, y), the verifier checks that c and y are in the range $\mathbb{Z}_q$, and if so, verifies that $\mathsf{H}(g^y \cdot pk^{-c}, m) = c$. If and only if all tests succeed, the verifier outputs 1, and 0 otherwise.

For correctness, we observe that for a signature $\sigma = (c, y)$ generated by Schnorr.Sig for key sk, we have that $y = r + c \cdot sk \bmod q$ for the randomness r used in the signing step. But then $g^y \cdot pk^{-c} = g^{r+c \cdot sk} \cdot g^{-c \cdot sk} = g^r \bmod p$ derived in the verification matches the value $R = g^r \bmod p$ computed by the signer. Hence, the hash function evaluation in the verification also maps $\mathsf{H}(g^y \cdot pk^{-c}, m)$ to c and verification succeeds.

2.2. Unforgeability

In this section, we discuss the basic notion of unforgeability. We also revisit the previous schemes in light of achieved security guarantees.

2.2.1. *Discussion*

Intuitively, it is straightforward to spell out what we expect from a secure signature scheme, namely, that no one can forge signatures. To formalize this, we have to consider what an adversary is able to do in an attack, and when the adversary wins. We start with the latter and follow the work by Goldwasser et al. (1988):

– *Total break*: The adversary is able to compute the signer's secret key.

– *Universal forgery*: The adversary is able to find a functionally equivalent algorithm to the signer's procedure.

– *Selective forgery*: The adversary is able to forge a signature for an a priori chosen message.

– *Existential forgery*: The adversary is able to forge a signature for an arbitrary, possibly meaningless message.

Note that from the signer's perspective, the first two items, a total break and a universal forgery, are usually equivalently harmful. One could also argue if the name "existential forgery" is fortunate, given that it does not suffice that such a message *exists* but that the adversary must be able to pinpoint the message.

As mentioned before, the other dimension for defining unforgeability refers to the adversary's attack capabilities. Here, the work by Goldwasser et al. (1988) instantaneously considered the strongest form of attack, called *adaptive chosen-message attacks*, where the adversary can first see signatures of chosen messages, where each message is chosen adaptively after having learned the signatures for the previous messages. However, sometimes it is also reasonable to consider weaker attack forms:

– *Key-only attack*: In a key-only attack, the adversary only receives the verification key and is supposed to output a forgery.

– *Non-adaptive chosen-message attack*: In a non-adaptive chosen-message attack, the adversary gets to see signatures for chosen messages before trying to produce a forgery, but the messages are determined at the beginning. Here, we can further distinguish between the cases that the adversary can choose the messages before or after having received the verification key.

– *One-time attack*: In a one-time attack, the adversary mounts a chosen-message attack but only gets to see one signature for a chosen message, before trying to produce a forgery. The chosen message may, or may not, depend on the public key. Schemes resilient against such attacks are also called one-time signature schemes.

– *Adaptive chosen-message attack*: As mentioned before, in such attacks, the adversary can ask for signatures of an arbitrary number of messages, where the next message is determined after having learned the previous signatures.

The relaxed security notions are useful because there are conversions for achieving the stronger variants. First note that one-time signature schemes are comparably easy to construct. Lamport (1979) shows a simple construction based on any one-way function, albeit this solution is quite expensive in terms of the signature length. If one has a one-time signature scheme, then, using Merkle trees (Merkle 1988), one gets a signature scheme that allows to sign an unbounded number of messages (Merkle 1990). This construction idea has meanwhile evolved into practical hash-based signature schemes such as SPHINCS$^+$ (Aumasson et al. 2020).

For the non-adaptive to adaptive transformation, there are two paths. One is to use the Even–Goldreich–Micali construction (Even et al. 1996). It starts with a scheme which is existentially unforgeable under random (and thus non-adaptively chosen) messages, and combines it with a one-time signature scheme. The key pair (sk_{rnd}, pk_{rnd}) consists of a pair for the scheme for random messages. To sign a message m, one generates a new key pair (sk_{ot}, pk_{ot}) for the one-time scheme, signs the message m under sk_{ot} and finally certifies pk_{ot} by signing it with sk_{rnd}. The signature of the combined scheme consists of the two signatures for m (under sk_{ot})

and for pk_{ot} (under sk_{rnd}), together with pk_{ot}. Note that we only sign random "messages" pk_{ot} under the key pk_{rnd} such that security against such attacks suffices.

The other possibility is to use chameleon hashes (Krawczyk and Rabin 2000). These are probabilistic hash functions $H(pk_{ch}, m, r)$, which have a public key pk_{ch} and map an input message m with randomness r to some hash value h. There is also a secret key sk_{ch} that allows to later find appropriate randomness r' to a given message m' such that $H(pk_{ch}, m', r') = h$ again maps to the same hash value. Such chameleon hashes can be built, for instance, under the discrete logarithm assumption, letting $H(pk_{ch}, m, r) = g^m \cdot pk_{ch}^r \mod p$. Knowledge of the secret key $sk_{ch} \in \mathbb{Z}_q^*$ with $pk_{ch} = g^{sk_{ch}} \mod p$ allows to find r' to a given m', m, r such that hash value coincide: $r' \leftarrow sk_{ch}^{-1} \cdot (m - m') + r \mod q$. In contrast, given only the public key pk_{ch}, finding such collisions $(m, r) \neq (m', r')$ is infeasible under the discrete logarithm assumption.

The signature transformation using chameleon hashes first hashes each message to be signed under such a chameleon hash function, such that security essentially follows the hash-and-sign principle. The public key for the chameleon hash function becomes part of the verification key. The signer does not need knowledge of the secret key of the chameleon function; only the security reduction takes advantage of it. It allows the reduction to first generate non-adaptively hashes to random messages, and once the adversary picks each message adaptively, to bend the hash value to the previously selected one with the help of sk_{ch}.

2.2.2. Existential unforgeability under chosen-message attacks

From now on we focus on the strongest type of attacks, existential unforgeability under chosen-message attacks. This notion brings forward a seemingly paradoxical situation, pointed out by Goldwasser et al. (1988), especially since they discussed factoring-based signatures: We must be able to sign arbitrary messages for the adversary, suggesting that we must know the factorization in order to do so. But for a security reduction, at the same time we must also be able to use the adversary's forgery strategy to derive a factorization algorithm. Indeed, the first version of the paper above was entitled "A 'Paradoxical' Solution to the Signature Problem" (Goldwasser et al. 1984), also explaining that one can in principle overcome this dilemma. The argument is roughly that the reduction may simulate the view of the adversary in an indistinguishable environment with a slightly different public key or secret key, supporting signature generation but still enabling us to derive the desired contradiction for the adversary's forgery for a new message.

In the following definition, we exclude trivial attacks, caused by the fact that digital signatures can be cloned easily. Assume that the adversary, in the chosen-message attack, requests a signature σ for some message m. Then, it would be trivial for the adversary to duplicate this message-signature pair digitally. One may argue if this is actually a valid attack since the signer has deliberately authenticated this message m. Hence, we exclude such duplication attacks in the definition below. For this, we collect all genuinely signed messages in a set $\mathcal{Q}$ and call the adversary only successful if it forges a signature for a new message not in this set $\mathcal{Q}$. The set $\mathcal{Q}$ is maintained by the game and updated with each signature request. We model the possibility to learn signatures by giving $\mathcal{A}$ access to a signing oracle $\mathcal{O}(sk, \cdot)$:

DEFINITION 2.4 (EUF-CMA).– *A signature scheme* $S = (\mathsf{S.KGen}, \mathsf{S.Sig}, \mathsf{S.Vf})$ *is existentially unforgeable under adaptive chosen-message attacks (EUF-CMA) if for any PPT adversary* $\mathcal{A}$ *the advantage*

$$\boldsymbol{Adv}_{S,\mathcal{A}}^{\text{EUF-CMA}}(\lambda) := \Pr\left[\boldsymbol{Exp}_{S,\mathcal{A}}^{\text{EUF-CMA}}(\lambda)\right]$$

is negligible, where

$\boldsymbol{Exp}_{S,\mathcal{A}}^{\text{EUF-CMA}}(\lambda)$		$\mathcal{O}(sk, m)$
1 $\mathcal{Q} \leftarrow \emptyset$		*1* $\sigma \leftarrow_\$ \mathsf{S.Sig}(sk, m)$
2 $(sk, pk) \leftarrow_\$ \mathsf{S.KGen}(1^\lambda)$		*2* $\mathcal{Q} \leftarrow \mathcal{Q} \cup \{m\}$
3 $(m^*, \sigma^*) \leftarrow_\$ \mathcal{A}^{\mathcal{O}(sk, \cdot)}(pk)$		*3* *return* σ
4 *return* 1 *iff*		
$\mathsf{S.Vf}(pk, m^*, \sigma^*) = 1$ *and* $m^* \notin \mathcal{Q}$		

Note that we have chosen an asymptotic notion to bound the success probability $\mathbf{Adv}_{S,\mathcal{A}}^{\text{EUF-CMA}}(\lambda)$ of the PPT adversary $\mathcal{A}$ for secure signature schemes. Alternatively, we could also use concrete security bounds and call a signature scheme (t, q, ϵ)-EUF-CMA if for any adversary $\mathcal{A}$ with resources at most t and making at most q signature queries, we have $\mathbf{Adv}_{S,\mathcal{A}}^{\text{EUF-CMA}} \leq \epsilon$. Here, the adversary's resources are usually measured in terms of run time (in some machine model), hence the character t. But we may also use other measures such as space requirements.

2.2.3. *Unforgeability of practical schemes*

We discuss here briefly what is known about the security of the two practical signature schemes presented in section 2.1.2, namely, the DSA and the Schnorr schemes.

2.2.3.1. *Digital signature algorithm*

The DSA scheme has been proposed by NIST without an accompanying security proof. It is clear that it relies on the hardness of computing discrete logarithms – otherwise an adversary could derive the secret key from the public key – and that one must not re-use the same randomness for creating signatures for different messages. See, for example, Vaudenay (2003), for further requirements. Although these are necessary conditions, as of today, we still do not have a convincing proof for the EUF-CMA security.

Several intermediate results about the security of *derivates* of DSA and its elliptic curve version exist, alas the results for the original algorithms is limited. A critical aspect in all of these results for (EC)DSA is the so-called conversion function f, mapping group elements from $\langle g \rangle$ to integers in $\mathbb{Z}_q$, as required in the signature generation step when computing $r \leftarrow f(g^k)$. In the original DSA scheme, this function is simply defined as $f(X) = (X \bmod q)$; in the ECDSA version, it maps the elliptic curve point to the x-coordinate.

Brown (2005) shows that, in the generic group model, DSA and ECDSA can be shown to be EUF-CMA if one makes additional assumptions about the hash function and the conversion function. However, as pointed out by Stern et al. (2002), the proof would also show that the ECDSA scheme is strongly unforgeable (see definition below) – which it is probably not (see section 2.3.3). Fersch et al. (2016) gave a proof for DSA and ECDSA under the discrete logarithm assumption, decomposing the conversion function and idealizing one part of this decomposition. It is unclear what this result means for the genuine conversion functions in DSA and ECDSA.

2.2.3.2. *Schnorr signatures*

For the Schnorr signature scheme, we have a security proof in the random oracle model (Bellare and Rogaway 1993), assuming the hardness of computing discrete logarithms. In the random oracle model, one models the deployed hash function H as a random function. The proof can be found in Pointcheval and Stern (1996, 2000). It uses the so-called forking strategy, causing a rather loose security bound. We state the bound here in the version of Bellare and Neven (2006), saying that an adversary winning in the EUF-CMA-experiment against the Schnorr scheme with probability ϵ, when making at most q_H random oracle requests, yields an algorithm against the discrete logarithm problem with roughly the same running time and with success probability approximately $\sqrt{q_H \cdot \epsilon}$. In other words, when settling for an acceptable security level for the discrete logarithm problem in the group, one must take into account that the upper bound against forgers for the signature scheme becomes quadratic and thus significantly larger.

The loss in the reduction from forgeries against the Schnorr signature scheme to the discrete-logarithm problem seems inevitable. Seurin (2012) gave strong evidence that the linear loss q_H in the security bound is inherent. His result rules out algebraic reductions with tighter bounds, assuming the one-more discrete logarithm problem. The non-tightness for generic reductions was later confirmed by Fleischhacker et al. (2019).

Concerning the assumption about the hash function being a random oracle, Neven et al. (2009) gave a security proof for the Schnorr signature scheme under standard assumptions about the hash function, but relying on the generic group model. In the analysis, they use a conversion function f mapping elements from the idealized group to bit strings for computing $H(f(R), m)$. Brown (2015b,a) later raised the question if the wrong choice of the conversion function allowed for attacks. It remains open if the "right" conversion function resurrects the security proof.

Concerning other possibility to avoid the strong random oracle model, there are meta-reduction results suggesting that this is infeasible. Paillier and Vergnaud (2005) showed that algebraic reductions cannot be used to show security of Schnorr signatures against key-only attacks, assuming the one-more discrete logarithm problem. Fischlin and Fleischhacker (2013) have complemented this, also under the one-more discrete logarithm assumption, for reductions which do not program the random oracle but which run only a single resettable instance of the adversary.

2.3. Strong unforgeability

In the EUF-CMA-definition above, we exclude attacks where the adversary copies a previously signed message in the forgery. In the experiment, this is captured by stipulating $m^* \notin Q$ for the forgery attempt m^* has not been queried before. Here, we discuss a stronger security property that prevents the adversary from transforming signatures. In other words, the adversary cannot even produce a new signature to a previously signed message.

2.3.1. *Discussion*

Strong unforgeability of signatures prevents malleability attacks where the adversary modified a pair (m, σ) into a related pair (m, σ^*) for the same message. This is, for example, useful in situations where the signature is part of a ciphertext and one aims to show chosen-ciphertext security of the encryption scheme. In such a chosen-ciphertext attack, the adversary receives a challenge ciphertext c and tries to determine some information about the encapsulated message. To do so, the adversary is allowed to query for decryptions of *different* ciphertexts c^*. If the challenge ciphertext c contained a malleable signature σ, then the encryption attacker could possibly maul this signature into another signature σ^* without affecting the authenticity of the signed data, and submit the modified ciphertext c^* to the decryption oracle to learn the original message.

Indeed, until recently, the usage of strongly unforgeable schemes has mainly been used to ensure non-malleability in ciphertexts (e.g. Canetti et al. 2004) and zero-knowledge proofs (e.g. Sahai 1999). Recently, however, strong unforgeability of signatures has gained quite some attention in the area of cryptocurrencies where signatures are used to authenticate money transfers. There, the issue of signatures which are not strongly unforgeable have emerged under the term transaction malleability attacks.

In a cryptocurrency like Bitcoin transactions used to carry a transaction identifier *TxID*, which was a (double) SHA256 hash value of the raw transaction data *transaction* and the signature information *scriptSig*:

$$TxID = H(H(transaction, scriptSig)).$$

Suppose now that Alice transferred some amount to Bob with this transaction identifier *TxID*, but Bob modified the signature in *scriptSig* to some other valid signature (which may be possible if the signature scheme was not strongly unforgeable). This resulted in another valid transaction under a different identifier

$$TxID^* = H(H(transaction, scriptSig^*)),$$

yet still transferring the money to Bob. If now Bob complained that he had not received the amount from transaction *TxID*, correctly claiming that the original transaction identifier does not appear on the ledger, then Alice might have been tricked into re-issuing the transfer, making Bob effectively receive the amount twice.

Besides the attack on the cryptographic property of the signature scheme, an adversary may also target the (ambiguous) encodings of signatures and transaction data, aiming to produce syntactically different but semantically equivalent transactions. That is, modifying *transaction* in such a way would also yield a different identifier *TxID**. While these attacks sound rather theoretical, transaction malleability has led to the fall of the Bitcoin exchange MtGox in 2014 (Decker and Wattenhofer 2014). To be fair, the attack on MtGox seemed to have targeted the encoding of signatures and transaction data, rather than the malleability of the signature scheme.

Note that one can fix the transaction malleability of the signature scheme by switching to a strongly unforgeable scheme. Indeed, Bitcoin has slightly modified the signature scheme, making it more robust against known malleability attacks; we will discuss this later in section 2.3.3. In order to cover also other transaction malleability attacks, Bitcoin has moved the signature out of the identifier computation with the soft fork *SegWit* in 2017.

2.3.2. *Strong existential unforgeability under chosen-message attacks*

We extend the EUF-CMA-definition above and now store the message-signature pairs generated in the signature queries in $\mathcal{Q}$. The adversary then needs to produce a forgery where either the message is new, or where at least the signature for the message in the forgery is new. This is captured by demanding that $(m^*, \sigma^*) \notin \mathcal{Q}$:

DEFINITION 2.5 (SEUF-CMA).– *A signature scheme* $\mathsf{S} = (\mathsf{S.KGen}, \mathsf{S.Sig}, \mathsf{S.Vf})$ *is strongly existentially unforgeable under adaptive chosen-message attacks* (SEUF-CMA) *if for any PPT adversary $\mathcal{A}$ the advantage*

$$\mathbf{Adv}_{\mathsf{S},\mathcal{A}}^{\mathrm{SEUF\text{-}CMA}}(\lambda) := \Pr\left[\mathbf{Exp}_{\mathsf{S},\mathcal{A}}^{\mathrm{SEUF\text{-}CMA}}(\lambda)\right]$$

is negligible, where

$\mathbf{Exp}_{\mathsf{S},\mathcal{A}}^{\mathrm{SEUF\text{-}CMA}}(\lambda)$	$\mathcal{O}(sk, m)$
1 $\mathcal{Q} \leftarrow \emptyset$	*1* $\sigma \leftarrow_\$ \mathsf{S.Sig}(sk, m)$
2 $(sk, pk) \leftarrow_\$ \mathsf{S.KGen}(1^\lambda)$	*2* $\mathcal{Q} \leftarrow \mathcal{Q} \cup \{(m, \sigma)\}$
3 $(m^*, \sigma^*) \leftarrow_\$ \mathcal{A}^{\mathcal{O}(sk, \cdot)}(pk)$	*3* *return* σ
4 *return* 1 *iff*	
$\quad$ $\mathsf{S.Vf}(pk, m^*, \sigma^*) = 1$ *and* $(m^*, \sigma^*) \notin \mathcal{Q}$	

As in the case of EUF-CMA, we can also define a concrete version of (t, q, ϵ)-SEUF-CMA security.

2.3.3. *Strong unforgeability of practical schemes*

We discuss here quickly the question of strong unforgeability of (EC)DSA and Schnorr signatures. This is easy for the case of Schnorr's scheme, where this is enforced by design: The security reduction of basic unforgeability of the scheme simultaneously shows strong unforgeability.

For DSA, the situation is less clear. The result by Fersch et al. (2016) shows strong unforgeability of DSA, assuming again an idealized conversion function under the discrete logarithm assumption. For the elliptic curve variant ECDSA, it is known that the scheme does *not* provide strong unforgeability. The reason lies in the bad interplay between elliptic curve cryptography and the conversion function, mapping to the x-coordinate. To see this, it is instructive to write the main verification check additively, as common for elliptic curves:

$$r = x\text{-coordinate}(s^{-1} \cdot \mathsf{H}(m) \cdot g + s^{-1} \cdot r \cdot pk).$$

It is known that for any point $S = (S_x, S_y)$ on the curve, the (additive) inverse point $-S$ is also on the curve. In fact, it holds $-S = (S_x, -S_y)$ such that the points S and $-S$ coincide in the x-coordinate. This allows an adversary to modify a given signature (r, s) into another valid signature $(r, -s \bmod q)$ for the same message:

$$(-s)^{-1} \cdot \mathsf{H}(m) \cdot g + (-s)^{-1} \cdot r \cdot pk = -(s^{-1} \cdot \mathsf{H}(m) \cdot g + s^{-1} \cdot r \cdot pk)$$

and hence the x-coordinate of the group element for verification of $-s \bmod q$ maps to the same one as for s.

Note that Bitcoin, on top of the soft fork *SegWit* moving the signature out of the transaction hash, also enforced that only the smaller (encoded) value of s, $-s \bmod q$ can appear in a valid signature. This prevents the attack above but it does not show that ECDSA with this modification is strongly unforgeable. There may still be other malleability attacks on ECDSA, although currently none is known.

2.3.4. *Building strongly unforgeable schemes*

There are several options to make an EUF-CMA-secure signature scheme strongly unforgeable. First, turning any EUF-CMA-secure signature scheme into a strongly unforgeable one can be done generically. That is, since an EUF-CMA-secure scheme implies the existence of one-way functions, and one-way functions suffice to build sEUF-CMA-secure signatures (Goldreich 2004, Section 6.5.2), we immediately have a feasibility result. However, this solution is far from being practical.

A more efficient transformation has been presented by Steinfeld et al. (2007). It relies on a chameleon hash function $H(pk_{ch}, m, r)$, as introduced in section 2.2.1. For such a chameleon hash function, one can adapt the randomness r to r' for a given message m' via the secret key sk_{ch}. Without the secret key, the hash function is collision resistant. An important observation is that common chameleon hashes have a built-in strong form of collision resistance in the sense that it is even hard to find $(m, r) \neq (m', r')$, that is, to find a different r' to a given $m = m'$ and r which collides. This suggests a close relation to strong unforgeability.

The idea of the transformed signature scheme is to have the signer first hash a fixed message m_0 and signature σ_0 under some chameleon hash key pk_{ch} with randomness r_0, and then hash the result h again under an independent chameleon key pk'_{ch} under randomness r'. Only then one signs the final hash value under the (possibly not strongly unforgeable) signature scheme, but then adapts the randomness of the first hash scheme to match the original message m and the final signature σ:

$\underline{\text{Sig}_{\text{strong}}((sk, sk_{ch}, pk_{ch}, pk'_{ch}), m)}$

1   let m_0, σ_0 be fixed values
2    $h \leftarrow H(pk_{ch}, (m_0, \sigma_0), r_0)$ for random r_0
3    $h' \leftarrow H(pk'_{ch}, h, r')$ for random r'
4    $\sigma \leftarrow_\$ \text{Sig}(sk, h')$
5   use sk_{ch} to find r such that $h = H(pk_{ch}, (m, \sigma), r)$
6   return $\sigma_{\text{strong}} = (\sigma, r, r')$

Formally, the key generation algorithm for the transformed scheme thus generates a signature key pair (sk, pk) for the underlying scheme, two independent key pairs for the chameleon hash functions (sk_{ch}, pk_{ch}) and (sk'_{ch}, pk'_{ch}), dropping the secret key sk'_{ch}, and outputs the key pair $sk_{strong} = (sk, sk_{ch}, pk_{ch}, pk'_{ch})$ and $pk_{strong} = (pk, pk_{ch}, pk'_{ch})$. Verification consists of re-computing the hash values and verifying the final signature for the second hash value.

Intuitively, the transformed signature scheme is strongly unforgeable because any modification of σ, r, or r' in the final signature σ_{strong} requires to find a collision in the chameleon hash functions, or to forge a signature for a new hash under the underlying signature scheme. We note that the two nested chameleon hashes are necessary in the proof to switch between different chameleon trapdoors. In principle, they could be combined into a single chameleon hash supporting multiple secret keys.

2.4. Summary

We have defined the common security notions EUF-CMA and sEUF-CMA for signature schemes. The former guarantees that adversaries cannot produce valid forgeries for previously unsigned messages. The latter one ensures also that one cannot find a fresh signature for a signed message. We have then described how one can transform EUF-CMA-secure schemes into strongly secure ones via chameleon hashes. The transformation is quite efficient, although it adds some overhead.

We have also discussed security of two practical signatures schemes, (EC)DSA and Schnorr. Although the Schnorr scheme provides sEUF-CMA-security under the discrete logarithm assumption in the random oracle model – with a loose security bound – the security status of (EC)DSA is currently open. The only guaranteed fact is that ECDSA is not strongly unforgeable.

2.5. References

Aumasson, J.-P., Bernstein, D.J., Beullens, W., Dobraunig, C., Eichlseder, M., Fluhrer, S., Gazdag, S.-L., Hülsing, A., Kampanakis, P., Kölbl, S., et al. (2020). Shincs$^+$: Algorithm specifications and supporting documentation [Online]. Available at: https://sphincs.org/data/sphincs+-round3-specification.pdf

Bai, S., Ducas, L., Kiltz, E., Lepoint, T., Lyubashevsky, V., Schwabe, P., Seiler, G., Stehle, D. (2020). Crystals-dilithium: Algorithm specifications and supporting documentation [Online]. Available at: https://pq-crystals.org/dilithium/data/dilithium-specification-round3.pdf

Bellare, M. and Neven, G. (2006). Multi-signatures in the plain public-key model and a general forking lemma. In *ACM CCS 2006*, Juels, A., Wright, R.N., De Capitani di Vimercati, S. (eds). ACM Press.

Bellare, M. and Rogaway, P. (1993). Random oracles are practical: A paradigm for designing efficient protocols. In *ACM CCS 93*, Denning, D.E., Pyle, R., Ganesan, R., Sandhu, R.S., Ashby, V. (eds). ACM Press.

Brown, D.R.L. (2005). Generic groups, collision resistance, and ECDSA. *Designs, Codes and Cryptography*, 35(1), 119–152.

Brown, D.R.L. (2015a). A flaw in a theorem about Schnorr signatures. Cryptology ePrint Archive, Report 2015/509 [Online]. Available at: https://eprint.iacr.org/2015/509.

Brown, D.R.L. (2015b). Short Schnorr signatures require a hash function with more than just random-prefix resistance. Cryptology ePrint Archive, Report 2015/169 [Online]. Available at: https://eprint.iacr.org/2015/169.

Canetti, R., Halevi, S., Katz, J. (2004). Chosen-ciphertext security from identity-based encryption. In *EUROCRYPT 2004*, vol. 3027 of *LNCS*, Cachin, C., Camenisch, J. (eds). Springer, Heidelberg.

Decker, C. and Wattenhofer, R. (2014). Bitcoin transaction malleability and MtGox. In *ESORICS 2014, Part II*, vol. 8713 of *LNCS*, Kutylowski, M., Vaidya, J. (eds). Springer, Heidelberg.

Even, S., Goldreich, O., Micali, S. (1996). On-line/off-line digital signatures. *Journal of Cryptology*, 9(1), 35–67.

Fersch, M., Kiltz, E., Poettering, B. (2016). On the provable security of (EC)DSA signatures. In *ACM CCS 2016*, Weippl, E.R., Katzenbeisser, S., Kruegel, C., Myers, A.C., Halevi, S. (eds). ACM Press.

Fiat, A. and Shamir, A. (1987). How to prove yourself: Practical solutions to identification and signature problems. In *CRYPTO'86*, vol. 263 of *LNCS*, Odlyzko, A.M. (ed.). Springer, Heidelberg.

Fischlin, M. and Fleischhacker, N. (2013). Limitations of the meta-reduction technique: The case of Schnorr signatures. In *EUROCRYPT 2013*, vol. 7881 of *LNCS*, Johansson, T., Nguyen, P.Q. (eds). Springer, Heidelberg.

Fleischhacker, N., Jager, T., Schröder, D. (2019). On tight security proofs for Schnorr signatures. *Journal of Cryptology*, 32(2), 566–599.

Goldreich, O. (2004). *Foundations of Cryptography: Basic Applications*, volume 2. Cambridge University Press, Cambridge, UK.

Goldwasser, S., Micali, S., Rivest, R.L. (1984). A "paradoxical" solution to the signature problem (extended abstract). In *25th FOCS*. IEEE Computer Society Press.

Goldwasser, S., Micali, S., Rivest, R.L. (1988). A digital signature scheme secure against adaptive chosen-message attacks. *SIAM Journal on Computing*, 17(2), 281–308.

Krawczyk, H. and Rabin, T. (2000). Chameleon signatures. In *NDSS 2000*. The Internet Society, Reston, VA.

Lamport, L. (1979). Constructing digital signatures from a one-way function. Technical Report SRI-CSL-98, SRI International Computer Science Laboratory.

Merkle, R.C. (1988). A digital signature based on a conventional encryption function. In *CRYPTO'87*, vol. 293 of *LNCS*, Pomerance, C. (ed.). Springer, Heidelberg.

Merkle, R.C. (1990). A certified digital signature. In *CRYPTO'89*, vol. 435 of *LNCS*, Brassard, G. (ed.). Springer, Heidelberg.

National Institute of Standards and Technology (1994). Digital signature standard (DSS). FIPS PUB 186, Federal Information Processing Standards Publication.

National Institute of Standards and Technology (2013). Digital signature standard (DSS). FIPS PUB 186-4, Federal Information Processing Standards Publication.

National Institute of Standards and Technology (2015). Secure hash standard (SHS). FIPS PUB 180-4, Federal Information Processing Standards Publication.

Neven, G., Smart, N.P., Warinschi, B. (2009). Hash function requirements for Schnorr signatures. *Journal of Mathematical Cryptology*, 3(1), 69–87.

Paillier, P. and Vergnaud, D. (2005). Discrete-log-based signatures may not be equivalent to discrete log. In *ASIACRYPT 2005*, vol. 3788 of *LNCS*, Roy, B.K. (ed.). Springer, Heidelberg.

Pointcheval, D. and Stern, J. (1996). Security proofs for signature schemes. In *EUROCRYPT'96*, vol. 1070 of *LNCS*, Maurer, U.M. (ed.). Springer, Heidelberg.

Pointcheval, D. and Stern, J. (2000). Security arguments for digital signatures and blind signatures. *Journal of Cryptology*, 13(3), 361–396.

Sahai, A. (1999). Non-malleable non-interactive zero knowledge and adaptive chosen-ciphertext security. In *40th FOCS*. IEEE Computer Society Press.

Schnorr, C.-P. (1990). Efficient identification and signatures for smart cards. In *CRYPTO'89*, vol. 435 of *LNCS*, Brassard, G. (ed.). Springer, Heidelberg.

Schnorr, C.-P. (1991). Efficient signature generation by smart cards. *Journal of Cryptology*, 4(3), 161–174.

Seurin, Y. (2012). On the exact security of Schnorr-type signatures in the random oracle model. In *EUROCRYPT 2012*, vol. 7237 of *LNCS*, Pointcheval, D., Johansson, T. (eds). Springer, Heidelberg.

Steinfeld, R., Pieprzyk, J., Wang, H. (2007). How to strengthen any weakly unforgeable signature into a strongly unforgeable signature. In *CT-RSA 2007*, vol. 4377 of *LNCS*, Abe, M. (ed.). Springer, Heidelberg.

Stern, J., Pointcheval, D., Malone-Lee, J., Smart, N.P. (2002). Flaws in applying proof methodologies to signature schemes. In *CRYPTO 2002*, vol. 2442 of *LNCS*, Yung, M. (ed.). Springer, Heidelberg.

Vaudenay, S. (2003). The security of DSA and ECDSA. In *PKC 2003*, vol. 2567 of *LNCS*, Desmedt, Y. (ed.). Springer, Heidelberg.

3

Zero-Knowledge Proofs

Ivan VISCONTI

University of Salerno, Italy

3.1. Introduction

Consider the following typical scenario: Peggy claims something and then tells Victor: "It's true, trust me". Victor would like to get evidence that the claim is true since he does not fully trust Peggy. At the same time, Peggy does not want to reveal some confidential information that would prove the truthfulness of her claim. If Trinity, a third party that both Peggy and Victor fully trust, is willing to help, then Peggy could just reveal everything she knows about the claim to Trinity, and Trinity, once convinced that the claim is true, could inform Victor about the veracity of the claim, forgetting at the same time the information received from Peggy. Nevertheless, Peggy and Victor would like to resolve their disputes without involving others, and therefore they wonder, in the absence of a trusted third party, how Victor can be convinced of the veracity of a claim while still preserving Peggy's privacy.

In 1985, Goldwasser et al. formalized the above two-party game introducing the notion of "interactive zero-knowledge proof system". In the above scenario, Peggy would play the role of a prover P, while Victor would play the role of a verifier V. The claim is formalized as an instance x that is claimed to belong to a language L. Both P and V know x and the description of L and engage in some well-defined exchange of messages so that in the end P is able to convince V that $x \in L$. This is a basic correctness property that is named "completeness" and corresponds to Peggy being able to convince Victor when her claim is true. In case Peggy maliciously tries

Asymmetric Cryptography,
coordinated by David POINTCHEVAL. © ISTE Ltd. 2022.

to prove a false claim, the protection for Victor is named "soundness" and requires that V at the end of the interaction is convinced about the veracity of a false claim (i.e. $x \notin L$ but V gets convinced that $x \in L$) with low probability even when interacting with an adversary P^*. The protection for Peggy in case an adversary Victor is interested in learning some confidential information is named "zero knowledge" (ZK). In order to properly define the absence of a leak of confidential information, Goldwasser et al. introduced the simulation paradigm: the information that an adversary V^* learns during the exchange of messages with P is something that essentially V^* knew already, in the sense that V^* could generate the same information without interacting with P but just running a special efficient algorithm called a simulator.

The simulation paradigm has revolutionized the way security of systems is assessed, becoming a de facto gold standard to formalize the protection of confidential data. The research on zero-knowledge proof systems has been extraordinarily active for many years, allowing to understand what can and what can not be proven in zero-knowledge considering many natural scenarios.

This chapter will present some of the most influential notions and results concerning zero-knowledge proofs, discussing both theoretical and practical achievements.

3.2. Notation

With the sake of simplifying the notation we will use $\epsilon(\cdot)$ to denote a negligible function (i.e., for every constant c and all sufficiently large n it holds that $\epsilon(n) < 1/n^c$). Given an $\mathcal{NP}$ language L, we consider the polynomial-time relation R_L consisting of pairs (x, w) such that $x \in L$ and w is a witness for an efficient (i.e., polynomial in $|x|$) membership verification procedure for L.

3.3. Classical zero-knowledge proofs

The most common way to define a zero-knowledge proof system assumes that both P and V are probabilistic polynomial-time (PPT) interactive algorithms, the language L is in $\mathcal{NP}$, P and V know x and moreover P knows a witness w such that $(x, w) \in R_L$. The output of V at the end of the above execution is usually denoted by $\langle P(w), V \rangle(x)$. We now provide a definition of interactive proof system that is commonly used in literature.

DEFINITION 3.1.– *A proof system* $\Pi = (P, V)$ *for an $\mathcal{NP}$-language L is a pair of PPT interactive algorithms satisfying the following two properties.*

Completeness: For all $(x, w) \in R_L$, $\Pr[\langle P(w), V \rangle(x) = 1] = 1$.

Soundness: *There exists a negligible function ϵ such that for every $x \notin L$ and for every adversary $P^\star$,* $\Pr[\langle P^\star, V \rangle(x) = 1] < \epsilon(|x|)$.

Remark on completeness: The above completeness requirement is pretty natural but in some cases it might be too stringent and a failure with negligible probability is sometimes tolerated.

Remark on soundness: The above soundness requirement protects an honest verifier even from an unbounded malicious prover. A relaxed, but still extremely useful soundness requirement focuses instead on experiments in which $P^\star$ runs in polynomial time. Such a form of "computationally sound" proof system is called an argument system. Most of the content of this chapter that generically refers to proof systems applies to argument systems as well. Obviously, positive results for proof systems are valid also for argument systems. Instead, negative results for proof systems might not hold for argument systems since they are less demanding.

Remark on PPT P and V: Some research directions investigated the cases where completeness considers a computationally unbounded honest prover that does need a witness and/or a computationally unbounded honest verifier. For simplicity and concreteness, we will always assume that P and V are efficient.

Proofs of knowledge: The soundness requirement considers the case of $x \notin L$ only. There are cases in which a claim cannot be false and thus soundness is useless. There are also cases where it is essential not only that P convinces V but also that any $P^\star$ that is successful in convincing V for some $x \in L$ must know a witness w such that $(x, w) \in R_L$. Bellare and Goldreich (1993) defined a knowledge extraction property requiring the existence of an algorithm (i.e. an extractor) that is able to compute a witness w for an instance x with an effort that depends on the success probability of $P^\star$ when proving $x \in L$. Very roughly, if $P^\star$ can prove $x \in L$ with non-negligible probability, then the extractor can compute a valid witness in polynomial time. Two-party protocols enjoying completeness and the above special knowledge property are called proofs of knowledge.

3.3.1. *Zero knowledge*

Proof systems defined as above are trivial to construct: P can just send w to V that can check that $(x, w) \in R_L$, therefore giving in output 1 or 0 according to the check.

However going back to the initial scenario where Peggy was interested in protecting the confidentiality of her private input w, there is a need to design more sophisticated proof systems. Obviously, one should first define what it means for a proof system to protect the privacy of the input of the prover.

Privacy by design: Requiring that w remains private can be tricky: the adversary $V^\star$ might already have some partial information about w and thus one cannot just say that at the end of the proof V^* should know nothing about w. Moreover, V^* might initially know nothing about w but could learn a function of it still without knowing w in full, and this might be a sufficient guarantee in some cases. However, depending on the application, even partial information on w acquired during the execution of the proof system could correspond to a serious leak of confidential information. Goldwasser et al. (1985) faced the challenging task of finding a rigorous definition that could guarantee full data confidentiality so that it can be safely used in all possible scenarios. Using current buzzwords they had to formalize the concept of "privacy by design", their breakthrough paved the road for a clean and robust way to assess the validity of a cryptographic protocol in protecting the involved information.

The simulation paradigm: In order to define the ineffectiveness of the attempts of V^* in learning something about w when interacting with P, Goldwasser et al. suggested that V^* should have been able to produce the same information on its own, without interacting with P. The above intuition might seem natural and straightforward; still, it is certainly a very non-trivial concept to define and has been revolutionary in the last decades.

The definition of Goldwasser et al. requires the existence of an efficient algorithm S, referred to as a *simulator*, that knows the same information of V^* and can produce essentially the same output that V^* would produce after interacting with P. Notice that P knows a witness w for x while S might not have this information. This simple observation already rules out the trivial proof system in which P sends the witness to V (i.e. it would not be simulatable, and thus it is not zero knowledge).

Black-box versus non-black-box simulation: There are various caveats to properly define a run of S. First of all, S needs some "connection" with V^* in order to produce essentially the same output. This connection has been defined in two ways. The first is known as *black-box* simulation, and requires that there is just one S that can emulate the output of any V^*, as long as S has black-box access to V^*. The second is known as *non-black-box* simulation, and allows consideration of a specific S for every specific V^*. In the black-box case, S does not know how V^* computes its messages, while in the non-black-box case S knows everything about V^*. Intuitively, it is clear that a black-box simulator is also a valid non-black-box simulator and thus designing black-box zero-knowledge proofs is seemingly harder than non-black-box ones. Surprisingly, for about 15 years there has been no clean way to exploit the additional power of a non-black-box simulator, until the breakthrough of Barak (2001).

The running time of the simulator: The fact that S performs some work on top of V^* suggests it is more tolerant when limiting the running time of S, which can go significantly beyond the one of V^* but still remaining efficient. Due to the fact that in some cases (e.g. in constant-round protocols with black-box simulation), there can be some unlucky runs of S that do not quickly manage to get from V^* what is needed to produce a correct output, S is allowed to run in "expected" (rather than strict) polynomial time.

Indistinguishability flavors: The output of S might not be identical to the one of a specific run of V^* when interacting with P. Indeed, clearly the view of V^* includes messages computed by P with some randomness r and w, but S does not know r and w. Therefore, the output of S is only required to be "essentially" the same as V^* meaning that the distribution of the output of V^* in a run with P should be indistinguishable from the distribution of the output of S. The above indistinguishability is computational when the distinguisher is PPT, obtaining computational zero knowledge. If instead the distinguisher is unbounded, then the simulation is called statistical or perfect zero knowledge, depending on the fact that the two distributions are statistically close or identical. We will always assume that V^* is efficient, even though in the literature there have been a few cases without this (natural) restriction.

Everlasting zero knowledge: Statistical and perfect zero knowledge are of great importance. They model forward security; indeed, they guarantee that the confidentiality of the witness is preserved forever, even in case in the future there will be unbounded computing power. Obtaining everlasting zero knowledge is demanding. One has either to consider some specific (e.g. graph isomorphism) $\mathcal{NP}$ languages only (rather than considering any $\mathcal{NP}$ language) or to consider argument (rather than proof) systems. Indeed, obtaining statistical zero-knowledge proofs for all $\mathcal{NP}$ implies that the polynomial hierarchy collapses (Fortnow 1987; Aiello and Håstad 1987), which is commonly conjectured to be unlikely.

Auxiliary input: The input of V^* includes in addition to the instance x also an auxiliary information z that can, for instance, correspond to data collected previously and on top of which V^* might compute its messages when playing with P. Since S receives the same input of V^*, S will also receive z as input. Goldreich and Oren (1994) showed that adding an auxiliary input to V^* is essential to make sure that zero knowledge is preserved under sequential composition (i.e. one can prove in zero knowledge multiple claims one after the other and still there is not a risk for the confidentiality of the witnesses) or that is correctly used as subprotocol.

DEFINITION 3.2.– *A proof system* $\Pi = (P, V)$ *for an* $\mathcal{NP}$-*language L is black-box computational (respectively, statistical, perfect) zero knowledge if there exists an expected PPT algorithm S such that for any PPT algorithm* V^* *any* $(x, w) \in R_L$ *and any* $z \in \{0, 1\}^*$, *the following two distributions are computationally (respectively, statistically, perfectly) indistinguishable:*

$$\{\langle P(w), V^*(z)\rangle(x)\}, \{S^{V^*}(x, z)\}.$$

Deniability of ZK proofs: The fact that V^* can run a simulator and thus can self-generate an indistinguishable transcript of the conversation with a prover makes ZK proofs deniable (i.e. a ZK proof does not leave any evidence that a proof has been given). In turn, this guarantees that ZK proofs are non-transferable, in the sense that V^* does not acquire the capability to convince other verifiers.

3.4. How to build a zero-knowledge proof system

Once we have a solid definition, the following step is to design systems that provide such robust security. There are many techniques and approaches that can be used to design[1] ZK proof systems. Here, we will consider one of them.

V has something in mind, and P using the witness can obtain it: Since V^* must learn no additional information about w from the interaction with P, a natural strategy to design a ZK proof system consists of allowing P to leverage knowledge of w in order to understand and use something that V (and thus V^*) privately knows and that would be essentially impossible to guess for P^* when the claim is false. This approach can allow P to convince V and at the same time protects w since the information that V^* receives is something that could be generated from what V^* knew already. How do we actually implement such a high-level idea?

The myth of X-ray glasses: In the 1970s, some glasses were sold with the promise that they had an X-ray feature allowing therefore to watch beyond capabilities of human eyes. For instance, sellers of those glasses claimed that they could be used to see through clothes. Here, we will assume that a seller claims that its glasses allow to identify the color of the shirt that is immediately under a sweater. For the sake of understanding how one can implement the above approach for designing ZK proof systems, we will give a toy example where a seller tries to convince a potential buyer about the seemingly magic feature of those glasses. The goal of this toy example is to give an intuition of how properties, like completeness, soundness and ZK can coexist in one protocol.

Proving the effectiveness of X-ray glasses preserving privacy: Clearly, the seller plays the role of P and the buyer plays the role of V. P and V meet in a room in which there is only a table and P gives two shirts to V, one is red and the other one is pink. V gives to P a pile of k (e.g. $k = 100$) envelopes where the ith envelope has the number i written on it. P shows that these k envelopes are the only ones in her possession. P turns toward a corner and V standing in the opposite corner of the room tosses privately a coin. If the result is heads, then V will wear first the pink shirt, then

---

1 While in this chapter we will consider ZK proofs for $\mathcal{NP}$-complete problems, languages like graph isomorphism have been extensively studied and they admit perfect ZK proofs (Goldreich et al. 1986) even in constant rounds (Bellare et al. 1990).

the red shirt and then the sweater; if the result is tails, then V will wear first the red shirt, then the pink shirt and finally the sweater. Once V is ready, P can turn toward V and using the magic glasses P can identify the color of the shirt that is right after the sweater. P then writes the color red or pink on a piece of paper that is then inserted into the first envelope. P then seals the envelope and leaves it on the table. Then V takes the sweater out so that P can see the color of the external shirt. They repeat the above game using at the ith iteration the ith envelope. Finally, after k iterations, P opens all envelopes therefore revealing all colors and V checks that they correspond in all iterations to the colors of the selected shirts. If this is the case, then V is convinced about the capabilities of the glasses.

Informal analysis: If the claim is true and both players are honest, the glasses always can identify the correct color, and therefore P will succeed in all k tests efficiently with probability 1, satisfying the completeness requirement. If instead the claim is false[2], P^* has only probability 1/2 to succeed in every test, therefore the probability of succeeding in all k tests is $1/2^k$ and this can be extremely low using a proper value for k. This guarantees soundness. Which information can be obtained by V^*? Notice that the only information revealed by P is about the color of the external shirt that V^* was wearing in every test, and this is an information that V^* clearly knew already before opening the envelopes. Therefore, the concept of non-revealing additional information seems to be satisfied. However, this is not enough since the definition requires the existence of a simulator that without the power of the glasses but having access to V^* can actually produce the same output of V^*. The design of a simulator in this case is simple: the simulator at the ith iteration will just try to guess selecting either pink or red randomly. If the selected color is correct, the simulator continues with the next iteration. Otherwise, the simulator will use a time machine to travel to the past selecting the other color and making sure to continue to the $(i+1)$th iteration with that correctly guessed other color at the ith iteration.

Is the use of a time machine just a cheat? While we currently do not have time machines in the real world, they are actually trivial when considering algorithms. After a run of an algorithm, one can run it again with the same identical initial inputs until a given point is reached and then the next input is changed. This use of a time machine is called *rewind* and has crucially allowed the design of zero-knowledge proofs until Barak showed how to leverage the non-black-box definition. Notice that V^* is not forced to follow honest behavior. Indeed, instead of tossing a coin he could adaptively decide the order of the shirts. This explains why the simulator cannot simply toss a coin on its own, but instead needs to activate V^*.

---

2 For simplicity, we are considering only two cases: either glasses always work or they are completely useless.

Risks of simpler approaches: It is certainly natural to think that the seller could simply give the glasses to the buyer that therefore could extensively test them. In this way, the buyer can simply check the effectiveness of the glasses on its own. Unfortunately, giving the glasses to the buyer might correspond to a leak of confidential information. The buyer could, for instance, use the glasses (e.g. watching the buyer) for its own advantage beyond the goal of just receiving a convincing proof that they work properly. Another risky approach consists of a seller revealing to the buyer the design that allowed her to construct the glasses. Obviously, this second approach would give too much information to the buyer who later on can decide to have its own production of such glasses. The need of envelopes in the protocol is more subtle: it makes sure that $V^\star$ is informed about the guess of P only after $V^\star$ clearly knows the color of the external shirt. Indeed, the sweater is taken off before the envelope is opened. Without envelopes, therefore, with P announcing the color, $V^\star$ might have more chances to learn something from the proof (e.g. without ever taking off the sweater $V^\star$ could learn the color of the underlying shirt that perhaps has been blindly selected and put on before entering the room).

3.4.1. *ZK proofs for all $\mathcal{NP}$*

ZK proofs exist for all $\mathcal{NP}$ languages assuming just the existence of any one-way function[3], a basic hardness assumption in cryptography (Goldreich et al. 1986). To see this, one can consider the ZK proof of Blum (1986) for the language of Hamiltonian graphs that is $\mathcal{NP}$-complete and thus can be used starting with any language in $\mathcal{NP}$.

Proving in ZK that a graph is Hamiltonian: The work of P and V is pretty similar to the one illustrated above about X-ray glasses. P holds a cycle C as witness proving that a graph G known also to V is Hamiltonian. While P is not observed by V, P computes a random permutation of the nodes of G obtaining a graph G', puts every bit of the adjacency matrix of G' in a different envelope and puts the envelopes on the table in the presence of V. V then tosses a coin and if the output is heads, then P opens the envelopes and gives the permutation to V that checks that the content of the envelopes and the permutation match the original graph G. If instead the output is tails, then P opens only those envelopes that show a cycle inside the adjacency matrix of G'. The above process is repeated $|x|$ times, each time starting with a new permutation and thus new envelopes. The envelope is used to freeze the value stored in it while it remains hidden until the opening phase. In cryptography, commitment schemes implement digital envelopes and can be constructed using any one-way function (Naor 1991) guaranteeing unconditional immutability of the value encoded in the envelope. The above protocol is public coin in the sense that the messages of V are independent of the ones of P and purely consist of sending random bits.

---

3 One-way functions are essentially necessary for ZK proof systems (Ostrovsky and Wigderson 1993).

Informal analysis: Completeness holds since P knows both C and the selected permutation and thus can correctly complete the task, both in case of heads and tails. Soundness holds because when G has no cycle, then once the envelopes are on the table there is at least one value among heads and tails that would defeat $P^\star$. Therefore, in $|x|$ executions $P^\star$ succeeds only with negligible probability. Zero knowledge holds because there exists a simulator that can try to guess the output of the next coin tossed[4] by $V^\star$. Whenever the simulator fails it can go back through a rewind and then repeat that iteration until the same coin is selected by $V^\star$, but this time the simulator will be able to pass the test and continue with the next iteration.

The adaptive $V^\star$: The above unspecified number of repetitions gives a hint about the flexibility with the running time of the simulator that runs in *expected* polynomial time. An (unlikely) unbounded number of repetitions might happen when $V^\star$ tosses a coin in a way that depends on its current view (that includes the envelopes) and could change at each rewind. $V^\star$ can even decide to abort (e.g. not to play until the end) the execution of the protocol.

3.4.2. *Round complexity*

The round complexity of ZK proof systems has been intensively investigated by researchers. The above protocol for Hamiltonian graphs requires a number of communication rounds that depends on the size of the common input.

A simple modification of Blum's protocol consists of running $\log |x|$ tests in parallel. This will require more rewinds during the simulation since S will have to predict a $\log |x|$-bit string, but still S can run in expected polynomial time. On the other hand, the resulting round complexity will be $\omega(1)$. Indeed, for each test, $P^\star$ will have probability $1/|x|$ to pass the test on a false instance, and thus it can pass $\omega(1)$ of such tests with negligible probability only. This round complexity is optimal for public-coin ZK argument systems with black-box simulation as shown in Goldreich and Krawczyk (1996). Instead, with non-black-box simulation, one can get a constant-round public coin ZK argument system (Barak 2001).

Assuming statistically hiding commitments (e.g. a 2-round scheme exists assuming the existence of families of collision resistant hash functions (Halevi and Micali 1996) [CRHFs]), one can obtain a five-round ZK proof system. Essentially all the tests are played in parallel but in addition the coins used by V are frozen at the onset of the protocol committing to them. Katz (2008) showed that a 4-round black-box ZK proof system for all $\mathcal{NP}$ implies that the polynomial hierarchy collapses. When considering argument systems, the situation changes. Bellare et al.

---

4 Note that by knowing in advance the output of the next coin one can prepare the envelopes so that the test can pass successfully even without knowing a cycle in G.

(1997) showed a four-round construction assuming one-way functions only. This is optimal for black-box simulation in light of the lower bound of Goldreich and Krawczyk (1996). It remains open the possibility of constructing[5] a three-round ZK argument system with non-black-box simulation, and that would be optimal in light of the lower bound of Goldreich and Oren (1994). Under certain assumptions on program obfuscation, there are negative results about constant-round public-coin non-black-box ZK proofs (Kalai et al. 2017) and three-round non-black-box ZK proofs (Fleischhacker et al. 2018).

Statistical zero-knowledge arguments for $\mathcal{NP}$ were proposed in Brassard et al. (1990), a four-round construction from CRHFs was shown in Bellare et al. (1997) and their assumption has been then relaxed in Bitansky and Paneth (2019). A four-round perfect ZK argument system based on claw-free permutations has been shown in Hazay and Venkitasubramaniam (2018).

3.5. Relaxed security in proof systems

The protection of the confidentiality of the input in a proof system can be defined in several other ways. In this section, we will overview some notions that are easier to achieve compared to ZK.

3.5.1. *Honest-verifier ZK*

In a classical ZK proof system, V^* can arbitrarily deviate from the prescribed protocol and this complicates the design of the simulator. A more friendly setting consists of a verifier that is honest when computing its messages, but still interested in combining the transcript of the conversation, its auxiliary input and its randomness to obtain more information than the mere truthfulness of the claim. This notion models in particular post-execution corruption, where the verifier is honest during the execution but later on it is corrupted and the adversary has access to the stored information about priorly played protocols. This notion is named honest-verifier ZK (HVZK) and is significantly simpler to achieve. Indeed, a public-coin proof system like the one of Blum for Hamiltonian graphs allows the simulator to predict the challenges with probability 1 when the verifier is honest. This is due to the fact that the simulator knows the randomness that V^* receives in input. In turn, the simulation is straight line (i.e. no rewind is needed), there is no abort and thus S runs in strict polynomial-time.

---

5 We are not considering constructions based on non-falsifiable assumptions like the knowledge of exponent assumption (Bellare and Palacio 2004).

3.5.2. *Witness hiding/indistinguishability*

Feige and Shamir (1990a) proposed two relaxed security notions for proof systems that instead of relying on the simulation paradigm focus on weaker guarantees about the secrecy of the witness.

Witness indistinguishability: The first security notion makes sense when there are multiple witnesses proving that $x \in L$. Fiat and Shamir defined witness indistinguishability (WI) as a protection for the witness used by P out of all possible witnesses that could have been used. WI requires that for any pair of possible witnesses V^* has no significant advantage in distinguishing the one used by P. WI can be defined considering perfect, statistical and computational indistinguishability, similarly to ZK. WI is a weaker security guarantee than ZK since it potentially allows V^* to obtain during the proof some useful information. Indeed, WI clearly does not satisfy deniability as there exist one-round WI (i.e. non-interactive WI (NIWI)) proof systems for all $\mathcal{NP}$ (Groth et al. 2006a), and a NIWI proof is obviously transferable.

Witness hiding: The second notion considers any $\mathcal{NP}$ language that has a generator of hard instances (i.e. given a parameter k, an instance of length k is generated and no PPT adversary can find a corresponding witness with non-negligible probability). Fiat and Shamir defined witness hiding (WH) of a proof system enforcing that no PPT V^*, receiving a proof computed by P for a randomly generated hard instance, can compute with non-negligible probability a corresponding witness. Note that in the above definition V^* might be able to compute part of a witness or a function of it, while in ZK this is in general not feasible. On the other hand, WH is a non-trivial notion (e.g. the trivial proof system where P just sends w to V clearly is not WH).

WH/WI beyond ZK limits: It is known that when there exist multiple witnesses for a single instance, then WI implies WH, that is, any WI proof system is also WH. WI is a notion that is closed under parallel and concurrent composition. This means that any WI proof system preserves its security also when the adversary can run multiple instances of the protocol in parallel and even concurrently with full control over the scheduling of the messages. Such forms of composition are instead way more problematic in ZK proof systems as we will discuss later.

WH/WI proof systems can be achieved with a better round complexity than ZK proof systems. Blum's protocol for Hamiltonian graphs composed in parallel is a 3-round WI proof system for all $\mathcal{NP}$ based on the existence of one-to-one one-way functions. Moreover, Dwork and Naor (2000) showed a 2-round WI proof system for all $\mathcal{NP}$ named ZAP that is public coin, has a reusable first round (i.e. multiple statements can be proven by reusing the same first round of the verifier) and assumes the existence of a non-interactive ZK (NIZK) proof systems in the common random string model. An NIWI proof system for all $\mathcal{NP}$ assuming a decisional-linear assumption for bilinear groups was given in Groth et al. (2006a). A statistical ZAP was given in Badrinarayanan et al. (2020), and by Goyal et al. (2020) assuming quasi-polynomial hardness of LWE and in Jain and Jin (2021) assuming sub-exponential DDH, while without the public-coin property a construction based on a quasi-polynomial decision-linear assumption for bilinear groups has been given in Lombardi et al. (2020).

Interestingly, while as discussed above WI and thus WH have been achieved way beyond what can be done in ZK, until recently such gap has been evident only when an instance admits multiple witnesses. A recent work of Bitansky et al. (2019) showed various positive results about WH argument systems for all $\mathcal{NP}$.

FLS paradigm: Feige et al. (1990) proposed a new technique to construct ZK proof systems. Their approach consists of adding to the claim $x \in L$ an auxiliary claim T that is generated during the interaction of P and V or obtained from an external entity. The auxiliary claim T is generated in a way that allows S to have a corresponding witness w_T. Instead, when V is honest T should be false[6]. Once the auxiliary claim is formed, the ZK proof system can just continue with a WI proof system where the prover P of the ZK proof system runs the prover of the WI proof system for the claim $x \in L \vee T$. Obviously, P will use w as witness in the WI proof system while S will use w_T.

An example of a typical (Feige and Shamir 1990b) way to implement the preamble that generates T consists of asking V to give (therefore playing as prover) a WH proof of knowledge of a witness corresponding to a hard instance that V generates at the onset of the protocol. Clearly, a polynomial-time P^* will not be able to get w_T and will fail with the WI proof. The simulator can instead run the extractor associated with the proof of knowledge obtaining w_T and can then use it in the WI proof. The resulting protocol is therefore a ZK argument system.

3.5.3. Σ-*Protocols*

One of the most popular privacy-preserving proof systems is known as Σ-protocol. It consists of three messages, is public coin and guarantees some special soundness and special HVZK properties. Special soundness requires that given two accepting transcripts with identical first messages and different second messages (e.g. (a, c, z) and (a, c', z') with $c \neq c'$) for a statement $x \in L$ one can efficiently compute a witness w such that $(x, w) \in R_L$. Special HVZK requires that for any $x \in L$ and any c, the distribution of the output of a special simulator on input (x, c) consists of pairs (a, z) such that (x, a, c, z) is indistinguishable from the distribution of the transcript

---

6 It can be true when the goal is to obtain an argument system, but in this case it should be hard for P^* to compute w_T.

produced by an honest prover when proving $x \in L$ and receiving c as a challenge. There exist very practical Σ-protocols for several useful languages. The most popular one is the Σ-protocol of Schnorr (1991) for proving knowledge of a discrete logarithm.

Σ-protocols have appealing features. Cramer et al. (1994) showed how to efficiently compose Σ-protocols to prove that at least k out of n instances are true, without disclosing which one is true (i.e. a proof of partial knowledge). There is also a simple way to perform an AND composition, and thus Σ-protocols can be very useful to (confidentially) show possession of credential satisfying access control policies.

3.6. Non-black-box zero knowledge

The FLS paradigm has been crucially used to break the black-box simulation barrier. Barak (2001) succeeded for the first time in finding a way to exploit the knowledge of the code of $V^\star$ during the simulation with the goal of creating a trapdoor claim that the simulator can leverage to complete the proof.

If the simulator knows the code of the verifier, what can be done in the design of a protocol so that the simulator can take advantage of it? The answer applying the FLS paradigm is the following: for proving $x \in L$, P should run a WI proof system to prove the claim "$x \in L$ or I know your code". The honest prover can use the legitimate witness to run the WI proof system and thus completeness holds. The malicious prover is stuck since both sub-statements are hard to prove. The simulator can just use the code of $V^\star$ as witness in the WI proof system. While the above idea looks, after the fact, pretty straightforward, there are significant technical problems behind the proper formalization of "I know your code". Indeed, the code of $V^\star$ can be of any polynomial size and thus the size of the witness of the simulator is not bounded by a fixed polynomial. In other words, the WI proof cannot just be Blum's protocol but it must be a special WI proof system with a communication complexity that can be made essentially independent of the witness size. This was solved by Barak starting with succinct arguments for $\mathcal{NP}$ of Kilian (1992).

The result of Barak has shown how to obtain constant-round public-coin zero knowledge for $\mathcal{NP}$. This result is impossible to achieve for non-trivial languages when sticking with black-box simulation only. Goyal et al. (2014) have shown that the above results can be obtained requiring only a black-box use of CRHFs.

3.7. Advanced notions

In this section, we will discuss more demanding notions of ZK proof systems that offer additional features/security.

3.7.1. *Publicly verifiable zero knowledge*

When running a ZK proof system, the prover can convince one verifier only. While this might seem a limitation, it offers the nice feature of making the proof non-transferable. Indeed, in case a malicious V^* tries to forward the transcript to some other party, the transcript will be by itself meaningless since V^* could have generated the transcript on its own running the simulator. However, there can be cases requiring the prover to compute a proof that is ZK but at the same time the proof must be verifiable by any verifier. In a publicly verifiable ZK proof system, the above transferability issue is actually a plus since a V^* that forwards the proof is actually helping with the goal that as many verifiers as possible end up verifying the veracity of the claim.

NIZK: The problem of obtaining a publicly verifiable proof was studied in Blum et al. (1988) where Blum et al. considered a scenario where a single message is generated by the prover non-interactively, therefore a NIZK proof system. In order to circumvent the obvious[7] impossibility of NIZK in the classical setting, in Blum et al. (1988) a third party Trinity, assumed to behave honestly by everybody, computes a string with a specific distribution. Using this common reference string one can compute a NIZK proof therefore achieving simultaneously completeness, soundness and ZK. While the original results of Blum et al. (1988) required Trinity to be involved for every proof, Feige et al. (1990) showed how to design a NIZK proof system for all $\mathcal{NP}$ assuming the existence of special trapdoor permutations, allowing the common reference string to be reused for any polynomial number of proofs. This result was achieved precisely showing the FLS paradigm in action, creating an auxiliary claim in the common reference string that can be controlled by the simulator. Then they showed a NIWI proof system using the common reference string. An additional feature is that the common reference string can be just a random string, therefore one can potentially start with a physical phenomena that produces public randomness rather than involving Trinity. Perfect NIZK has been achieved by Groth et al. (2006b) relying on the subgroup decision assumption. A NIZK proof system for $\mathcal{NP}$ from LWE has been recently shown in Peikert and Shiehian (2019) and a statistical NIZK argument system for $\mathcal{NP}$ from sub-exponential DDH has been shown in Jain and Jin (2021).

The Fiat–Shamir transform: Using the Fiat–Shamir transform (Fiat and Shamir 1987), Σ-protocols can be converted into NIZK argument systems in the programmable random oracle model when the message of V is sufficiently large. This means that whenever a NIZK is needed and the random oracle heuristic is

---

7 With one message only the simulator computing accepting proofs for any statement can be used by P^* to violate soundness. Instead, the simulator computing accepting proofs for truthful statements only clearly shows that the language is in BPP (i.e. one can efficiently check on its own if an instance is or is not in the language, and thus there is no need to receive a proof).

acceptable, one can just focus on a Σ-protocol that is easier to design than a regular ZK proof system. Moreover, Lindell (2015) and Ciampi et al. (2016c) showed how to obtain NIZK from Σ-protocols using both a common reference string and a non-programmable random oracle.

Other models: Publicly verifiable ZK has been achieved in several other models (i.e. under different setup assumptions). Here, we mention two of them. NIZK has been achieved in the multi-string (Groth and Ostrovsky 2007) model that relaxes the common reference string model. Publicly verifiable zero knowledge has been achieved with a specific assumption on blockchains (Scafuro et al. 2021) tolerating that after the proof is given, the blockchain can be completely compromised.

3.7.2. Concurrent ZK and more

The classical definition of a ZK proof system considers only adversaries that run the protocol in isolation, without knowing anything of what is happening around them until the protocol is over. This is clearly not always realistic and thus various forms of compositions of executions of ZK proofs have been considered. While sequential composition comes essentially for free, the situation is way more complicated when considering other forms of composition.

Parallel and concurrent ZK: Parallel composition assumes that multiple instances of the ZK proof system are played in parallel (i.e. when it is the turn of the prover to play, it plays in all instances, and the same does the verifier when it is its turn). Unlike WI, ZK is not closed under parallel and concurrent composition. This means that a ZK protocol is not necessarily simulatable when multiple executions are played in parallel or concurrently. It is easy to see why this limitation holds: typical ZK proof systems have a simulator that tries to predict with non-negligible probability the next message of the verifier in order to perform only a polynomial number of rewinds. When composing multiple instances the amount of information that the simulator is supposed to predict quickly grows, the probability of predicting the next messages becomes negligible and the number of rewinds becomes super-polynomial, violating the required efficiency of the simulation. The above explanation issue applies in particular to black-box simulation with public-coin protocols. Using commitment schemes, one can design constant-round ZK proof systems that are secure also under parallel composition.

The situation is more complicated in case of concurrent composition. Indeed, as shown in Canetti et al. (2001), constant-round black-box (even just bounded) concurrent zero knowledge is impossible with sub-logarithmic round complexity. The additional difficulty introduced by the concurrent composition of executions of a ZK proof system is due to the adversarial scheduling of messages. Indeed, the simulator, by rewinding $V^\star$ to complete a session, could waste the previous work done to complete another session. On the positive side, in Prabhakaran et al. (2002) they showed that a slightly super-logarithmic number of rounds is sufficient for black-box concurrent zero knowledge.

Non-black-box simulation was immediately used in Barak (2001) to obtain a constant-round bounded-concurrent zero-knowledge argument system. It took a long path to finally obtain a constant-round concurrent zero knowledge argument system presented in Chung et al. (2015) assuming indistinguishability obfuscation.

Non-malleable ZK and universally composable ZK: The fact that a ZK proof is deniable and does not leak information about the witness does not limit an adversary to take advantage of it. Indeed, still exploiting the concurrent composition of instances of a ZK poof system, an adversary could decide to play as V^* in a first session and as P^* in a second session with the goal of leveraging messages exchanged in the first session in order to succeed in the second session. One can, for instance, imagine Peggy proving to Victor knowledge of the discrete logarithm of a group element while at the same time Victor proves to Trinity knowledge of the discrete logarithm of another group element without actually knowing the discrete logarithm, but only leveraging the fact that the two group elements are somehow correlated. Such attack has been studied initially in Dolev et al. (1991) where Dolev et al. considered the above scenario motivating the notion of non-malleable zero-knowledge proofs. Ciampi et al. (2017) showed that similarly to the classical notion of ZK, there exists a four-round non-malleable zero-knowledge argument of knowledge assuming one-way functions only. The case with polynomially many sessions has been shown to have a complexity similar to the one of concurrent zero knowledge (Barak et al. 2006).

When a ZK proof system is played concurrently with other protocols, there can be additional issues due to the fact that for technical reasons the simulator cannot rewind and does not have the code of the adversary. These limitations are enforced by the framework of Canetti (2001) where the notion of universally composability (UC) is presented. Given such limits, UC ZK is clearly impossible without some special "help" that can allow black-box straight-line simulation. Various tricks have been proposed to make this possible. Here, we recall that the use of a common reference string is one of such possible tricks. Indeed, it allows straight-line black-box simulation and can be used to obtain non-malleable NIZK and UC NIZK (De Santis et al. 2001).

3.7.3. *ZK with stateless players*

The classical definition of a ZK proof system assumes that honest players are stateful and when playing the next message they know exactly the history of the conversation.

Resettable ZK: Canetti et al. (2000) proposed a natural strengthening of the classical notion proposing a setting where the honest prover is stateless. The motivation of Canetti et al. (2000) started from the use of smart cards implementing provers in ZK proofs, and the possibility that a smart card could be reset to its initial state. Therefore, they defined resettable ZK (rZK) to capture the idea that $V^\star$ can somehow rewind the prover, resetting it to a previous state. Canetti et al. have shown techniques that allow in many cases to obtain rZK from concurrent ZK without penalizing the round complexity and the underlying assumptions.

Resettably sound ZK: Following the same spirit, Barak et al. (2001) considered the case of a stateless verifier and a $P^\star$ that is able to rewind it, introducing the notion of resettable soundness (res-sound). They showed that res-sound black-box ZK is impossible for non-trivial languages. They also showed how to use Barak's non-black-box simulation technique to design a res-sound ZK argument assuming CRHFs. The assumption was improved to one-way functions in Chung et al. (2013b); Bitansky and Paneth (2013) and the round complexity was reduced to 4 in Chung et al. (2014).

Simultaneously resettable ZK: Barak et al. (2001) considered also the setting where both P and V are stateless, referring to it as simultaneously resettable zero knowledge. They only conjectured the feasibility of this very strong security notion. Deng et al. (2009) gave a positive answer formally confirming that the conjecture was true, by showing a res-sound rZK argument system assuming one-to-one one-way functions, CRHFs and ZAPs. The gap in terms of computational assumptions with ZK arguments has been filled in Chung et al. (2013a) where Chung et al. showed a res-sound rZK argument system assuming one-way functions.

3.7.4. *Delayed-input proof systems*

Even though we have assumed so far that P receives as input both instance and witness already when computing the first message, there are cases where knowledge of the input can be postponed. Lapidot and Shamir (1991) showed a three-round WI proof system for Hamiltonian graphs (and thus for all $\mathcal{NP}$) that requires instance and witness only when playing the last round. Looking at more practical protocols, many Σ-protocols (e.g. the one of Schnorr) have this special feature named "delayed input". This means that the first two messages can be pre-processed obtaining better efficiency especially when delayed-input proof systems are used inside larger protocols. Obviously, this feature is not very relevant when interactive proofs become non-interactive in the random oracle model. However, there are scenarios where the need for deniability or for unconditional soundness might actually suggest to stick with interactive proofs. Notice that while delaying the selection of the input at the last round adds flexibility, it also introduces potential issues since both $P^\star$ and $V^\star$ might have a role in adaptively deciding the inputs in order to succeed in their attacks.

The OR composition of Cramer et al. (1994) unfortunately does not preserve the delayed-input property of the underlying Σ-protocols. Indeed, even when starting with two Σ-protocols that satisfy the delayed-input property, the compound Σ-protocol obtained through (Cramer et al. 1994) forces P to know the instances already when computing the first message. Alternative OR compositions have been proposed in Ciampi et al. (2016a) and Ciampi et al. (2016b) obtaining practical delayed-input WI proofs of partial knowledge starting from practical delayed-input Σ-protocols.

3.8. Conclusion

ZK proofs are extremely powerful. They can be used to enforce honest computations and therefore they simplify the task of designing cryptographic protocols. While for a long time the focus on ZK proofs was mainly related to open questions of theoretical interest, nowadays there is a major effort to obtain practical constructions and to use them in deployed applications (e.g. privacy-preserving cryptocurrencies). After an extraordinary past, the research on ZK proofs is still blooming.

3.9. References

Aiello, W. and Håstad, J. (1987). Perfect zero-knowledge languages can be recognized in two rounds. In *28th FOCS*. IEEE Computer Society Press.

Badrinarayanan, S., Fernando, R., Jain, A., Khurana, D., Sahai, A. (2020). Statistical ZAP arguments. In *EUROCRYPT 2020, Part III*, vol. 12107 of *LNCS*, Canteaut, A., Ishai, Y. (eds). Springer, Heidelberg.

Barak, B. (2001). How to go beyond the black-box simulation barrier. In *42nd FOCS*. IEEE Computer Society Press.

Barak, B., Goldreich, O., Goldwasser, S., Lindell, Y. (2001). Resettably-sound zero-knowledge and its applications. In *42nd FOCS*. IEEE Computer Society Press.

Barak, B., Prabhakaran, M., Sahai, A. (2006). Concurrent non-malleable zero knowledge. In *47th FOCS*. IEEE Computer Society Press.

Bellare, M. and Goldreich, O. (1993). On defining proofs of knowledge. In *CRYPTO'92*, vol. 740 of *LNCS*, Brickell, E.F. (ed.). Springer, Heidelberg.

Bellare, M. and Palacio, A. (2004). The knowledge-of-exponent assumptions and 3-round zero-knowledge protocols. In *CRYPTO 2004*, vol. 3152 of *LNCS*, Franklin, M. (ed.). Springer, Heidelberg.

Bellare, M., Micali, S., Ostrovsky, R. (1990). Perfect zero-knowledge in constant rounds. In *22nd ACM STOC*. ACM Press.

Bellare, M., Jakobsson, M., Yung, M. (1997). Round-optimal zero-knowledge arguments based on any one-way function. In *EUROCRYPT'97*, vol. 1233 of *LNCS*, Fumy, W. (ed.). Springer, Heidelberg.

Bitansky, N. and Paneth, O. (2013). On the impossibility of approximate obfuscation and applications to resettable cryptography. In *45th ACM STOC*, Boneh, D., Roughgarden, T., Feigenbaum, J. (eds). ACM Press.

Bitansky, N. and Paneth, O. (2019). On round optimal statistical zero knowledge arguments. In *CRYPTO 2019, Part III*, vol. 11694 of *LNCS*, Boldyreva, A., Micciancio, D. (eds). Springer, Heidelberg.

Bitansky, N., Khurana, D., Paneth, O. (2019). Weak zero-knowledge beyond the black-box barrier. In *51st ACM STOC*, Charikar, M., Cohen, E. (eds). ACM Press.

Blum, M. (1986). How to prove a theorem so no one else can claim it. *Proceedings of the International Congress of Mathematicians*, Berkeley, CA.

Blum, M., Feldman, P., Micali, S. (1988). Non-interactive zero-knowledge and its applications (extended abstract). In *20th ACM STOC*. ACM Press.

Brassard, G., Crépeau, C., Yung, M. (1990). Everything in NP can be argued in perfect zero-knowledge in a bounded number of rounds (extended abstract). In *EUROCRYPT'89*, vol. 434 of *LNCS*, Quisquater, J.-J., Vandewalle, J. (eds). Springer, Heidelberg.

Canetti, R. (2001). Universally composable security: A new paradigm for cryptographic protocols. In *42nd FOCS*. IEEE Computer Society Press.

Canetti, R., Goldreich, O., Goldwasser, S., Micali, S. (2000). Resettable zero-knowledge (extended abstract). In *32nd ACM STOC*. ACM Press.

Canetti, R., Kilian, J., Petrank, E., Rosen, A. (2001). Black-box concurrent zero-knowledge requires omega (log n) rounds. In *33rd ACM STOC*. ACM Press.

Chung, K.-M., Ostrovsky, R., Pass, R., Visconti, I. (2013a). Simultaneous resettability from one-way functions. In *54th FOCS*. IEEE Computer Society Press.

Chung, K.-M., Pass, R., Seth, K. (2013b). Non-black-box simulation from one-way functions and applications to resettable security. In *45th ACM STOC*, Boneh, D., Roughgarden, T., Feigenbaum, J. (eds). ACM Press.

Chung, K.-M., Ostrovsky, R., Pass, R., Venkitasubramaniam, M., Visconti, I. (2014). 4-round resettably-sound zero knowledge. In *TCC 2014*, vol. 8349 of *LNCS*, Lindell, Y. (ed.). Springer, Heidelberg.

Chung, K.-M., Lin, H., Pass, R. (2015). Constant-round concurrent zero-knowledge from indistinguishability obfuscation. In *CRYPTO 2015, Part I*, vol. 9215 of *LNCS*, Gennaro, R., Robshaw, M.J.B. (eds). Springer, Heidelberg.

Ciampi, M., Persiano, G., Scafuro, A., Siniscalchi, L., Visconti, I. (2016a). Improved OR-composition of sigma-protocols. In *TCC 2016-A, Part II*, vol. 9563 of *LNCS*, Kushilevitz, E., Malkin, T. (eds). Springer, Heidelberg.

Ciampi, M., Persiano, G., Scafuro, A., Siniscalchi, L., Visconti, I. (2016b). Online/offline OR composition of sigma protocols. In *EUROCRYPT 2016, Part II*, vol. 9666 of *LNCS*, Fischlin, M., Coron, J.-S. (eds). Springer, Heidelberg.

Ciampi, M., Persiano, G., Siniscalchi, L., Visconti, I. (2016c). A transform for NIZK almost as efficient and general as the Fiat–Shamir transform without programmable random oracles. In *TCC 2016-A, Part II*, vol. 9563 of *LNCS*, Kushilevitz, E., Malkin, T. (eds). Springer, Heidelberg.

Ciampi, M., Ostrovsky, R., Siniscalchi, L., Visconti, I. (2017). Delayed-input non-malleable zero knowledge and multi-party coin tossing in four rounds. In *TCC 2017, Part I*, vol. 10677 of *LNCS*, Kalai, Y., Reyzin, L. (eds). Springer, Heidelberg.

Cramer, R., Damgård, I., Schoenmakers, B. (1994). Proofs of partial knowledge and simplified design of witness hiding protocols. In *CRYPTO'94*, vol. 839 of *LNCS*, Desmedt, Y. (ed.). Springer, Heidelberg.

De Santis, A., Di Crescenzo, G., Ostrovsky, R., Persiano, G., Sahai, A. (2001). Robust non-interactive zero knowledge. In *CRYPTO 2001*, vol. 2139 of *LNCS*, Kilian, J. (ed.). Springer, Heidelberg.

Deng, Y., Goyal, V., Sahai, A. (2009). Resolving the simultaneous resettability conjecture and a new non-black-box simulation strategy. In *50th FOCS*. IEEE Computer Society Press.

Dolev, D., Dwork, C., Naor, M. (1991). Non-malleable cryptography (extended abstract). In *23rd ACM STOC*. ACM Press.

Dwork, C. and Naor, M. (2000). Zaps and their applications. In *41st FOCS*. IEEE Computer Society Press.

Feige, U., Lapidot, D., Shamir, A. (1990). Multiple non-interactive zero knowledge proofs based on a single random string (extended abstract). In *31st FOCS*. IEEE Computer Society Press.

Feige, U. and Shamir, A. (1990a). Witness indistinguishable and witness hiding protocols. In *22nd ACM STOC*. ACM Press.

Feige, U. and Shamir, A. (1990b). Zero knowledge proofs of knowledge in two rounds. In *CRYPTO'89*, vol. 435 of *LNCS*, Brassard, G. (ed.). Springer, Heidelberg.

Fiat, A. and Shamir, A. (1987). How to prove yourself: Practical solutions to identification and signature problems. In *CRYPTO'86*, vol. 263 of *LNCS*, Odlyzko, A.M. (ed.). Springer, Heidelberg.

Fleischhacker, N., Goyal, V., Jain, A. (2018). On the existence of three round zero-knowledge proofs. In *EUROCRYPT 2018, Part III*, vol. 10822 of *LNCS*, Nielsen, J.B., Rijmen, V. (eds). Springer, Heidelberg.

Fortnow, L. (1987). The complexity of perfect zero-knowledge (extended abstract). In *19th ACM STOC*, Aho, A. (ed.). ACM Press.

Goldreich, O. and Krawczyk, H. (1996). On the composition of zero-knowledge proof systems, *SIAM Journal on Computing*, 25(1), 169–192.

Goldreich, O., Micali, S., Wigderson, A. (1986). Proofs that yield nothing but their validity and a methodology of cryptographic protocol design (extended abstract). In *27th FOCS*. IEEE Computer Society Press.

Goldreich, O. and Oren, Y. (1994). Definitions and properties of zero-knowledge proof systems. *Journal of Cryptology*, 7(1), 1–32.

Goldwasser, S., Micali, S., Rackoff, C. (1985). The knowledge complexity of interactive proof-systems (extended abstract). In *17th ACM STOC*. ACM Press.

Goyal, V., Ostrovsky, R., Scafuro, A., Visconti, I. (2014). Black-box non-black-box zero knowledge. In *46th ACM STOC*, Shmoys, D.B. (ed.). ACM Press.

Goyal, V., Jain, A., Jin, Z., Malavolta, G. (2020). Statistical zaps and new oblivious transfer protocols. In *EUROCRYPT 2020, Part III*, vol. 12107 of *LNCS*, Canteaut, A., Ishai, Y. (eds). Springer, Heidelberg.

Groth, J. and Ostrovsky, R. (2007). Cryptography in the multi-string model. In *CRYPTO 2007*, vol. 4622 of *LNCS*, Menezes, A. (ed.). Springer, Heidelberg.

Groth, J., Ostrovsky, R., Sahai, A. (2006a). Non-interactive zaps and new techniques for NIZK. In *CRYPTO 2006*, vol. 4117 of *LNCS*, Dwork, C. (ed.). Springer, Heidelberg.

Groth, J., Ostrovsky, R., Sahai, A. (2006b). Perfect non-interactive zero knowledge for NP. In *EUROCRYPT 2006*, vol. 4004 of *LNCS*, Vaudenay, S. (ed.). Springer, Heidelberg.

Halevi, S. and Micali, S. (1996). Practical and provably-secure commitment schemes from collision-free hashing. In *CRYPTO'96*, vol. 1109 of *LNCS*, Koblitz, N. (ed.). Springer, Heidelberg.

Hazay, C. and Venkitasubramaniam, M. (2018). Round-optimal fully black-box zero-knowledge arguments from one-way permutations. In *TCC 2018, Part I*, vol. 11239 of *LNCS*, Beimel, A., Dziembowski, S. (eds). Springer, Heidelberg.

Jain, A. and Jin, Z. (2021). Non-interactive zero knowledge from sub-exponential DDH. In *EUROCRYPT 2021, Part I*, vol. 12696 of *LNCS*, Canteaut, A., Standaert, F.-X. (eds). Springer, Heidelberg.

Kalai, Y.T., Rothblum, G.N., Rothblum, R.D. (2017). From obfuscation to the security of Fiat–Shamir for proofs. In *CRYPTO 2017, Part II*, vol. 10402 of *LNCS*, Katz, J., Shacham, H. (eds). Springer, Heidelberg.

Katz, J. (2008). Which languages have 4-round zero-knowledge proofs? In *TCC 2008*, vol. 4948 of *LNCS*, Canetti, R. (ed.). Springer, Heidelberg.

Kilian, J. (1992). A note on efficient zero-knowledge proofs and arguments (extended abstract). In *24th ACM STOC*. ACM Press.

Lapidot, D. and Shamir, A. (1991). Publicly verifiable non-interactive zero-knowledge proofs. In *CRYPTO'90*, vol. 537 of *LNCS*, Menezes, A.J., Vanstone, S.A. (eds). Springer, Heidelberg.

Lindell, Y. (2015). An efficient transform from sigma protocols to NIZK with a CRS and non-programmable random oracle. In *TCC 2015, Part I*, vol. 9014 of *LNCS*, Dodis, Y., Nielsen, J.B. (eds). Springer, Heidelberg.

Lombardi, A., Vaikuntanathan, V., Wichs, D. (2020). Statistical ZAPR arguments from bilinear maps. In *EUROCRYPT 2020, Part III*, vol. 12107 of *LNCS*, Canteaut, A., Ishai, Y. (eds). Springer, Heidelberg.

Naor, M. (1991). Bit commitment using pseudorandomness. *Journal of Cryptology*, 4(2), 151–158.

Ostrovsky, R. and Wigderson, A. (1993). One-way fuctions are essential for non-trivial zero-knowledge. *Second Israel Symposium on Theory of Computing Systems, ISTCS 1993, Natanya, Israel, June 7–9, 1993.* IEEE Computer Society.

Peikert, C. and Shiehian, S. (2019). Noninteractive zero knowledge for NP from (plain) learning with errors. In *CRYPTO 2019, Part I*, vol. 11692 of *LNCS*, Boldyreva, A., Micciancio, D. (eds). Springer, Heidelberg.

Prabhakaran, M., Rosen, A., Sahai, A. (2002). Concurrent zero knowledge with logarithmic round-complexity. In *43rd FOCS*. IEEE Computer Society Press.

Scafuro, A., Siniscalchi, L., Visconti, I. (2021). Publicly verifiable zero knowledge from (collapsing) blockchains. In *PKC 2021, Part II*, vol. 12711 of *LNCS*, Garay, J. (ed.). Springer, Heidelberg.

Schnorr, C.-P. (1991). Efficient signature generation by smart cards. *Journal of Cryptology*, 4(3), 161–174.

4

Secure Multiparty Computation

Yehuda LINDELL
Coinbase, San Francisco, United States

Protocols for secure multiparty computation (MPC) enable a set of parties to interact and compute a joint function of their private inputs while revealing nothing but the output. The potential applications for MPC are huge: privacy-preserving auctions, private DNA comparisons, private machine learning, threshold cryptography, and so on. Due to this, MPC has been an intensive topic of research in academia ever since it was introduced in the 1980s by Yao (1986) for the two-party case, and by Goldreich et al. (1986) for the multiparty case. Recently, MPC has become efficient enough to be used in practice, and has made the transition from an object of theoretical study to a technology being used in industry. In this chapter, we will review what MPC is, what problems it solves and how it is being currently used.

We note that the examples and references brought in this review chapter are far from comprehensive, and due to the lack of space many highly relevant works are not cited.

4.1. Introduction

Distributed computing considers the scenario where a number of distinct, yet connected, computing devices (or parties) wish to carry out a joint computation of some function. For example, these devices may be servers who hold a distributed database system, and the function to be computed may be a database update of some kind. The aim of *secure* MPC is to enable parties to carry out such distributed

Asymmetric Cryptography,
coordinated by David POINTCHEVAL. © ISTE Ltd. 2022.

computing tasks in a secure manner. Although distributed computing often deals with questions of computing under the threat of machine crashes and other inadvertent faults, secure MPC is concerned with the possibility of deliberately malicious behavior by some adversarial entity (these have also been considered in the distributed literature where they are called Byzantine faults). That is, it is assumed that a protocol execution may come under "attack" by an external entity, or even by a subset of the participating parties. The aim of this attack may be to learn private information or cause the result of the computation to be incorrect. Thus, two important requirements on any secure computation protocol are *privacy* and *correctness*. The privacy requirement states that nothing should be learned beyond what is absolutely necessary; more exactly, parties should learn their output and nothing else. The correctness requirement states that each party should receive its correct output. Therefore, the adversary must not be able to cause the result of the computation to deviate from the function that the parties had set out to compute.

Secure MPC can be used to solve a wide variety of problems, enabling the utilization of data without compromising privacy. Consider, for example, the problem of comparing a person's DNA against a database of cancer patients' DNA, with the goal of finding if the person is in a high risk group for a certain type of cancer. Such a task clearly has important health and societal benefits. However, DNA information is highly sensitive and should not be revealed to private organizations. This dilemma can be solved by running a secure MPC that reveals only the category of cancer that the person's DNA is close to (or none). In this example, the privacy requirement ensures that only the category of cancer is revealed, and nothing else about anyone's DNA (neither the DNA of the person being compared nor the DNA of the patients in the database). Furthermore, the correctness requirement guarantees that a malicious party cannot change the result (e.g. make the person think that they are at risk of a type of cancer, and therefore need screening).

In another example, consider a trading platform where parties provide offers and bids, and are matched whenever an offer is greater than a bid (with, for example, the price of the trade being some function of the offer and bid prices). In such a scenario, it can be beneficial from a game theoretic perspective to not reveal the parties' actual offers and bids (since this information can be used by others in order to artificially raise prices or provide bids that are lower than their utility). Privacy here guarantees that only the match between buyer and seller and the resulting price is revealed, and correctness would guarantee that the price revealed is the correct one according to the function (and not some lower value, for example). It is interesting to note that in some cases privacy is more important (like in the DNA example), whereas in others correctness is more important (like in the trading example). In any case, MPC guarantees both of these properties and so on.

4.1.1. *A note on terminology*

In the literature, beyond secure MPC, there are also references to secure function evaluation (SFE). These notions overlap significantly, and are often used synonymously. In addition, special cases of MPC often have their own names. Two examples are private set intersection (PSI) that considers the secure computation of the intersection of private sets, and threshold cryptography that considers the secure computation of digital signatures and decryption, where no single party holds the private key.

4.2. Security of MPC

4.2.1. *The definitional paradigm*

As we have mentioned above, the setting that we consider is one where an adversarial entity controls some subset of the parties and wishes to attack the protocol execution. The parties under the control of the adversary are called corrupted and follow the adversary's instructions. Secure protocols should withstand any adversarial attack (where the exact power of the adversary will be discussed later). In order to formally claim and prove that a protocol is secure, a precise definition of security for MPC is required. A number of different definitions have been proposed and these definitions aim to ensure a number of important security properties that are general enough to capture most (if not all) MPC tasks. We now describe the most central of these properties:

1) *Privacy*: No party should learn anything more than its prescribed output. In particular, the only information that should be learned about other parties' inputs is what can be derived from the output itself. For example, in an auction where the only bid revealed is that of the highest bidder, it is clearly possible to derive that all other bids were lower than the winning bid. However, nothing else should be revealed about the losing bids.

2) *Correctness*: Each party is guaranteed that the output that it receives is correct. To continue with the example of an auction, this implies that the party with the highest bid is guaranteed to win, and no party including the auctioneer can influence this.

3) *Independence of Inputs*:   Corrupted parties must choose their inputs independently of the honest parties' inputs. This property is crucial in a sealed auction, where bids are kept secret and parties must fix their bids independently of others. We note that independence of inputs is *not* implied by privacy. For example, it may be possible to generate a higher bid, without knowing the value of the original one. Such an attack can actually be carried out on some encryption schemes (i.e. given an encryption of $100, it is possible to generate a valid encryption of $101, without knowing the original encrypted value).

4) *Guaranteed Output Delivery*: Corrupted parties should not be able to prevent honest parties from receiving their output. In other words, the adversary should not be able to disrupt the computation by carrying out a "denial of service" attack.

5) *Fairness*: Corrupted parties should receive their outputs if and only if the honest parties also receive their outputs. The scenario where a corrupted party obtains output and an honest party does not should not be allowed to occur. This property can be crucial, for example, in the case of contract signing. Specifically, it would be very problematic if the corrupted party received the signed contract and the honest party did not. Note that guaranteed output delivery implies fairness, but the converse is not necessarily true.

We stress that the above list does *not* constitute a definition of security, but rather a set of requirements that should hold for any secure protocol. Indeed, one possible approach to defining security is to just generate a list of separate requirements (as above) and then say that a protocol is secure if all of these requirements are fulfilled. However, this approach is not satisfactory for the following reasons. First, it may be possible that an important requirement was missed. This is especially true because different applications have different requirements, and we would like a definition that is general enough to capture all applications. Second, the definition should be simple enough so that it is trivial to see that *all* possible adversarial attacks are prevented by the proposed definition.

The standard definition today (Canetti 2000) following previous studies (Goldreich et al. 1987; Goldwasser and Levin 1991; Beaver 1992; Micali and Rogaway 1992) therefore formalizes security in the following general way. As a mental experiment, consider an "ideal world" in which an external trusted (and incorruptible) party is willing to help the parties carry out their computation. In such a world, the parties can simply send their inputs to the trusted party, who then computes the desired function and passes each party its prescribed output. Since the only action carried out by a party is that of sending its input to the trusted party, the only freedom given to the adversary is in choosing the corrupted parties' inputs. Note that all of the above-described security properties (and more) hold in this ideal computation. For example, privacy holds because the only message ever received by a party is its output (and so it cannot learn any more than this). Likewise, correctness holds since the trusted party cannot be corrupted and so will always compute the function correctly.

Of course, in the "real world", there is no external party that can be trusted by all parties. Rather, the parties run some protocol among themselves without any help, and some of them are corrupted and colluding. Despite this, a secure protocol should emulate the so-called "ideal world". That is, a real protocol that is run by the parties (in a world where no trusted party exists) is said to be secure, if no adversary can do more harm in a real execution that in an execution that takes place in the ideal world. This can be formulated by saying that for any adversary carrying out a successful attack in the real world, there exists an adversary that successfully carries out an attack with the same effect in the ideal world. However, successful adversarial attacks *cannot* be carried out in the ideal world. We therefore conclude that all adversarial attacks on protocol executions in the real world must also fail.

More formally, the security of a protocol is established by comparing the outcome of a real protocol execution to the outcome of an ideal computation. That is, for any adversary attacking a real protocol execution, there exists an adversary attacking an ideal execution (with a trusted party) such that the input/output distributions of the adversary and the participating parties in the real and ideal executions are essentially the same. Thus, a real protocol execution "emulates" the ideal world. This formulation of security is called the ideal/real simulation paradigm. In order to motivate the usefulness of this definition, we describe why all the properties described above are implied. Privacy follows from the fact that the adversary's output is the same in the real and ideal executions. Since the adversary learns nothing beyond the corrupted party's outputs in an ideal execution, the same must be true for a real execution. Correctness follows from the fact that the honest parties' outputs are the same in the real and ideal executions, and from the fact that in an ideal execution, the honest parties all receive correct outputs as computed by the trusted party. Regarding independence of inputs, notice that in an ideal execution, all inputs are sent to the trusted party before any output is received. Therefore, the corrupted parties know nothing of the honest parties' inputs at the time that they send their inputs. In other words, the corrupted parties' inputs are chosen independently of the honest parties' inputs, as required. Finally, guaranteed output delivery and fairness hold in the ideal world because the trusted party always returns all outputs. The fact that it also holds in the real world again follows from the fact that the honest parties' outputs are the same in the real and ideal executions.

We remark that in some cases, the definition is relaxed to exclude fairness and guaranteed output delivery. The level of security achieved when these are excluded is called "security with abort", and the result is that the adversary may be able to obtain output while the honest parties do not. There are two main reasons why this relaxation is used. First, in some cases, it is impossible to achieve fairness; it is impossible to achieve fair coin tossing for two parties (Cleve 1986). Second, in some cases, more efficient protocols are known when fairness is not guaranteed. Thus, if the application does not require fairness (and in particular in cases where only one party receives output), this relaxation is helpful.

4.2.2. Additional definitional parameters

4.2.3. Adversarial power

The above informal definition of security omits one very important issue: the power of the adversary that attacks a protocol execution. As we have mentioned, the adversary controls a subset of the participating parties in the protocol. However, we have not defined what power such an adversary has. We describe the two main parameters defining the adversary: its allowed adversarial behavior (i.e. does the adversary just passively gather information or can it instruct the corrupted parties to act maliciously) and its corruption strategy (i.e. when or how parties come under the "control" of the adversary):

1) *Allowed adversarial behavior*: The most important parameter that must be defined relates to the actions that corrupted parties are allowed to take. There are three main types of adversaries:

a) Semi-honest adversaries: In the semi-honest adversarial model, even corrupted parties correctly follow the protocol specification. However, the adversary obtains the internal state of all the corrupted parties (including the transcript of all the messages received), and attempts to use this to learn information that should remain private. This is a rather weak adversarial model, but a protocol with this level of security does guarantee that there is no inadvertent data leakage. In some cases, this is sufficient, although in today's adversarial environment, it is often insufficient. Semi-honest adversaries are also called "honest-but-curious" and "passive". (Sometimes, fail-stop adversaries are also considered; these are essentially semi-honest adversaries who may also halt the protocol execution early.)

b) Malicious adversaries: In this adversarial model, the corrupted parties can *arbitrarily* deviate from the protocol specification, according to the adversary's instructions. In general, providing security in the presence of malicious adversaries is preferred, as it ensures that no adversarial attack can succeed. Malicious adversaries are also called "active".

c) Covert adversaries (Aumann and Lindell 2010): This type of adversary may behave maliciously in an attempt to break the protocol. However, the security guarantee provided is that if it does attempt such an attack, then it will be detected with some specified probability that can be tuned to the application. We stress that unlike in the malicious model, if the adversary is not detected then it may successfully cheat (e.g. learn an honest party's input). This model is suited to settings where some real-world penalty can be associated with an adversary being detected, and the adversary's expectation is to lose overall if it attempts an attack.

2) *Corruption strategy*: The corruption strategy deals with the question of when and how parties are corrupted. There are three main models:

a) Static corruption model: In this model, the set of parties controlled by the adversary is fixed before the protocol begins. Honest parties remain honest throughout and corrupted parties remain corrupted.

b) Adaptive corruption model: Rather than having a fixed set of corrupted parties, adaptive adversaries are given the capability of corrupting parties during the computation. The choice of who to corrupt, and when, can be arbitrarily decided by the adversary and may depend on its view of the execution (for this reason it is called adaptive). This strategy models the threat of an external "hacker" breaking into a machine during an execution, or a party who is honest initially and later changes its behavior. We note that in this model, once a party is corrupted, it remains corrupted from that point on.

c) Proactive security model (Ostrovsky and Yung 1991; Canetti and Herzberg 1994): This model considers the possibility that parties are corrupted for a certain period of time only. Thus, honest parties may become corrupted throughout the computation (like in the adaptive adversarial model), but corrupted parties may also become honest. The proactive model makes sense in cases where the threat is an external adversary who may breach networks and break into services and devices, and secure computations are ongoing. When breaches are discovered, the systems are cleaned and the adversary loses control of some of the machines, making the parties honest again. The security guarantee is that the adversary can only learn what it derived from the local state of the machines that it corrupted, while they were corrupted. Such an adversary is sometimes called mobile.

There is no "right" model when considering the above. Rather, the specific definition used and adversary considered depends on the application and the threats being dealt with.

4.2.4. Modular sequential and concurrent composition

In reality, a secure MPC protocol is not run in isolation; rather it is part of a system. In Canetti (2000), it was proven that if you run an MPC protocol as part of a larger system, then it still behaves in the same way as if an incorruptible trusted party carried out the computation for the parties. This powerful theorem is called modular composition, and it enables larger protocols to be constructed in a modular way using secure sub-protocols, as well as analyzing a larger system that uses MPC for some of the computations.

One important question in this context is whether or not the MPC protocol itself runs at the same time as other protocols. In the setting of *sequential composition*, the MPC protocol can run as a subprotocol of another protocol with arbitrary other messages being sent before and after the MPC protocol. However, the MPC protocol itself must be run without any other messages being sent in parallel. This is called the stand-alone setting, and is the setting considered by the basic definition of security of Canetti (2000). The sequential modular composition theorem of Canetti (2000) states that in this setting, the MPC protocol indeed behaves like a computation carried out by a trusted third party.

In some (many) cases, MPC protocols are run at the same time as other instances of itself, other MPC protocols, and other insecure protocols. In these cases, a protocol proven secure under the aforementioned stand-alone definition of security may not actually remain secure. A number of definitions were proposed to deal with this setting; the most popular of these is that of universal composability (Canetti 2001). Any protocol proven secure according to this definition is guaranteed to behave like an ideal execution, irrespective of what other protocols run concurrently to it. As such, this is the gold standard of MPC definitions. However, it does come at a price (both of efficiency and assumptions required on the system setup).

4.2.5. *Important definitional implications*

4.2.6. *The ideal model and using MPC in practice*

The ideal/real paradigm for defining security actually has some very important implications for the use of MPC in practice. Specifically, in order to *use* an MPC protocol, all a practitioner needs to do is to consider the security of their system when an incorruptible trusted party carries out the computation for which MPC is used. If the system is secure in this case, then it will remain secure even when the real MPC protocol is used (under the appropriate composition case). This means that non-cryptographers need not understand anything about *how* MPC protocols work, or even how security is defined. The ideal model provides a clean and easy to understand abstraction that can be utilized by those constructing systems.

4.2.7. *Any inputs are allowed*

Although the ideal model paradigm provides a simple abstraction, as described above, there is a subtle point that is sometime misunderstood. An MPC protocol behaves like an ideal execution; as such, the security obtained is analogous to that of an ideal execution. However, in an ideal execution, adversarial parties may input any values that they wish, and indeed there is no generic way of preventing this. Thus, if two people wish to see who earns a higher salary (without revealing any more than this one bit of information), then nothing stops one of them from inputting the maximum possible value as their salary (and then behaving honestly in the MPC protocol itself), with the result being that the output is that they earn more. Thus, if the security of an application depends on the party's using *correct inputs*, then mechanisms must be used to enforce this. For example, it is possible to require signed inputs, and have the signature be verified as part of the MPC computation. Depending on the specific protocol, this can add significant cost.

4.2.8. *MPC secures the process, but not the output*

Another subtlety that is often misunderstood is that MPC secures the process, meaning that nothing is revealed by the computation itself. However, this does not mean that the output of the function being computed does not reveal sensitive information. For an extreme example, consider two people computing the average of their salaries. It is indeed true that nothing but the average will be output, but given a person's own salary and the average of both salaries, they can derive the exact salary of the other person. Thus, just using MPC does not mean that all privacy concerns are solved. Rather, MPC secures the computing process, and the question of what functions should and should not be computed due to privacy concerns still needs to be addressed. In some cases, like threshold cryptography, this question is not an issue (since the output of cryptographic functions does not reveal the key, assuming that it is secure). However, in other cases, it may be less clear. The best tool currently available for analysis of what function to compute is differential privacy (Dwork et al. 2006; Dwork 2008).

4.3. Feasibility of MPC

The above-described definition of security seems to be very restrictive in that no adversarial success is tolerated, and the protocol should behave as if a trusted third party is carrying out the computation. Thus, one may wonder whether it is even possible to obtain secure protocols under this definition, and if yes, for which distributed computing tasks. Perhaps surprisingly, powerful feasibility results have been established, demonstrating that in fact, *any* distributed computing task (function) can be securely computed, in the presence of malicious adversaries. We now briefly state the most central of these results. Let n denote the number of participating parties, and let t denote a bound on the number of parties that may be corrupted (where the identity of the corrupted parties is unknown):

1) For $t < n/3$ (i.e. when less than one-third of the parties can be corrupted), secure multiparty protocols with fairness and guaranteed output delivery can be achieved for any function with computational security assuming a synchronous point-to-point network with authenticated channels (Goldreich et al. 1987), and with information-theoretic security assuming the channels are also private (Ben-Or et al. 1988; Chaum et al. 1988).

2) For $t < n/2$ (i.e. in the case of a guaranteed honest majority), secure multiparty protocols with fairness and guaranteed output delivery can be achieved for any function with computational and information-theoretic security, assuming that the parties also have access to a broadcast channel (Goldreich et al. 1987; Rabin and Ben-Or 1989).

3) For $t \geq n/2$ (i.e. when the number of corrupted parties is not limited), secure multiparty protocols (without fairness or guaranteed output delivery) can be achieved (Yao 1986; Goldreich et al. 1987).

In the setting of concurrent composition described at the end of section 4.2.2, it has also been shown that any function can be securely computed (Canetti 2001; Canetti et al. 2002).

In summary, secure multiparty protocols exist for any distributed computing task. This fact is what provides its huge potential – whatever needs to be computed can be computed securely! We stress, however, that the aforementioned feasibility results are *theoretical*, meaning that they demonstrate that this is possible in principle. They do not consider the practical efficiency costs incurred; these will be mentioned in section 4.4.6.

We conclude this section with a caveat. The above feasibility results are proven in specific models, and under cryptographic hardness and/or setting assumptions. It is beyond the scope of this review to describe these details, but it is important to be aware that they need to be considered.

4.4. Techniques

Over the past three decades, many different techniques have been developed for constructing MPC protocols with different properties and for different settings. It is way beyond the scope of this paper to even mention all of the techniques, and we highly recommend reading Evans et al. (2018) for an extremely well-written and friendly introduction to MPC, including a survey of the major techniques. Nevertheless, we will provide a few simple examples of how MPC protocols are constructed in order to illustrate how it can work.

4.4.1. *Shamir secret sharing*

MPC protocols for an honest majority typically utilize secret sharing as a basic tool. We will therefore begin by briefly describing Shamir's secret sharing scheme (Shamir 1979).

A secret sharing scheme solves the problem of a dealer who wishes to share a secret s among n parties, so that any subset of $t + 1$ or more of the parties can reconstruct the secret, yet no subset of t or fewer parties can learn anything about the secret. A scheme that fulfills these requirements is called a $(t + 1)$-out-of-n-threshold secret-sharing scheme.

Shamir's secret sharing scheme utilizes the fact that for any for $t + 1$ points on the two-dimensional plane $(x_1, y_1), \ldots, (x_{t+1}, y_{t+1})$ with unique x_i, there exists a unique polynomial $q(x)$ of degree at most t such that $q(x_i) = y_i$ for every i. Furthermore, it is possible to efficiently reconstruct the polynomial $q(x)$, or any specific point on it. One way to do this is with the Lagrange basis polynomials $\ell_1(x), \ldots, \ell_t(x)$, where reconstruction is carried out by computing $q(x) = \sum_{i=1}^{t+1} \ell_i(x) \cdot y_i$. From here on, we will assume that all computations are in the finite field $\mathbb{Z}_p$ for a prime $p > n$.

Given the above, in order to share a secret s, the dealer chooses a random polynomial $q(x)$ of degree at most t under the constraint that $q(0) = s$. (Concretely, the dealer sets $a_0 = s$ and chooses random coefficients $a_1, \ldots, a_t \in \mathbb{Z}_p$, and sets $q(x) = \sum_{i=0}^{t} a_i \cdot x^i$.) Then, for every $i = 1, \ldots, n$, the dealer provides the ith party with the share $y_i = q(i)$; this is the reason why we need $p > n$, so that different shares can be given to each party. Reconstruction by a subset of any t parties works by simply interpolating the polynomial to compute $q(x)$ and then deriving $s = q(0)$. Although $t + 1$ parties can completely recover s, it is not hard to show that *any* subset of t or fewer parties cannot learn anything about s. This is due to the fact that they have t or fewer points on the polynomial, and so there exists a polynomial going through these points and the point $(0, s)$ for every possible $s \in \mathbb{Z}_p$. Furthermore, since the polynomial is random, all polynomials are equally likely, and so all values of $s \in \mathbb{Z}_p$ are equally likely.

4.4.2. *Honest-majority MPC with secret sharing*

The first step in most protocols for *general* MPC (i.e. protocols that can be used to compute any function) is to represent the function being computed as a Boolean or arithmetic circuit. In the case of honest-majority MPC based on secret sharing, the arithmetic circuit (composed of multiplication and addition gates) is over a finite field $\mathbb{Z}_p$ with $p > n$, as above. We remark that arithmetic circuits are Turing complete, and so any function can be represented in this form. The parties participating in the MPC protocol are all provided this circuit, and we assume that they can all communicate securely with each other. The protocol for semi-honest adversaries (see below for what is needed for the case of malicious adversaries) consists of the following phases:

1) *Input sharing*: In this phase, each party shares its input with the other parties, using Shamir's secret sharing. That is, for each input wire to the circuit, the party whose input is associated with that wire plays the dealer in Shamir's secret sharing to share the value to all parties. The secret sharing used is $(t+1)$-out-of-n, with $t = \lfloor \frac{n-1}{2} \rfloor$ (thus, the degree of the polynomial is t). This provides security against any minority of corrupted parties, since no such minority can learn anything about the shared values. Following this step, the parties hold secret shares of the values on each input wire.

2) *Circuit evaluation*: In this phase, the parties evaluate the circuit one gate at a time, from the input gates to the output gates. The evaluation maintains the invariant that for every gate for which the parties hold $(t+1)$-out-of-n sharings of the values on the two input wires, the result of the computation is a $(t+1)$-out-of-n secret sharing of the value on the output wire of the gate.

a) Computing addition gates: According to the invariant, each party holds a secret sharing of the values on the input wires to the gate; we denote these polynomials by $a(x)$ and $b(x)$ and this means that the ith party holds the values $a(i)$ and $b(i)$. The output wire of this gate should be a $(t+1)$-out-of-n secret sharing of the value $a(0) + b(0)$. This is easily computed by the ith party locally setting its share on the output wire to be $a(i)+b(i)$. Observe that by defining the polynomial $c(x) = a(x)+b(x)$, this means that the ith party holds $c(i)$. Furthermore, $c(x)$ is a degree-t polynomial such that $c(0) = a(0)+b(0)$. Thus, the parties hold a valid $(t+1)$-out-of-n secret sharing of the value $a(0) + b(0)$, as required. Observe that no communication is needed in order to compute addition gates.

b) Computing multiplication gates: Once again, we denote the polynomials on the input wires to the gate by $a(x)$ and $b(x)$. As for an addition gate, the ith party can locally multiply its shares to define $c(i) = a(i) \cdot b(i)$. By the properties of polynomial multiplication, this defines a polynomial $c(x)$ such that $c(0) = a(0) \cdot b(0)$. Thus, $c(x)$ is a sharing of the correct value (the product of the values on the input wires). However, $c(x)$ is of degree-$2t$, and thus this is a $(2t+1)$-out-of-n secret sharing and not a $(t+1)$-out-of-n secret sharing. In order to complete the computation of the multiplication gate, it is therefore necessary for the parties to carry out a *degree reduction* step to securely reduce the degree of the polynomial shared among the parties from $2t$ to t, without changing its value at 0. Before proceeding to describe this, observe that since $t < n/2$, the shares held by the n parties do fully determine the polynomial $c(x)$ of degree $2t + 1$.

In order to compute the degree reduction step, we use a basic idea from Damgård and Nielsen (2007) (although they have a far more efficient way of realizing it than what we describe here). Assume that the parties all hold two independent secret sharings of an unknown random value r, the first sharing via a polynomial of degree-$2t$ denoted $R_{2t}(x)$, and the second sharing via a polynomial of degree-t denoted $R_t(x)$. Note that $R_{2t}(0) = R_t(0) = r$. Then, each party can locally compute its share of the degree-$2t$ polynomial $d(x) = c(x) - R_{2t}(x)$ by setting $d(i) = c(i) - R_{2t}(i)$. Note that both $c(x)$ and $R_{2t}(x)$ are of degree-$2t$. Next, the parties reconstruct $d(0) = a(0) \cdot b(0) - r$ by sending all of their shares to all other parties. Finally, the ith party for all $i = 1, \ldots, n$ computes its share on the output wire to be $c'(i) = R_t(i) + d(0)$.

Observe that $c'(x)$ is of degree t since $R_t(x)$ is of degree t, and it is defined by adding a constant $d(0)$ to $R_t(x)$. Next, $c'(0) = a(0) \cdot b(0)$ since $R_t(0) = r$ and $d(0) = a(0) \cdot b(0) - r$; thus r cancels out when summing the values. Thus, the parties hold a valid $(t+1)$-out-of-n secret sharing of the product of the values on the input wires, as required. Furthermore, note that the value $d(0)$ that is revealed to all parties does not leak any information since $R_t(x)$ perfectly masks all values of $c(x)$, and in particular it masks the value $a(0) \cdot b(0)$.

It remains to show how the parties generate two independent secret sharings of an unknown random value r via polynomials of degree $2t$ and t. This can be achieved by the ith party, for all $i = 1, \ldots, n$, playing the dealer and sharing a random value r_i via a degree-$2t$ polynomial $R_{2t}^i(x)$ and via a degree-t polynomial $R_t^i(x)$. Then, upon receiving such shares from each of the parties, the ith party for all $i = 1, \ldots, n$ defines its shares of $R_{2t}(x)$ and $R_t(x)$ by computing $R_{2t}(i) = \sum_{j=1}^n R_{2t}^j(i)$ and $R_t(i) = \sum_{j=1}^n R_t^j(i)$. Since all parties contribute secret random values $r_1, \ldots, r_n$ and we have that $r = \sum_{j=1}^n r_j$, it follows that no party knows r.

3) *Output reconstruction*: Once the parties have obtained shares on the output wires, they can obtain the outputs by simply sending their shares to each other and reconstructing the outputs via interpolation. Observe that it is also possible for different parties to obtain different outputs, if desired. In this case, the parties send the shares for reconstruction only to the relevant parties who are supposed to obtain the output on a given wire.

The above protocol is secure for *semi-honest adversaries*, as long as less than $n/2$ parties are corrupted. This is because the only values seen by the parties during the computation are secret shares (that reveal nothing about the values they hide) and opened $d(0)$ values that reveal nothing about the actual values on the wires due to the independent random sharings used each time. Note that in order to achieve security in the presence of *malicious adversaries* who may deviate from the protocol specification, it is necessary to utilize different methods to prevent cheating. See Beerliová-Trubíniová and Hirt (2008); Chida et al. (2018); Furukawa and Lindell (2019) for a few examples of how to efficiently achieve security in the presence of malicious adversaries.

4.4.3. *Private set intersection*

In section 4.4.2, we described an approach to *general* secure computation that can be used to securely compute any function. In many cases, these general approaches turn out to actually be the most efficient (especially when considering malicious adversaries). However, in some cases, the specific structure of the function being solved enables us to find faster, tailored solutions. In this and the next section, we present two examples of such functions.

In a private set intersection protocol, two parties with private sets of values wish to find the intersection of the sets, without revealing anything but the elements in the intersection. In some cases, some function of the intersection is desired, like its size only. There has been a lot of work on this problem, with security for both semi-honest and malicious adversaries, and with different efficiency goals (few rounds, low communication, low computation, etc.). In this section, we will describe the idea behind the protocol of Kolesnikov et al. (2016); the actual protocol is far more complex, but we present the conceptually simple idea underlying their construction.

A pseudorandom function F is a keyed function with the property that outputs of the function on known inputs look completely random. Thus, for any given list of elements $x_1, \ldots, x_n$, the series of values $F_k(x_1), \ldots, F_k(x_n)$ looks random. In particular, given $F_k(x_i)$, it is infeasible to determine the value of x_i. In the following simple protocol, we utilize a tool called *oblivious pseudorandom function evaluation*. This is a specific type of MPC protocol where the first party inputs k and the second party inputs x, and the second party receives $F_k(x)$ while the first party learns nothing about x (note that the second party learns $F_k(x)$ but nothing beyond that; in particular, k remains secret). Such a primitive can be built in many ways, and we will not describe them here.

Now, consider two parties with respective sets of private elements; denote them $x_1, \ldots, x_n$ and $y_1, \ldots, y_n$, respectively (for simplicity, we assume that their lists are of the same size, although this is not needed). Then, the protocol proceeds as follows:

1) The first party chooses a key k for a pseudorandom function.

2) The two parties run n oblivious pseudorandom function evaluations: in the ith execution, the first party inputs k and the second party inputs y_i. As a result, the second party learns $F_k(y_1), \ldots, F_k(y_n)$ while the first party learns nothing about $y_1, \ldots, y_n$.

3) The first party locally computes $F_k(x_1), \ldots, F_k(x_n)$ and sends the list to the second party. It can compute this since it knows k.

4) The second party computes the intersection between the lists $F_k(y_1), \ldots, F_k(y_n)$ and $F_k(x_1), \ldots, F_k(x_n)$, and outputs all values y_j for which $F_k(y_j)$ is in the intersection. (The party knows these values since it knows the association between y_j and $F_k(y_j)$.)

The above protocol reveals nothing but the intersection since the first party learns nothing about $y_1, \ldots, y_n$ from the oblivious pseudorandom function evaluations, and the second party learns nothing about values of x_j that are not in the intersection since the pseudorandom function hides the preimage values. This is therefore secure in the semi-honest model. It is more challenging to achieve security in the malicious model. For example, a malicious adversary could use a different key for the first element and later elements, and then have the result that the value y_1 is in the output if and only if it was the first element of the second party's list.

The most efficient private set intersection protocols today use advanced hashing techniques, and can process millions of items in a few seconds (Kolesnikov et al. 2016; Pinkas et al. 2018, 2019).

4.4.4. *Threshold cryptography*

The aim of threshold cryptography is to enable a set of parties to carry out cryptographic operations, without any single party holding the secret key. This can be used to ensure multiple signatories on a transaction, or alternatively to protect secret keys from being stolen by spreading key shares out on different devices (so that the attacker has to breach all devices in order to learn the key). We demonstrate a very simple protocol for two-party RSA, but warn that for more parties (and other schemes), it is much more complex.

RSA is a public-key scheme with public-key (e, N) and private-key (d, N). The basic RSA function is $y = x^e \bmod N$, and its inverse function is $x = y^d \bmod N$. RSA is used for encryption and signing, by padding the message and other techniques. Here, we relate to the *raw* RSA function, and show how the inverse can be computed securely among two parties, where neither party can compute the function itself. In order to achieve this, the system is set up with the first party holding (d_1, N) and the second party holding (d_2, N), where d_1 and d_2 are random under the constraint that $d_1 + d_2 = d$. (More formally, the order in the exponent is $\phi(N)$ – Euler's function – and therefore the values $d_1, d_2 \in \mathbb{Z}_{\phi(N)}$ are random under the constraint that $d_1 + d_2 = d \bmod \phi(N)$.) In order to securely compute $y^d \bmod N$, the first party computes $x_1 = y^{d_1} \bmod N$, the second party computes $x_2 = y^{d_2} \bmod N$, and these values are exchanged between them. Then, each party computes $x = x_1 \cdot x_2 \bmod N$, verifies that the output is correct by checking that $x^e = y \bmod N$ and if yes outputs x. Observe that this computation is correct since

$$x = y^{d_1} \cdot y^{d_2} \bmod N = y^{d_1 + d_2 \bmod \phi(N)} \bmod N = y^d \bmod N.$$

In addition, observe that given the output x and its share d_1 of the private exponent, the first party can compute $x_2 = y/y^{d_1} \bmod N$ (this is correct since $x_2 = y^{d_2} = y^{d_1 + d_2 - d_1} = y/y^{d_1} \bmod N$). This means that the first party does not learn anything more than the output from the protocol, since it can generate the messages that it receives in the protocol by itself from its own input and the output.

We stress that full-blown threshold cryptography supports quorum approvals involving many parties (e.g. requiring $(t + 1)$-out-of-n parties to sign, and maintaining security for any subset of t corrupted parties). This needs additional tools, but can also be done very efficiently (see Shoup (2000) and references within). Recently, there has been a lot of interest in threshold ECDSA due to its applications to protecting cryptocurrencies (Lindell 2017; Gennaro and Goldfeder 2018; Lindell and Nof 2018; Doerner et al. 2019).

4.4.5. *Dishonest-majority MPC*

In section 4.4.2, we described a general protocol for MPC that is secure as long as an adversary cannot corrupt more than a minority of the parties. In the case of a dishonest majority, including the important special case of two parties (with one corrupted), completely different approaches are needed. There has been a very large body of work in this direction, from the initial protocols of Yao (1986); Goldreich et al. (1987); Beaver et al. (1990) that focused on feasibility, and including a lot of recent work focused on achieving concrete efficiency. There is so much work in this direction that any attempt to describe it here will do it a grave injustice. We therefore refer the reader to Evans et al. (2018) for a description of the main approaches, including the GMW oblivious transfer approach (Goldreich et al. 1987; Ishai et al. 2003), garbled circuits (Yao 1986; Beaver et al. 1990), cut-and-choose (Lindell and Pinkas 2007), SPDZ (Damgård et al. 2012), TinyOT (Nielsen et al. 2012), MPC in the head (Ishai et al. 2008) and so on. (We stress that for each of these approaches, there have been many follow-up works, achieving increasingly better efficiency.)

4.4.6. *Efficient and practical MPC*

The first 20 years of MPC research focused primarily on feasibility: how to define and prove security for multiple adversarial and network models, under what cryptographic and setup assumptions it is possible to achieve MPC, and so on. The following decade saw a large body of research around making MPC more and more efficient. The first steps of this process were purely algorithmic and focused on reducing the overhead of the cryptographic primitives. Following this, other issues were considered that had significant impact: the memory and communication, utilization of hardware instructions like AES-NI and so on. In addition, since most general protocols require the circuit representation of the function being computed, and circuits are hard to manually construct, special-purpose MPC compilers from code to circuits were also constructed. These compilers are tailored to be sensitive to the special properties of MPC. For example, in many protocols XOR gates are computed almost for free (Kolesnikov and Schneider 2008), in contrast to AND/OR gates that cost. These compilers therefore minimize the number of AND gates, even at the expense of considerably more XOR gates. In addition, the computational cost of some protocols is dominated by the circuit size, while in others it is dominated by the circuit depth. Thus, some compilers aim to generate the smallest circuit possible, while others aim to generate a circuit with the lowest depth. See Hastings et al. (2019) for a survey on general-purpose compilers for MPC and their usability. The combination of these advancements led to performance improvements of many orders of magnitude in just a few years, paving the way for MPC to be fast enough to be used in practice for a wide variety of problems. See Evans et al. (2018, Chapter 4) for a description of a few of the most significant of these advancements.

4.5. MPC use cases

There are many great theoretical examples of where MPC can be helpful. It can be used to compare no-fly lists in a privacy-preserving manner, to enable private DNA comparisons for medical and other purposes, to gather statistics without revealing anything but the aggregate results and so on. Up until very recently, these theoretical examples of usage were almost all we had to say about the potential benefits of MPC. However, the situation today is very different. MPC is now being used in multiple real-world use cases and usage is growing fast.

We will conclude this review chapter with some examples of MPC applications that have been actually deployed.

4.5.1. *Boston wage gap (Lapets et al. 2018)*

The Boston Women's Workforce Council used MPC in 2017 in order to compute statistics on the compensation of 166,705 employees across 114 companies, comprising roughly 16% of the Greater Boston area workforce. The use of MPC was crucial, since companies would not provide their raw data due to privacy concerns. The results showed that the gender gap in the Boston area is even larger than previously estimated by the U.S. Bureau of Labor Statistics. This is a powerful example demonstrating that MPC can be used for social good.

4.5.2. *Advertising conversion (Ion et al. 2017)*

In order to compute accurate conversion rates from advertisements to actual purchases, Google computes the *size* of the intersection between the list of people shown an advertisement to the list of people actually purchasing the advertised goods. When the goods are not purchased online and so the purchase connection to the shown advertisement cannot be tracked, Google and the company paying for the advertisement have to share their respective lists in order to compute the intersection size. In order to compute this without revealing anything but the size of the intersection, Google utilizes a protocol for privacy-preserving set intersection. The protocol used by Google is described in Ion et al. (2017). Although this protocol is far from the most efficient known today, it is simple and meets their computational requirements.

4.5.3. *MPC for cryptographic key protection (Unbound Security; Sepior; Curv)*

As described in section 4.4.4, threshold cryptography provides the ability to carry out cryptographic operations (like decryption and signing) without the private key being held in any single place. A number of companies are using threshold cryptography as an alternative to legacy hardware for protecting cryptographic keys. In this application, MPC is not run between different parties holding private information. Rather, a single organization uses MPC to generate keys and compute cryptographic operations, without the key ever being in a single place where it can be stolen. By placing the key shares in different environments, it is very hard for an adversary to steal all shares and obtain the key. In this setting, the proactive model described in section 4.2.2 is the most suitable. Another use of MPC in this context is for protecting the signing keys used for protecting cryptocurrencies and other digital assets. Here, the ability to define general quorums enables the cryptographic enforcement of strict policies for approving financial transactions or to share keys between custody providers and clients.

4.5.4. *Government collaboration (Sharemind)*

Different governmental departments hold information about citizens, and significant benefit can be obtained by correlating that information. However, the privacy risks involved in pooling private information can prevent governments from doing this. For example, in 2000, Canada scrapped a program to pool citizen information, under criticism that they were building a "big brother database". Utilizing MPC, Estonia collected encrypted income tax records and higher education records to analyze if students who work during their degree are more likely to fail than those focusing solely on their studies. By using MPC, the government was guaranteed that all data protection and tax secrecy regulations were followed without losing data utility.

4.5.5. *Privacy-preserving analytics (Duality)*

Machine learning usage is increasing rapidly in many domains. MPC can be used to run machine learning models on data without revealing the model (which contains precious intellectual property) to the data owner, and without revealing the data to the model owner. In addition, statistical analyses can be carried out between organizations for the purpose of anti-money laundering, risk score calculations and so on.

4.6. Discussion

Secure MPC is a fantastic example of success in the long game of research (Vardi 2019). For the first 20 years of MPC research, no applications were in sight, and it was questionable whether or not MPC would ever be used. In the past decade, the state of MPC usability has undergone a radical transformation. In this time, MPC has not only become fast enough to be used in practice, but it has received industry recognition and has made the transition to a technology that is deployed in practice. MPC still requires great expertise to deploy, and additional research breakthroughs are needed to make secure computation practical on large data sets and for complex problems, and to make it easy to use for non-experts. The progress from the past few years, and the large amount of applied research now being generated paints a positive future for MPC in practice. Together with this, deep theoretical work in MPC continues, ensuring that applied MPC solutions stand on strong scientific foundations.

4.7. References

Asharov, G. and Lindell, Y. (2017). A full proof of the BGW protocol for perfectly secure multiparty computation. *Journal of Cryptology*, 30(1), 58–151.

Aumann, Y. and Lindell, Y. (2010). Security against covert adversaries: Efficient protocols for realistic adversaries. *Journal of Cryptology*, 23(2), 281–343.

Beaver, D. (1992). Foundations of secure interactive computing. In *CRYPTO'91*, vol. 576 of *LNCS*, Feigenbaum, J. (ed.). Springer, Heidelberg.

Beaver, D., Micali, S., Rogaway, P. (1990). The round complexity of secure protocols (extended abstract). In *22nd ACM STOC*. ACM Press.

Beerliová-Trubíniová, Z. and Hirt, M. (2008). Perfectly-secure MPC with linear communication complexity. In *TCC 2008*, vol. 4948 of *LNCS*, Canetti, R. (ed.). Springer, Heidelberg.

Ben-Or, M., Goldwasser, S., Wigderson, A. (1988). Completeness theorems for non-cryptographic fault-tolerant distributed computation (extended abstract). In *20th ACM STOC*. ACM Press.

Canetti, R. (2000). Security and composition of multiparty cryptographic protocols. *Journal of Cryptology*, 13(1), 143–202.

Canetti, R. (2001). Universally composable security: A new paradigm for cryptographic protocols. In *42nd FOCS*. IEEE Computer Society Press.

Canetti, R. and Herzberg, A. (1994). Maintaining security in the presence of transient faults. In *CRYPTO'94*, vol. 839 of *LNCS*, Desmedt, Y. (ed.). Springer, Heidelberg.

Canetti, R., Lindell, Y., Ostrovsky, R., Sahai, A. (2002). Universally composable two-party and multi-party secure computation. In *34th ACM STOC*. ACM Press.

Chaum, D., Crépeau, C., Damgård, I. (1988). Multiparty unconditionally secure protocols (extended abstract). In *20th ACM STOC*. ACM Press.

Chida, K., Genkin, D., Hamada, K., Ikarashi, D., Kikuchi, R., Lindell, Y., Nof, A. (2018). Fast large-scale honest-majority MPC for malicious adversaries. In *CRYPTO 2018, Part III*, vol. 10993 of *LNCS*, Shacham, H., Boldyreva, A. (eds). Springer, Heidelberg.

Cleve, R. (1986). Limits on the security of coin flips when half the processors are faulty (extended abstract). In *18th ACM STOC*. ACM Press.

Curv (n.d.). Available at: www.curv.co.

Damgård, I. and Nielsen, J.B. (2007). Scalable and unconditionally secure multiparty computation. In *CRYPTO 2007*, vol. 4622 of *LNCS*, Menezes, A. (ed.). Springer, Heidelberg.

Damgård, I., Pastro, V., Smart, N.P., Zakarias, S. (2012). Multiparty computation from somewhat homomorphic encryption. In *CRYPTO 2012*, vol. 7417 of *LNCS*, Safavi-Naini, R., Canetti, R. (eds). Springer, Heidelberg.

Doerner, J., Kondi, Y., Lee, E., Shelat, A. (2019). Threshold ECDSA from ECDSA assumptions: The multiparty case. In *2019 IEEE Symposium on Security and Privacy*. IEEE Computer Society Press.

Duality (n.d.). Available at: duality.cloud.

Dwork, C. (2008). Differential privacy: A survey of results. In *Theory and Applications of Models of Computation, 5th International Conference, TAMC 2008*, vol. 4978 of *LNCS*, Agrawal, M., Du, D., Duan, Z., Li, A. (eds). Springer, Heidelberg.

Dwork, C., McSherry, F., Nissim, K., Smith, A. (2006). Calibrating noise to sensitivity in private data analysis. In *TCC 2006*, vol. 3876 of *LNCS*, Halevi, S., Rabin, T. (eds). Springer, Heidelberg.

Evans, D., Kolesnikov, V., Rosulek, M. (2018). A pragmatic introduction to secure multi-party computation. *Foundations and Trends® in Privacy and Security*, 2(2–3), 70–246.

Furukawa, J. and Lindell, Y. (2019). Two-thirds honest-majority MPC for malicious adversaries at almost the cost of semi-honest. In *ACM CCS 2019*, Cavallaro, L., Kinder, J., Wang, X., Katz, J. (eds). ACM Press.

Gennaro, R. and Goldfeder, S. (2018). Fast multiparty threshold ECDSA with fast trustless setup. In *ACM CCS 2018*, Lie, D., Mannan, M., Backes, M., Wang, X. (eds). ACM Press.

Goldreich, O., Micali, S., Wigderson, A. (1986). Proofs that yield nothing but their validity and a methodology of cryptographic protocol design (extended abstract). In *27th FOCS*. IEEE Computer Society Press.

Goldreich, O., Micali, S., Wigderson, A. (1987). How to play any mental game or A completeness theorem for protocols with honest majority. In *19th ACM STOC*, Aho, A. (ed.). ACM Press.

Goldwasser, S. and Levin, L.A. (1991). Fair computation of general functions in presence of immoral majority. In *CRYPTO'90*, vol. 537 of *LNCS*, Menezes, A.J., Vanstone, S.A. (eds). Springer, Heidelberg.

Hastings, M., Hemenway, B., Noble, D., Zdancewic, S. (2019). SoK: General purpose compilers for secure multi-party computation. In *2019 IEEE Symposium on Security and Privacy*. IEEE Computer Society Press.

Ion, M., Kreuter, B., Nergiz, E., Patel, S., Saxena, S., Seth, K., Shanahan, D., Yung, M. (2017). Private intersection-sum protocol with applications to attributing aggregate ad conversions. Cryptology ePrint Archive, Report 2017/738 [Online]. Available at: https://eprint.iacr.org/2017/738.

Ishai, Y., Kilian, J., Nissim, K., Petrank, E. (2003). Extending oblivious transfers efficiently. In *CRYPTO 2003*, vol. 2729 of *LNCS*, Boneh, D. (ed.). Springer, Heidelberg.

Ishai, Y., Prabhakaran, M., Sahai, A. (2008). Founding cryptography on oblivious transfer – efficiently. In *CRYPTO 2008*, vol. 5157 of *LNCS*, Wagner, D. (ed.). Springer, Heidelberg.

Kolesnikov, V. and Schneider, T. (2008). Improved garbled circuit: Free XOR gates and applications. In *ICALP 2008, Part II*, vol. 5126 of *LNCS*, Aceto, L., Damgård, I., Goldberg, L.A., Halldórsson, M.M., Ingólfsdóttir, A., Walukiewicz, I. (eds). Springer, Heidelberg.

Kolesnikov, V., Kumaresan, R., Rosulek, M., Trieu, N. (2016). Efficient batched oblivious PRF with applications to private set intersection. In *ACM CCS 2016*, Weippl, E.R., Katzenbeisser, S., Kruegel, C., Myers, A.C., Halevi, S. (eds). ACM Press.

Lapets, A., Jansen, F., Albab, K.D., Issa, R., Qin, L., Varia, M., Bestavros, A. (2018). Accessible privacy-preserving web-based data analysis for assessing and addressing economic inequalities. In *Proceedings of the 1st ACM SIGCAS Conference on Computing and Sustainable Societies, COMPASS 2018*, Zegura, E.W. (ed.). ACM Press.

Lindell, Y. (2017). Fast secure two-party ECDSA signing. In *CRYPTO 2017, Part II*, vol. 10402 of *LNCS*, Katz, J., Shacham, H. (eds). Springer, Heidelberg.

Lindell, Y. and Nof, A. (2018). Fast secure multiparty ECDSA with practical distributed key generation and applications to cryptocurrency custody. In *ACM CCS 2018*, Lie, D., Mannan, M., Backes, M., Wang, X. (eds). ACM Press.

Lindell, Y. and Pinkas, B. (2007). An efficient protocol for secure two-party computation in the presence of malicious adversaries. In *EUROCRYPT 2007*, vol. 4515 of *LNCS*, Naor, M. (ed.). Springer, Heidelberg.

Micali, S. and Rogaway, P. (1992). Secure computation (abstract). In *CRYPTO'91*, vol. 576 of *LNCS*, Feigenbaum, J. (ed.). Springer, Heidelberg.

Nielsen, J.B., Nordholt, P.S., Orlandi, C., Burra, S.S. (2012). A new approach to practical active-secure two-party computation. In *CRYPTO 2012*, vol. 7417 of *LNCS*, Safavi-Naini, R., Canetti, R. (eds). Springer, Heidelberg.

Ostrovsky, R. and Yung, M. (1991). How to withstand mobile virus attacks (extended abstract). In *10th ACM PODC*, Logrippo, L. (ed.). ACM Press.

Pinkas, B., Schneider, T., Zohner, M. (2018). Scalable private set intersection based on OT extension. *ACM Transactions on Privacy and Security*, 21(2), 7:1–7:35.

Pinkas, B., Rosulek, M., Trieu, N., Yanai, A. (2019). SpOT-light: Lightweight private set intersection from sparse OT extension. In *CRYPTO 2019, Part III*, vol. 11694 of *LNCS*, Boldyreva, A., Micciancio, D. (eds). Springer, Heidelberg.

Rabin, T. and Ben-Or, M. (1989). Verifiable secret sharing and multiparty protocols with honest majority (extended abstract). In *21st ACM STOC*. ACM Press.

Sepior (n.d.). Available at: sepior.com.

Shamir, A. (1979). How to share a secret. *Communications of the Association for Computing Machinery*, 22(11), 612–613.

Sharemind (n.d.). Available at: sharemind.cyber.ee.

Shoup, V. (2000). Practical threshold signatures. In *EUROCRYPT 2000*, vol. 1807 of *LNCS*, Preneel, B. (ed.). Springer, Heidelberg.

Unbound Security (n.d.). Available at: www.unboundsecurity.com.

Vardi, M.Y. (2019). The long game of research. *Communications of the Association for Computing Machinery*, 62(9), 7.

Yao, A.C.-C. (1986). How to generate and exchange secrets (extended abstract). In *27th FOCS*. IEEE Computer Society Press.

5

Pairing-Based Cryptography

Olivier BLAZY

Ecole Polytechnique, Palaiseau, France

With the emergence of public-key cryptography, through the seminal paper from Diffie and Hellman (1976), an emphasis has been placed on studying the discrete logarithm problem. Assuming a cyclic group $(\mathbb{G}, \cdot)$ of order p, this problem consists of, given elements g, h in the group, finding a scalar s in $\mathbb{Z}_p$ such that $h = g^s$. In carefully chosen groups, this problem is assumed to be hard. In 1985, both Koblitz (1987) and Miller (1986) proposed to use elliptic curves to instantiate such groups.

In their paper, Diffie and Hellman presented an application through a key exchange (see Chapter 9). In such a protocol, two users commonly referred to as Alice and Bob want to obtain a shared secret key by exchanging information over a public channel. To do so, they each pick a random scalar a (respectively, b), then send g^a (respectively, g^b), and receiving the element from the other compute the shared key $K = (g^b)^a$ (respectively, $(g^a)^b$). This leads to the introduction of the decisional Diffie–Hellman problem, where given g, g^a, g^b, g^c one has to guess whether $c = ab$. It is easy to see that if this problem is hard, then the discrete logarithm problem is hard.

A natural question quickly arises when looking at their protocol: can it be extended to three participants while remaining one-round and resistant to eavesdropping?

This chapter is going to look deeper into this question, via the positive answer given in 2000 by Joux (2004), and independently by R. Sakai, K. Ohgishi, and M. Kasahara and the various doors it opened in cryptography (or at least a selection thereof).

Asymmetric Cryptography,
coordinated by David POINTCHEVAL. © ISTE Ltd. 2022.

5.1. Introduction

5.1.1. *Notations*

Throughout the chapter, we are going to follow those conventions.

– Groups will be denoted by bold letters according to the standard convention. When we do not consider any pairing, or we are in the symmetric case, we will use the group $\mathbb{G}$, in case of asymmetric pairings the groups will be $\mathbb{G}_1$ and $\mathbb{G}_2$. The target group will always be $\mathbb{G}_T$.

– Group generators will be noted by lowercase letters ($g \in \mathbb{G}$), possibly with indices denoting the groups ($g_1 \in \mathbb{G}_1$).

– In addition:

- e will be the non-degenerated bilinear form of pairing (see below).

- λ will be the security parameter, and 1^λ will be a string composed of λ concatenated 1.

- p will be a prime number, generally the order of the groups. (In that case, p has often λ bits.)

– If required, the group law will be noted "·" but may be forgotten.

5.1.2. *Generalities*

DEFINITION 5.1.– *Hard problem: A function* $f : \mathbb{N} \to \mathcal{R}$ *is said to be negligible, if* $\forall c \in \mathbb{N}, \exists k_0 \in \mathbb{N}, \forall k \geq k_0 : |f(k)| < k^{-c}$. *A problem is said to be hard, if there exists no polynomial time algorithm solving it with non-negligible probability.*

DEFINITION 5.2.– *Cyclic group: A cyclic group is a tuple* $(p, \mathbb{G}, g)$ *where* $\mathbb{G}$ *is a group entirely generated by g where* $g^p = 1_{\mathbb{G}}$. *(The neutral element of* $\mathbb{G}$.*)*

DEFINITION 5.3.– *Bilinear groups: A bilinear group is a tuple* $(p, \mathbb{G}_1, \mathbb{G}_2, \mathbb{G}_T, e, g_1, g_2)$ *where* $\mathbb{G}_1, \mathbb{G}_2$ *and* $\mathbb{G}_T$ *are cyclic groups of prime order p, generated respectively, by* g_1, g_2 *and* $e(g_1, g_2)$, $e : \mathbb{G}_1 \times \mathbb{G}_2 \to \mathbb{G}_T$ *is a non-degenerated bilinear form, that is:*

$$\forall X \in \mathbb{G}_1, \forall Y \in \mathbb{G}_2, \forall x, y \in \mathbb{Z}_p : e(X^x, Y^y) = e(X, Y)^{xy}$$

and $e(g_1, g_2)$ *does indeed generate the prime order group* $\mathbb{G}_T$. *In the following, we will suppose there exists a polynomial time algorithm that takes* 1^λ *as input, and which outputs such bilinear groups.*

Such groups are commonly instantiated on elliptic curves on which such pairings can be defined as bilinear forms. Galbraith et al. (2006) have split such instantiations in three main types, with associated computational assumptions detailed later:

– Type I, where $\mathbb{G}_1 = \mathbb{G}_2$, and $g_1 = g_2$, those groups are said to be symmetric and can be simplified in $(p, \mathbb{G}, \mathbb{G}_T, e, g)$. This first case often leads to problems based on the Decisional Linear (DLin) assumption.

– Type II, if there exists a computationally efficient homomorphism from $\mathbb{G}_2$ in $\mathbb{G}_1$, but none from $\mathbb{G}_1$ to $\mathbb{G}_2$. This case often leads to problems based on the eXternal Diffie–Hellman (XDH) assumption.

– Type III, if such efficient homomorphism does not exist in either way. This last case often leads to problems based on the Symmetric eXternal Diffie–Hellman (SXDH) assumption.

NOTE.– As pointed out in the original paper, there always exists an homomorphism between cyclic groups of the same order; however, in Types II and III, it is assumed that it is as hard as computing the discrete logarithm, hence the emphasis on the word *efficient*.

5.2. One small step for man, one giant leap for cryptography

Pairings were initially motivated by two reasons. On the one hand, being able to compute $e(g, g^a)$ allows to move a discrete logarithm problem on the curve (between g, g^a) to a discrete logarithm problem on a finite field (between $e(g, g), e(g, g)^a$) where one can apply sub-exponential algorithms. This was at the core of the MOV attacks, as given by Menezes et al. (1993). However, in those cases, the existence of pairings was seen as a bad thing (in term of security), as they made building secure discrete logarithm-based protocols more difficult.

This meant, that instead, one had to search and look for a type of curves, where this feature was considered at the creation, to be able to use it *on purpose* during protocol creations. This was the second goal trying to find a way to securely extend the Diffie–Hellman key exchange to a three-party protocol. While classical techniques could have been used at the cost of cumbersome extra rounds, here the goal was to be able to do everything, asynchronously, in a single pass. As a result, this possibility presented a real improvement compared to the state of the art.

The basic steps are very similar to classical Diffie–Hellman, Alice, Bob and this time Carol, each generate a scalar s in $\mathbb{Z}_p$ and once this is done send the associated group element g^s to the other. Now, Alice receiving B and C from Bob and Carol is able to use the pairing to compute $K = e(B, C)^a = e(g, g)^{abc}$.

One can easily see in Figure 5.1 that every flow can be asynchronous and they can be sent in any order, without waiting for the recipient to be online. In addition, the final key obtained by all participants is $K = e(g, g)^{abc} = e(g^a, g^b)^c = e(g^a, g^c)^b = e(g^b, g^c)^a$

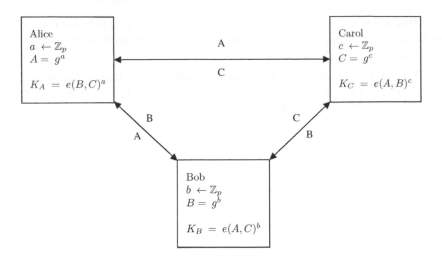

Figure 5.1. *Representation of Joux tripartite Diffie–Hellman exchange*

5.2.1. *Opening Pandora's box, demystifying the magic*

At the core of most pairing computations, their lies the Miller's algorithm. We present in Figure 5.2 the double-and-add version, which is more efficient than the original version, while remaining compact to describe.

There are two main approaches to define pairings on elliptic curves, namely the Tate and the Weil pairings.

They allowed to provide maps such that:

– the base groups are subgroups of the rational points of an elliptic curve E defined over an extension $\mathbb{F}_{p^k}$ of $\mathbb{F}_p$;

– the target group is the subgroup of r-roots of unity of $\mathbb{F}_{q^k}^*$, or at a high level it can be viewed as the group $(\mathbb{F}_{q^k}^*, \times)$ where the group law is the field multiplication over $\mathbb{F}_{q^k}^*$;

– using the Miller's algorithm (see Figure5.2), one can compute the pairing e.

5.2.1.1. *The Weil pairing*

Historically, the first pairing used on elliptic curves was the one defined by Weil. It is not so common to use it nowadays; however, it remains a good stepping stone to introduce the Tate one.

Algorithm: Miller's algorithm for Weierstrass coordinate

Input: $r \in \mathbb{N}, I = [\log r, ..., 0], P = (x_P, y_P) \in E[r](K), Q = (x_Q, y_Q) \in E(K)$.

Output: $f_{r,P}(Q)$

(1) Compute the binary decomposition of $r = \sum_{i \in I} b_i 2^i$.

(2) Set $T = P, f_1 = f_2 = 1$

(3) For $i \in I \setminus 0$, compute:

(i) $\alpha = \frac{3x_T^2 + a}{2y_T}$, in other word, the slope of the tangent of E at T.

(ii) Set $x_{2T} = \alpha^2 - 2x_T, y_{2T} = -\alpha x_{2T} - x_T - y_T$.

(iii) Update $f_1 = f_1^2(y_Q - y_T - \alpha(x_Q - x_T)), f_2 = f_2^2(x_Q, +2x_T - \alpha^2)$.

(iv) Update $T = 2T$.

(v) If $b_i = 1$, compute: (a) $\alpha = \frac{y_P - y_T}{x_P - x_T}$, the slope of the line between P and T.

(b) Set $x_{P+T} = \alpha^2 - x_P - x_T, y_{P+T} = -\alpha(x_{P+T} - x_T) - y + T$.

(c) Update $f_1 = f_1(y_Q - y_T - \alpha(x_Q - x_T)), f_2 = f_2^2(x_Q, +x_P + x_T - \alpha^2)$.

(d) $T = T + P$.

(4) To handle 0, set $f_1 = f_1(x_Q - x_T)$ and return it.

Figure 5.2. *Miller's algorithm for Weierstrass coordinate*

THEOREM.– Given an elliptic curve E defined over a finite field $\mathbb{K}$, and $R \leq 2$ an integer prime with the characteristic of $\mathbb{K}$, and P, Q two points of r-torsion on E, then the value:

$$e_{W,r} = (-1)^r \frac{f_{r,P}(Q)}{f_{r,Q}(P)}$$

is well defined when $P \neq Q$ and both $P, Q \neq 0_E$. To extend the definition to the whole domain, one can then set $e_{W,r}(0_E, P) = e_{W,r}(P, 0_E) = e_{W,r}(P, P) = 1$. In this case, the resulting operation is a pairing, called the Weil pairing. One should be careful; this pairing is alternate, so $e_{W,r}(P, Q) = e_{W,r}(Q, P)^{-1}$.

NOTE.– In cryptographic applications, we consider $\mathbb{K} = \mathbb{F}_q$ with q a prime. We call the embedding degree k, the smallest k such that $r | q^k - 1$. This leads to $\mathbb{F}_{q^k} = \mathbb{F}_q(\mathsf{Im}(e_{W,r}))$

5.2.1.2. *The Tate pairing*

This pairing was originally described by Tate for number fields (Tate 1958), and then updated by Frey and Rück (1994) for finite fields. In order to tailor our presentation for cryptographical use, we restrict ourselves to $\mathbb{K} = \mathbb{F}_q$, and an embedding degree k corresponding to r.

THEOREM.– Let E be an elliptic curve, r a prime number dividing the cardinal of $E(\mathbb{F}_q)$, P a point of the r-torsion defined over $\mathbb{F}_{q^k}$ and Q a point of the curve defined over $\mathbb{F}_{q^k}$. Let R be any point of the curve, such that both R and $Q + R$ are different from P and 0_E. Then one can define (independently from R):

$$e_{T,r}(P,Q) = \left(\frac{f_{r,P}(Q+R)}{f_{r,P}(R)} \right)^{\frac{q^k-1}{r}}$$

This defines a non-degenerated pairing, called the Tate pairing.

NOTE.– In practice, when Q is not a multiple of P (e.g. when they are in different groups), one can simply take $R = 0_E$, and just compute $e_{T,r}(P,Q) = f_{r,P}(Q)^{\frac{q^k-1}{r}}$. Doing so also allows to avoid complications, which could arise in a normal run of Miller's algorithm.

5.2.2. *A new world of assumptions*

Before exploring the new protocols that can be built using pairings, one has to pay attention to hypotheses that can still exist on curves admitting an efficient pairing.

On the plus side, due to the bilinearity of the pairing operation, one can see that the discrete logarithm problem in $\mathbb{G}_1, \mathbb{G}_2$ can be reduced to the discrete logarithm in $\mathbb{G}_T$.

In the symmetric setting, one can see that the decisional Diffie–Hellman assumption becomes trivial to break. Anyone being given a challenge $g, A = g^a, B = g^b, C = g^c$ can simply compute $e(A, B), e(g, C)$ and check for equality. If this is the case, then $c = ab$.

One of the core assumptions, when considering pairings, is the bilinear Diffie–Hellman (BDH) problem.

DEFINITION 5.4.– *Bilinear Diffie–Hellman (BDH): Let $\mathcal{BG}$ be a bilinear group generator. We say that the BDH assumption holds in $\mathcal{BG}$ if for every PPT $\mathcal{A}$:*

$$\Pr\left[D = e(g,g)^{abc} \,\middle|\, \begin{array}{l} \text{bgp} := (p, \mathbb{G}, \mathbb{G}_T, e) \leftarrow \mathcal{BG}(1^\lambda), a, b, c \leftarrow \mathbb{Z}_p \\ D \leftarrow \mathcal{A}(\text{bgp}, (g^a, g^b, g^c)) \end{array} \right] = \text{negl}(\lambda)$$

Like for most problems, it is possible to define a decisional version (arguably slightly weaker) that proves useful in various schemes.

Having elements in the target group in the hypothesis could be cumbersome, so other families of hypotheses have been introduced in order to have cleaner version of the problem. Depending on the type of curves used, they each have their uses.

DEFINITION 5.5.– *Decisional linear (DLin (Boneh et al. 2004)): The decisional linear hypothesis says that in a multiplicative group $(p, \mathbb{G}, g)$ when we are given $(g^x, g^y, g^{\alpha x}, g^{\beta y}, g^\psi)$ for unknown random $\alpha, \beta, x, y \in \mathbb{Z}_p$, it is hard to decide whether $\psi = \alpha + \beta$.*

DEFINITION 5.6.– *External Diffie–Hellman in $\mathbb{G}_1$ (XDH (Boneh et al. 2004)): This variant of the previous hypothesis states that in a type II bilinear group, given $(g_1^\mu, g_1^\nu, g_1^\psi)$ for unknown $\mu, \nu \in \mathbb{Z}_p$, it is hard to decide whether $\psi = \mu\nu$. (In other words, DDH is hard in $\mathbb{G}_1$.) A variant can say that DDH is hard in $\mathbb{G}_2$.*

DEFINITION 5.7.– *Symmetric external Diffie–Hellman (SXDH (Ateniese et al. 2005)): This last variant, used mostly in type III bilinear groups, states that DDH is hard in both $\mathbb{G}_1$ and $\mathbb{G}_2$.*

5.2.2.1. *One assumption to rule them all*

In 2013, Escala et al. (2013) proposed a framework generalizing those hypotheses. They proposed to view a problem as a matrix of group elements, together with a challenge vector (once again composed of group elements), and the decisional problems now consists of guessing whether the vector is in the span of the matrix or not. Such an approach has several advantages, as it allows to quickly scale hypothesis to any size, then it allows to unify some approaches on pairing-based cryptography, and lattices (and even code-based theory) by presenting un-noisy version of the problems.

In addition, the authors managed to show the existence of unexploited assumptions whose difficulty is similar to classical ones but which admits a shorter representation.

For $s \in \{1, 2\}$ and scalars $(a_{ij}) \in \mathbb{Z}_p^{\beta \times \alpha}$ we denote $\mathbf{A}_s$ the matrix

$$\mathbf{A}_s = \begin{pmatrix} g_s^{a_{11}} & \cdots & g_s^{a_{1\alpha}} \\ \vdots & \ddots & \vdots \\ g_s^{a_{\beta 1}} & \cdots & g_s^{a_{\beta\alpha}} \end{pmatrix} \in \mathbb{G}_s^{\beta \times \alpha}.$$

DEFINITION 5.8.– *Let $m, k \in \mathbb{N}$, such that $m > k$. We call $\mathcal{D}_k[m, k]$ a matrix distribution if it outputs matrices in $\mathbb{Z}_p^{m \times k}$ of full rank k in polynomial time (without loss of generality, we assume the first k rows of $\mathbf{M} \leftarrow \mathcal{D}_k[m, k]$ form an invertible matrix). We write $\mathcal{D}_k := \mathcal{D}_k[k + 1, k]$.*

DEFINITION 5.9.– *For all adversary $\mathcal{A}$, for $s \in \{1, 2\}$, the advantage function is defined as follows:*

$$\mathsf{Adv}_{\mathcal{A}, \mathbb{G}_s}^{\mathsf{mddh}}(\lambda) = |\Pr[\mathcal{A}(\mathbf{U}_s, \mathbf{U}\mathbf{x}_s) = 1] - \Pr[\mathcal{A}(\mathbf{U}_s, \mathbf{z}_s) = 1]|$$

where $\mathbf{U} \leftarrow \mathcal{D}_k$, $\mathbf{x} \leftarrow \mathbb{Z}_p^k$ *and* $\mathbf{z} \leftarrow \mathbb{Z}_p^{k+1}$ *(the index s meaning the use of group elements in* $\mathbb{G}_s$ *with the corresponding scalars as exponents). The* mddh *assumption states that* $\mathsf{Adv}_{\mathcal{A},\mathbb{G}_s}^{\mathsf{mddh}}(\lambda)$ *is negligible in λ for all* ppt *adversary $\mathcal{A}$.*

From this, one can find classical assumptions: $\mathcal{D}_1$ is simply the classical decisional Diffie–Hellman assumption.

Then for a given k, one can single out three main assumptions:

1) The uniform assumption $\mathcal{D}_k$, where all coefficients are sampled at random.

2) The linear assumption $\mathcal{DL}_k$, where $a_{ij} = 0 \iff i \neq j \wedge i < k + 1$, and $a_{(k+1)j} = 1$. In this case, $\mathcal{DL}_2$ is simply the decisional linear assumption.

3) The cascade assumption $\mathcal{DC}_k$, where $a_{ij} = 0 \iff j \neq i \wedge j - 1 \neq i$, and $a_{ij} = 1 \iff i = j - 1$.

$$\mathcal{D}_2 : \mathbf{A} = \begin{pmatrix} g^{a_{11}} & g^{a_{12}} \\ g^{a_{21}} & g^{a_{22}} \\ g^{a_{31}} & g^{a_{32}} \end{pmatrix}, \mathcal{DL}_2 : \mathbf{A} = \begin{pmatrix} g^{a_{11}} & 1_{\mathbb{G}} \\ 1_{\mathbb{G}} & g^{a_{22}} \\ g & g \end{pmatrix}, \mathcal{DC}_2 : \mathbf{A} = \begin{pmatrix} g^{a_{11}} & 1_{\mathbb{G}} \\ g & g^{a_{22}} \\ 1_{\mathbb{G}} & g \end{pmatrix}$$

Figure 5.3. *Examples of the assumptions, in the case $k = 2$*

NOTE.– It should be noted, that in the case where $k = 1$, those three assumptions are the same. It should also be noted that the uniform variant is harder than the two others; in other words, for any ppt adversary $\mathcal{A}$, there exist ppt adversaries $\mathcal{B}, \mathcal{C}$ such that $\mathsf{Adv}_{\mathcal{A},\mathcal{G}_s}^{\mathsf{unif}}(\lambda) \leq \mathsf{Adv}_{\mathcal{B},\mathcal{G}_s}^{\mathsf{lin}}(\lambda)$ and $\mathsf{Adv}_{\mathcal{A},\mathcal{G}_s}^{\mathsf{unif}}(\lambda) \leq \mathsf{Adv}_{\mathcal{C},\mathcal{G}_s}^{\mathsf{casc}}(\lambda)$.

All those assumptions can be shown to be hard in the generic group model, where law operations are applied by calling an oracle, and inputs are available to the reduction.

The main goal of these news assumptions was to prepare to define compact versions:

1) The incremental linear assumption $\mathcal{IL}_k$, where $a_{ij} = 0 \iff i \neq j \wedge i < k+1$, $a_{(k+1)j} = 1$ and $a_{ij} = a + i - 1$ otherwise.

2) The symmetric cascade assumption is even more simple $\mathcal{SC}_k$, where $a_{ij} = 0 \iff j \neq i \wedge j - 1 \neq i$, $a_{ij} = 1 \iff i = j - 1$, and $a_{ij} = a$ otherwise.

When counting the elements needed to represent a problem, $\mathcal{D}_k$ needs $k(k + 1)$ group elements, where both $\mathcal{C}_k, \mathcal{L}_k$ only need k of them, and $\mathcal{SC}_k, \mathcal{IL}_k$ require only 1.

$$\mathcal{IL}_2 : \mathbf{A} = \begin{pmatrix} g^a & 1_\mathbb{G} \\ 1_\mathbb{G} & g^{a+1} \\ g & g \end{pmatrix}, \mathcal{SC}_2 : \mathbf{A} = \begin{pmatrix} g^a & 1_\mathbb{G} \\ g & g^a \\ 1_\mathbb{G} & g \end{pmatrix}$$

Figure 5.4. *Compact version of the assumptions, in the case* $k = 2$

Figure 5.5 shows the hierarchy between the various assumptions. For a given k, the symmetric cascade and the incremental linear assumption are equivalent. They are both stronger (easier to break) than the cascade and linear assumptions. And those two are stronger than the generic matrix assumption. It should however be noted that there are no known relation between the cascade assumption and the linear assumption.

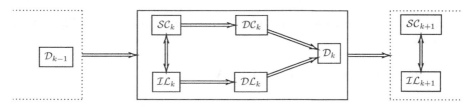

Figure 5.5. *Hierarchy of matrix assumptions*

In addition, as a $k + 1$ linear map allows to break any k-matrix Diffie–Hellman assumption, we can also determine that we can rank the assumption by increasing k, with them getting harder to break when k increases.

DEFINITION 5.10.– *For all adversary $\mathcal{A}$, the advantage function* $\mathrm{Adv}_{\mathcal{A},\mathcal{BG}}^{\mathrm{bmddh}}(\lambda)$ *is defined by*

$$|\Pr[\mathcal{A}(\mathbf{V}_1, \mathbf{V}_2, \mathbf{V}\mathbf{y}_1, \mathbf{V}\mathbf{y}_2) = 1] - \Pr[\mathcal{A}(\mathbf{V}_1, \mathbf{V}_2, \mathbf{z}_1, \mathbf{z}_2) = 1]|$$

where $\mathbf{V} \leftarrow \mathcal{D}_k$, $\mathbf{y} \leftarrow \mathbb{Z}_p^k$ *and* $\mathbf{z} \leftarrow \mathbb{Z}_p^{k+1}$. *The* bmddh *assumption states that* $\mathrm{Adv}_{\mathcal{A},\mathcal{BG}}^{\mathrm{bmddh}}(\lambda)$ *is negligible in λ for all* ppt *adversary $\mathcal{A}$.*

NOTE.– The bilateral variant (bmddh) is provably no weaker (in the generic group model) than the unilateral variant in the symmetric bilinear groups. Bilateral variant of the DLIN assumption in asymmetric pairings has already been used in prior works (Libert et al. 2015; Agrawal and Chase 2017) and has been used in a matrix-based generalized form in Fuchsbauer and Gay (2018). We further note that bmddh[1] is not secure and one can only use bmddh[k] for $k \geq 2$.

DEFINITION 5.11.– *For all adversary $\mathcal{A}$, for $s \in \{1,2\}$, the advantage function is defined as follows:*

$$\mathsf{Adv}_{\mathcal{A},\mathbb{G}_s}^{\mathsf{ker-dh}}(\lambda) = \Pr[\mathbf{z} \in \mathbf{orth}(\mathbf{U}) | \mathbf{z}_{3-s} \leftarrow \mathcal{A}(\mathbf{U}_s)]$$

where $\mathbf{U} \leftarrow \mathcal{D}_k$. *The* $\mathsf{ker-dh}$ *assumption states that* $\mathsf{Adv}_{\mathcal{A},\mathbb{G}_s}^{\mathsf{ker-dh}}(\lambda)$ *is negligible in* λ *for all* ppt *adversary* $\mathcal{A}$.

NOTE.– The winning condition is efficiently checkable using the pairing function: $\mathbf{z} \in \mathbf{orth}(\mathbf{U}) \iff e(\mathbf{z}^\top{}_1, \mathbf{U}_2) = \mathbf{1}_T \iff e(\mathbf{U}^\top{}_1, \mathbf{z}_2) = \mathbf{1}_T$. Morillo et al. (2016) showed that mddh $\Rightarrow$ ker $-$ dh, that is, for any ppt adversary $\mathcal{A}$, there exists a ppt adversary $\mathcal{B}$ such that $\mathsf{Adv}_{\mathcal{A},\mathbb{G}_s}^{\mathsf{ker-dh}}(\lambda) \leq \mathsf{Adv}_{\mathcal{B},\mathbb{G}_s}^{\mathsf{mddh}}(\lambda)$.

DEFINITION 5.12.– *For all adversary $\mathcal{A}$, the advantage function* $\mathsf{Adv}_{\mathcal{A},\mathcal{BG}}^{\mathsf{bker-dh}}(\lambda)$ *is defined by*

$$\Pr[\mathbf{z} \in \mathbf{orth}(\mathbf{V}) | \mathbf{z}_1 \text{ OR } \mathbf{z}_2 \leftarrow \mathcal{A}(\mathbf{V}_1, \mathbf{V}_2)]$$

where $\mathbf{V} \leftarrow \mathcal{D}_k$. *The* $\mathsf{bker-dh}$ *assumption states that* $\mathsf{Adv}_{\mathcal{A},\mathcal{BG}}^{\mathsf{bker-dh}}(\lambda)$ *is negligible in* λ *for all* ppt *adversary* $\mathcal{A}$.

NOTE.– Once again, bker $-$ dh[1] is not secure and one can only use bker $-$ dh[k] for $k \geq 2$.

Following (Morillo et al. 2016), it is easy to show that bmddh $\Rightarrow$ bker $-$ dh, that is, for any ppt adversary $\mathcal{A}$, there exists a ppt adversary $\mathcal{B}$ such that $\mathsf{Adv}_{\mathcal{A},\mathcal{BG}}^{\mathsf{bker-dh}}(\lambda) \leq \mathsf{Adv}_{\mathcal{B},\mathcal{BG}}^{\mathsf{bmddh}}(\lambda)$.

5.3. A new world of cryptographic protocols at your fingertips

The discrete logarithm problem allowed to introduce a linear one-way function $\mathcal{F}_a : g \in \mathbb{G} \rightarrow g^a$; however, there was no way to check that two pairs of input and outputs were generated by the same function, or not without giving explicitly the secret trapdoor a.

Thanks to pairings, given two pairs of input and output, one can now check that they were generated by the same function, without having to reveal the trapdoor. Given $(x_1, y_1), (x_2, y_2)$, one can simply compare $e(x_1, y_2)$ and $e(x_2, y_1)$ without having to know explicitly the discrete logarithm.

This extra verification allows to overcome limitation from *pure* discrete Logarithm-based constructions, where there was no way to combine elements without knowing the secret.

5.3.1. *Identity-based encryption made easy*

In 1984, A. Shamir introduced the concept of identity-based encryption (see Chapter 7). For 17 years, building such a scheme remained an open question (at least in the academic circles).

However, only 1 year after the introduction of pairings, the extra magical step they provide allowed the emergence of a practical instantiation of this primitive by Boneh and Franklin (2001). They simply exploited the fact that the pairing allows to combine three elements:

– a hash value of the identity mapped into the group, with unknown discrete logarithm (while it exists, and will be known by the simulator only in the security analysis);

– an encapsulation (whose discrete logarithm is only known by the emitter);

– a master public key (whose discrete logarithm is known by the central authority).

In Figure 5.6, we represent the identity-based key encapsulation mechanism (IBKEM) associated with the Boneh–Franklin construction. To obtain their identity-based encryption, one then simply has to use the generated key as the nonce for a one time occurrence of the message.

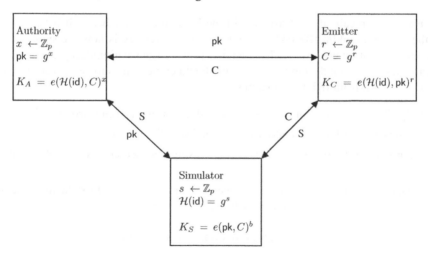

Figure 5.6. *Representation of Boneh–Franklin identity-based key encapsulation mechanism as a tripartie Diffie–Hellman exchange*

Of course, one key participant is missing from such a protocol, the user. In this case, he/she would receive from the authority an intermediate value mixing the hash evaluation on his identity with the secret key: $\mathsf{usk}[\mathsf{id}] = \mathcal{H}(\mathsf{id})^x$. Interestingly, he can check whether the authority sent the correct value by checking whether: $e(\mathsf{usk}[\mathsf{id}], g) = e(\mathcal{H}(\mathsf{id}), \mathsf{pk})$.

We can see that any outsider would only see three group elements, without knowing a single discrete logarithm. This is exactly the setting of the tripartite Diffie–Hellman as originally introduced and a posteriori it should come to no surprise that getting the latter leads to an efficient (and secure) construction of such an identity-based scheme.

5.3.2. *Efficient deterministic compact signature*

Until the emergence of pairings, most existing discrete-logarithm based schemes were variations of the ElGamal signature scheme (ElGamal 1985). Those schemes have two main drawbacks: the signature is composed of two scalars and the signature has to be probabilistic.

However, in 2001, Boneh et al. (2001) introduced an extra compact deterministic signature that can be provably shown to be secure under the computational Diffie–Hellman assumption in the Random Oracle Model.

Figure 5.7 recalls the construction of the BLS signature scheme. It is very close to the Boneh–Franklin IBKEM, where the user's secret key is now the signature σ, and the verification consists of checking the correct encapsulation/decapsulation for a randomness $r = 1$ on the emitter side. This should come to no surprise because of the Naor transform from IBE to Signatures.

CRS: $(p, \mathbb{G}, \mathbb{G}_T, e)$, $\mathcal{H}$ a collision resistant hash function mapping strings to $\mathbb{G}$.

– KeyGen(1^λ): Picks a random $x \in \mathbb{Z}_p$, and sets $\mathsf{sk} = x, \mathsf{pk} = g^x$.

– Sign(sk, M): To sign a message M using the secret key, simply outputs $\mathcal{H}(M)^x \in \mathbb{G}$.

– KeyGen(pk, σ, M): To check whether a signature σ is valid for the message M under the verification key, pk checks whether $e(\sigma, g) = e(\mathcal{H}(M), \mathsf{pk})$.

Figure 5.7. *Boneh–Lynn–Shacham signature scheme*

One can see that all the difficulty of the signature is being able to compute σ from $g, g^x, \mathcal{H}(M)$, in other words, solving this instance of the computational Diffie–Hellman problem.

The pairings here are crucial; on the one hand, they allow a public verification of the signatures without any trapdoor, and on the other hand, because they are non-degenerated they ensure that if the equation holds, then the σ provided is the solution to the computational Diffie–Hellman challenge.

5.4. References

Agrawal, S. and Chase, M. (2017). FAME: Fast attribute-based message encryption. In *ACM CCS 2017*, Thuraisingham, B.M., Evans, D., Malkin, T., Xu, D. (eds). ACM Press.

Ateniese, G., Camenisch, J., Hohenberger, S., de Medeiros, B. (2005). Practical group signatures without random oracles. Cryptology ePrint Archive, Report 2005/385 [Online]. Available at: https://eprint.iacr.org/2005/385.

Boneh, D. and Franklin, M.K. (2001). Identity-based encryption from the Weil pairing. In *CRYPTO 2001*, vol. 2139 of *LNCS*, Kilian, J. (ed.). Springer, Heidelberg.

Boneh, D., Lynn, B., Shacham, H. (2001). Short signatures from the Weil pairing. In *ASIACRYPT 2001*, vol. 2248 of *LNCS*, Boyd, C. (ed.). Springer, Heidelberg.

Boneh, D., Boyen, X., Shacham, H. (2004). Short group signatures. In *CRYPTO 2004*, vol. 3152 of *LNCS*, Franklin, M. (ed.). Springer, Heidelberg.

Diffie, W. and Hellman, M.E. (1976). New directions in cryptography. *IEEE Transactions on Information Theory*, 22(6), 644–654.

ElGamal, T. (1985). A public key cryptosystem and a signature scheme based on discrete logarithms. *IEEE Transactions on Information Theory*, 31(4), 469–472.

Escala, A., Herold, G., Kiltz, E., Ràfols, C., Villar, J. (2013). An algebraic framework for Diffie–Hellman assumptions. In *CRYPTO 2013, Part II*, vol. 8043 of *LNCS*, Canetti, R., Garay, J.A. (eds). Springer, Heidelberg.

Frey, G. and Rück, H.-G. (1994). A remark concerning m-divisibility and the discrete logarithm in the divisor class group of curves. *Mathematics of Computation*, 62(206), 865–874.

Fuchsbauer, G. and Gay, R. (2018). Weakly secure equivalence-class signatures from standard assumptions. In *PKC 2018, Part II*, vol. 10770 of *LNCS*, Abdalla, M., Dahab, R. (eds). Springer, Heidelberg.

Galbraith, S., Paterson, K., Smart, N. (2006). Pairings for cryptographers. Cryptology ePrint Archive, Report 2006/165 [Online]. Available at: https://eprint.iacr.org/2006/165.

Joux, A. (2004). A one round protocol for tripartite Diffie–Hellman. *Journal of Cryptology*, 17(4), 263–276.

Koblitz, N. (1987). Elliptic curve cryptosystems. *Mathematics of Computation*, 48(177), 203–209.

Libert, B., Peters, T., Joye, M., Yung, M. (2015). Compactly hiding linear spans – Tightly secure constant-size simulation-sound QA-NIZK proofs and applications. In *ASIACRYPT 2015, Part I*, vol. 9452 of *LNCS*, Iwata, T., Cheon, J.H. (eds). Springer, Heidelberg.

Menezes, A.J., Okamoto, T., Vanstone, S.A. (1993). Reducing elliptic curve logarithms to logarithms in a finite field. *IEEE Transactions on Information Theory*, 39(5), 1639–1646.

Miller, V.S. (1986). Use of elliptic curves in cryptography. In *CRYPTO'85*, vol. 218 of *LNCS*, Williams, H.C. (ed.) Springer, Heidelberg.

Morillo, P., Ràfols, C., Villar, J.L. (2016). The kernel matrix Diffie–Hellman assumption. In *ASIACRYPT 2016, Part I*, vol. 10031 of *LNCS*, Cheon, J.H., Takagi, T. (eds). Springer, Heidelberg.

Tate, J. (1958). wc-groups over p-adic fields. *Séminaire Bourbaki : années 1956/57 – 1957/58, exposés 137–168*, 4(1958), exposé 156.

6

Broadcast Encryption and Traitor Tracing

Duong Hieu Phan
Telecom Paris – Institut Polytechnique de Paris, France

6.1. Introduction

The oldest goal of cryptography is to allow parties to communicate in a secure manner over an insecure channel which might be under adversarial control. Nowadays, confidentiality remains one of the main goals, besides authentication and integrity.

Classical standard protocols for confidentiality, named *encryption*, are implemented in a "one-to-one" communication framework: a sender encrypts the message and sends the ciphertext to a receiver who has the secret key to decrypt the ciphertext. The objective, from a security point of view, is to prevent an outside attacker (who observes and may be able to interact with the system) to break the confidentiality, that is, to recover some information about the original message. The situation will not be exactly the same when one generalizes "one-to-one" to "one-to-many" communication, a.k.a. multi-receiver encryption, where the sender needs to send a secret message to many receivers. At first glance, one might think that the trivial solution consisting of sharing a common secret key among all legitimate receivers would be sufficient. However, this is not the case, mainly because the security notions in "one-to-many" communications need to be extended to meet practical requirements. As the old saying goes: when a secret is known by more than one person, it is not a secret anymore. Therefore, if a common secret key

Asymmetric Cryptography,
coordinated by David POINTCHEVAL. © ISTE Ltd. 2022.

is shared among all the receivers, then one of the receivers can give it to the adversary. Consequently, on the one hand, the confidentiality of the whole system is totally broken, and on the other hand, we have no idea who the source of secret leakage is and we cannot detect and exclude this dishonest user (commonly called a traitor), since all the receivers have the same secret key.

In "one-to-many" communications, there are new fundamental security requirements for the security to deal with access control and traceability.

– Access control guarantees that only legitimate or target users have the right to decrypt the message. The resulting schemes are generally called *broadcast encryption* (BE in short). In practical applications, such as pay-TV, the target set is often very large and contains almost all the users except some non-paying ones (who should be revoked from the system), the target set is implicitly determined via the revoked set and the corresponding system is commonly called a *revocation scheme*. Broadcast encryption and revocation schemes can be covered by more general primitives such as attribute-based encryption that is presented in Chapter 7. However, when applying a general framework to a concrete primitive, this often results in impractical schemes. We will give a discussion about recent advancements of this approach at the end of this chapter.

– While access control is quite natural to be considered in "one-to-many" communications, traceability is a new property which is "orthogonal" to the main objectives of classical cryptographic systems. Since one cannot totally prevent receivers from leaking their secret keys in "one-to-many" communications, we should discourage them from doing this. In fact, when a user joins the system and commits himself to respect the security requirement by not revealing any secret information, and if the user knows that the source of any secret information leakage will be detected, then dishonest users are deterred from revealing their secret. A multi-receiver encryption scheme with the ability to trace traitors is called a *traitor tracing* (TT).

Before giving a technical overview of broadcast encryption and TT, let us discuss some impacts in practice of these primitives.

PRACTICAL IMPACT.– Broadcast encryption and TT have received quite a lot of attention due to their practical impact, especially in pay-TV and in positioning systems. In the context of pay-TV, piracy has an increasingly alarming and direct impact on the revenues of broadcasters. In Loebbecke and Fischer (2005), it specifies that "the European Association for the Protection of Encrypted Works and Services (AEPOC) estimates that annual revenues from pirate cards and manipulated set-top boxes in the EU amount to at least one billion euros" (AEPOC, 2003). Another report from Datamonitor estimates that between 2004 and 2010, the loss for broadcast operators would have been around 681 million euros for a 3.2 billion euros benefit over the same period. Recent years have witnessed the emergence of a growing global black economy based on piracy. In the context of positioning systems, we can look at the Galileo European project to build a global navigation satellite system (whose cost is estimated at 3.4 billion euros); broadcast methods are at the core of Galileo to operate group management, that is, to allow or deny access to some of its services.

Due to a large number of potential multi-receiver scenarios, it is highly unlikely that a single solution will fit them all. This motivates a trade-off between efficiency parameters and security levels. The goal is to construct schemes that are flexible enough to fit a variety of scenarios in a way that is optimal (or close to optimal) and of which the security levels are rigorously investigated. This chapter is therefore devoted to present an overview of the different techniques for designing broadcast encryption and TT.

6.2. Security notions for broadcast encryption and TT

The main goal of a BE scheme is to enable the sender of a message to choose any subset of users (called the *target set* or the *privileged set*) to which the message will be encrypted. The target set can be directly determined by the sender or can be implicitly determined via its complement (the revoked set). In the latter case, the resulting scheme is called a *revocation scheme*.

Theoretically, it requires N bits to uniquely identify a subset of a set of size N. However, if the size r of the revoked set is small, it is sufficient to identify the revoked users, which can be done using $r \log N$ bits. The same technique applies if the target set is small. In practice, we should notice that the target set is quite stable (e.g. in pay-TV, the target set is almost stable during the whole month) and we only need to communicate the modifications between two periods. It was often sufficient to consider group key distribution where one user is added to or removed from the target group: it corresponds to a broadcast encryption where one user is added or removed from the target set. In general, it is widely accepted – which we also follow in this chapter – that the size of the description of the target set is not taken into account when broadcast encryption schemes are compared.

DEFINITIONS.– Broadcast encryption is conventionally formalized as *broadcast encapsulation* in which a session key is produced and this session key is required to be indistinguishable from random, under the adversarial view. Such a scheme can provide public encryption functionality in combination with a symmetric encryption through the hybrid encryption (a.k.a. KEM-DEM) paradigm (Cramer and Shoup 2003). Formally, a (public-key) *dynamic* broadcast encapsulation scheme is a tuple of four algorithms BE $=$ (Setup, Join, Encaps, Decaps) where: Setup(1^k) outputs (msk, ek) containing the master secret key and the (initial) encryption key; Join(msk, i) outputs the key pair (sk_i, pk_i) for user i, and updates system parameters to include the information of the users i (by appending pk_i to ek and sk_i to msk); Encaps(ek, S) for a set of users S outputs (H, K) containing a ciphertext (a.k.a. key header) and a session key (for a revocation scheme, one replaces S by R to define the target set); Decaps(ek, sk_i, S, H) outputs K if $i \in S$ (or $i \notin R$ in a revocation scheme) and $\perp$ otherwise.

In some static schemes, the setup algorithm takes as input N the number of users and returns the secret keys for all users. This can be made compliant with our definition by defining msk to contain the concatenation of the users' secret keys and defining Join to simply return the ith key contained in msk.

The correctness requirement is that for any subset S of users and for any $i \in S$: If [(msk, ek) $\leftarrow$ Setup(1^k), $K_i \leftarrow$ Join(msk, i), $(H, K) \leftarrow$ Encaps(ek, S)] then Decaps(K_i, S, H) = K. For revocation schemes, the definition is the same except that S is replaced with R, and we require that $i \notin R$.

TRACEABILITY.– We can add traceability in a broadcast encryption to get a *trace&revoke* scheme. Formally, a trace&revoke encapsulation scheme is a broadcast encapsulation scheme with an additional tracing algorithm Trace$^{\mathbb{D}}$($R_{\mathbb{D}}$, pk, msk): the TT algorithm interacts in a black-box manner with a pirate decoder $\mathbb{D}$ that is built from a certain set T of traitors. The algorithm takes as input a subset $R_{\mathbb{D}} \subset [N]$ (suppose that, at the time of tracing, there are N users in the system and $R_{\mathbb{D}}$ can be adversarially chosen), the public key pk, the master key msk and outputs a set $T_{\mathbb{D}} \subseteq [N]$. Under the conditions that the target set $S_{\mathbb{D}} = ([N] - R_{\mathbb{D}})$ contains at least one traitor and the pirate decoder $\mathbb{D}$ is "efficient" to decrypt ciphertexts (i.e. decrypts with some non-negligible probability), then the tracing algorithm outputs at least one traitor in $S_{\mathbb{D}}$, that is, $\emptyset \neq T_{\mathbb{D}} \subseteq T \cap S_{\mathbb{D}}$.

The above definition captures both the functionalities of revoking users and tracing traitors in a general black-box model. However, there are many other models for tracing such as *non-black-box tracing*, *single-key black-box tracing* and *black-box confirmation* models (Boneh and Franklin 1999) and tracing for *stateful pirates* (Kiayias and Yung 2002b). The objective of the tracing procedure could also be relaxed in some situation where it might be sufficient for the authority to disable pirate decoders. In a *bounded model*, one supposes that the maximum number of traitors is bounded by some parameter t.

A TT scheme is in fact a trace&revoke scheme without the possibility to revoke users, namely the target set is always set to be the whole set of users. The combination of traceability and revocation is challenging and they are often studied independently.

SECURITY NOTIONS.– The strongest security model, namely the adaptive CCA security game for a dynamic broadcast encryption, can be modeled as a classical CCA game between a challenger and an adversary: The challenger runs Setup(1^k) to initialize the system and gives the adversary the encryption key; the adversary has adaptive access to oracles to decrypt chosen ciphertexts, to join new users to the system and to corrupt some of them getting back all their secret keys; the adversary finally outputs a set S of receivers it wants to attack which must not contain any corrupted user; the challenger then computes $(H, K) \leftarrow \mathsf{Encaps}(\mathsf{ek}, S)$, then flips a coin $b \xleftarrow{\$} \{0, 1\}$ and sets $K_b = K$, $K_{1-b} \xleftarrow{\$} \mathcal{K}$ and returns (S, H, K_0, K_1) to the adversary; the adversary then continues to have adaptive access to oracles, except to corrupt users in S and outputs his guess bit b'. The adversary wins the game iff $|\Pr[b' = b] - \frac{1}{2}|$ is non-negligible.

In the CCA1 version, the adversary has access to the decryption oracle only before the challenge phase. In the CPA version, the adversary does not have access to the decryption oracle.

6.3. Overview of broadcast encryption and TT

Broadcast encryption was first described by Fiat and Naor (1994). BE then did not receive much attention until the beginning of the years 2000, when Naor et al. (2001) presented their (symmetric-key) subset-cover framework along with a security model and a security analysis. Since then, many BE schemes have been proposed and the subset cover framework has become the basis for many subsequent proposals, including Dodis and Fazio (2003), who proposed the first public-key broadcast encryption.

Boneh et al. (2005) are first to propose a fully collusion-resistant public-key broadcast encryption in which the ciphertext size is constant. They proposed two schemes, respectively, CPA and CCA secure, both in the selective model of security where the adversary is required to choose the corrupted users before the setup.

Adaptive security is proposed by Gentry and Waters (2009) where the authors give several schemes, which achieve adaptive CPA security, including two broadcast encryption schemes and two identity-based broadcast encryption (IBBE) schemes, one of them achieves constant-size ciphertexts in the random oracle model. The schemes proposed in Waters (2009) and Lewko et al. (2010), respectively, a broadcast encryption and a revocation scheme, are the only secure schemes under static assumptions (as opposed to the so called q-type ones). Lewko et al. (2010) also propose an identity-based revocation scheme, which is proved selective CPA secure.

Dynamic broadcast encryption is proposed in Delerablée et al. (2007) where they design CPA secure schemes with only partially adaptive security. Strictly speaking, their scheme is a *revocation* scheme in which the set of revoked users is selected at the time of encryption, and in turn, any user outside of the revoked set is able to decrypt. Delerablée (2007) proposes identity-based broadcast encryption and gives a selective CPA secure scheme. Based on BGW scheme, a constant-size adaptive CCA secure *inclusive-exclusive* broadcast encryption scheme is proposed in Phan et al. (2013), in which one can act both as a broadcast encryption and as a revocation scheme at the same time. A concrete evaluation of this scheme can be found in Dubois et al. (2013).

Very recently, Agrawal and Yamada (2020b) achieved optimal broadcast encryption from attribute-based encryption. As broadcast functionality can be expressed as a policy circuit with linear size in width (by simply checking whether the user is in the target set or not), their main idea is to propose an ABE scheme whose size is independent from width. They also give instantiation based on the learning with errors assumption (LWE) along with assumptions on bilinear maps. However, this construction could only be proven secure in the generic bilinear group. Their improved work (Agrawal and Yamada 2020a) relies on the Knowledge of OrthogonALity Assumption (KOALA) (Beullens and Wee 2019) on bilinear groups and it is still open to construct an optimal broadcast encryption from standard assumptions.

The first formal definition of TT scheme appears (Chor et al. 1994, 2000) in which the construction requires storage, decryption time complexity of $O(t^2 \log^2 t \log(N/t))$ and communication complexity of $O(t^3 \log^4 t \log(N/t))$, where N is the size of the users and t is the upper bound on the number of traitors. Stinson and Wei (1998) later suggest explicit combinatorial constructions that achieve better efficiency for small values of t and N.

Boneh and Franklin (1999) present an efficient public-key TT scheme with deterministic tracing, up to t traitors, based on an algebraic approach. Its communication, storage and decryption complexities are all $O(t)$. The authors also introduce the notion of *non-black-box traceability*: given a "valid" key extracted from a pirate device (constructed using the keys of at most t users), one recovers the identity of at least one traitor. This is in contrast with the notion of *black-box tracing* where the traitor's identity can be uncovered by only observing the pirate decoder's replies on "well crafted" ciphertexts. Unfortunately, Kiayias and Yung (2001) show that black-box tracing cannot be efficient (say, in polynomial time) in this type of scheme whenever the number of traitors is super-logarithmic. The Boneh-Franklin scheme can however achieve *black-box confirmation*: given a superset of the traitors, it is guaranteed to find at least one traitor and no innocent suspect is incriminated. Boneh et al. (2006) and Boneh and Waters (2006) propose TT schemes that withstand any number of traitors (*full traceability*) while requiring a sub-linear ciphertext length of $O(\sqrt{N})$; Zhandry (2020) moreover improves this result to $O(N^{\frac{1}{3}})$. Recently, Boneh and Zhandry (2014) propose a fully collusion-resistant scheme with poly-log size parameters. It relies on indistinguishability obfuscation (Garg et al. 2013), of which security foundation remains to be studied and practicality remains to be exhibited.

Pfitzmann (1996) introduces the notion of *asymmetric* TT. In this model, the tracer uncovers some secret information about the traitor that was a priori unknown to the system manager. Thus, the result of the tracing algorithm provides evidence of the malicious behavior. Further results in this direction are in Kurosawa and Desmedt (1998); Kurosawa and Yoshida (2002); Kiayias and Yung (2002a). The notion of *public traceability*, that is, the possibility of running tracing procedure on public information, was put forth in Chabanne et al. (2005). Some schemes (Chabanne et al. 2005; Phan et al. 2006; Boneh and Waters 2006; Boneh and Zhandry 2014; Ling et al. 2014) achieve public traceability and some others achieve a stronger notion than public traceability, namely the non-repudiation, but the setup in these schemes require some interactive protocol between the manager and each user, such as a secure 2-party computation protocol in Pfitzmann (1996), a commitment protocol in Pfitzmann and Waidner (1997) or an oblivious polynomial evaluation in Watanabe et al. (2001); Komaki et al. (2001); Kiayias and Yung (2002a).

Alternative TT solutions (Fiat and Tassa 2001; Berkman et al. 2000; Safavi-Naini and Wang 2003a) have also been proposed to fight against leakage of the decrypted content than against leakage of the decryption material.

A class of schemes relying on the use of collusion-secure codes (Boneh and Shaw 1995, 1998; Tardos 2003) has been introduced by Kiayias and Yung (2002c). These code-based schemes enjoy many nice and desirable properties: they support black-box tracing and the ratio between the ciphertexts and the plaintexts is constant. However, since these schemes use collusion-secure codes for both the ciphertext and the key used in the decoders, the sizes of the ciphertexts and keys are quite large. Another drawback of Kiayias and Yung (2002c); Chabanne et al. (2005) comes from the use of an all-or-nothing transform (AONT; Rivest 1997) to prevent deletion of keys from the pirate decoders as a way to escape the tracing procedure based on the underlying collusion-secure code. Billet and Phan (2008) and Boneh and Naor (2008) independently proposed schemes with constant-size ciphertext by relying on robust collusion-secure code (Safavi-Naini and Wang 2003b; Sirvent 2007). Subsequently, efficient robust codes were proposed in Nuida (2010) and Boneh et al. (2010). These schemes become quite competitive but their drawbacks remain the large private key size.

The first lattice-based TT scheme is introduced in Ling et al. (2014). This scheme is in the bounded model in which the security relies on the hardness of a new variant of the LWE problem, called k-LWE. This is an analog of the k-SIS problem introduced in Boneh and Freeman (2011). The Boneh–Freeman reduction from SIS to k-SIS suffers from an exponential loss in k and the authors in Ling et al. (2014) improved and extended it to an LWE to k-LWE reduction with a polynomial loss in k. The resulting TT scheme is therefore as effective as the underlying LWE encryption.

As originally observed in Gafni et al. (1999), TT schemes are most useful when combined with revocation schemes; such trace&revoke approach consists of first uncovering the compromised decryption keys and then revoking their decryption capabilities, thus making pirate decoders useless. We can name some schemes in this category (Naor and Pinkas 2001; Tzeng and Tzeng 2001; Naor et al. 2001; Dodis and Fazio 2002, 2003; Kim et al. 2003; Dodis et al. 2005; Boneh and Waters 2006; Ngo et al. 2013).

Recently, a new line of research for building trace&revoke schemes has emerged (Nishimaki et al. 2016; Kowalczyk et al. 2016; Agrawal and Rosen 2017; Agrawal et al. 2017; Goyal et al. 2018a, 2019a, 2019b). Nishimaki et al. (2016) provided a generic construction for trace&revoke from functional encryption schemes. Functional encryption (Sahai and Waters 2005; Boneh et al. 2011) is a generalization of public-key encryption allowing fine-grained access to encrypted data. We note that the strongest constructions in Nishimaki et al. (2016) are based on the existence of indistinguishability obfuscation (Barak et al. 2001), for which we do not at present have any candidate construction based on well-established hardness assumptions. One may also instantiate the NWZ compiler with a bounded-collusion functional encryption scheme, which can be based on standard assumptions such as the existence of public-key encryption (Gorbunov et al. 2012) or sub-exponential time hardness of learning with errors (LWE) (Goldwasser et al. 2013; Agrawal and Rosen 2017). For trace&revoke, this results in a construction that supports public black-box traceability and adaptive security in addition to anonymity of honest users and an exponential size universe of identities. However, the generic nature of their construction results in loss of concrete efficiency. For instance, when based on the bounded-collusion FE of Gorbunov et al. (2012), the resulting scheme has a ciphertext size growing at least as $O((r + t)^5 \mathcal{P}oly(\lambda))$ where r is the maximum size of the list of revoked users and t the maximum coalition size. By relying on learning with errors, this blowup can be improved to $O((r + t)^4 \mathcal{P}oly(\lambda))$ but at the cost of relying on heavy machinery such as attribute-based encryption (Gorbunov et al. 2013) and fully homomorphic encryption (Goldwasser et al. 2013). Additionally, this construction must also rely on complexity leveraging for adaptive security and learning with errors with sub-exponential error rates. The bounded-collusion FE of Agrawal and Rosen (2017) leads to better asymptotic bounds $O((r + t)^3 \mathcal{P}oly(\lambda))$ but suffers from large polynomial factors which hurt concrete efficiency. The paper by Agrawal et al. (2017) revisits the connection between functional encryption and trace-and-revoke systems and observes that the notion of FE required for bounded-collusion trace&revoke schemes is significantly weaker than that considered by Nishimaki et al. (2016): rather than FE for polynomial sized circuits, a weak variant of *inner-product* functional encryption (IPFE) (Abdalla et al. 2015; Agrawal et al. 2016) suffices. Consequently, efficient trace&revoke with black-box confirmation under standard assumptions, namely the DCR, LWE and DDH assumptions, are proposed in Agrawal et al. (2017) with ciphertext and key sizes that are *linear* in the sum of revoked list size r and maximum coalition size t. The construction of practical trace&revoke schemes in a full-collusion model still remains a challenge.

In the next sections, we will discuss the most relevant techniques in designing BE and TT schemes.

6.4. Tree-based methods

Combinatorial broadcast encryption schemes are mainly based on a tree structure or on a fingerprinting code. Tree-based schemes support revocation but have limited capacity dealing with tracing traitors, while code-based ones provide traceability but very few support revocation.

SUBSET-COVER FRAMEWORK.– The subset-cover framework is put forth by Aiello et al. (1998) and Naor et al. (2001) (which is also equivalent to the notion of an exclusive set system (Kumar and Russell 2003)). This is a powerful tool to design efficient trace&revoke systems. It captures the ideas from previously proposed TT systems and forms the basis of the so-called NNL scheme used in the content protection system for HD-DVDs known as AACS (AACS LA n.d.).

In the subset-cover framework, the set N of users in the system is covered by a collection of subsets S_i such that $\cup_i S_i \supset N$ and $S_i \cap N \neq \emptyset$. This covering is not a partition of N and the sets S_i rather overlap. To every subset S_i corresponds a long-term secret key L_i, and every user that belongs to S_i is provided with this secret key (or in an equivalent way, with some material that allows him to derive this secret key). Therefore, every user u of the system is given a collection of long-term keys $\{L_{i_k}\}$ that together form his/her secret key, which we denote by sk_u.

In order to broadcast a content M, the center uses a standard hybrid scheme: a session key K is first drawn randomly and used to encrypt the content (with an encryption scheme E') before being encapsulated under multiple long-term keys (with another encryption scheme E). The long-term keys L_{i_k}, for $k = 1, \ldots, l$, are chosen so that the corresponding subsets $S_{i_1}, \ldots, S_{i_l}$ only cover the set of users entitled to decrypt. Therefore, the center broadcasts ciphertexts of the form:

$$\left[\left(i_1, E_{L_{i_1}}(K) \right), \left(i_2, E_{L_{i_2}}(K) \right), \ldots, \left(i_l, E_{L_{i_l}}(K) \right) \parallel E'_K(M) \right]$$

To decrypt, a valid decoder for user u performs the following sequence of operations: it first looks for an index i_j in the first element of each of the l pairs $(i_k, E_{i_k}(K))$ such that $L_{i_j} \subset sk_u$. If no index corresponds, the decoder does not decrypt; otherwise, the decoder uses L_{i_j} to decrypt the associated encrypted session key $E_{i_j}(K)$ and then decrypts the payload $E'_K(M)$.

Since the system is built to handle revoked users, let us also denote by R the set of revoked users in the system at any point in time. In order to prevent them (individually but also together as a collusion) from accessing the encrypted content $E'_K(M)$, the collection $S_{i_1}, \ldots, S_{i_l}$ is specially crafted so that: $\bigcup_{k=1}^{l} S_{i_k} = N \setminus R$.

Two of the most efficient trace&revoke schemes under this framework are the complete subtree scheme and the subset difference scheme.

COMPLETE SUBTREE SCHEME.– In this scheme, the users correspond to the leaves of a complete binary tree, whereas the collection of subsets S_i exactly corresponds to all the possible subtrees in the complete tree. When $|N| = 2^n$, the complete binary tree is of depth n and there are exactly n subtrees that contain a given leaf. Figure 6.1 shows a covering using six subsets of twelve users that excludes four revoked users (depicted in black). This subset scheme complies with the bifurcation property since any subset (or equivalently any subtree of the complete binary tree) can be split into two subsets of equal size (the two subtrees rooted at the two descendants of the root of the original subtree). Regarding the key assignment, each user represented by a leaf u in the complete binary tree is provided with the keys L_i associated with the nodes i on the path from the leaf u to the root.

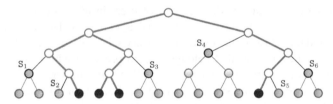

Figure 6.1. *Complete subtree: leaves correspond to users, $S_1, \ldots, S_6$ consist of the covering that excludes revoked users (in black) while allowing other users to decrypt. This is derived from the Steiner tree associated to the set of revoked users R*

Covering algorithm: In the case of the complete subtree, the covering used to exclude the $r = |R|$ revoked users from N is the collection of subsets that hang off the Steiner tree of the revoked leaves. (The Steiner tree of the revoked leaves is the minimal subtree of the complete binary tree that connects all the revoked leaves to the root and it is unique.) Since any user only knows the keys from its leaf to the root and since this path is included in the Steiner tree for revoked users, these users cannot decrypt anymore. This algorithm produces coverings of size $O(r \log(N/r))$.

SUBSET DIFFERENCE SCHEME.– The subset difference scheme has been introduced to lower the number of subsets required to partition the set of legitimate users $N \setminus R$. It improves the above complete subtree scheme by a factor of $\log(N/r)$ (therefore independent of the total number of users N) in terms of bandwidth usage for the headers.

Recall that S_i denotes the full binary subtree of the complete binary tree rooted at node i. Now, for each node j in S_i different from i, let us denote by $S_{i,j}$ the binary subtree rooted at node i of which the full binary subtree rooted at node j has been removed. By this definition, the covering algorithm, used to exclude the $r = |\mathsf{R}|$ revoked users, only needs $O(r)$ subsets. An example output of this procedure is shown in Figure 6.4.

To achieve this level of performance, the number of possible subsets has been tremendously increased. A user will need to know all the keys $L_{i,j}$ such that he/she belongs to the subtree rooted at i but not to the subtree rooted at j. However, it would be impossible for each device to store such a large number of long-term keys. This is why a key derivation procedure has been designed to allow the derivation of most of the $O(N)$ long-term keys: a user only needs to store $O(\log^2(N))$ keys. Each node i in the full binary tree is first assigned a random label LABEL_i, then labels $\mathsf{LABEL}_{i,j}$ together with their corresponding long-term keys $L_{i,j}$ are deduced (in a pseudo-random way) from label LABEL_i. The key derivation procedure then works as follows: from each LABEL_i, a pseudo-random value $\mathsf{LABEL}_{i,j}$ is obtained for each sub-node j using the tree-based construction proposed by Goldreich et al. (1984); from this value $\mathsf{LABEL}_{i,j}$, a long-term key $L_{i,j}$ is eventually deduced (in a pseudo-random way). Each user is then provided with labels $\mathsf{LABEL}_{i,j}$ for all nodes i that are on the path from the leaf that represents the user to the root and all nodes j hanging off this path.

This key assignment ensures that every user in the subtree rooted at node i but not in the subtree rooted at node j is able to derive $L_{i,j}$ while every user in the subtree rooted at node j is not able to derive $L_{i,j}$.

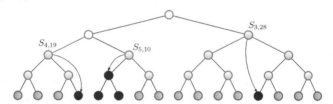

Figure 6.2. *Subset difference: leaves correspond to users and black nodes are not able to derive the necessary information to decrypt. Therefore,* $S_{4,19}$ *prevents user 19 from decrypting,* $S_{5,10}$ *prevents users 20 and 21 from decrypting and* $S_{3,28}$ *prevents user* 28 *from decrypting. All other users are able to decrypt*

The tracing procedure: The idea is to refine the covering initially used to broadcast ciphertexts so that the pirate decoder cannot decrypt with probability p higher than some threshold. To this end, the authors of Naor et al. (2001) suggest to use a hybrid argument: the pirate box is provided with "ciphertexts" with payload $E'_K(M)$ and headers of type j (for $j = 1, \ldots, l$):

$$\left(i_1, E_{L_{i_1}}(R)\right), \ldots, \left(i_j, E_{L_{i_j}}(R)\right), \left(i_{j+1}, E_{L_{i_{j+1}}}(K)\right), \ldots, \left(i_l, E_{L_{i_l}}(K)\right)$$

where R is some randomly chosen element independent from K. If we denote by p_j the probability that the pirate box correctly decrypts the specially crafted ciphertexts of type j, there must exist an index t such that $|p_t - p_{t-1}| \geq \frac{p}{l}$ and therefore some traitor belongs to S_{i_t}. The tracer then iterates this basic procedure, applying it to an arbitrary covering of S_{i_t} until either S_{i_t} contains a single element (which thus matches a traitor) or the pirate box cannot decrypt above the threshold (and no one is accused of being a traitor, but the new partition renders the pirate box useless). It is showed that this tracing procedure is correct as soon as the revocation scheme satisfies a so-called "bifurcation property": every subset can be split into two subsets of roughly the same size. This is the case for the two schemes *complete subtree* and *subset difference*.

Limitation of traceability: Because the ciphertext in the tracing procedure must contain nodes at the lower levels of the tree, the pirate can adapt the strategy to defeat the tracer by using the high level nodes so that the ciphertext gets bigger and bigger; this is the idea in the pirate evolution attack in Kiayias and Pehlivanoglu (2007). Another shortcoming in these tree-based schemes (as well as in many other combinatorial schemes) is that subkeys of different users can be combined to build a pirate decoder; therefore, a traitor can publish some subkeys while remaining anonymous and the pirate decoder can be constructed from a public collaborative database as shown in Billet and Phan (2009). Note that these pirate decoders in Kiayias and Pehlivanoglu (2007) and Billet and Phan (2009) are imperfect (they can only decrypt ciphertexts of size lower than certain bound, say 1 GB) but still very practical.

6.5. Code-based TT

Fingerprinting with collusion-secure codes allows one to identify a digital document among several copies of it by embedding a fingerprint (a codeword). Such an identification scheme must be resilient to collusions of traitors trying to remove their fingerprints so as to escape identification. Therefore, collusion secure codes share some properties with TT. However, the main assumption here, called the *marking assumption*, is that the traitors from a collusion are only able to identify the positions where the digits from their respective codewords differ; such positions are called *detectable positions*. This assumption especially makes sense with fingerprinting data: apart from the codewords, the documents are identical, and it is easy to uncover places where two copies of a document differ.

Among the first constructions are the identifiable parent property (IPP) codes introduced in Chor et al. (1994). These codes are defined over large alphabets and can be obtained from linear codes or from combinatorial constructions. If the condition that a traitor is always correctly identified in IPP can be relaxed, that is, a tracing algorithm may fail with some negligible probability, then more efficient construction can be achieved. Randomized collusion secure codes, which can be seen as "relaxed" binary IPP codes, have first been proposed by Boneh and Shaw (1995). These codes are more efficient than linear codes based IPP codes. In Boneh–Shaw codes, the length of the codewords is $O(N^3 \log(N/\epsilon))$ for fully collusion-resistant codes and $O(c^4 \log(N/\epsilon))$ for codes resisting collusions of at most c traitors. Tardos later introduces a new construction in Tardos (2003) and proves that the size of its codewords is optimal: a length of $O(c^2 \log(N/\epsilon))$ is enough to resist collusions of at most c traitors.

We will first give a definition of an IPP code, then explain the general framework of constructing TT schemes which relies on any IPP code, including the most important case of collusion-secure code.

IPP CODES.– Let $\mathcal{Q}$ be an alphabet set containing q symbols. If $C = \{w_1, w_2, \ldots, w_N\} \subset \mathcal{Q}^\ell$, then C is called a q-ary code of size N and length ℓ. Each $w_i \in C$ is called a codeword and we write $w_i = (w_{i,1}, w_{i,2}, \ldots, w_{i,\ell})$, where $w_{i,j} \in \mathcal{Q}$ is called the jth component of the codeword w_i.

We define *descendants* of a subset of codewords as follows. Let $X \subset C$ and $u = (u_1, \ldots, u_\ell) \in \mathcal{Q}^\ell$. The word u is called a descendant of X if for any $1 \leq j \leq \ell$, the jth component u_j of u is equal to a jth component of a codeword in X. In this case, codewords in X are called *parent codewords* of u. For example, $(3, 2, 1, 3)$ is a descendant of the three codewords $(3, 1, 1, 2)$, $(1, 2, 1, 3)$ and $(2, 2, 2, 2)$. We denote by $\mathsf{Desc}(X)$ the set of all descendants of X. For a positive integer c, denote by $\mathsf{Desc}_c(C)$ the set of all descendants of subsets of up to c codewords. Codes with IPP (IPP codes) are defined below.

DEFINITION 6.1.– *A code C is called c-IPP if, for any $u \in \mathsf{Desc}_c(C)$, there exists $w \in C$ such that for any $X \subset C$, if $|X| \leq c$ and $u \in \mathsf{Desc}(X)$ then $w \in X$.*

In a c-IPP code, given a descendant $u \in \mathsf{Desc}_c(C)$, we can always identify at least one of its parent codewords. It is also required that the tracing is *error-free* and a traitor is always correctly identified. There are many constructions (Stinson and Wei 1999; Silverberg et al. 2001; Trung and Martirosyan 2005) of c-IPP codes.

Binary c-IPP codes (with more than two codewords) do not exist, thus in any c-IPP code, the alphabet size $q \geq 3$. However, if the condition on error-free tracing is relaxed then binary codes, called then *collusion secure codes* (Boneh and Shaw 1995), can be achieved. Therefore, in collusion secure codes, there is an error parameter that specifies the probability that the tracing algorithm fails to output the correct parent codeword. As mentioned, the most efficient codes are Tardos's collusion secure codes.

CODE-BASED TT SCHEMES.– At a high level, the idea is to first define a q-user sub-scheme which is resilient against a single traitor, and then "concatenate" v instantiations of this sub-scheme according to the q-ary IPP code $\mathcal{C}$; in particular, each user $i \in [1, n]$ is associated with a codeword $\omega^{(i)}$ in $\mathcal{C}$, and given the decryption key $\mathsf{sk}_i := (k_{1,\omega_1^{(i)}}, \ldots, k_{v,\omega_v^{(i)}})$, where $\omega_j^{(i)}$ is the jth bit of the codeword $\omega^{(i)}$, and $k_{j,0}, \ldots, k_{j,q-1}$ are the keys for the jth instantiation of the basic two-user sub-scheme. The session key K is decomposed into random sub-keys as $K = K_1 \oplus K_2 \cdots \oplus K_l$ and then each K_i is encrypted with each of the $k_{i,j}$ to form a sub-ciphertext $c_{i,j}$. The whole ciphertext contains all sub-ciphertexts and the decryption is realized in a natural way: each user i decrypts sub-ciphertext $c_{j,\omega_j^{(i)}}$ with its secret key $k_{j,\omega_j^{(i)}}$ to get K_j for any $j = 1, \ldots l$ and finally gets K. Here is an example of a TT scheme with three-ary IPP code.

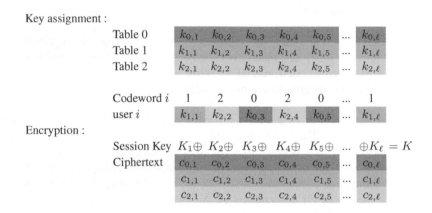

CONSTANT-SIZE CIPHERTEXT WITH ROBUST FINGERPRINTING CODES.– Independently from Billet and Phan (2008) and Boneh and Naor (2008), TT schemes from robust fingerprinting codes were considered: instead of decomposing the session key K into l parts, we simply decompose it into u parts, for some u much smaller than l. This helps to reduce the ciphertext size from $O(lq)$ to $O(uq)$. When u is a constant and the code is binary (i.e. $q = 2$), the ciphertext size is constant. However, under this encryption, if the adversary erases some position in his codeword, then he can still decrypt a large part of the ciphertexts. The parameter u is to amplify the probability of not being able to decrypt the ciphertext. For example, if the adversary erases half of the positions, then he has a probability of success of about $\frac{1}{2^u}$ and thus, to be effective, the adversary cannot erase too many positions of his codeword. With standard fingerprinting codes, one cannot trace back the traitors. This requires using robust fingerprinting codes that exactly deal with tracing adversaries who can erase some parts of their codewords. This requires a stronger definition of a feasible set:

$$FS^\star(w_1, \ldots, w_t) = \{w \in \{0,1\}^n \mid \forall i \in [n] : (w[i] = \star) \vee (\exists j \in [t] : w[i] = w_j[i])\}.$$

The scheme (Billet and Phan 2008) is described as in Figure 6.3.

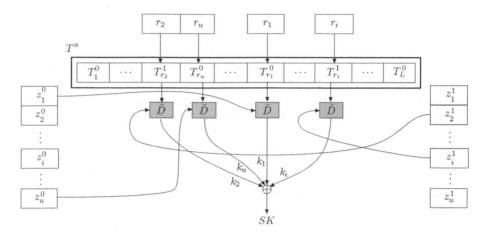

Figure 6.3. *The* HEADER *is made of the values* r_i, $z_i^{(0)}$ *and* $z_i^{(1)}$ *and the decoder of user a has access to table* T^a *consisting of* $T^a[i] = k_{i,j}$. *Using its bit string* I^a, *user a selects the correct values* z_i *to be decrypted: here, user a selects* $z_1^{(0)}$, $z_2^{(1)}$, $\ldots$, $z_i^{(1)}$, $\ldots$, $z_u^{(0)}$. *User a then decrypts these values with the corresponding keys* $T^a[k_1]$, $\ldots$, $T^a[k_u]$ *from table* T^a. *The decrypted keys* $k_1, \ldots, k_u$ *are further combined together to form the session key* $SK = k_1 \oplus \cdots \oplus k_u$

Robust fingerprinting codes are constructed by Safavi-Naini and Wang (2003b) and Sirvent (2007). The previous studies (Nuida 2010; Boneh et al. 2010) give the most efficient constructions to date.

6.6. Algebraic schemes

TRAITOR TRACING FROM REPRESENTATION PROBLEM.– This has been introduced by Boneh and Franklin (1999). *Representation problem*: We let $G_q = <g>$ be a cyclic group of prime order q for which we write its group operation multiplicatively. When $y = \Pi_{i=1}^{k} h_i^{\delta_i}$, we say that $\vec{d} = (\delta_1, \ldots, \delta_k) \in \mathbb{Z}_q^n$ is a representation of y with respect to the basis $(h_1, \ldots, h_k) \in G_q^n$. It is shown that, unless one can solve the discrete logarithm problem, from one representation it is hard to produce another representation. More generally, Boneh–Franklin showed that, still under discrete logarithm assumption, from $t < k$ representations, the only way to produce another representation is to compute a convex combination of the t known representations.

The representation problem was first used in the context of incremental hashing (Bellare et al. 1994) and digital signets (Dwork et al. 1996). The digital signet is particularly close to TT as it aims to protect digital content from redistribution by an authorized user. Note first of all that the authority, when generating $y = g^a, h_i = g_i^\alpha$, knows all α_i and can generate as many representations as it wants (just by arbitrarily generating $\delta_1, \ldots, \delta_{k-1}$ and set $\delta_k = (a - \Sigma_{i=1}^{k-1} \alpha_i \delta_i) \alpha_k^{-1}$). The main idea in designing a digital signet is then to give each user a representation of y w.r.t the basis $h_1, \ldots, h_k$ so that this representation contains personal information of the user (the authority can do this by defining δ_1 to be the hash of personal information for example). Therefore, any redistribution of the individual representation will also disclose personal information.

Boneh and Franklin are the first to use the representation problem to trace traitors, generalizing the ElGamal encryption to the multi-receiver setting. We can look at the ElGamal in the following way, from the representation problem: the basis contains only one element $h_1 = g$, the public key is y and the secret key is the representation δ such that $y = g^\delta$. To encrypt a message m, the ciphertext is defined to be my^r, g^r. Because the basis contains only one element, there is a unique representation and the scheme does not support multi-receiver encryption. The idea of Boneh and Franklin is to extend the basis to k elements $h_1, \ldots, h_k$ and each user's secret key is a representation $\delta_1, \ldots, \delta_k$. The ciphertext is now composed of $my^r, h_1^r, \ldots, h_k^r$. Because $(\delta_1, \ldots, \delta_k)$ is a representation of y w.r.t the basis $h_1, \ldots, h_k$, it is also a representation of y^r w.r.t the basis $h_1^r, \ldots, h_k^r$ and the user can thus recover m.

To support multi-receiver encryption, it is sufficient for the basis to contain two elements. However, for the purpose of TT, it needs to contain $2k$ elements $h_1, \ldots, h_{2k}$ to achieve traceability up to k traitors. As we mentioned above, Boneh and Franklin showed that, unless breaking the discrete logarithm problem, the only way for the adversary to produce a new representation of y is to linearly combine its known representations. This leads to the idea of using linear error-correcting code for tracing. Indeed, consider any linear error-correcting code A (codewords generated by the columns of A) that can correct up to k errors and its parity check matrix H. If we associate each user to a row of H, then from any linear combination of up to k corrupted rows of H, one can trace back the corrupted rows. This is derived directly from the error-correcting property: given d which is a linear combination of up to k corrupted rows of H, that is, $d = wB$ for an unknown vector w of weight at most k; the goal is to find w. We can do this by first computing any v satisfying $vB = d$ by linear algebra; we know then $v - w$ is a codeword of A and thus v is deviated from a codeword with at most k errors; the correction of the error of v will directly provide us with the "error" w.

In fact, Boneh and Franklin use for A as a Reed–Solomon code corresponding to a Vandermonde matrix and the white-box tracing follows the above intuition. A more challenging point is the black-box tracing where one does not know any pirate key d. The black-box tracing, which is in fact quite expensive, relies on the black-box confirmation: given a superset of the traitors, it is guaranteed to find at least one traitor and no innocent suspect is incriminated.

REVOCATION FROM REDUNDANCY.– The main idea in many revocation systems is that the revoked users get redundant information from the ciphertext and thus have less information than the legitimate users. This difference prevents revoked users (even the collusion of all of them) from decrypting ciphertexts while allowing legitimate users to successfully decrypt ciphertexts.

Polynomial interpolation in exponent (Naor and Pinkas 2001): At a high level, the main idea is to use a *t-out-of-N* secret sharing and the scheme can revoke up to $t - 1$ users. For simplicity, we can suppose that the number of revoked users r is equal to $t - 1$ (if the effective number of revoked users is less than $t - 1$ then we can add "dummy" users to the revoked list). The system works as follows: a secret is divided into N shares and each user who joins the system receives a share; the ciphertext contains $t - 1$ shares that cover all the revoked users; each non-revoked user adds its share to have t shares that can decrypt the ciphertext while the revoked users only get $t - 1$ shares in total and cannot decrypt even if they all collude. In order to implement this idea, Naor and Pinkas use secret sharing in the exponent and randomize the ciphertext.

More formally, the authority chooses a global polynomial P of degree $t - 1$ in the setup, then chooses and publishes a random element x_i for each user i. The secret key for user i is $P(x_i)$ and all the values $g^{P(x_i)}$ and $g^{P(0)}$ are published. To revoke a set of users $(1, 2, ..., t - 1)$, a broadcaster chooses a random element r then sets the session key $K = g^{rP(0)}$. The ciphertext is composed of $t - 1$ elements $g^{rP(x_j)}, j \in 1, ..., t - 1$. Each non-revoked user owns t shares and can perform a polynomial interpolation in the exponent to recover the session key, while the revoked users have at most $t - 1$ shares and get no information from the ciphertext. It is worth noticing that the Naor–Pinkas method can be combined with the Boneh–Franklin method to achieve a trace&revoke scheme.

Two equations technique: In the Naor–Pinkas schemes, by defining a global polynomial across the whole system, the bound on the number of revoked user is fixed (below the degree of the polynomial) in the setup and the scheme will be totally broken if the size of the collusion goes beyond this bound. In Lewko et al. (2010), in order to avoid this limitation, still basing on revocation by redundant equations, a new *two equation* method for decryption is introduced. A ciphertext will be encrypted such that a certain set $S = \{ID_1, ..., ID_r\}$ will be revoked from decrypting it. The ciphertext consists of $O(r)$ group elements in which a ciphertext component for each

ID_i. When decrypting, a user ID will apply his secret key to each component. If $ID \neq IDi$, the user will get two independent equations and be able to extract the ith decryption share. However, if the user is revoked and $ID = ID_i$ for some i, then the user will only get two dependent equations of a two variable formula and thus be unable to extract the decryption share. To prevent the collusion, the key shares are randomized to each user to prevent combination of decryption shares. The authors then proposed a cancelation technique based on pairings.

PAIRING-BASED CONSTRUCTION.– Polynomial commitment: The use of polynomial commitment was first used by Feldman in 1988 for verifiable secret sharing. The idea is to commit all the coefficients a_i of a polynomial $f(x) = \Sigma_{i=0}^{k} a_i x^i$, say $y_i = g^{a_i}$. Thus, anyone can compute $g^{f(u)}$ for any u. Any user can therefore verify whether its share $(u, f(u))$ is correct. Kurosawa and Desmedt then used this feature for TT. In their scheme, each user u has as secret key $(u, f(u))$. The idea is that, to encrypt a session key s, one gives as ciphertext $sy_0^r, y_1^r, \ldots, y_k^r$ and g^r. Each user can thus compute $sg^{rf(u)}$ from $sy_0^r, y_1^r, \ldots, y_k^r$ and then $g^{rf(u)} = (g^r)^{f(u)}$ to retrieve s.

At first glance, the scheme is secure as from an evaluation of the polynomial, one cannot deduce another evaluation at another point. However, the scheme was broken in Stinson and Wei (1999) by showing that traitors can decrypt using a linear sum of their keys without calculating another private key.

Since the application of pairings in tripartite key exchange (Joux 2000) and in identity-based cryptography (Sakai et al. 2000; Boneh and Franklin 2001), the use of pairings has exploded in the construction of almost all kinds of cryptographic primitives. We refer to Chapter 5 for a detailed presentation of pairing-based cryptography.

Pairings provide a powerful tool to combine encrypted elements in a meaningful way: Even if we have no information about the exponents a and b in committed values g^a, g^b, from a pairing, we can still compute an element with the multiplication of exponent ab, say $e(g, g)^{ab}$. This gives a possibility to cancel out personalized elements. For example, if a personalized key of an user u is $g^{\frac{1}{f(u)}}$ and anyone can compute $g^{rf(x)}$ for any x, then a user can compute the pairing $e(g^{\frac{1}{f(u)}}, g^{rf(x)})$ to get the session key $e(g, g)^r$ which is independent from its personal information. This is exactly the idea that Tô et al. (2003) introduced to avoid a linear attack as KD by putting the inverse of $f(u)$ in the user's secret key. In decryption, the user can publicly compute $g^{rf(u)}$ and then combine it with the secret key $g^{\frac{1}{f(u)}}$ to get $e(g, g)^r$.

However, in Chabanne et al. (2005), it is shown that the adversary can also take advantage from the pairings and give a more disastrous attack on Tô et al.'s (2003) scheme as only one user can produce a pirate decoder while remaining totally anonymous. In fact, they can rewrite the session key as

$$e(g^{\frac{1}{f(u)}}, g^{rf(x)}) = e(g^{\frac{1}{f(u)}}, \Pi g^{ra_i u^i}) = \Pi e(g^{\frac{u^i}{f(u)}}, g^{ra_i})$$

and thus, by giving $g^{\frac{u^i}{f(u)}}$, anyone can decrypt ciphertexts. Even worse, the pirate can also randomize $g^{\frac{u^i}{f(u)}}$ in such a way that these values are perfectly unlinkable to u and thus the pirate key is untraceable.

The authors in Chabanne et al. (2005) then proposed the first two-user pairing-based scheme (which is a variant of the Boneh–Franklin scheme) and achieve a very nice property of public traceability, from the bilinear group property. However, the use of pairings is most useful to achieve fully collusion resistance (Boneh et al. 2005).

BGW constant-size ciphertext: Aggregation of ciphertexts: One of the very interesting uses of pairings is to aggregate data. The best-known example is undoubtedly the aggregation of the BLS signature (Boneh et al. 2003), which is now widely used in the blockchain. Later, Boneh et al. (2005) introduced a method to construct a fully collusion-resistant broadcast scheme with constant-size ciphertext. This can be seen as a technique of aggregating many individual ciphertexts into one ciphertext. Intuition at a high level in the BGW scheme can be described as follows.

The pairing allows us to do one-time multiplication on the hidden exponents in the target group without knowing them. One can obtain a variant of ElGamal encryption where the decryption does not need to know the discrete logarithm. Given a bilinear group of prime order p with a generator g and a public key g, g^α, for a random $\alpha \in \mathbb{Z}_p$. The ciphertext in ElGamal encryption is g^r, for a random $r \in \mathbb{Z}_p$ which encapsulates a session key $g^{\alpha r}$. The user must know α to get $g^{\alpha r}$ from g^r. With a bilinear group, from g^α, one can compute $e(g^\alpha, g^\alpha) = e(g, g)^{\alpha^2}$ and therefore with the ciphertext g^r, the corresponding encapsulated session key is naturally set to be $e(g, g)^{\alpha^2 r}$. The nice thing is that the user does not need to know the exponent α to decrypt. Indeed, by adding another generator h in the public key and an element $(hg^\alpha)^r$ in the ciphertext, then starting from a secret key h^α, the user can retrieve the session key like:

$$e(g^\alpha, (hg^\alpha)^r)/e(h^\alpha, g^r) = e(g, g)^{\alpha^2 r}$$

Without disclosing the exponent α, the above encryption can be extended to multiple users. For each $i \in \mathbb{N}$, denote by $g_i = g^{\alpha^i}$ and $h_i = h^{\alpha^i}$. One associates each user, for $i = 1, \ldots, n$, with a public key g_i and a secret key h_i. Then the session key is set to be $e(g, g)^{\alpha^{n+1} r}$ which can be calculated from g_1, g_n, for a random

$r \in \mathbb{Z}_p$. As above, for the user i to obtain this session key, the ciphertext contains g^r and $(hg^{\alpha^{n+1-i}})^r$. At this point, the session key is common for all users. However, in order for any user i in a set S to be able to decrypt, we must add the element $(hg^{\alpha^{n+1-i}})^r$ to the ciphertext and the ciphertext size is thus linear in the size of the target set S. The interesting technique is to aggregate all these ciphertexts into a single element $(h\Pi_{i \in S}g^{\alpha^{n+1-i}})^r$. Each user $i \in S$ then can factor this element into $(hg^{\alpha^{n+1-i}})^r$ and $(\Pi_{i \in S, j \neq i}g^{\alpha^{n+1-j}})^r$. The latter redundant term can be canceled out with the help of new added public elements $g_{n+2}, \ldots g_{2n}$ as:

$$e(g, g_{n+1})^r = e(g_i, (h\Pi_{j \in S}g_{n+1-j})^r)/e(g^r, h_i\Pi_{j \in S, j \neq i}g_{n+1-j+i}).$$

The security is then based on a new type of assumption called bilinear Diffie–Hellman exponent assumption which states that from $h, g, g_1, \ldots, g_n$, $g_{n+2}, \ldots, g_{2n}$, it is hard to compute $e(h, g_{n+1})$. The final scheme contains $g, h, g_1, \ldots, g_n, g_{n+2}, \ldots, g_{2n}$ as public key, h_i as secret key for user i and $(g^r, (h\Pi_{i \in S}g^{\alpha^{n+1-i}})^r)$ as ciphertext to encapsulate the session key $e(g, g_{n+1})^r$.

Inversion technique: The DPP scheme (Delerablée et al. 2007): Delerablée et al. introduced the inversion technique that helps to construct the first dynamic revocation scheme. The main idea is to generate a value x_u to each user u and then, in the decryption phase, to force the user to multiply a group element by $\frac{1}{x_r - x_u}$ for each revoked user r. This means that every revoked user has to divide by 0 during decryption, which leads to a procedure failure. The construction requires a pairing in prime-order groups, but it does not matter whether the pairing is symmetric or not. The security guarantee is actually stronger than the static security level: The adversary is allowed to corrupt users immediately before they join. The master secret key and the user secret keys consist of a scalar value and one group element from each of the groups $\mathbb{G}_1, \mathbb{G}_2$; the encryption key consists of one group element from each of the groups $\mathbb{G}_1, \mathbb{G}_2$ and one from the target group $\mathbb{G}_T$. For each user, a scalar, an element from the group $\mathbb{G}_2$ and an element from the target group are added to the encryption key. The ciphertext consists of one element from each of the groups $\mathbb{G}_1, \mathbb{G}_2$ plus a scalar and an element from $\mathbb{G}_2$ for each revoked user.

Another modification of the public-key scheme makes it non-dynamic, but allows to achieve constant-size ciphertexts at the expense of linear size decryption keys.

Fully collusion-resistant TT: BSW scheme: We recall that a trivial way to construct a multi-receiver scheme is to encrypt independently to each user: the ciphertext contains many components; each of them is an individual encryption of the session key for a user. We can then apply the *linear tracing technique* which consists of replacing step by step each component by a random element: when we modify a component, it only affects one user and therefore, if the pirate decoder decrypts differently from one step to the next, we can detect a traitor. Now, in order to achieve a sub-linear size ciphertext, we should deal with "dependent" component problems because a component in the ciphertext must be related to many users. The task of the tracer becomes quite challenging because each time the ciphertext is modified, many users are affected and it is not easy to detect the traitor.

Boneh et al. (2006) introduce a method to deal with this problem and propose the first fully collusion-resistant TT scheme with sub-linear ciphertext size, in which they took benefit from the bilinearity of pairings to arrange the users in a matrix. In such a way, each user is identified by a couple of parameters: row position and column position. The main idea that allows to use the linear tracing technique is to produce a probe ciphertext for any position (i, j) in such a way that: any user at position (x, y) will be able to decrypt the message if and only if $(x > i)$ or $(x = i, y \geq j)$. This requires to randomize row components and column components in a smart way. In fact, Boneh et al. need to use pairings on composite order groups, say $e : G \times G \to G_T$ such that G is of composite order pq and if g_p is an element from the order p subgroup (which is called G_p) and g_q is an element from the order q subgroup (which is called G_q), then $e(g_p, g_q) = 1$. Each ciphertext contains $m = \sqrt{N}$ "well-formed" row components in G and m "well-formed" column components in G. The user (x, y) can successfully decrypt if the row component and the column component are of type (well-formed, well-formed). Now, the tracer produces a probe ciphertext in which:

– column ciphertext components are well formed in both G_p and G_q subgroups for columns greater than or equal to j; well formed in the G_q subgroup but random in the G_p subgroup for a column that is less than j;

– row ciphertext components are completely random for rows less than i , well formed elements in the G_q subgroup for rows greater than i and are well formed in both subgroups for row i.

We can see that the ciphertext structure will lead to restrictions on the decryption: it can be successful for a user (x, y) if and only if $x > i$ or $x = i, y \geq j$. Indeed:

– if $x > i$, then, because the row ciphertext components are well formed elements in the G_q subgroup, even if the column ciphertext components are randomized with an element in G_p, the randomized part is canceled out and the (row component, column component) for (x, y) looks like (well-formed, well-formed);

– if $x = i$ and $y \leq j$, then the (row component, column component) for (x, y) looks like (well-formed, well-formed);

– if $x = i$ and $y < j$ or $x < i$, then the (row component, column component) are randomized either in G_q or in G_p and are thus not of type (well-formed, well-formed) and the decryption fails.

The security analysis requires some assumptions, in particular the bilinear subgroup decision assumption which requires that, given $g_p, g_q \in G$, a random order p element in G_T is indistinguishable from a random element in G_T. We remark however that, because the ciphertext size is of $O(\sqrt{N})$, the scheme is more about theoretical interest than of practical interest.

Trace&Revoke. Boneh and Waters (2006) further improve the BSW scheme by providing broadcast functionality. Their scheme is a combination of the BGW scheme and the BSW scheme, in which they make use of the broadcast technique from the BGW and of the tracing technique from the BSW scheme, the ciphertext size remains $O(\sqrt{N})$.

6.7. Lattice-based approach with post-quantum security

Since the pioneering work of Ajtai (1996), there have been a number of proposals of cryptographic schemes with security relying on the worst-case hardness of standard lattice problems, such as the decision gap shortest vector problem with polynomial gap (see the surveys by Micciancio and Regev (2009); Regev (2010)). These schemes enjoy very strong security guarantees: security relies on *worst-case* hardness assumptions for problems expected to be *exponentially hard* to be solved (with respect to the lattice dimension n), even with quantum computers. At the same time, they often enjoy great asymptotic efficiency, as the basic operations are matrix-vector multiplications in dimension $\tilde{O}(n)$ over a ring of cardinality $\leq \mathcal{P}oly(n)$. A breakthrough result in that field is the introduction of the learning with errors problem by Regev (2005), who shows it to be at least as hard as worst-case lattice problems and exploited it to derive an elementary encryption scheme. Gentry et al. (2008) show that Regev's scheme may be adapted so that a manager can generate a large number of secret keys for the same public key. As a result, the latter encryption scheme, called dual-Regev, can be naturally extended into a multi-receiver encryption scheme. In Ling et al. (2014), the authors build TT schemes from this dual-Regev LWE-based encryption scheme, which also enjoys public traceability. To trace the traitors, the authors extend the LWE problem and introduce the k-LWE problem, in which k hint vectors (the leaked keys) are given out.

The k-LWE problem can be interpreted as a dual of the k-SIS problem introduced by Boneh and Freeman (2011). Intuitively, in both k-LWE and k-SIS, it is given as input $A \in \mathbb{Z}_q^{m \times n}$ along with k small hints $\vec{x}_1, \ldots, \vec{x}_k \in \mathbb{Z}^m$ s.t $\vec{x}_i A = \vec{0} \mod q$. The k-SIS solver is required to output a new vector $\vec{x}$, linearly independent from $\vec{x}_1, \ldots, \vec{x}_k$ such that $\vec{x} A = \vec{0} \mod q$, while the k-LWE solver is required to distinguish between

$$\frac{1}{q} \cdot U\left(\operatorname{Im}\left(A\right)\right) + \nu_\alpha^m \quad \text{and} \quad \frac{1}{q} \cdot U\left(\operatorname{Span}_{i \leq k}\left(\vec{x}_i\right)^\perp\right) + \nu_\alpha^m.$$

where $\mathrm{Im}(A) = \{A\vec{s} : \vec{s} \in \mathbb{Z}_q^n\} \subseteq \mathbb{Z}_q^m$, $U(X)$ denotes the uniform distribution over X, $\mathrm{Span}(X)$ denotes the set of all linear combinations of elements of X and ν_α denotes the one-dimensional Gaussian distribution with standard deviation α.

Under the hardness of the above k-LWE problem, one can implement the classical method of linear tracing in the black-box confirmation: start with a target set of suspected users, say $1, \ldots, k$, containing all traitors; send to the pirate decoder probe ciphertexts sampled from $\frac{1}{q} \cdot U\left(\mathrm{Span}_{i \le k}\left(\vec{x}_i\right)^{\perp}\right) + \nu_\alpha^m$ which are indistinguishable from normal ciphertexts; then remove one by one of them in the target set until the decoder cannot decrypt anymore and one can then find out a traitor, because the pirate cannot distinguish two consecutive distributions of probe ciphertexts if the removed user is not a traitor. Concerning the hardness of k-SIS and k-LWE problem, Boneh–Freeman reduction (Boneh and Freeman 2011) from SIS to k-SIS suffers from an exponential loss in k while Ling et al. (2014) presents a reduction with a polynomial loss in k, thus showing that their proposed LWE TT is almost as efficient as the LWE encryption.

CONSTRUCTIONS FROM ADVANCED PRIMITIVES.– Broadcast encryption and TT are often considered to be among the simplest of the advanced primitives. Interestingly, in the last few years, a very active line of research focuses on constructing broadcast encryption, TT and trace&revoke systems from more general or powerful advanced primitives, in particular attribute-based encryption, functional encryption, multi-linear maps and indistinguishability obfuscation (Boneh and Zhandry 2014; Nishimaki et al. 2016; Kowalczyk et al. 2016; Agrawal et al. 2017; Goyal et al. 2018a, 2018b, 2019a, 2019b; Kowalczyk et al. 2018; Chen et al. 2018; Agrawal and Yamada 2020b,a; Zhandry 2020). We can think of broadcast encryption as a special type of attribute-based encryption and traceability is often achieved on the basis of anonymity (which allows to implement the linear tracing technique). Therefore, by weakening the required notion of advanced primitives and through modern techniques developed for advanced primitives, many works have succeeded in proving security under more and more standard assumptions. They contribute to advancing the search for optimal schemes with the strongest notions of security. Nonetheless, the ultimate goal of building optimal or practical trace&revoke schemes in the full-collusion model remains open.

6.8. References

AACS LA (n.d.). AACS specifications [Online]. Available at: http://www.aacsla.com/specifications/.

Abdalla, M., Bourse, F., De Caro, A., Pointcheval, D. (2015). Simple functional encryption schemes for inner products. In *PKC 2015*, vol. 9020 of *LNCS*, Katz, J. (ed.). Springer, Heidelberg.

Agrawal, S. and Rosen, A. (2017). Functional encryption for bounded collusions, revisited. In *TCC 2017, Part I*, vol. 10677 of *LNCS*, Kalai, Y., Reyzin, L. (eds). Springer, Heidelberg.

Agrawal, S., Libert, B., Stehlé, D. (2016). Fully secure functional encryption for inner products, from standard assumptions. In *CRYPTO 2016, Part III*, vol. 9816 of *LNCS*, Robshaw, M., Katz, J. (eds). Springer, Heidelberg.

Agrawal, S., Bhattacherjee, S., Phan, D.H., Stehlé, D., Yamada, S. (2017). Efficient public trace and revoke from standard assumptions: Extended abstract. In *ACM CCS 2017*, Thuraisingham, B.M., Evans, D., Malkin, T., Xu, D. (eds). ACM Press.

Agrawal, S. and Yamada, S. (2020a). CP-ABE for circuits (and more) in the symmetric key setting. In *TCC 2020, Part I*, vol. 12550 of *LNCS*, Pass, R., Pietrzak, K. (eds). Springer, Heidelberg.

Agrawal, S. and Yamada, S. (2020b). Optimal broadcast encryption from pairings and LWE. In *EUROCRYPT 2020, Part I*, vol. 12105 of *LNCS*, Canteaut, A., Ishai, Y. (eds). Springer, Heidelberg.

Aiello, W., Lodha, S., Ostrovsky, R. (1998). Fast digital identity revocation (extended abstract). In *CRYPTO'98*, vol. 1462 of *LNCS*, Krawczyk, H. (ed.). Springer, Heidelberg.

Ajtai, M. (1996). Generating hard instances of lattice problems (extended abstract). In *28th ACM STOC*. ACM Press.

Barak, B., Goldreich, O., Impagliazzo, R., Rudich, S., Sahai, A., Vadhan, S.P., Yang, K. (2001). On the (im)possibility of obfuscating programs. In *CRYPTO 2001*, vol. 2139 of *LNCS*, Kilian, J. (ed.). Springer, Heidelberg.

Bellare, M., Goldreich, O., Goldwasser, S. (1994). Incremental cryptography: The case of hashing and signing. In *CRYPTO'94*, vol. 839 of *LNCS*, Desmedt, Y. (ed.). Springer, Heidelberg.

Berkman, O., Parnas, M., Sgall, J. (2000). Efficient dynamic traitor tracing. In *Proceedings of the Eleventh Annual ACM-SIAM Symposium on Discrete Algorithms*, San Francisco, CA, ACM/SIAM.

Beullens, W. and Wee, H. (2019). Obfuscating simple functionalities from knowledge assumptions. In *PKC 2019, Part II*, vol. 11443 of *LNCS*, Lin, D., Sako, K. (eds). Springer, Heidelberg.

Billet, O. and Phan, D.H. (2008). Efficient traitor tracing from collusion secure codes. In *ICITS 08*, vol. 5155 of *LNCS*, Safavi-Naini, R. (ed.). Springer, Heidelberg.

Billet, O. and Phan, D.H. (2009). Traitors collaborating in public: Pirates 2.0. In *EUROCRYPT 2009*, vol. 5479 of *LNCS*, Joux, A. (ed.). Springer, Heidelberg.

Boneh, D. and Franklin, M.K. (1999). An efficient public key traitor tracing scheme. In *CRYPTO'99*, vol. 1666 of *LNCS*, Wiener, M.J. (ed.). Springer, Heidelberg.

Boneh, D. and Franklin, M.K. (2001). Identity-based encryption from the Weil pairing. In *CRYPTO 2001*, vol. 2139 of *LNCS*, Kilian, J. (ed.). Springer, Heidelberg.

Boneh, D. and Freeman, D.M. (2011). Linearly homomorphic signatures over binary fields and new tools for lattice-based signatures. In *PKC 2011*, vol. 6571 of *LNCS*, Catalano, D., Fazio, N., Gennaro, R., Nicolosi, A. (eds). Springer, Heidelberg.

Boneh, D. and Naor, M. (2008). Traitor tracing with constant size ciphertext. In *ACM CCS 2008*, Ning, P., Syverson, P.F., Jha, S. (eds), ACM Press.

Boneh, D. and Shaw, J. (1995). Collusion-secure fingerprinting for digital data (extended abstract). In *CRYPTO'95*, vol. 963 of *LNCS*, Coppersmith, D. (ed.). Springer, Heidelberg.

Boneh, D. and Shaw, J. (1998). Collusion-secure fingerprinting for digital data. *IEEE Transactions on Information Theory*, 44(5), 1897–1905.

Boneh, D. and Waters, B. (2006). A fully collusion resistant broadcast, trace, and revoke system. In *ACM CCS 2006*, Juels, A., Wright, R.N., De Capitani di Vimercati, S. (eds). ACM Press.

Boneh, D. and Zhandry, M. (2014). Multiparty key exchange, efficient traitor tracing, and more from indistinguishability obfuscation. In *CRYPTO 2014, Part I*, vol. 8616 of *LNCS*, Garay, J.A., Gennaro, R. (eds). Springer, Heidelberg.

Boneh, D., Gentry, C., Lynn, B., Shacham, H. (2003). Aggregate and verifiably encrypted signatures from bilinear maps. In *EUROCRYPT 2003*, vol. 2656 of *LNCS*, Biham, E. (ed.). Springer, Heidelberg.

Boneh, D., Gentry, C., Waters, B. (2005). Collusion resistant broadcast encryption with short ciphertexts and private keys. In *CRYPTO 2005*, vol. 3621 of *LNCS*, Shoup, V. (ed.). Springer, Heidelberg.

Boneh, D., Sahai, A., Waters, B. (2006). Fully collusion resistant traitor tracing with short ciphertexts and private keys. In *EUROCRYPT 2006*, vol. 4004 of *LNCS*, Vaudenay, S. (ed.). Springer, Heidelberg.

Boneh, D., Kiayias, A., Montgomery, H.W. (2010). Robust fingerprinting codes: A near optimal construction. In *Proceedings of the 10th ACM Workshop on Digital Rights Management*, Chicago, IL, October 4.

Boneh, D., Sahai, A., Waters, B. (2011). Functional encryption: Definitions and challenges. In *TCC 2011*, vol. 6597 of *LNCS*, Ishai, Y. (ed.). Springer, Heidelberg.

Chabanne, H., Phan, D.H., Pointcheval, D. (2005). Public traceability in traitor tracing schemes. In *EUROCRYPT 2005*, vol. 3494 of *LNCS*, Cramer, R. (ed.). Springer, Heidelberg.

Chen, Y., Vaikuntanathan, V., Waters, B., Wee, H., Wichs, D. (2018). Traitor-tracing from LWE made simple and attribute-based. In *TCC 2018, Part II*, vol. 11240 of *LNCS*, Beimel, A., Dziembowski, S. (eds). Springer, Heidelberg.

Chor, B., Fiat, A., Naor, M. (1994). Tracing traitors. In *CRYPTO'94*, vol. 839 of *LNCS*, Desmedt, Y. (ed.). Springer, Heidelberg.

Chor, B., Fiat, A., Naor, M., Pinkas, B. (2000). Tracing traitors. *IEEE Transactions on Information Theory*, 46(3), 893–910.

Cramer, R. and Shoup, V. (2003). Design and analysis of practical public-key encryption schemes secure against adaptive chosen ciphertext attack. *SIAM Journal on Computing*, 33(1), 167–226.

Delerablée, C. (2007). Identity-based broadcast encryption with constant size ciphertexts and private keys. In *ASIACRYPT 2007*, vol. 4833 of *LNCS*, Kurosawa, K. (ed.). Springer, Heidelberg.

Delerablée, C., Paillier, P., Pointcheval, D. (2007). Fully collusion secure dynamic broadcast encryption with constant-size ciphertexts or decryption keys. In *PAIRING 2007*, vol. 4575 of *LNCS*, Takagi, T., Okamoto, T., Okamoto, E., Okamoto, T. (eds). Springer, Heidelberg.

Dodis, Y. and Fazio, N. (2002). Public-key broadcast encryption for stateless receivers. In *ACM Digital Rights Management – DRM '02*, vol. 2696 of *LNCS*. Springer, Heidelberg.

Dodis, Y. and Fazio, N. (2003). Public key trace and revoke scheme secure against adaptive chosen ciphertext attack. In *PKC 2003*, vol. 2567 of *LNCS*, Desmedt, Y. (ed.). Springer, Heidelberg.

Dodis, Y., Fazio, N., Kiayias, A., Yung, M. (2005). Scalable public-key tracing and revoking. *Journal of Distributed Computing*, 17(4), 323–347.

Dubois, R., Dugardin, M., Guillevic, A. (2013). Golden sequence for the PPSS broadcast encryption scheme with an asymmetric pairing. Cryptology ePrint Archive, Report 2013/477 [Online]. Available at: https://eprint.iacr.org/2013/477.

Dwork, C., Lotspiech, J.B., Naor, M. (1996). Digital signets: Self-enforcing protection of digital information (preliminary version). In *28th ACM STOC*. ACM Press.

Fiat, A. and Naor, M. (1994). Broadcast encryption. In *CRYPTO'93*, vol. 773 of *LNCS*, Stinson, D.R. (ed.). Springer, Heidelberg.

Fiat, A. and Tassa, T. (2001). Dynamic traitor tracing. *Journal of Cryptology*, 14(3), 211–223.

Gafni, E., Staddon, J., Yin, Y.L. (1999). Efficient methods for integrating traceability and broadcast encryption. In *CRYPTO'99*, vol. 1666 of *LNCS*, Wiener, M.J. (ed.). Springer, Heidelberg.

Garg, S., Gentry, C., Halevi, S., Raykova, M., Sahai, A., Waters, B. (2013). Candidate indistinguishability obfuscation and functional encryption for all circuits. In *54th FOCS*. IEEE Computer Society Press.

Gentry, C. and Waters, B. (2009). Adaptive security in broadcast encryption systems (with short ciphertexts). In *EUROCRYPT 2009*, vol. 5479 of *LNCS*, Joux, A. (ed.). Springer, Heidelberg.

Gentry, C., Peikert, C., Vaikuntanathan, V. (2008). Trapdoors for hard lattices and new cryptographic constructions. In *40th ACM STOC*, Ladner, R.E., Dwork, C. (eds). ACM Press.

Goldreich, O., Goldwasser, S., Micali, S. (1984). How to construct random functions (extended abstract). In *Symposium on Foundations of Computer Science – FOCS 84*. IEEE.

Goldwasser, S., Kalai, Y.T., Popa, R.A., Vaikuntanathan, V., Zeldovich, N. (2013). Reusable garbled circuits and succinct functional encryption. In *45th ACM STOC*, Boneh, D., Roughgarden, T., Feigenbaum, J. (eds). ACM Press.

Gorbunov, S., Vaikuntanathan, V., Wee, H. (2012). Functional encryption with bounded collusions via multi-party computation. In *CRYPTO 2012*, vol. 7417 of *LNCS*, Safavi-Naini, R., Canetti, R. (eds). Springer, Heidelberg.

Gorbunov, S., Vaikuntanathan, V., Wee, H. (2013). Attribute-based encryption for circuits. In *45th ACM STOC*, Boneh, D., Roughgarden, T., Feigenbaum, J. (eds). ACM Press.

Goyal, R., Koppula, V., Russell, A., Waters, B. (2018a). Risky traitor tracing and new differential privacy negative results. In *CRYPTO 2018, Part I*, vol. 10991 of *LNCS*, Shacham, H., Boldyreva, A. (eds). Springer, Heidelberg.

Goyal, R., Koppula, V., Waters, B. (2018b). Collusion resistant traitor tracing from learning with errors. In *50th ACM STOC*, Diakonikolas, I., Kempe, D., Henzinger, M. (eds). ACM Press.

Goyal, R., Koppula, V., Waters, B. (2019a). New approaches to traitor tracing with embedded identities. In *TCC 2019, Part II*, vol. 11892 of *LNCS*, Hofheinz, D., Rosen, A. (eds). Springer, Heidelberg.

Goyal, R., Quach, W., Waters, B., Wichs, D. (2019b). Broadcast and trace with N^ϵ ciphertext size from standard assumptions. In *CRYPTO 2019, Part III*, vol. 11694 of *LNCS*, Boldyreva, A., Micciancio, D. (eds). Springer, Heidelberg.

Joux, A. (2000). A one round protocol for tripartite Diffie–Hellman. In *Algorithmic Number Theory*, Bosma, W. (ed.). Springer, Heidelberg.

Kiayias, A. and Pehlivanoglu, S. (2007). Pirate evolution: How to make the most of your traitor keys. In *CRYPTO 2007*, vol. 4622 of *LNCS*, Menezes, A. (ed.). Springer, Heidelberg.

Kiayias, A. and Yung, M. (2001). Self protecting pirates and black-box traitor tracing. In *CRYPTO 2001*, vol. 2139 of *LNCS*, Kilian, J. (ed.). Springer, Heidelberg.

Kiayias, A. and Yung, M. (2002a). Breaking and repairing asymmetric public-key traitor tracing. In *Digital Rights Management – DRM '02*, vol. 2696 of *LNCS*, Feigenbaum, J. (ed.). Springer, Heidelberg.

Kiayias, A. and Yung, M. (2002b). On crafty pirates and foxy tracers. In *Security and Privacy in Digital Rights Management – DRM 2001*, vol. 2320 of *LNCS*, Sander, T. (ed.). Springer, Heidelberg.

Kiayias, A. and Yung, M. (2002c). Traitor tracing with constant transmission rate. In *EUROCRYPT 2002*, vol. 2332 of *LNCS*, Knudsen, L.R. (ed.). Springer, Heidelberg.

Kim, C.H., Hwang, Y.H., Lee, P.J. (2003). An efficient public key trace and revoke scheme secure against adaptive chosen ciphertext attack. In *ASIACRYPT 2003*, vol. 2894 of *LNCS*, Laih, C.-S. (ed.). Springer, Heidelberg.

Komaki, H., Watanabe, Y., Hanaoka, G., Imai, H. (2001). Efficient asymmetric self-enforcement scheme with public traceability. In *PKC 2001*, vol. 1992 of *LNCS*, Kim, K. (ed.). Springer, Heidelberg.

Kowalczyk, L., Malkin, T., Ullman, J., Zhandry, M. (2016). Strong hardness of privacy from weak traitor tracing. In *TCC 2016-B, Part I*, vol. 9985 of *LNCS*, Hirt, M., Smith, A.D. (eds). Springer, Heidelberg.

Kowalczyk, L., Malkin, T., Ullman, J., Wichs, D. (2018). Hardness of non-interactive differential privacy from one-way functions. In *CRYPTO 2018, Part I*, vol. 10991 of *LNCS*, Shacham, H., Boldyreva, A. (eds). Springer, Heidelberg.

Kumar, R. and Russell, A. (2003). A note on the set systems used for broadcast encryption. In *14th SODA*. ACM-SIAM.

Kurosawa, K. and Desmedt, Y. (1998). Optimum traitor tracing and asymmetric schemes. In *EUROCRYPT'98*, vol. 1403 of *LNCS*, Nyberg, K. (ed.). Springer, Heidelberg.

Kurosawa, K. and Yoshida, T. (2002). Linear code implies public-key traitor tracing. In *PKC 2002*, vol. 2274 of *LNCS*, Naccache, D., Paillier, P. (eds). Springer, Heidelberg.

Lewko, A.B., Sahai, A., Waters, B. (2010). Revocation systems with very small private keys. In *2010 IEEE Symposium on Security and Privacy*. IEEE Computer Society Press.

Ling, S., Phan, D.H., Stehlé, D., Steinfeld, R. (2014). Hardness of k-LWE and applications in traitor tracing. In *CRYPTO 2014, Part I*, vol. 8616 of *LNCS*, Garay, J.A., Gennaro, R. (eds). Springer, Heidelberg.

Loebbecke, C. and Fischer, M. (2005). Pay TV piracy and its effects on pay TV provision. *Journal of Media Business Studies*, 2(2), 17–34.

Micciancio, D. and Regev, O. (2009). Lattice-based cryptography. In *Post-Quantum Cryptography*, Bernstein, D.J., Buchmann, J., Dahmen, E. (eds). Springer, Heidelberg.

Naor, M. and Pinkas, B. (2001). Efficient trace and revoke schemes. In *FC 2000*, vol. 1962 of *LNCS*, Frankel, Y. (ed.). Springer, Heidelberg.

Naor, D., Naor, M., Lotspiech, J. (2001). Revocation and tracing schemes for stateless receivers. In *CRYPTO 2001*, vol. 2139 of *LNCS*, Kilian, J. (ed.). Springer, Heidelberg.

Ngo, H.Q., Phan, D.H., Pointcheval, D. (2013). Black-box trace&revoke codes. *Algorithmica*, 67(3), 418–448.

Nishimaki, R., Wichs, D., Zhandry, M. (2016). Anonymous traitor tracing: How to embed arbitrary information in a key. In *EUROCRYPT 2016, Part II*, vol. 9666 of *LNCS*, Fischlin, M., Coron, J.-S. (eds). Springer, Heidelberg.

Nuida, K. (2010). A general conversion method of fingerprint codes to (more) robust fingerprint codes against bit erasure. In *ICITS 09*, vol. 5973 of *LNCS*, Kurosawa, K. (ed.). Springer, Heidelberg.

Pfitzmann, B. (1996). Trials of traced traitors. In *Information Hiding*, vol. 1174 of *LNCS*, Anderson, R. (ed.). Springer, Heidelberg.

Pfitzmann, B. and Waidner, M. (1997). Asymmetric fingerprinting for larger collusions. In *ACM CCS 97*, Graveman, R., Janson, P.A., Neuman, C., Gong, L. (eds). ACM Press.

Phan, D., Safavi-Naini, R., Tonien, D. (2006). Generic construction of hybrid public key traitor tracing with full-public-traceability. In *ICALP 2006, Part II*, vol. 4052 of *LNCS*, Bugliesi, M., Preneel, B., Sassone, V., Wegener, I. (eds). Springer, Heidelberg.

Phan, D.H., Pointcheval, D., Shahandashti, S.F., Strefler, M. (2013). Adaptive CCA broadcast encryption with constant-size secret keys and ciphertexts. *International Journal of Information Security*, 12(4), 251–265.

Regev, O. (2005). On lattices, learning with errors, random linear codes, and cryptography. In *37th ACM STOC*, Gabow, H.N., Fagin, R. (eds). ACM Press.

Regev, O. (2010). On the complexity of lattice problems with polynomial approximation factors. In *The LLL Algorithm – Survey and Applications*, Nguyen, P.Q., Vallée, B. (eds). Information Security and Cryptography, Springer, Heidelberg.

Rivest, R.L. (1997). All-or-nothing encryption and the package transform. In *FSE'97*, vol. 1267 of *LNCS*, Biham, E. (ed.). Springer, Heidelberg.

Safavi-Naini, R. and Wang, Y. (2003a). Sequential traitor tracing. *IEEE Transactions on Information Theory*, 49(5), 1319–1326.

Safavi-Naini, R. and Wang, Y. (2003b). Traitor tracing for shortened and corrupted fingerprints. In *DRM 2003*, vol. 2696 of *LNCS*, Feigenbaum, J. (ed.). Springer, Heidelberg.

Sahai, A. and Waters, B.R. (2005). Fuzzy identity-based encryption. In *EUROCRYPT 2005*, vol. 3494 of *LNCS*, Cramer, R. (ed.). Springer, Heidelberg.

Sakai, R., Ohgishi, K., Kasahara, M. (2000). Cryptosystems based on pairing. In *SCIS 2000*, Okinawa, Japan.

Silverberg, A., Staddon, J., Walker, J.L. (2001). Efficient traitor tracing algorithms using list decoding. In *ASIACRYPT 2001*, vol. 2248 of *LNCS*, Boyd, C. (ed.). Springer, Heidelberg.

Sirvent, T. (2007). Traitor tracing scheme with constant ciphertext rate against powerful pirates. In *Proceedings of the Workshop on Coding and Cryptography (WCC'07)*, Versailles, France.

Stinson, D.R. and Wei, R. (1998). Combinatorial properties and constructions of traceability schemes and frameproof codes. *SIAM Journal on Discrete Mathematics*, 11(1), 41–53.

Stinson, D.R. and Wei, R. (1999). Key preassigned traceability schemes for broadcast encryption. In *SAC 1998*, vol. 1556 of *LNCS*, Tavares, S.E., Meijer, H. (eds). Springer, Heidelberg.

Tardos, G. (2003). Optimal probabilistic fingerprint codes. In *35th ACM STOC*. ACM Press.

Tô, V.D., Safavi-Naini, R., Zhang, F. (2003). New traitor tracing schemes using bilinear map. In *Digital Rights Management – DRM '03*, Feigenbaum, J., Sander, T., Yung, M. (eds). ACM Press.

Trung, T.V. and Martirosyan, S. (2005). New constructions for IPP codes. *Designs, Codes and Cryptography*, 35(2), 227–239.

Tzeng, W.-G. and Tzeng, Z.-J. (2001). A public-key traitor tracing scheme with revocation using dynamic shares. In *PKC 2001*, vol. 1992 of *LNCS*, Kim, K. (ed.). Springer, Heidelberg.

Watanabe, Y., Hanaoka, G., Imai, H. (2001). Efficient asymmetric public-key traitor tracing without trusted agents. In *CT-RSA 2001*, vol. 2020 of *LNCS*, Naccache, D. (ed.). Springer, Heidelberg.

Waters, B. (2009). Dual system encryption: Realizing fully secure IBE and HIBE under simple assumptions. In *CRYPTO 2009*, vol. 5677 of *LNCS*, Halevi, S. (ed.). Springer, Heidelberg.

Zhandry, M. (2020). New techniques for traitor tracing: Size $N^{1/3}$ and more from pairings. In *CRYPTO 2020, Part I*, vol. 12170 of *LNCS*, Micciancio, D., Ristenpart, T. (eds). Springer, Heidelberg.

7

Attribute-Based Encryption

Romain GAY
IBM Research Zurich, Switzerland

7.1. Introduction

In this chapter, we present encryption schemes with fine-grained access to the encrypted plaintext, as opposed to the all-or-nothing access achieved by traditional public-key encryption schemes. These are referred to as attribute-based encryption schemes (ABE). Namely, in an ABE scheme, the setup generates a public key and a so-called master secret key. The public key can be used by anyone to encrypt a plaintext associated with a policy access that can be represented for instance as a Boolean formula. There is an additional algorithm that given as input the master secret key and an attribute generates a user secret key (for that specific attribute). Decryption takes a ciphertext and a user secret key, and succeeds in recovering the plaintext if and only if the attribute of the user secret key satisfies the formula embedded in the ciphertext. If an adversary gets hold of some user secret keys, where none which is supposed to decrypt, then the confidentiality of the encrypted plaintext is preserved.

We present here ABE schemes from pairing groups (which are described at length in Chapter 5). We follow a modular approach, where the ABE is obtained starting with a simple statistical primitive called predicate encoding that only satisfies a weak notion of security (only secure when one user secret key is corrupted), which is then generically transformed into a secret-key ABE, that is, an ABE where the encryption algorithm requires the master-secret key (and not just the public key). Finally, this secret-key ABE itself is turned into an ABE, where the encryption is public-key.

Asymmetric Cryptography,
coordinated by David POINTCHEVAL. © ISTE Ltd. 2022.

Figure 7.1 describes this two-step approach. When instantiated with existing predicate encodings, this generic construction yields ABE for different classes of access polices, such as Boolean formulae or identity-based encryption (IBE). We also provide such predicate encodings for completeness and to illustrate the versatility of the modular approach.

Organization of the chapter: In the first section, we recall some basics about pairing groups and the computational assumptions of use (more details are provided in Chapter 5). In the second section, we give the definition of predicate encodings and give some concrete constructions for IBE and Boolean formulae. In the third section, we show how to generically convert a predicate encoding into a secret-key ABE, then into an ABE (where the encryption algorithm is public-key). We conclude by a brief historical note on ABE.

7.2. Pairing groups

Here, we recall some definitions from Chapter 5 but with our notations. Throughout this chapter, we write column vectors as $(x_1, \ldots, x_n) \in \mathbb{Z}^n$ and row vectors as $(u_1 | \cdots | u_n) \in \mathbb{Z}^{1 \times n}$.

7.2.1. *Cyclic groups*

We use a PPT algorithm $\mathsf{GGen}(1^\lambda)$ that on input the security parameter (in unary) $\lambda \in \mathbb{N}$ generates a cyclic group $\mathbb{G}$ of order p, where p is a 2λ-bit prime. We use additive bracket notations, where P is a generator of $\mathbb{G}$, and for all $a \in \mathbb{Z}_p$, we write $[a] = aP \in \mathbb{G}$. Similarly for any matrix $\mathbf{A} \in \mathbb{Z}_p^{m \times m}$, we write $[\mathbf{A}] = \mathbf{A}P \in \mathbb{G}^{m \times n}$, where the multiplication is performed component-wise. This choice of notations implies that for all matrices $\mathbf{A}, \mathbf{B} \in \mathbb{Z}_p^{m \times n}$, $[\mathbf{A}] + [\mathbf{B}] = [\mathbf{A} + \mathbf{B}]$.

We say the DDH assumption holds with respect to GGen if for all PPT adversaries $\mathcal{A}$, there exists a negligible function ν such that for all $\lambda \in \mathbb{N}$: $\mathsf{Adv}_{\mathcal{A}}^{\mathsf{GGen}}(\lambda) \leq \nu(\lambda)$, where the advantage $\mathsf{Adv}_{\mathcal{A}}^{\mathsf{GGen}}(\lambda)$ is defined as follows:

$$
\mathsf{Adv}_{\mathcal{A}}^{\mathsf{GGen}}(\lambda) = \left| 1/2 - \Pr \left[\begin{array}{c} \mathsf{GGen}(1^\lambda) \to \mathbb{G}, \mathbf{a}, \mathbf{u} \leftarrow_R \mathbb{Z}_p^2, \\ r \leftarrow_R \mathbb{Z}_p \, b \leftarrow_R \{0,1\} \\ t_0 = (\mathbb{G}, [\mathbf{a}], [\mathbf{a}r]), t_1 = (\mathbb{G}, [\mathbf{a}], [\mathbf{u}]) \\ \mathcal{A}(t_b) \to b' \end{array} : b = b' \right] \right|.
$$

7.2.2. *Pairing groups*

We use a PPT algorithm $\mathsf{PGGen}(1^\lambda)$ that on input the security parameter (in unary) $\lambda \in \mathbb{N}$ generates groups $\mathbb{G}_1, \mathbb{G}_2, \mathbb{G}_T$ of order p, where p is a 2λ-bit prime, generated, respectively, by P_1, P_2, P_T. For all $s \in \{1, 2, T\}$ and $\mathbf{A} \in \mathbb{Z}_p^{m \times n}$, we write $[\mathbf{A}]_s = \mathbf{A}P_s \in \mathbb{G}_s^{m \times n}$. These groups are equipped with a non-degenerate bilinear map $e : \mathbb{G}_1 \times \mathbb{G}_2 \rightarrow \mathbb{G}_T$ such that for all $a, b \in \mathbb{Z}_p$, $e([a]_1, [b]_2) = [ab]_T$. For matrices $\mathbf{A}$ and $\mathbf{B}$ of matching dimension, we have $e([\mathbf{A}]_1, [\mathbf{B}]_2) = [\mathbf{AB}]_T$. For any $s \in \{1, 2, T\}$, we say DDH holds with respect to PGGen in $\mathbb{G}_s$ if for all PPT adversaries $\mathcal{A}$, there exists a negligible function ν such that for all $\lambda \in \mathbb{N}$: $\mathsf{Adv}_{\mathcal{A}}^{\mathsf{PGGen}, s}(\lambda) \leq \nu(\lambda)$, where the advantage $\mathsf{Adv}_{\mathcal{A}}^{\mathsf{PGGen}, s}(\lambda)$ is defined as $\mathsf{Adv}_{\mathcal{A}}^{\mathsf{GGen}}(\lambda)$, but using $\mathbb{G}_s$ instead of $\mathbb{G}$.

7.3. Predicate encodings

7.3.1. Definition

DEFINITION 7.1 (Predicate Encoding).– *Let p be a prime, $|\mathsf{ct}|, |\mathsf{usk}|, n, s \in \mathbb{N}$ and $\mathcal{P} \subseteq \{P : \{0, 1\}^s \rightarrow \{0, 1\}\}$. A predicate encoding with respect to $(p, |\mathsf{ct}|, |\mathsf{usk}|, n, \mathcal{P})$ is a tuple of polynomial-time deterministic algorithms (EncCt, EncKey, Decode) that fulfills the syntax, correctness and security properties described below.*

7.3.1.1. Syntax

– $\mathsf{EncCt}(P) \rightarrow \mathbf{C}$. Given as input a predicate $P \in \mathcal{P}$, it outputs a matrix $\mathbf{C} \in \mathbb{Z}_p^{n \times |\mathsf{ct}|}$.

– $\mathsf{EncKey}(\mathsf{att}) \rightarrow \mathbf{K}$. Given as input an attribute $\mathsf{att} \in \{0, 1\}^s$, it outputs a matrix $\mathbf{K} \in \mathbb{Z}_p^{(n+1) \times |\mathsf{usk}|}$.

– $\mathsf{Decode}(P, \mathsf{att}) \rightarrow \mathbf{d}$. Given as input a predicate $P \in \mathcal{P}$ and an attribute $\mathsf{att} \in \{0, 1\}^s$, it outputs a vector $\mathbf{d} \in \mathbb{Z}_p^{|\mathsf{ct}| + |\mathsf{usk}|}$.

7.3.1.2. Correctness

For all $P \in \mathcal{P}$ and $\mathsf{att} \in \{0, 1\}^s$ such that $P(\mathsf{att}) = 1$, writing $\mathbf{C} = \mathsf{EncCt}(P) \in \mathbb{Z}_p^{n \times |\mathsf{ct}|}$, $\mathbf{K} = \mathsf{EncKey}(\mathsf{att}) \in \mathbb{Z}_p^{(n+1) \times |\mathsf{usk}|}$ and $\mathbf{d} = \mathsf{Decode}(P, \mathsf{att}) \in \mathbb{Z}_p^{|\mathsf{ct}| + |\mathsf{usk}|}$, we have: $\left(\frac{\mathbf{0}^\top}{\mathbf{C}} \middle| \mathbf{K} \right) \mathbf{d} = (1, 0, \dots, 0) \in \mathbb{Z}_p^{n+1}$, where $\mathbf{0}^\top \in \mathbb{Z}_p^{1 \times |\mathsf{ct}|}$.

7.3.1.3. Security

For all $P \in \mathcal{P}$ and $\mathsf{att} \in \{0, 1\}^s$ such that $P(\mathsf{att}) = 0$, the vector $(1, 0, \dots, 0) \in \mathbb{Z}_p^{n+1}$ is not in the column span of $\left(\frac{\mathbf{0}^\top}{\mathbf{C}} \middle| \mathbf{K} \right)$.

7.3.1.4. *Equivalent definition of security*

For all $P \in \mathcal{P}$ and att $\in \{0,1\}^s$ such that $P(\text{att}) = 0$, the following distributions are equal:

$$\left\{ \alpha \leftarrow_R \mathbb{Z}_p, \mathbf{v} \leftarrow_R \mathbb{Z}_p^n : \left(\alpha, (\alpha, \mathbf{v})^\top \left(\frac{\mathbf{0}^\top}{\mathbf{C}} \middle| \mathbf{K} \right) \right) \right\}$$

$$= \left\{ \alpha \leftarrow_R \mathbb{Z}_p, \mathbf{v} \leftarrow_R \mathbb{Z}_p^n : \left(\alpha, (0, \mathbf{v})^\top \left(\frac{\mathbf{0}^\top}{\mathbf{C}} \middle| \mathbf{K} \right) \right) \right\}.$$

7.3.2. Constructions

We present two constructions of predicate encodings. The first one corresponds to IBE, where the predicate is simply the equality between two identities that belong to a large space. The second is a predicate encoding for predicates that are represented by read-once monotone span programs (we recall the definition of the latter), which capture Boolean read-once formulae.

7.3.2.1. *Identity-based encryption*

Let p be a prime, $|\text{ct}| = 1, |\text{usk}| = 1, n = 2, s = \lfloor \log(p) \rfloor$ and $\mathcal{P} = \{P_{\text{id}} : \{0,1\}^s \rightarrow \{0,1\}\}$ is the set of predicates P_{id} defined for all id $\in \{0,1\}^s$ as $P_{\text{id}}(\text{id}') = 1$ if id $=$ id′, $P_{\text{id}}(\text{id}') = 0$ otherwise. We present a predicate encoding with respect to $(p, |\text{ct}|, |\text{usk}|, n, \mathcal{P})$, where we interpret any bit string id $\in \{0,1\}^s$ as an integer in $\mathbb{Z}_p$ in the straightforward way.

– EncCt(id): Given id $\in \mathbb{Z}_p$, it outputs the matrix $\mathbf{C} \in \mathbb{Z}_p^{2 \times 1}$ such that for all $(v_1, v_2) \in \mathbb{Z}_p^2$, $\mathbf{C}^\top(v_1, v_2) = v_1 + \text{id}v_2 \in \mathbb{Z}_p$.

– EncKey(id): Given id $\in \mathbb{Z}_p$, it outputs the matrix $\mathbf{K} \in \mathbb{Z}_p^{3 \times 1}$ such that for all $(\alpha, v_1, v_2) \in \mathbb{Z}_p^3$, $\mathbf{K}^\top(\alpha, v_1, v_2) = \alpha + v_1 + \text{id}v_2 \in \mathbb{Z}_p$.

– Decode(id, id′): If id $=$ id′, it outputs the vector $\mathbf{d} = (-1, 1) \in \mathbb{Z}_p^2$.

Correctness: Let id $\in \mathbb{Z}_p$, $\mathbf{C} = \text{EncCt}(\text{id})$, $\mathbf{K} = \text{EncKey}(\text{id})$ and $\mathbf{d} = \text{Decode}(\text{id}, \text{id}')$. For all $\alpha, v_1, v_2 \in \mathbb{Z}_p$, we have $(\alpha, v_1, v_2)^\top \left(\frac{\mathbf{0}^\top}{\mathbf{C}} \middle| \mathbf{K} \right) \mathbf{d} = -(v_1 + \text{id}v_2) + \alpha + v_1 + \text{id}v_2 = \alpha$. □

Security: Consider the map $H_{v_1, v_2} : \mathbb{Z}_p \rightarrow \mathbb{Z}_p$ defined for all $v_1, v_2 \in \mathbb{Z}_p$ as $H_{v_1, v_2}(\text{id}) = v_1 + \text{id}v_2$. The security of the encoding follows readily from the pairwise independence of this map, which states that for all inputs id, id′ $\in \mathbb{Z}_p$, id $\neq$ id′, the distribution $\{v_1, v_2 \leftarrow_R \mathbb{Z}_p : (H_{v_1, v_2}(\text{id}), H_{v_1, v_2}(\text{id}'))\}$ is uniform over $\mathbb{Z}_p^2$. The proof of this well-known property is recalled in lemma 7.1. □

LEMMA 7.1 (Pairwise independence).– *For all* $\mathrm{id}, \mathrm{id}' \in \mathbb{Z}_p$, $\mathrm{id} \neq \mathrm{id}'$, *the distribution* $\{v_1, v_2 \leftarrow_R \mathbb{Z}_p : (H_{v_1, v_2}(\mathrm{id}), H_{v_1, v_2}(\mathrm{id}'))\}$ *is uniform over* $\mathbb{Z}_p^2$, *where* H_{v_1, v_2} *is defined above.*

Proof. The matrix $\begin{pmatrix} 1 & 1 \\ \mathrm{id} & \mathrm{id}' \end{pmatrix}$ is invertible for $\mathrm{id} \neq \mathrm{id}'$, since $\det \begin{pmatrix} 1 & 1 \\ \mathrm{id} & \mathrm{id}' \end{pmatrix} = \mathrm{id}' - \mathrm{id}$.

Thus, the distribution $\left\{ \mathbf{v} \leftarrow_R \mathbb{Z}_p^2 : \begin{pmatrix} 1 & 1 \\ \mathrm{id} & \mathrm{id}' \end{pmatrix} \mathbf{v} \right\}$ is uniform over $\mathbb{Z}_p^2$.   □

7.3.2.2. *Read-once monotone span programs*

We start by recalling the definition of read-once monotone span programs.

DEFINITION 7.2 (Read-Once MSP).– *Let p be a prime, $\ell, s \in \mathbb{N}$ and $\mathbf{M} \in \mathbb{Z}_p^{\ell \times s}$. We say $\mathbf{x} \in \{0,1\}^s$ satisfies $\mathbf{M}$ if the vector $(1, 0, \ldots, 0) \in \mathbb{Z}_p^\ell$ is in the column span of $\mathbf{M_x}$, which denotes the collection of vectors $(\mathbf{M}_i)_{i \in [s], x_i = 1}$ where $\mathbf{M}_i$ denotes the ith column of $\mathbf{M}$. That is, $\mathbf{x}$ satisfies $\mathbf{M}$ if there exist constants $\omega_1, \ldots, \omega_s \in \mathbb{Z}_p$ such that $\sum_{i \in [s], x_i = 1} \omega_i \mathbf{M}_i = (1, 0, \ldots, 0)$. Observe that the constants $\{\omega_i\}_{i \in [s]}$ can be computed in time polynomial in the size of the matrix $\mathbf{M}$ via Gaussian elimination.*

As we will see later, MSP are convenient to use in the context of ABE, and they capture the predicates that can be expressed as Boolean formulae. Namely, every Boolean formula ϕ that is monotone (only uses positive literals) and read-once (each variable is used as a literal at most once) can be turned efficiently into a matrix $\mathbf{M}_\phi$ (whose size grows with the size of ϕ) such that for all $\mathbf{x} \in \{0,1\}^s$, we have $\phi(\mathbf{x}) = 1$ if and only if $\mathbf{x}$ satisfies $\mathbf{M}$ (as per definition 7.2).

We recall a useful lemma regarding the statistical security of MSP, whose proof is given in Karchmer and Wigderson (1993).

LEMMA 7.2 (Security of MSP).– *Let $\mathbf{M} \in \mathbb{Z}_p^{\ell \times s}$ and $\mathbf{x} \in \{0,1\}^s$ that does not satisfy $\mathbf{M}$ (as per definition 7.2). The following distributions are identical:* $\{\alpha \leftarrow \mathbb{Z}_p, \mathbf{v} \leftarrow \mathbb{Z}_p^{\ell-1} : (\alpha, (\alpha, \mathbf{v})^\top \mathbf{M}_i)_{i \in [s], x_i = 1}\}$ *and* $\{\alpha \leftarrow \mathbb{Z}_p, \mathbf{v} \leftarrow \mathbb{Z}_p^{\ell-1} : (\alpha, (0, \mathbf{v})^\top \mathbf{M}_i)_{i \in [s], x_i = 1}\}$.

We now present a predicate encoding for read-once MSP, that is, with respect to $(p, |\mathrm{ct}|, |\mathrm{usk}|, n, \mathcal{P})$ where p is a prime, $\ell, s \in \mathbb{N}$, $n = \ell + s$, $|\mathrm{ct}| = s$, $|\mathrm{usk}| = s + 1$ and $\mathcal{P} = \{P_\mathbf{M} : \{0,1\}^s \to \{0,1\}\}$ is the set of predicates $P_\mathbf{M}$ defined for all $\mathbf{M} \in \mathbb{Z}_p^{\ell \times s}$ as follows. $P_\mathbf{M}$ takes as input an attribute $\mathbf{x} = (x_1, \ldots, x_s) \in \{0,1\}^s$, and outputs 1 if $\mathbf{x}$ satisfies $\mathbf{M}$ as per definition 7.2.

– EncCt(M): Given $\mathbf{M} \in \mathbb{Z}_p^{\ell \times s}$, it outputs the matrix $\mathbf{C} \in \mathbb{Z}_p^{n \times |\mathrm{ct}|}$ such that for all $\mathbf{u} \in \mathbb{Z}_p^s, \mathbf{v} \in \mathbb{Z}_p^{\ell-1}, \gamma \in \mathbb{Z}_p$, $\mathbf{C}^\top(\mathbf{u}, \mathbf{v}, \gamma) = (u_1 + (\gamma, \mathbf{v})^\top \mathbf{M}_1, \ldots, u_s + (\gamma, \mathbf{v})^\top \mathbf{M}_s) \in \mathbb{Z}_p^{|\mathrm{ct}|}$, where $\mathbf{M}_j$ denotes the ith column of $\mathbf{M}$.

– EncKey($\mathbf{x}$): Given $\mathbf{x} \in \{0,1\}^s$, it outputs the matrix $\mathbf{K} \in \mathbb{Z}_p^{(n+1) \times |\text{usk}|}$ such that for all $\mathbf{u} \in \mathbb{Z}_p^s, \mathbf{v} \in \mathbb{Z}_p^{\ell-1}, \gamma, \alpha \in \mathbb{Z}_p, \mathbf{K}(\alpha, \mathbf{u}, \mathbf{v}, \gamma) = (\alpha + \gamma, x_1 u_1, \ldots, x_s u_s) \in \mathbb{Z}_p^{|\text{usk}|}$.

– Decode($\mathbf{M}, \mathbf{x}$): If $\mathbf{x}$ satisfies $\mathbf{M}$, it computes $\omega_1, \ldots, \omega_s \in \mathbb{Z}_p$ such that $\sum_{i \in [s], x_i = 1} \omega_i \mathbf{M}_i = (1, 0, \ldots, 0)$ and outputs the vector $\mathbf{d} := (-x_1 \omega_1, \ldots, -x_s \omega_s, 1, \omega_1, \ldots, \omega_s) \in \mathbb{Z}_p^{|\text{ct}| + |\text{usk}|}$.

Roughly speaking, each value u_i contained in the encoding EncKey($\mathbf{x}$) allows the decryption to unpad the value $(\gamma, \mathbf{v})^\top \mathbf{M}_i$ from the encoding EncCt($\mathbf{M}$). If enough of those values are recovered, then the value γ can be obtained, which itself unpads the value α. If enough of those values remain padded, then γ is statistically hidden, and so does α.

Correctness: Let $\mathbf{M} \in \mathbb{Z}_p^{\ell \times s}, \mathbf{C} = \text{EncCt}(\mathbf{M}), \mathbf{x} \in \{0,1\}^s$ that satisfies $\mathbf{M}$, $\mathbf{K} = \text{EncKey}(\mathbf{x})$, and $\mathbf{d} = \text{Decode}(\mathbf{M}, \mathbf{x})$. For all $\alpha, \gamma, \in \mathbb{Z}_p, \mathbf{u} \in \mathbb{Z}_p^s, \mathbf{v} \in \mathbb{Z}_p^{\ell-1}$, we have $(\alpha, \mathbf{u}, \mathbf{v}, \gamma)^\top \left(\dfrac{\mathbf{0}^\top}{\mathbf{C}} \middle| \mathbf{K} \right) \mathbf{d} = -\sum_{i \in [s], x_i = 1} \omega_i \left(x_i u_i + (\gamma, \mathbf{v})^\top \mathbf{M}_i \right) + \gamma + \alpha + \sum_{i \in [s], x_i = 1} \omega_i x_i u_i = \alpha$.   □

Security: Let $\mathbf{M} \in \mathbb{Z}_p^{\ell \times s}, \mathbf{C} = \text{EncCt}(\mathbf{M}), \mathbf{x} \in \{0,1\}^s$ that does not satisfy $\mathbf{M}$ and $\mathbf{K} = \text{EncKey}(\mathbf{x})$. The following distributions are equal: $\left\{ \gamma \leftarrow_R \mathbb{Z}_p, \mathbf{u} \leftarrow_R \mathbb{Z}_p^s, \mathbf{v} \leftarrow_R \mathbb{Z}_p^{\ell-1} : \left(u_1 x_1, \ldots, u_s x_s, (u_i + (\gamma, \mathbf{v})^\top \mathbf{M}_i)_{i \in [s]} \right) \right\} = \left\{ \gamma \leftarrow_R \mathbb{Z}_p, \mathbf{u}, \mathbf{r} \leftarrow_R \mathbb{Z}_p^s, \mathbf{v} \leftarrow_R \mathbb{Z}_p^{\ell-1} : \left(u_1 x_1, \ldots, u_s x_s, (u_i + (\gamma, \mathbf{v})^\top \mathbf{M}_i)_{i \in [s], x_i = 1}, (r_i)_{i \in [s], x_i = 0} \right) \right\} = \left\{ \mathbf{u}, \mathbf{r} \leftarrow_R \mathbb{Z}_p^s, \mathbf{v} \leftarrow_R \mathbb{Z}_p^{\ell-1} : \left(u_1 x_1, \ldots, u_s x_s, (u_i + (0, \mathbf{v})^\top \mathbf{M}_i)_{i \in [s], x_i = 1}, (r_i)_{i \in [s], x_i = 0} \right) \right\}$, where the last equality follows from the statistical security of MSP. Note that the last distribution does not depend on $\gamma \leftarrow_R \mathbb{Z}_p$. Thus, the secret α is masked by the random γ.   □

7.4. Attribute-based encryption

7.4.1. *Definition*

DEFINITION 7.3 (ABE).– *Let s be a polynomial, and $\{\mathcal{P}_\lambda\}_{\lambda \in \mathbb{N}}$ be a family such that for all $\lambda \in \mathbb{N}$, $\mathcal{P}_\lambda$ is a set of predicates on $s(\lambda)$-bits inputs, that is, $\mathcal{P}_\lambda \subseteq \{P : \{0,1\}^{s(\lambda)} \to \{0,1\}\}$. An ABE for $\{\mathcal{P}_\lambda\}_{\lambda \in \mathbb{N}}$ is a tuple of PPT algorithms (Setup, Enc, KeyGen, Dec) that fulfills the syntax, correctness and security properties described below.*

7.4.1.1. Syntax

– Setup(1^λ) → (mpk, msk). Given as input the security parameter $\lambda \in \mathbb{N}$ (in unary), it outputs a master public key mpk and a master secret key msk.

– Enc(mpk, P) → (ct, kem). Given as input the master public key mpk and a predicate $P \in \mathcal{P}_\lambda$, it outputs a ciphertext ct and a symmetric key kem in a key space $\mathcal{K}_\lambda$.

– KeyGen(msk, att) → usk. Given as input the master secret key msk and an attribute att $\in \{0, 1\}^{s(\lambda)}$, it outputs a user secret key usk.

– Dec(mpk, ct, usk) → kem. Given as input the master public key mpk, a ciphertext ct and a user secret key usk, it outputs a symmetric key kem.

7.4.1.2. Correctness

For all $\lambda \in \mathbb{N}$, all (mpk, msk) in the support of Setup(1^λ), all $P \in \mathcal{P}_\lambda$, all (ct, kem) in the support of Enc(mpk, P), all attributes att $\in \{0, 1\}^{s(\lambda)}$ such that $P(\text{att}) = 1$, all usk in the support of KeyGen(msk, att), we have: Dec(mpk, ct, usk) = kem.

7.4.1.3. Security

For all PPT stateful adversaries $\mathcal{A}$ and all ABE $\mathcal{ABE}$ = (Setup, Enc, KeyGen, Dec), we define the following advantage function:

$$\text{Adv}_{\mathcal{A}}^{\mathcal{ABE}}(\lambda) = \left| 1/2 - \Pr \left[\begin{array}{c} \text{Setup}(1^\lambda) \to (\text{mpk}, \text{msk}) \\ \mathcal{A}^{\mathcal{O}_{\text{KeyGen}}(\cdot)}(\text{mpk}) \to P \\ \text{Enc}(\text{mpk}, P) \to (\text{ct}, \text{kem}) \\ b \leftarrow_R \{0, 1\}, \text{kem}_0 = \text{kem}, \text{kem}_1 \leftarrow_R \mathcal{K}_\lambda \\ \mathcal{A}^{\mathcal{O}_{\text{KeyGen}}(\cdot)}(\text{ct}, \text{kem}_b) \to b' \end{array} : b = b' \right] \right|,$$

where the oracle $\mathcal{O}_{\text{KeyGen}}$, when given as input an attribute att $\in \{0, 1\}^{s(\lambda)}$, outputs KeyGen(msk, att). We say $\mathcal{A}$ is an *admissible* adversary if it chooses a predicate P and queries its oracle $\mathcal{O}_{\text{KeyGen}}$ on inputs $\text{att}_1, \ldots, \text{att}_q$ such that $P(\text{att}_i) = 0$ for all $i = 1, \ldots, q$. That is, none of the queried user secret keys decrypt the challenge ciphertext. We say $\mathcal{ABE}$ is secure if for all PPT admissible adversaries $\mathcal{A}$, there exists a negligible function ν such that for all $\lambda \in \mathbb{N}$, $\text{Adv}_{\mathcal{A}}^{\mathcal{ABE}}(\lambda) \leq \nu(\lambda)$.

7.4.1.4. Secret-key ABE

We say an ABE is secret-key if the encryption algorithm takes as an additional input the master secret key. Note that security is defined above for an adversary that receives a single ct-kem pair, whereas real-world attacks involve many such pairs. For a (public-key) ABE, security with many ct-kem pairs is implied by security with one ct-kem pair straightforwardly. However, this implication does not hold for secret-key

ABE. Otherwise said, the security definition given above is weak for secret-key ABE. This is not an issue since secret-key ABE will only be used as a building block for public-key ABE.

7.4.2. *A modular construction*

In this section, we show how to transform generically predicate encodings into secret-key ABE, then into ABE (see Figure 7.1).

predicate encoding	secret-key ABE	ABE
statistical $\rightarrow$ one-ct (secret-key) one-usk	computational (pairing-free) one-ct (secret-key) many-usk	$\rightarrow$ computational (pairing) many-ct (public-key) many-usk

Figure 7.1. *Security features of predicate encoding, secret-key ABE and ABE*

7.4.2.1. *From predicate encodings to secret-key ABE*

Let s be a polynomial and $\{P_\lambda : \{0,1\}^{s(\lambda)} \rightarrow \{0,1\}\}_{\lambda \in \mathbb{N}}$ be a family of predicates. Assume there exists a PPT algorithm GGen such that for all $\lambda \in \mathbb{N}$, $\mathsf{GGen}(1^\lambda)$ outputs a group $\mathbb{G}_\lambda$ of prime order p_λ, and such that the DDH assumption holds with respect to GGen. Assume there exist polynomials $|\mathsf{ct}|, |\mathsf{usk}|, n$ such that for all $\lambda \in \mathbb{N}$, there exists a predicate encoding $(\mathsf{EncCt}_\lambda, \mathsf{EncKey}_\lambda, \mathsf{Decode}_\lambda)$ with respect to $(p_\lambda, |\mathsf{ct}|(\lambda), |\mathsf{usk}|(\lambda), n(\lambda), P_\lambda)$. Then, the construction presented below is a secret-key ABE. Note that to keep notations light, we do not explicitly write the dependency on λ from here on. We describe informally the transformation from predicate encodings to secret-key ABE in Figure 7.2.

predicate encoding	secret-key ABE
$\mathsf{ct} = \mathbf{u}^\top \mathbf{C}$ $\rightarrow$ $\mathsf{usk} = (\alpha, \mathbf{u})^\top \mathbf{K}$	$\mathsf{ct} = \mathbf{U}^\top \mathbf{C}$ $\mathsf{usk} = [\alpha, \mathbf{U}a r]^\top \mathbf{K}, [ar]$

Figure 7.2. *Transformation from predicate encoding to secret-key ABE. Here,* $\mathbf{C} = \mathsf{EncCt}(P)$ *for a predicate P and* $\mathbf{K} = \mathsf{EncKey}(\mathsf{att})$ *for attribute* $\mathsf{att} \in \{0,1\}^s$

– $\mathsf{Setup}(1^\lambda)$: $\mathsf{GGen}(1^\lambda) \rightarrow \mathbb{G}$ of order p, $\mathbf{U} \leftarrow_R \mathbb{Z}_p^{n \times 2}$, $\alpha \leftarrow_R \mathbb{Z}_p$, $\mathbf{a} \leftarrow_R \mathbb{Z}_p^2$, $\mathsf{msk} = (\mathbf{U}, \alpha, [\mathbf{a}], [\mathbf{U}\mathbf{a}])$, $\mathsf{mpk} = \mathbb{G}$. It outputs $(\mathsf{mpk}, \mathsf{msk})$.

– $\mathsf{Enc}(\mathsf{msk}, \mathsf{mpk}, P)$: $\mathsf{EncCt}(P) \rightarrow \mathbf{C} \in \mathbb{Z}_p^{n \times |\mathsf{ct}|}$, $\mathsf{ct} = (\mathbf{U}^\top \mathbf{C}, P)$, $\mathsf{kem} = [\alpha] \in \mathbb{G}$. It outputs $(\mathsf{ct}, \mathsf{kem})$.

– KeyGen(msk, att): EncKey(att) $\rightarrow$ $\mathbf{K} \in \mathbb{Z}_p^{(n+1) \times |\text{usk}|}$, $r \leftarrow \mathbb{Z}_p$, usk $=$ $([\alpha, \mathbf{U}ar]^\top \mathbf{K}, [ar], \text{att})$. It outputs usk.

– Dec(mpk, ct, usk): Parse ct $= (\mathbf{V}, P)$ with $\mathbf{V} \in \mathbb{Z}_p^{2 \times |\text{ct}|}$ and usk $=$ $([\mathbf{w}^\top], [\mathbf{z}], \text{att})$ with $[\mathbf{w}^\top] \in \mathbb{G}^{1 \times |\text{usk}|}$, $[\mathbf{z}] \in \mathbb{G}^2$. Decode$(P, \text{att}) \rightarrow \mathbf{d} \in \mathbb{Z}_p^{|\text{ct}| + |\text{usk}|}$. It outputs $([\mathbf{z}]^\top \mathbf{V} | [\mathbf{w}^\top]) \mathbf{d} \in \mathbb{G}$.

Correctness: Let P and att such that $P(\text{att}) = 1$. The encryption Enc(msk, mpk, P) outputs ct $= (\mathbf{U}^\top \mathbf{C}, P)$ where $\mathbf{C} = \text{EncCt}(P)$. The user secret key generation KeyGen(msk, att) outputs usk $= ([\alpha, \mathbf{U}ar]^\top \mathbf{K}, [ar], \text{att})$ where $\mathbf{K} = \text{EncKey}(\text{att})$. Decryption computes $([ar]^\top \mathbf{U}^\top \mathbf{C} | [\alpha, \mathbf{U}ar]^\top \mathbf{K}) \mathbf{d} =$ $[\alpha, \mathbf{U}ar]^\top \left(\dfrac{\mathbf{0}^\top}{\mathbf{C}} \middle| \mathbf{K} \right) \mathbf{d} = [\alpha]$ where the last equality follows from the correctness of the predicate encoding.

Security: We show that the secret-key ABE is secure if DDH holds with respect to GGen and the predicate encoding is secure. Namely, we show that for all admissible PPT adversaries $\mathcal{A}$ making q user secret key queries, there exists a PPT algorithm $\mathcal{B}$ and a negligible function ν such that for all $\lambda \in \mathbb{N}$: $\text{Adv}_{\mathcal{A}}^{\mathcal{ABE}}(\lambda) \leq 2q \cdot \text{Adv}_{\mathcal{B}}^{\text{GGen}}(\lambda) + \nu(\lambda)$, where $\mathcal{ABE} = (\text{Setup}, \text{Enc}, \text{KeyGen}, \text{Dec})$ denotes the ABE scheme above.

We proceed using a series of hybrid games, described below. For any $i \in \mathbb{N}$, we denote by Adv_i the probability (taken over the random coins of the adversary $\mathcal{A}$ and Game_i) that Game_i outputs 1 when interacting with the adversary $\mathcal{A}$.

– $\text{Game}_0(1^\lambda)$: This is the game that corresponds to the security definition (see definition 7.3); thus, we have $\text{Adv}_{\mathcal{A}}^{\mathcal{ABE}}(\lambda) = \text{Adv}_0$. For completeness, we describe the game here. It runs Setup$(1^\lambda) \rightarrow$ (mpk, msk) where msk $= (\mathbf{U}, \alpha, [\mathbf{a}], [\mathbf{U}\mathbf{a}])$ and mpk $= \mathbb{G}$. It sends mpk to the adversary $\mathcal{A}$. When $\mathcal{A}$ sends the query att to its oracle $\mathcal{O}_{\text{KeyGen}}$, the game computes KeyGen(msk, att) $\rightarrow$ usk $= ([\alpha, \mathbf{U}ar]^\top \mathbf{K}, [ar], \text{att})$ and returns usk to $\mathcal{A}$. At some point, $\mathcal{A}$ sends a predicate P, upon which the game samples $b \leftarrow_R \{0,1\}$, computes Enc(msk, mpk, P) $\rightarrow$ $\Big(\text{ct} = (\mathbf{U}^\top \mathbf{C}, P), \text{kem} = [\alpha]\Big)$. It sets $\text{kem}_0 = [\alpha]$ and $\text{kem}_1 \leftarrow_R \mathbb{G}$. It returns (ct, kem_b) to $\mathcal{A}$. At some point, $\mathcal{A}$ sends a guess b', upon which the game ends and outputs 1 if $b' = b$, 0 otherwise.

– $\text{Game}_i(1^\lambda)$: This game is defined for all $i \in \{0, \ldots, q\}$, where q denotes the number of queries from $\mathcal{A}$ to its oracle $\mathcal{O}_{\text{KeyGen}}$. For the last $q - i$th queries to $\mathcal{O}_{\text{KeyGen}}$, Game_i computes usk exactly as for Game_0. However, it answers to the first ith queries as follows (the differences with Game_0 are highlighted). Given att $\in \{0,1\}^s$, it computes EncKey(att) $\rightarrow$ $\mathbf{K}$, $r \leftarrow_R \mathbb{Z}_p$, usk $= \big([\mathbf{0}, \mathbf{U}ar]^\top \mathbf{K}, [ar], \text{att}\big)$.

Note that $\text{Adv}_q = 0$, since in Game_q, none of the user secret keys given to $\mathcal{A}$ depend on the secret value $\alpha \in \mathbb{Z}_p$. Thus, in this last game, both kem_0 and kem_1 are identically distributed, namely, uniformly random (independent from everything else). Thus, to conclude the security proof, we show that for all $i \in [q]$, there exists a PPT algorithm $\mathcal{B}_i$ and a negligible function ν_i such that $\mathsf{Adv}_{i-1} - \mathsf{Adv}_i \leq 2\mathsf{Adv}_{\mathcal{B}_i}^{\mathsf{GGen}}(\lambda) + \nu_i(\lambda)$.

To do so, we introduce intermediate games defined below for all $i \in [q]$.

– $\underline{\mathsf{Game}_{i-1.1}(1^\lambda)}$: This game is as Game_{i-1} except for the ith query to $\mathcal{O}_{\mathsf{KeyGen}}$. This query is answered as follows (the differences with Game_{i-1} are highlighted). Given att $\in \{0,1\}^s$, it computes $\mathsf{EncKey}(\mathsf{att}) \rightarrow \mathbf{K}$, $\boxed{\mathbf{z} \leftarrow_R \mathbb{Z}_p^2}$, usk $= ([\alpha, \mathbf{Uz}]^\top \mathbf{K}, [\mathbf{z}], \mathsf{att})$. This transition is justified by the DDH assumption, which states that the following are computationally indistinguishable: $([\mathbf{a}], [\mathbf{a}r]) \approx_c ([\mathbf{a}], [\mathbf{z}])$ where $\mathbf{a}, \mathbf{z} \leftarrow_R \mathbb{Z}_p^2$ and $r \leftarrow_R \mathbb{Z}_p$. Namely, there exists a PPT algorithm $\mathcal{B}_{i.1}$ such that $\mathsf{Adv}_{i-1} - \mathsf{Adv}_{i-1.1} \leq \mathsf{Adv}_{\mathcal{B}_{i.1}}^{\mathsf{GGen}}(\lambda)$.

– $\underline{\mathsf{Game}_{i-1.2}(1^\lambda)}$: This game is as $\mathsf{Game}_{i-1.1}$ except for the ith query to $\mathcal{O}_{\mathsf{KeyGen}}$. This query is answered as follows (the differences with $\mathsf{Game}_{i-1.1}$ are highlighted). Given att $\in \{0,1\}^s$, it computes $\mathsf{EncKey}(\mathsf{att}) \rightarrow \mathbf{K}$, $\mathbf{z} \leftarrow_R \mathbb{Z}_p^2$, usk $= ([\boxed{\mathbf{0}}, \mathbf{Uz}]^\top \mathbf{K}, [\mathbf{z}], \mathsf{att})$. We show that the following are statistically close: $\mathsf{Adv}_{i-1.1} \approx_s \mathsf{Adv}_{i-1.2}$ with statistical distance $1/p$, using the security of the predicate encoding.

Write $\mathbf{C} = \mathsf{EncCt}(P)$ and $\mathbf{K} = \mathsf{EncKey}(\mathsf{att})$, where att is the ith query to $\mathcal{O}_{\mathsf{KeyGen}}$. We have (difference from one distribution to the next one are highlighted):

$$\left\{ \alpha \leftarrow_R \mathbb{Z}_p, \mathbf{a}, \mathbf{z} \leftarrow_R \mathbb{Z}_p^2, \mathbf{U} \leftarrow_R \mathbb{Z}_p^{n\times 2} : \left(\mathbf{U}^\top \mathbf{C}, \mathbf{a}, \mathbf{Ua}, \alpha, (\alpha, \mathbf{Uz})^\top \mathbf{K}\right) \right\}$$

$$\approx_s \left\{ \alpha \leftarrow_R \mathbb{Z}_p, \boxed{(\mathbf{a}|\mathbf{z}) \leftarrow_R \mathsf{GL}_2}, \mathbf{U} \leftarrow_R \mathbb{Z}_p^{n\times 2} : \left(\mathbf{U}^\top \mathbf{C}, \mathbf{a}, \mathbf{Ua}, \alpha, (\alpha, \mathbf{Uz})^\top \mathbf{K}\right) \right\}$$

$$= \left\{ \alpha \leftarrow_R \mathbb{Z}_p, (\mathbf{a}|\mathbf{z}) \leftarrow_R \mathsf{GL}_2, \boxed{\mathbf{a}^\perp s.t. \mathbf{a}^\top \mathbf{a}^\perp = 0, \mathbf{z}^\top \mathbf{a}^\perp = 1, \mathbf{u} \leftarrow_R \mathbb{Z}_p^n}, \mathbf{U} \right.$$
$$\left. \leftarrow_R \mathbb{Z}_p^{n\times 2} : \left(\mathbf{U}^\top \mathbf{C} + \boxed{\mathbf{a}^\perp \mathbf{u}^\top \mathbf{C}}, \mathbf{a}, \mathbf{Ua}, \alpha, (\alpha, \mathbf{Uz} + \mathbf{u})^\top \mathbf{K}\right) \right\}$$

$$= \left\{ \alpha \leftarrow_R \mathbb{Z}_p, (\mathbf{a}|\mathbf{z}) \leftarrow_R \mathsf{GL}_2, \mathbf{a}^\perp s.t. \mathbf{a}^\top \mathbf{a}^\perp = 0, \mathbf{z}^\top \mathbf{a}^\perp = 1, \mathbf{u} \leftarrow_R \mathbb{Z}_p^n, \mathbf{U} \right.$$
$$\left. \leftarrow_R \mathbb{Z}_p^{n\times 2} : \left(\mathbf{U}^\top \mathbf{C} + \mathbf{a}^\perp \mathbf{u}^\top \mathbf{C}, \mathbf{a}, \mathbf{Ua}, \alpha, (\boxed{\mathbf{0}}, \mathbf{Uz} + \mathbf{u})^\top \mathbf{K}\right) \right\}.$$

The first approximation $\approx_s$ relies on the fact that with probability less than $2/p$ over the random choices $\mathbf{a}, \mathbf{z} \leftarrow_R \mathbb{Z}_p^2$, the matrix $(\mathbf{a}|\mathbf{z}) \in \mathbb{Z}_p^2$ is non-singular. In that case, we can define $\mathbf{a}^\perp \in \mathbb{Z}_p^2$ to be the vector such that $\mathbf{a}^\top \mathbf{a}^\perp = 0$ and $\mathbf{z}^\top \mathbf{a}^\perp = 1$. We denote GL_2 the set of non-singular 2 by 2 matrices over $\mathbb{Z}_p$ – equipped with matrix multiplication, this is a group called general linear group.

The first equality follows from the fact that for all $\mathbf{a}^\perp \in \mathbb{Z}_p^2$, we have: $\{\mathbf{U} \leftarrow_R \mathbb{Z}_p^{n\times 2} : \mathbf{U}\} = \{\mathbf{U} \leftarrow_R \mathbb{Z}_p^{n\times 2}, \mathbf{u} \leftarrow_R \mathbb{Z}_p^n : \mathbf{U} + \mathbf{u}(\mathbf{a}^\perp)^\top\}$.

The last equality follows the security of the predicate encoding.

Then, note that $\mathsf{Game}_{i-1.2}$ is the same as Game_i except the ith query to $\mathcal{O}_{\mathsf{KeyGen}}$ is answered using a vector $[\mathbf{z}] \leftarrow_R \mathbb{G}^2$ instead of $[ar]$ with $r \leftarrow_R \mathbb{Z}_p$ in Game_i. These games are computationally indistinguishable by the DDH assumption, which states that $([\mathbf{a}], [\mathbf{z}]) \approx_c ([\mathbf{a}], [ar])$ where $\mathbf{a}, \mathbf{z} \leftarrow_R \mathbb{Z}_p^2, r \leftarrow_R \mathbb{Z}_p$. Namely, there exists a PPT algorithm $\mathcal{B}_{i.2}$ such that $\mathsf{Adv}_{i-1.2} - \mathsf{Adv}_i \leq \mathsf{Adv}_{\mathcal{B}_{i.2}}^{\mathsf{GGen}}(\lambda)$.

This completes the proof that Game_{i-1} is computationally indistinguishable from Game_i. The security bound is obtained by summing up the differences $\mathsf{Adv}_{i-1} - \mathsf{Adv}_i$ for all $i \in [q]$.   □

7.4.2.2. *From secret-key ABE to ABE*

Here, we show how to compile a secret-key ABE into an ABE. The underlying secret-key ABE is only apparent in the security proof. Namely, the security of the ABE will boil down to the use of a computational assumption on the ciphertext space, and the security of the secret-key variant of the ABE. The construction itself relies only on a predicate encoding.

Let s be a polynomial and $\{P_\lambda : \{0,1\}^{s(\lambda)} \to \{0,1\}\}_{\lambda \in \mathbb{N}}$ be a family of predicates. Assume there exists a PPT algorithm PGGen such that for all $\lambda \in \mathbb{N}$, $\mathsf{PGGen}(1^\lambda)$ outputs groups $\mathbb{G}_{1,\lambda}, \mathbb{G}_{2,\lambda}, \mathbb{G}_{T,\lambda}$ of prime order p_λ, equipped with a non-degenerate bilinear map $e_\lambda : \mathbb{G}_{1,\lambda} \times \mathbb{G}_{2,\lambda} \to \mathbb{G}_{T,\lambda}$ such that the DDH assumption holds in both $\mathbb{G}_{1,\lambda}, \mathbb{G}_{2,\lambda}$. Assume there exist polynomials $|ct|, |usk|, n$ such that for all $\lambda \in \mathbb{N}$, there exists a predicate encoding $(\mathsf{EncCt}_\lambda, \mathsf{EncKey}_\lambda, \mathsf{Decode}_\lambda)$ with respect to $(p_\lambda, |ct|(\lambda), |usk|(\lambda), n(\lambda), P_\lambda)$. Then, the construction presented below is a secure ABE. Note that to keep notations light, we do not explicitly write the dependency on λ from here on. As explained above, to prove security, we rely on the security of the secret-key variant of the ABE. We describe informally the transformation from the secret-key ABE to the ABE in Figure 7.3.

secret-key ABE	ABE
$ct = (\mathbf{u}_1 \mid \cdots \mid \mathbf{u}_n)\mathbf{C}$	$ct = [\mathbf{U}_1\mathbf{bs} \mid \cdots \mid \mathbf{U}_n\mathbf{bs}]_1\mathbf{C}, [\mathbf{bs}]_1$
$kem = [\alpha]$ $\to$	$kem = [\mathbf{k}^\top\mathbf{bs}]_T$
$usk = [\alpha, \mathbf{u}_1^\top ar, \ldots, \mathbf{u}_n^\top ar]^\top\mathbf{K}$	$usk = [\mathbf{k} \mid \mathbf{U}_1^\top ar \mid \cdots \mid \mathbf{U}_n^\top ar]_2\mathbf{K}$

Figure 7.3. *Transformation from secret-key ABE to ABE. Here,* $\mathbf{C} = \mathsf{EncCt}(P)$ *for a predicate P and $\mathbf{K} = \mathsf{EncKey}(\mathsf{att})$ for attribute* $\mathsf{att} \in \{0,1\}^s$

– $\mathsf{Setup}(1^\lambda)$: $\mathsf{PGGen}(1^\lambda) \to (\mathbb{G}_1, \mathbb{G}_2, \mathbb{G}_T)$ of order p, for all $i \in [n]$, $\mathbf{U}_i \leftarrow_R \mathbb{Z}_p^{2 \times 2}$, $\mathbf{k} \leftarrow_R \mathbb{Z}_p^2$, $\mathbf{a}, \mathbf{b} \leftarrow_R \mathbb{Z}_p^2$, $\mathsf{msk} = ([\mathbf{k}]_2, [\mathbf{a}]_2, ([\mathbf{U}_i^\top\mathbf{a}]_2)_{i \in [n]})$, $\mathsf{mpk} = ([\mathbf{b}]_1, ([\mathbf{U}_i\mathbf{b}]_1)_{i \in [n]}, [\mathbf{k}^\top\mathbf{b}]_T)$. It outputs $(\mathsf{mpk}, \mathsf{msk})$.

– Enc(mpk, P):   EncCt(P) $\rightarrow$ $\mathbf{C}$ $\in$ $\mathbb{Z}_p^{n \times |ct|}$, $s \leftarrow_R \mathbb{Z}_p$, ct $=$ $([\mathbf{U}_1 \mathbf{b}s| \cdots |\mathbf{U}_n \mathbf{b}s]_1 \mathbf{C}, [\mathbf{b}s]_1, P)$, kem $= [\mathbf{k}^\top \mathbf{b}s]_T \in \mathbb{G}_T$. It outputs (ct, kem).

– KeyGen(msk, att):   EncKey(att) $\rightarrow$ $\mathbf{K}$ $\in$ $\mathbb{Z}_p^{(n+1) \times |usk|}$, $r \leftarrow \mathbb{Z}_p$, usk $=$ $\left([\mathbf{k}|\mathbf{U}_1^\top \mathbf{a}r| \cdots |\mathbf{U}_n^\top \mathbf{a}r]_2 \mathbf{K}, [\mathbf{a}r]_2, \text{att}\right)$. It outputs usk.

– Dec(mpk, ct, usk): Parse ct $= ([\mathbf{V}]_1, [\mathbf{w}]_1, P)$ with $[\mathbf{V}]_1 \in \mathbb{G}_1^{2 \times |ct|}$ and $[\mathbf{w}]_1 \in \mathbb{G}_1^2$, usk $= ([\mathbf{Y}]_2, [\mathbf{z}]_2, \text{att})$ with $[\mathbf{Y}]_2 \in \mathbb{G}_2^{2 \times |usk|}$, $[\mathbf{z}]_2 \in \mathbb{G}_2^2$. Decode($P$, att) $\rightarrow \mathbf{d} \in \mathbb{Z}_p^{|ct|+|usk|}$, which we write as $\mathbf{d} = (\mathbf{d}_{ct}, \mathbf{d}_{usk})$ with $\mathbf{d}_{ct} \in \mathbb{Z}_p^{|ct|}$ and $\mathbf{d}_{usk} \in \mathbb{Z}_p^{|usk|}$. It outputs $e(\mathbf{d}_{ct}^\top [\mathbf{W}^\top]_1, [\mathbf{z}]_2) + e([\mathbf{w}]_1^\top, [\mathbf{Y}]_2 \mathbf{d}_{usk}) \in \mathbb{G}_T$.

Correctness: Let P and att be such that $P(\text{att}) = 1$. The encryption Enc(mpk, P) outputs ct $= ([\mathbf{U}_1 \mathbf{b}s| \cdots |\mathbf{U}_n \mathbf{b}s]_1 \mathbf{C}, [\mathbf{b}s]_1, P)$ where $\mathbf{C} = \text{EncCt}(P)$. The user secret key generation KeyGen(msk, att) outputs usk $= ([\mathbf{k}|\mathbf{U}_1^\top \mathbf{a}r| \cdots |\mathbf{U}_n^\top \mathbf{a}r]_2 \mathbf{K}, [\mathbf{a}r]_2, \text{att})$ where $\mathbf{K} = \text{EncKey(att)}$. Decryption computes $[(\mathbf{a}r)^\top (\mathbf{U}_1 \mathbf{b}s| \cdots |\mathbf{U}_n \mathbf{b}s) \mathbf{C} \mathbf{d}_{ct}]_T + [(\mathbf{b}s)^\top (\mathbf{k}| \cdots |\mathbf{U}_1^\top \mathbf{a}r| \cdots |\mathbf{U}_n^\top \mathbf{a}r) \mathbf{K} \mathbf{d}_{usk}]_T = [\alpha, u_1, \ldots, u_n]_T^\top \left(\dfrac{\mathbf{0}^\top}{\mathbf{C}} \middle| \mathbf{K} \right) \mathbf{d} = [\alpha]_T$ where $\alpha = \mathbf{k}^\top \mathbf{b}s$, $u_i = (\mathbf{a}r)^\top \mathbf{U}_i \mathbf{b}s$ and the last equality follows from the correctness of the predicate encoding.

Security: We show that the ABE is secure if DDH holds $\mathbb{G}_1$ and $\mathbb{G}_2$, and the predicate encoding is secure. Namely, we show that for all admissible PPT adversaries $\mathcal{A}$ making q user secret key queries, there exist PPT algorithms $\mathcal{B}_1$, $\mathcal{B}_2$, and a negligible function ν such that for all $\lambda \in \mathbb{N}$: $\text{Adv}_{\mathcal{A}}^{\mathcal{ABE}}(\lambda) \le \text{Adv}_{\mathcal{B}_1}^{\mathbb{G}_1}(\lambda) + 2q \cdot \text{Adv}_{\mathcal{B}_2}^{\mathbb{G}_2}(\lambda) + \nu(\lambda)$, where $\mathcal{ABE} = (\text{Setup, Enc, KeyGen, Dec})$ denotes the ABE scheme above.

We proceed using a series of hybrid games, described below. For any $i \in \mathbb{N}$, we denote by Adv_i the probability (taken over the random coins of the adversary $\mathcal{A}$ and Game_i) that Game_i outputs 1 when interacting with the adversary $\mathcal{A}$.

– $\underline{\text{Game}_0(1^\lambda)}$: This is the game that corresponds to the security definition (see definition 7.3); thus, we have $\text{Adv}_{\mathcal{A}}^{\mathcal{ABE}}(\lambda) = \text{Adv}_0$. For completeness, we describe the game here. It runs $\text{Setup}(1^\lambda) \rightarrow (\text{mpk, msk})$ where msk $= ([\mathbf{k}]_2, [\mathbf{a}]_2, ([\mathbf{U}_i^\top \mathbf{a}]_2)_i \in [n])$ and mpk $= ([\mathbf{b}]_1, ([\mathbf{U}_i \mathbf{b}]_1)_{i \in [n]}, [\mathbf{k}^\top \mathbf{b}]_T)$. It sends mpk to the adversary $\mathcal{A}$. When $\mathcal{A}$ sends the query att to its oracle $\mathcal{O}_{\text{KeyGen}}$, the game computes KeyGen(msk, att) $\rightarrow$ usk $= ([\mathbf{k}|\mathbf{U}_1^\top \mathbf{a}r| \cdots |\mathbf{U}_n^\top \mathbf{a}r]_2 \mathbf{K}, [\mathbf{a}r]_2, \text{att})$ and returns usk to $\mathcal{A}$. At some point, $\mathcal{A}$ sends a predicate P, upon which the game samples $b \leftarrow_R \{0,1\}$, computes Enc(msk, mpk, P) $\rightarrow$ ct $= ([\mathbf{U}_1 \mathbf{b}s| \cdots |\mathbf{U}_n \mathbf{b}s]_1 \mathbf{C}, [\mathbf{b}s]_1, P)$, kem $= [\mathbf{k}^\top \mathbf{b}s]_T$. It sets $\text{kem}_0 = [\mathbf{k}^\top \mathbf{b}s]_T$ and $\text{kem}_1 \leftarrow_R \mathbb{G}_T$. It returns (ct, kem_b) to $\mathcal{A}$. At some point, $\mathcal{A}$ sends a guess b', upon which the game ends and outputs 1 if $b' = b$, 0 otherwise.

– $\underline{\text{Game}_1(1^\lambda)}$: This game is as Game_0, except the challenge ciphertext is computed as follows (the differences with Game_0 are highlighted). Given P, it computes $\mathsf{EncCt}(P) \rightarrow \mathbf{C}$, $\mathbf{z} \leftarrow_R \mathbb{Z}_p^2$, $\mathsf{ct} = ([\mathbf{U}_1\mathbf{z}|\cdots|\mathbf{U}_n\mathbf{z}]_1\,\mathbf{C}, [\mathbf{z}]_1, P)$, $\mathsf{kem} = [\mathbf{k}^\top \mathbf{z}]_T$. These games are computationally indistinguishable by the DDH assumption in $\mathbb{G}_1$, which states that $([\mathbf{b}]_1, [\mathbf{b}s]_1) \approx_c ([\mathbf{b}]_1, [\mathbf{z}]_1)$ where $\mathbf{b}, \mathbf{z} \leftarrow_R \mathbb{Z}_p^2$, $s \leftarrow_R \mathbb{Z}_p$. Namely, there exists a PPT algorithm $\mathcal{B}_1$ such that $\mathsf{Adv}_0 - \mathsf{Adv}_1 \le \mathsf{Adv}_{\mathcal{B}_1}^{\mathbb{G}_1}(\lambda)$.

- $\mathsf{Game}_2(1^\lambda)$: This game is as Game_1, except the mpk and the challenge ciphertext are computed as follows (the differences with Game_1 are highlighted): $\mathsf{mpk} = ([\mathbf{b}]_1, ([\mathbf{U}_i\mathbf{b}]_1)_{i\in[n]}, [\mathbf{k}^\top\mathbf{b}]_T)$, $\mathsf{ct} = ([\mathbf{U}_1\mathbf{z}|\cdots|\mathbf{U}_n\mathbf{z}]_1\,\mathbf{C}, [\mathbf{z}]_1, P)$, $\mathsf{kem} = [\mathbf{k}^\top\mathbf{z}]_T$ where $(\mathbf{b}|\mathbf{z}) \leftarrow_R \mathsf{GL}_2$, as opposed to $\mathbf{b}, \mathbf{z} \leftarrow_R \mathbb{Z}_p^2$ in Game_1. Recall that GL_2 denotes the general linear group of degree 2, that is, the group of 2 by 2 non-singular matrices over $\mathbb{Z}_p$. Since the probability over the random choices of $\mathbf{b}, \mathbf{z} \leftarrow_R \mathbb{Z}_p^2$ that $(\mathbf{b}|\mathbf{z})$ is singular is less than $2/p$, these two games have statistical distance less than $2/p$.

- $\mathsf{Game}_3(1^\lambda)$: This game is as Game_2, except the challenge ciphertext and the user secret keys are computed as follows (the differences with Game_2 are highlighted): $\mathsf{ct} = ([\mathbf{U}_1\mathbf{z}+\mathbf{u}_1|\cdots|\mathbf{U}_n\mathbf{z}+\mathbf{u}_n]_1\,\mathbf{C}, [\mathbf{z}]_1, P)$, $\mathsf{kem} = [\mathbf{k}^\top\mathbf{z}+\alpha]_T$ with $\mathbf{u}_1,\ldots,\mathbf{u}_n \leftarrow_R \mathbb{Z}_p^2, \alpha \leftarrow_R \mathbb{Z}_p$; $\mathsf{usk} = ([\mathbf{k}+\alpha\mathbf{b}^\perp|\mathbf{U}_1^\top a r + \mathbf{b}^\perp\mathbf{u}_1^\top a r|\cdots|\mathbf{U}_n^\top a r + \mathbf{b}^\perp\mathbf{u}_n^\top a r]_2\mathbf{K}, [ar]_2, \mathsf{att})$, where $\mathbf{b}^\perp \in \mathbb{Z}_p^2$ is the vector such that $\mathbf{b}^\top\mathbf{b}^\perp = 0$ and $\mathbf{z}^\top\mathbf{b}^\perp = 1$. Game_3 and Game_2 are identically distributed, which comes from the fact that the two following distributions are equal: $\{\mathbf{U}_1,\ldots,\mathbf{U}_n \leftarrow_R \mathbb{Z}_p^{2\times 2}, (\mathbf{b}|\mathbf{z}) \leftarrow_R \mathsf{GL}_2, \mathbf{k} \leftarrow_R \mathbb{Z}_p^2 : ((\mathbf{U}_i)_{i\in[n]}, \mathbf{b}, \mathbf{z}, \mathbf{k})\} = \{\mathbf{U}_1,\ldots,\mathbf{U}_n \leftarrow_R \mathbb{Z}_p^{2\times 2}, (\mathbf{b}|\mathbf{z}) \leftarrow_R \mathsf{GL}_2, \mathbf{k} \leftarrow_R \mathbb{Z}_p^2, \mathbf{u}_1,\ldots,\mathbf{u}_n \leftarrow_R \mathbb{Z}_p^2, \alpha \leftarrow_R \mathbb{Z}_p : ((\mathbf{U}_i + \mathbf{u}_i^\top(\mathbf{b}^\perp)^\top)_{i\in[n]}, \mathbf{b}, \mathbf{z}, \mathbf{k}+\alpha\mathbf{b}^\perp)\}$, where $\mathbf{b}^\perp \in \mathbb{Z}_p^2$ is the vector such that $\mathbf{b}^\top\mathbf{b}^\perp = 0$ and $\mathbf{z}^\top\mathbf{b}^\perp = 1$. There is a post-processing algorithm that given an input distributed according the first distribution, produces an output distributed as specified by Game_2, whereas when given an input distributed according to the second distribution, the same post-processing algorithm produces an output distributed as specified by Game_3. Namely, the post-processing algorithm, upon receiving its input, samples $\mathbf{a} \leftarrow_R \mathbb{Z}_p^2$ and generates $\mathcal{A}$'s view straightforwardly.

Finally, we show that the security in Game_3 reduces to the security of the *secret-key* variant of the ABE, as presented above. Namely, we build a reduction $\mathcal{B}_3$ such that $\mathsf{Adv}_3 \le \mathsf{Adv}_{\mathcal{B}_3}^{\mathsf{sk}\text{-}\mathcal{ABE}}(\lambda)$, where $\mathsf{sk}\text{-}\mathcal{ABE}$ is the secret-key ABE obtained by transforming the predicate encoding $(\mathsf{EncCt}, \mathsf{EncKey}, \mathsf{Decode})$ as described a few pages above (using the cyclic group $\mathbb{G}_2$; see Figure 7.2). In fact, the vectors $\mathbf{u}_1,\ldots,\mathbf{u}_n \in \mathbb{Z}_p^2$ and the scalar $\alpha \in \mathbb{Z}_p$ introduced in Game_3 (highlighted above) serve as a secret key of the scheme $\mathsf{sk}\text{-}\mathcal{ABE}$. We now proceed to describe $\mathcal{B}_3$. It receives a public key $\mathsf{mpk} = \mathbb{G}_1$ from its security game. It samples $(\mathbf{b}|\mathbf{z}) \leftarrow_R \mathsf{GL}_2$, $\mathbf{U}_1,\ldots,\mathbf{U}_n \leftarrow_R \mathbb{Z}_p^{2\times 2}$ and sends $\mathsf{mpk} = ([\mathbf{b}]_1, ([\mathbf{U}_i\mathbf{b}]_1)_{i\in[n]}, [\mathbf{k}^\top\mathbf{b}]_T)$ to $\mathcal{A}$. It computes $\mathbf{b}^\perp \in \mathbb{Z}_p^2$ the vector such that $\mathbf{b}^\top\mathbf{b}^\perp = 0$ and $\mathbf{z}^\top\mathbf{b}^\perp = 1$. Whenever $\mathcal{A}$ queries its oracle $\mathcal{O}_{\mathsf{KeyGen}}$ on att, $\mathcal{B}_3$ queries its own oracle to get usk $= ([\alpha, \mathbf{u}_1^\top ar, \ldots, \mathbf{u}_n^\top ar]_2^\top \mathbf{K}, [ar]_2, \mathsf{att})$ where $\alpha \leftarrow_R \mathbb{Z}_p, \mathbf{a}, \mathbf{u}_1, \ldots, \mathbf{u}_n \leftarrow_R \mathbb{Z}_p^2$ are global parameters of sk-$\mathcal{ABE}$, whereas $r \leftarrow_R \mathbb{Z}_p$ is sampled freshly for each usk generation, and $\mathbf{K}$ $=$ EncKey(att). The reduction $\mathcal{B}_3$ sends usk $= ([\mathbf{k} + \alpha \mathbf{b}^\perp | \mathbf{U}_1 ar + \mathbf{b}^\perp \mathbf{u}_1^\top ar | \cdots | \mathbf{U}_n ar + \mathbf{b}^\perp \mathbf{u}_n^\top ar]_2 \mathbf{K}, [ar]_2, \mathsf{att})$ to $\mathcal{A}$, which it can compute since it knows the values $(\mathbf{U}_i)_{i \in [n]}$ and $\mathbf{k}, \mathbf{b}^\perp \in \mathbb{Z}_p^2$. When $\mathcal{A}$ sends the challenge P, $\mathcal{B}_3$ forwards it to its own security game to receive ct $= (\mathbf{u}_1 | \cdots | \mathbf{u}_n)\mathbf{C}$ where $\mathbf{C}$ = EncCt(P) and kem $= [\gamma]_2$, where $\gamma = \alpha$ or $\gamma \leftarrow_R \mathbb{Z}_p$, depending on the random bit chosen by the security game for sk-$\mathcal{ABE}$. Then, $\mathcal{B}_3$ sends ct $=$ $([\mathbf{U}_1 \mathbf{z} + \mathbf{u}_1 | \cdots | \mathbf{U}_n \mathbf{z} + \mathbf{u}_n]_1 \mathbf{C}, [\mathbf{z}]_1, P)$ and kem $= [\mathbf{k}^\top \mathbf{z} + \gamma]_T$, which it can computes since it knows the values $\mathbf{k}, \mathbf{b}, \mathbf{z}$ and $(\mathbf{U}_i)_{i \in [n]}$. It is clear that the output generated by $\mathcal{B}_3$ corresponds to the view of $\mathcal{A}$ in Game$_3$, and that its input is distributed according to the security game for the security of sk-$\mathcal{ABE}$. Thus, we have Adv$_3$ $\leq$ Adv$_{\mathcal{B}_3}^{\mathsf{sk}\text{-}ABE}(\lambda)$. Finally, by the security of sk-$\mathcal{ABE}$, proven a few pages above, we know there exists a PPT adversary $\mathcal{B}_2$ and a negligible function ν such that Adv$_{\mathcal{B}_3}^{\mathsf{sk}\text{-}ABE}(\lambda) \leq 2q \cdot$ Adv$_{\mathcal{B}_2}^{\mathsf{G}_2}(\lambda) + \nu(\lambda)$. Overall, we get Adv$_{\mathcal{A}}^{ABE}(\lambda) \leq$ Adv$_{\mathcal{B}_1}^{\mathsf{G}_1}(\lambda) + 2q \cdot$ Adv$_{\mathcal{B}_2}^{\mathsf{G}_2}(\lambda) + \nu(\lambda)$. $\qquad \square$

7.4.2.3. Chapter notes and history

First, the notion of IBE was put forth by Shamir (1984) as an alternative to traditional public-key infrastructure: in an IBE, any bit string that identifies a receiver (such as an email address or a social security number) can serve as a public key. One of the first construction was given in Boneh and Franklin (2001), from pairings. In doing so, they introduced the pairings for a constructive use in cryptography.

Later on, Sahai and Waters (2005) introduced the notion of fuzzy-IBE, where the identity of the ciphertext only has to approximately match that of the user secret key; they also envisioned more general access policy: the notion of ABE was born. Goyal et al. (2006) presented the first construction of ABE beyond IBE (for Boolean formulae), which also relies on pairings. Note that their original construction is key-policy: the policy (i.e. the Boolean formula) is embedded in the user secret key, and the attribute is used to produce the ciphertext. The notion we present in this chapter is reversed and referred to as ciphertext-policy ABE. It was introduced and built first in Bethencourt et al. (2007). A plethora of constructions for different families of predicates and using different sort of computational assumptions ensued. Most of them follow a proof paradigm originally introduced in Waters (2009), and referred to as the dual-system encryption methodology (this is also the case for the constructions presented in this chapter, although the presentation given here slightly differs from the original one). In an attempt to unify these works (and also to produce new ABE schemes), Attrapadung (2014) and Wee (2014) independently gave modular frameworks for building ABE from a simpler object: pair encodings and predicate encodings, respectively. Note that the former also has a computational variant that captures schemes that are not captured by predicate encodings. We choose the latter notion for simplicity in this chapter.

The first constructions of pairing-based ABE used symmetric pairings (where $\mathbb{G}_1 = \mathbb{G}_2$) and often times of composite order (instead of prime order as used here). Asymmetric pairings (where $\mathbb{G}_1 \neq \mathbb{G}_2$) give better performances for similar security levels, given they have less structure to exploit than their symmetric counterparts. Similarly, composite-order pairings are vastly outperformed by prime-order ones. In particular, the composite order must be hard to factor, which involves an order of several thousand bits, instead of a couple hundreds for the prime order for typical security levels (say, 128 bits). See Guillevic (2013) for a detailed efficiency comparison. On the other hand, composite-order pairings are easier to design schemes from, which is why they were first used historically. Significant research efforts went into converting composite-order schemes to prime-order schemes (in the context of ABE, we can cite, for instance, Okamoto and Takashima (2009); Lewko (2012)). We directly went for the state-of-the-art prime-order schemes in this chapter.

7.5. References

Attrapadung, N. (2014). Dual system encryption via doubly selective security: Framework, fully secure functional encryption for regular languages, and more. In *EUROCRYPT 2014*, vol. 8441 of *LNCS*, Nguyen, P.Q., Oswald, E. (eds). Springer, Heidelberg.

Bethencourt, J., Sahai, A., Waters, B. (2007). Ciphertext-policy attribute-based encryption. In *2007 IEEE Symposium on Security and Privacy*. IEEE Computer Society Press.

Boneh, D. and Franklin, M.K. (2001). Identity-based encryption from the Weil pairing. In *CRYPTO 2001*, vol. 2139 of *LNCS*, Kilian, J. (ed.). Springer, Heidelberg.

Goyal, V., Pandey, O., Sahai, A., Waters, B. (2006). Attribute-based encryption for fine-grained access control of encrypted data. In *ACM CCS 2006*, Juels, A., Wright, R.N., De Capitani di Vimercati, S. (eds). ACM Press. Cryptology ePrint Archive Report 2006/309.

Guillevic, A. (2013). Comparing the pairing efficiency over composite-order and prime-order elliptic curves. In *ACNS 13*, vol. 7954 of *LNCS*, Jacobson, M., Locasto, M., Mohassel, P., Safavi-Naini, R. (eds). Springer, Heidelberg.

Karchmer, M. and Wigderson, A. (1993). On span programs. In *Proceedings of the Eigth Annual Structure in Complexity Theory Conference 1993*. IEEE Computer Society.

Lewko, A.B. (2012). Tools for simulating features of composite order bilinear groups in the prime order setting. In *EUROCRYPT 2012*, vol. 7237 of *LNCS*, Pointcheval, D., Johansson, T. (eds). Springer, Heidelberg.

Okamoto, T. and Takashima, K. (2009). Hierarchical predicate encryption for inner-products. In *ASIACRYPT 2009*, vol. 5912 of *LNCS*, Matsui, M. (ed.). Springer, Heidelberg.

Sahai, A. and Waters, B.R. (2005). Fuzzy identity-based encryption. In *EUROCRYPT 2005*, vol. 3494 of *LNCS*, Cramer, R. (ed.). Springer, Heidelberg.

Shamir, A. (1984). Identity-based cryptosystems and signature schemes. In *CRYPTO'84*, vol. 196 of *LNCS*, Blakley, G.R., Chaum, D. (eds). Springer, Heidelberg.

Waters, B. (2009). Dual system encryption: Realizing fully secure IBE and HIBE under simple assumptions. In *CRYPTO 2009*, vol. 5677 of *LNCS*, Halevi, S. (ed.). Springer, Heidelberg.

Wee, H. (2014). Dual system encryption via predicate encodings. In *TCC 2014*, vol. 8349 of *LNCS*, Lindell, Y. (ed.). Springer, Heidelberg.

8

Advanced Signatures

Olivier SANDERS

Orange Labs, Rennes, France

8.1. Introduction

Today, authentication massively relies on digital signature mechanisms that act as real electronic stamps, as we saw in Chapter 2. Each of us uses these on a daily basis, whether browsing the Internet, paying by credit card or presenting official documentation with an electronic chip (passport, etc).

This approach modeled on traditional authentication methods (handwritten signatures, stamps, etc.) forms the implicit hypothesis that the problems of the real and digital worlds are the same. A simple example illustrates the limits of this reasoning. When going to the checkout, presenting the ID card to verify one's age does not create too many worries, since it is reasonable to think that the cashier will not keep hold of all the information contained in the ID card for tracing purposes or for other processes. This hypothesis unfortunately does not hold in the digital world where each piece of data is generally held automatically. In particular, it is legitimate to think that the same customer would have more qualms about sending a copy of their ID card via the Internet to access, for example, a website with adult-only content.

This example demonstrates two essential needs that we encounter in many cases of use that require authentication. There is first of all the need to limit the information

Asymmetric Cryptography,
coordinated by David POINTCHEVAL. © ISTE Ltd. 2022.

revealed only to what is strictly necessary. When a person has to prove that they are an adult, it is not the norm that, in order to do this, they must also send a whole series of information (name, date of birth, address, etc) such as that contained in their ID card. All the check should reveal is whether this person is or is not an adult. The second need is to limit the capacity to trace users once they have presented identification. If this person has to prove twice that they are an adult, then it should not be possible to link these items of "proof". Otherwise, this traceability risks leading in most cases to a precise identification of the person.

These two needs seem initially incompatible with the principle of digital signature authentication. First of all, a signature σ is created precisely to guarantee that a piece of data m has not been altered or truncated. By definition, σ can only be verified with complete knowledge of m, which seems to conflict with our first need. Then, the signature received for authentication is an element common to all the authentications of its holder and is itself an element that enables tracing. It is certainly possible to send, regularly, new signatures to alleviate this problem, as currently specified for connected vehicles (Petit et al. 2015), but this approach weighs heavily on public key infrastructures (PKI) which are then solicited much more often and, above all, do not protect against traceability involving these same infrastructures, which have the capacity to link all signatures to a single identity.

This need to hide some elements (the signature, all or part of the message) while still attesting some properties (in this instance, checking that the signature is valid) clearly call on *zero-knowledge* proof mechanisms presented in Chapter 3. In theory, these mechanisms are perfectly able to manage this type of relationship to be proved. In practice, the situation is more complex when it comes to obtaining an effective solution and it is in particular necessary to have a well-adapted pair (signature scheme S, *zero-knowledge* proof protocol Π), that is, one that can be proven effectively, using Π, the validity of a σ signature generated with S on a message m, without revealing m or σ. Generally, these are mainly signature schemes that are adapted to existing *zero-knowledge* proofs as we will see below. Such schemes will be called *advanced* in the remainder of this chapter.

In all cases, this need to interact suitably with *zero-knowledge* proofs has a fundamental consequence: it excludes all solutions where the message to be signed is hashed by means of a cryptographic hash function and so in particular all hash-and-sign approaches or approaches relying on the Fiat–Shamir heuristic (Fiat and Shamir 1987), which form the basis for the vast majority of signature schemes used in practice (see Pointcheval and Stern (2000) and the references therein). This near proscription of the hash function in advanced signatures largely explains their differences from their traditional counterparts. In particular, it resurrects the problem of long messages that can no longer simply be hashed to make them a convenient size.

Today, there is a wide variety of advanced signature constructions that reflect the variety of environments and *zero-knowledge* proof protocols used in cryptography. In this chapter, we will describe some of these more specifically, those that are fairly representative of the state-of-the-art. We will also show how they can be used to meet the needs outlined above using some primitives that are emblematic of cryptography for the protection of privacy.

8.2. Some constructions

8.2.1. *The case of scalar messages*

As explained above, advanced signature schemes were most often constructed with a well-specified *zero-knowledge* proof protocol in mind. Since 1976, and the seminal article by Diffie and Hellman (1976), public key encryption has relied essentially on groups $\mathbb{G}$ of prime order p. As explained in Chapter 5, it is often useful to consider the particular case of bilinear groups $(\mathbb{G}_1, \mathbb{G}_2, \mathbb{G}_T)$ provided with a pairing e.

Among their many advantages, prime order groups are compatible with *zero-knowledge* proof of knowledge of a discrete logarithm proposed by Schnorr (1990). In concrete terms, it is possible to prove very efficiently knowledge of scalars $x_1, x_2, \ldots, x_n \in \mathbb{Z}_p$ satisfying one or more relations $h = \prod_i g_i^{x_i}$ for $g_i, h \in \mathbb{G}$ elements.

To suit this type of proof, several signature schemes (Camenisch and Lysyanskaya 2003, 2004; Boneh and Boyen 2008; Pointcheval and Sanders 2016) supporting messages $m \in \mathbb{Z}_p$ have therefore been proposed. More precisely, these schemes present a verification equation where the messages appear as exponents, which corresponds perfectly to the Schnorr protocol. Another example of such schemes is the one proposed by Boneh and Boyen (2008), which we summarize below.

8.2.1.1. *Boneh–Boyen signatures*

– $\mathtt{Setup}(1^k)$: Given k the system's security parameter, this algorithm returns the description of bilinear groups pp $\leftarrow (p, \mathbb{G}_1, \mathbb{G}_2, \mathbb{G}_T, e)$.

– $\mathtt{Keygen}(\mathsf{pp})$: The algorithm selects two generators $g \in \mathbb{G}_1$ and $\widetilde{g} \in \mathbb{G}_2$ as well as a random scalar $x \xleftarrow{\$} \mathbb{Z}_p$ and calculates $\widetilde{X} \leftarrow \widetilde{g}^x$. The secret key sk is x and the public key pk is $(g, \widetilde{g}, \widetilde{X})$.

– $\mathtt{Sign}(\mathsf{sk}, m)$: given $m \in \mathbb{Z}_p$ the message to sign, the algorithm returns the signature $\sigma \leftarrow g^{\frac{1}{x+m}}$.

– $\mathtt{Verify}(m, \sigma, \mathsf{pk})$: To check the validity of a signature σ on a message m, this algorithm tests whether $e(\sigma, \widetilde{X} \cdot \widetilde{g}^m) = e(g, \widetilde{g})$ in which case it returns 1. Otherwise, it returns 0.

The scheme described above satisfies only a weak version of EUF-CMA security but it suffices in practice in many applications that we will see at the end of the chapter. The study of Boneh and Boyen (2008) explains nonetheless how to attain complete EUF-CMA security at the cost of a moderate increase in complexity. Moreover, a version capable of signing several messages at the same time has been described in Camenisch and Lysyanskaya (2004); Au et al. (2006) but we will not need that in this chapter. In our instance, by using bilinearity of pairing, the verification equation can simply be rewritten in the form

$$e(\sigma, \widetilde{g})^m = e(g, \widetilde{g}) \cdot e(\sigma^{-1}, \widetilde{X}).$$

Knowledge of the message m can therefore be proven by means of the Schnorr protocol mentioned above. It nevertheless remains to conceal the signature σ, which can be done by means of encryption or a commitment scheme. Unfortunately, this complexifies the relationship to be proven (since it then needs to be shown that the elements provided are encryption of a signature on a concealed message) and, hence, *zero-knowledge* proof.

To solve this problem, a very interesting alternative was proposed by Camenisch and Lysyanskaya (2004). The particularity of their scheme is in fact that any signature σ on a message $m \in \mathbb{Z}_p$ can be randomized, meaning it is possible to derive publicly (without knowledge of any particular secret) from σ a new signature σ' also valid on m. The important point for our example of use is that it is impossible, for anyone who does not know m, to know whether σ and σ' are valid on the same message. This means that in practice it is possible to transmit σ' "in clear" without any risk to anonymity. More generally, a user holding a certificate will be able to randomize it before each authentication so as to remain untraceable.

Camenisch and Lysyanskaya's original scheme suffers however from linear complexity in the number of messages to sign. In particular, the size of the signature increases with the number of messages to sign, which poses problems in cases such as identity data, where several elements (surname, first name, date of birth, etc.) must be validated. To solve this problem, Pointcheval and Sanders (2016) proposed a new scheme presenting the same features as Camenisch and Lysyanskaya (2004), but with a constant signature size. Conceptually, these two constructions are in fact very similar, so we will present only the most recent (Pointcheval and Sanders 2016) in this chapter.

8.2.1.2. *Pointcheval–Sanders signatures*

– $\mathtt{Setup}(1^k)$: Whatever k the security setting, this algorithm outputs the description pp $\leftarrow (p, \mathbb{G}_1, \mathbb{G}_2, \mathbb{G}_T, e)$ of type III bilinear groups.

– Keygen(pp, n): This algorithm generates $\widetilde{g} \stackrel{\$}{\leftarrow} \mathbb{G}_2$ and $(x, y_1, \ldots, y_n) \stackrel{\$}{\leftarrow} \mathbb{Z}_p^{n+1}$, then calculates $(\widetilde{X}, \widetilde{Y}_1, \ldots, \widetilde{Y}_n) \leftarrow (\widetilde{g}^x, \widetilde{g}^{y_1}, \ldots, \widetilde{g}^{y_n})$. The secret key sk is then defined as being $(x, y_1, \ldots, y_n)$ and the public key pk as being $(\widetilde{g}, \widetilde{X}, \widetilde{Y}_1, \ldots, \widetilde{Y}_n)$.

– Sign(sk, $m_1, \ldots, m_n$): To sign messages $m_1, \ldots, m_n$, this algorithm selects a random generator $h \stackrel{\$}{\leftarrow} \mathbb{G}_1^*$ and returns $\sigma \leftarrow (h, h^{(x + \sum y_j \cdot m_j)})$.

– Verify(pk, $(m_1, \ldots, m_n), \sigma$): Given a signature $\sigma = (\sigma_1, \sigma_2)$, the algorithm checks whether the conditions $\sigma_1 \neq 1_{\mathbb{G}_1}$ and $e(\sigma_1, \widetilde{X} \cdot \prod \widetilde{Y}_j^{m_j}) = e(\sigma_2, \widetilde{g})$ are met. It returns 1 if so and 0 if not.

As we explain in the introduction to this chapter, cases where there are several messages cannot simply be regulated with the help of a hash function. In this scheme, messages m_i are "mixed" using secret coefficients (y_i), which makes it possible to avoid compensation phenomena. Intuitively, in fact, it takes account of the fact that an adversary replacing m_1 with $m_1 + t$ for some $t \in \mathbb{Z}_p$ would be unable to adjust the other m_i to obtain a valid signature since he/she would not know the value $y_1 t$ to compensate. Here too, we might rewrite the verification equation in the form

$$\prod e(\sigma_1, \widetilde{Y}_j)^{m_j} = e(\sigma_1^{-1}, \widetilde{X}) \cdot e(\sigma_2, \widetilde{g})$$

to highlight the link with the Schnorr protocol. Each message in fact appears as an exponent, which makes it possible to prove knowledge with proofs (Schnorr 1990). The main difference with the Boneh–Boyen signature is that σ can this time be randomized as many times as necessary. Indeed, for any scalar $r \in \mathbb{Z}_p$, the signature $\sigma' = (\sigma_1^r, \sigma_2^r)$ satisfied the same relationship as before. Moreover, as soon as a single one of the messages m_i is secret, it is impossible to link σ and σ' under the DDH assumption in $\mathbb{G}_1$. This property remains true even if all the elements g^{m_i} are public, which will be useful for us in some use cases.

In all cases, this means that one can transmit σ' to authenticate and prove, with the help of the Schnorr protocol, knowledge of the messages m_i. The resulting protocol then achieves the untraceability and minimization properties of the data revealed, which we might expect from a modern authentication system. This construction, which seems quite basic, will in fact form the basis of a good number of written protocols at the end of the chapter.

8.2.2. *The case of non-scalar messages*

With regard to the performances displayed, as much by the signature schemes presented above as by the Schnorr protocol, it is tempting to think that our initial problem is solved perfectly. This would, however, ignore one characteristic of

Schnorr's proofs. These latter are in fact interactive and are not therefore suitable for use cases where authentication should be made by means of a publicly verifiable signature, even after the event. It is certainly possible to render this proof non-interactive by means of the Fiat–Shamir technique (Fiat and Shamir 1987), but this induces the need to prove security in the idealized model of the random oracle, which is not without security loss (Canetti et al. 1998, 2004).

In 2008 a major advance in *zero-knowledge* proofs was made by Groth and Sahai (2008), who proposed a new system of non-interactive proofs proved in the standard model, that is, without a random oracle. The strength of their system is that it covers a very broad range of relationships involving elements of bilinear groups, which earned them a place in an incalculable number of cryptographic protocols. Certainly, their effectiveness is not as good as the combination of Schnorr + Fiat–Shamir, but for many, the excess cost is acceptable with regard to the capacity to prove security in the standard model.

Unfortunately, these proofs, called Groth-Sahai, suffer from a limit that makes them almost incompatible with the signature schemes cited above. It is not in fact possible to use them to prove knowledge of scalars $m \in \mathbb{Z}_p$, which are messages of these same schemes. The system proposed by Groth and Sahai however makes it possible to prove knowledge of elements of groups $\mathbb{G}_1$ and $\mathbb{G}_2$, which will create another branch of advanced signatures, those that preserve the structure, that is, structure-preserving signatures (Abe et al. 2010).

This name comes from the fact that these signature mechanisms take as input elements of $\mathbb{G}_1$ and $\mathbb{G}_2$ and produce a signature formed of elements taken from these same groups, verifiable with the help of a pairing product. This specification is in fact a direct transposition of the Groth-Sahai proof capacities for which these mechanisms were specifically designed.

A very large number of constructions and variants have been proposed but we will only describe the one proposed by Abe et al. (2011) as this is today the most effective for type III asymmetric bilinear groups.

8.2.2.1. *AFGHO signatures*

– Setup(1^k): Given k, the security parameter, this algorithm returns the description pp $\leftarrow (p, \mathbb{G}_1, \mathbb{G}_2, \mathbb{G}_T, e)$ of type III bilinear groups.

– Keygen(pp, n): This algorithm generates $\widetilde{g} \xleftarrow{\$} \mathbb{G}_2$ and $(v, u_1, \ldots, u_n) \xleftarrow{\$} \mathbb{Z}_p^{n+1}$, then calculates $(U_1, \ldots, U_n) \leftarrow (g^{u_1}, \ldots, g^{u_n})$ and $\widetilde{V} \leftarrow \widetilde{g}^v$. The secret key sk is then defined as being $(v, u_1, \ldots, u_n)$ and the public key pk as being $(\widetilde{g}, \widetilde{V}, U_1, \ldots, U_n)$.

– Sign(sk, $\widetilde{M}_1, \ldots \widetilde{M}_n$): To sign messages $\widetilde{M}_1, \ldots \widetilde{M}_n \in \mathbb{G}_2$, this algorithm selects a random scalar $r \xleftarrow{\$} \mathbb{Z}_p^*$ and returns $R \leftarrow g^r$, $S = R^v$ and $\widetilde{T} \leftarrow (\widetilde{g} \prod_i \widetilde{M}_i^{u_i})^{\frac{1}{r}}$.

– Verify($\text{pk}, (\widetilde{M}_1, \ldots, \widetilde{M}_n), (R, S, \widetilde{T})$):   Given a signature $(R, S, \widetilde{T})$, the algorithm checks whether the conditions $e(R, \widetilde{V}) = e(S, \widetilde{g})$ and $e(R, T) \cdot \prod_i e(U_i, \widetilde{M}_i) = e(g, \widetilde{g})$ are met. It returns 1 if so and 0 if not.

The signature thus obtained can be randomized by selecting a scalar $t \xleftarrow{\$} \mathbb{Z}_p$ and by calculating $(R', S', \widetilde{T}') \leftarrow (R^t, S^t, \widetilde{T}^{\frac{1}{t}})$. Unfortunately, $(R, S, \widetilde{T})$ and $(R', S', \widetilde{T}')$ can be linked, since $e(R, \widetilde{T}) = e(R', \widetilde{T}')$ and it is therefore necessary to dissimulate at least $\widetilde{T}'$ after randomization.

In all cases, we note that this scheme satisfies all the Groth–Sahai proof criteria: it is possible to prove knowledge of signed messages and the latter are properly certified by $(R, S, \widetilde{T})$. It can therefore be used in practice in the same way as schemes from section 8.2.1, resulting in security in the standard model.

8.3. Applications

The examples given in the introduction to this chapter essentially highlight a need for untraceability and more generally a need to minimize the information revealed in each authentication. Depending on the instances of use, this need should however be reconciled with other imperatives, which led the cryptographic community to propose a wide variety of primitives, which we will summarize under the generic name of mechanisms for anonymous authentication. In this section, we will give some examples of them selected for their representativeness within the domain or for their industrial success. The aim of this section is to highlight the absolutely central role of the advanced signatures presented above in the construction of such mechanisms.

8.3.1. *Anonymous credentials*

The notion of anonymous credentials is quite broad because in cryptography it covers all the solutions where a user $\mathcal{U}$ obtains a certificate on its "attributes" from an entity $\mathcal{I}$, so as to then be able to convince, anonymously, any verifier $\mathcal{V}$ that its attributes satisfy some conditions. A typical example is the one of the ID card outlined in the introduction. Here, $\mathcal{U}$ would be a citizen obtaining for the first time a digital ID card from administration (so here playing the role of $\mathcal{I}$) certifying their attributes, in this case their surname, first name, address, date of birth, etc. This card could then be presented to a seller (playing the role of $\mathcal{V}$) so as to guarantee that $\mathcal{U}$ properly meets the conditions required for the purchase.

However, there is no uniform model for this notion, which haphazardly covers solutions where the certificate obtained from $\mathcal{I}$ can be used only once (e.g. Brands (2000); Fuchsbauer et al. (2015)), others that allow a single certificate to be presented several times untraceably but which require attributes to be revealed clearly (e.g. Camenisch et al. (2015); Fuchsbauer et al. (2019)) and to finish, constructions that are free of the previous limits but at the cost of greater complexity (e.g. Camenisch and Lysyanskaya (2004); Pointcheval and Sanders (2016); Sanders (2020)).

The recent model introduced by Fuchsbauer et al. (2019) allows multiple authentications and reduces security to the two following notions:

– *Unforgeability*: A user cannot convince an honest verifier that he/she benefits from a set of attributes $\mathbb{A} = \{a_1, \ldots, a_m\}$ for which he/she has not received any certificate. This remains true even if he/she has certificates each relating to a strict sub-set of $\mathbb{A}$ (collusion resistance) and if he/she has observed the authentication of another user possessing all these attributes.

– *Anonymity*: During authentication, no information about the user is leaked apart from the attributes he/she reveals. In particular, it is not possible to decide whether two authentications reflecting the same attributes $\mathbb{A}$ have involved the same user or two users who have both obtained a certificate reflecting (especially) $\mathbb{A}$.

To illustrate the subtleties created by this model, it is interesting to start from one of the advanced signatures described above, for example, that of Pointcheval and Sanders (2016), which we will denote using Σ below to avoid any confusion. At first glance, a construction of anonymous credentials could essentially be summarized as follows:

– IssuerKeygen: The algorithm generates a pair of keys $(\mathsf{sk}, \mathsf{pk})$ by executing $\Sigma.\mathsf{Keygen}$.

– (Obtain, Issue): To obtain a certificate on the $(a_1, \ldots, a_n)$ attributes, the user interacts with $\mathcal{I}$ which returns him/her a signature σ generated by executing $\mathsf{Sign}(\mathsf{sk}, a_1, \ldots, a_n)$.

– (Show, Verify): To prove that he/she has a certificate on a particular set $(a_{i_1}, \ldots, a_{i_m})$, the user randomizes σ before sending it to $\mathcal{V}$. He thus proves that the randomized signature σ' is as valid on $(a_{i_1}, \ldots, a_{i_m})$ as on the rest of the attributes of which he/she proves knowledge. More concretely, if $\sigma' = (\sigma'_1, \sigma'_2)$ and $\mathbb{I} = \{i_1, \ldots, i_m\}$, so $\mathcal{U}$ proves, using the Schnorr protocol mentioned above, knowledge of $\{a_i\}_{i \in [1,n] \setminus \mathbb{I}}$, elements such as:

$$\prod_{i \in [1,n] \setminus \mathbb{I}} (\sigma'_1, \widetilde{Y}_i)^{a_i} = e(\sigma'_2, \widetilde{g}) \cdot e(\sigma'_1, \prod_{i \in \mathbb{I}} \widetilde{Y}_i^{a_i})^{-1}$$

This draft solution considerably illustrates the advantages of advanced signatures. Signature randomization allows the signature to be sent in clear and the verification equation is perfectly compatible with the Schnorr protocol, which guarantees very good performances, certainly dependent on the number of attributes concealed. However, as it stands, this system does not completely satisfy the properties above.

Concerning anonymity, randomization helps, but is not enough in itself. In fact, a dishonest entity (potentially $\mathcal{I}$) is likely to know all the attributes $(a_1, \ldots, a_n)$ associated with a $\mathcal{U}^*$ user and can therefore test whether σ' is valid on this set to trace all the authentications carried out by $\mathcal{U}$. Moreover, we note that this same entity can then be authenticated in place of $\mathcal{U}$ because knowledge of σ' and $(a_1, \ldots, a_n)$ is sufficient to carry out the protocol $(\text{Show}, \text{Verify})$.

Fortunately, the solution to these two problems is very simple. It consists of adding to $\{a_1, \ldots, a_n\}$ a special "attribute" $a_0 \in \mathbb{Z}_p$ generated at random by the user $\mathcal{U}$ who will keep it secret (a_0 can then be seen as the secret key of $\mathcal{U}$). By generating the σ certificate on $\{a_0, \ldots, a_n\}$ this time, we will kill two birds with one stone. First of all, we ensure that no one can test the validity of σ' because no one (apart from $\mathcal{U}$) knows all the attributes already signed. Moreover, since a_0 is one of the hidden attributes, it is necessary to prove knowledge of it during the $(\text{Show}, \text{Verify})$ protocol, which excludes, here again, re-use of σ' by any entity other than $\mathcal{U}$.

It merely remains to explain how $\mathcal{U}$ can obtain a signature on $\{a_0, \ldots, a_n\}$ without revealing its secret a_0. For the signature of Pointcheval and Sanders (2016), it is enough to define the new public key $\text{pk} = (Y_0, \widetilde{X}, \widetilde{Y_0}, \widetilde{Y_1}, \ldots, \widetilde{Y_n}) \leftarrow (g^{y_0}, \widetilde{g}^x, \widetilde{g}^{y_0}, \widetilde{g}^{y_1}, \ldots, \widetilde{g}^{y_n})$. Thanks to this new element $Y_0 \in \mathbb{G}_1$, $\mathcal{U}$ can now transmit $C = Y_0^{a_0}$ to the signer and no longer a_0 directly[1]. The signer can then calculate the signature $(g^r, C^{r \cdot y_0} g^{r(x + \sum_{i=1}^{n} a_i \cdot y_i)})$ for a random scalar r, which is precisely a signature valid on $(a_0, \ldots, a_n)$ for the original protocol. This ability to sign committed messages is common to the advanced signatures in the previous section. The schemes presented in Camenisch and Lysyanskaya (2004); Boneh and Boyen (2008) proceed moreover in a way very similar to the one that has just been presented.

Thanks to this modification, the new protocol can be proven to be secure. This moreover involves the construction outlined in Pointcheval and Sanders (2016). Intuitively, the unforgeability of the anonymous credentials mechanism thus obtained relies on that of the Σ signature scheme. If an individual is able to present a signature σ' on a set of attributes $(a_1, \ldots, a_n)$ for which they have not obtained certificates, then this means that σ' is a forgery. Moreover, any repeat of a σ' presented by an honest user $\mathcal{U}^*$ is then impossible because the protocol $(\text{Show}, \text{Verify})$ requires proving knowledge of the secret a_0 of $\mathcal{U}^*$. As for anonymity, it relies on the following observation. The signature σ' transmitted by a user $\mathcal{U}^*$ is formed of a perfectly random element $\sigma_1 \in \mathbb{G}_1$ and a $\sigma_2 = \sigma_1^{x + \sum_{i=0}^{n} y_i \cdot a_i}$ element. The adversary $\mathcal{A}$ can therefore only identify $\mathcal{U}^*$ from σ_2. Let us suppose that $\mathcal{A}$ is powerful enough

---

[1] For security reasons, $\mathcal{U}$ should also prove knowledge of a_0, but this is done very effectively because of the Schnorr protocol.

to know the secret key of $\mathcal{I}$ and the attributes $(a_1, \ldots, a_n)$ linked to $\mathcal{U}^*$. He/she can then calculate

$$\tau = \sigma_2 \cdot \sigma_1^{-(x + \sum_{i=1} y_i \cdot a_i)} = \sigma_1^{y_0 \cdot a_0},$$

and even $\tau^{\frac{1}{y_0}} = \sigma_1^{u_0}$. He cannot however go any further since the DDH assumption assures us that $\sigma_1^{u_0}$ is indistinguishable from an element of $\mathbb{G}_1$ for $\mathcal{A}$, even with the knowledge of σ_1 and g^{u_0}. In other words, σ_2 is masked by a pseudo-random $\sigma_1^{u_0}$ value, which prevents $\mathcal{A}$ from obtaining any information about this element. Anonymity therefore relies directly on the DDH assumption, which is considered very reasonable in cryptography.

To finish, we can note that the protocol described above does not exactly deal with the problem described in the introduction. Indeed, this protocol, as it stands, simply makes it possible to reveal some attributes. In cases where the user has to prove that they are over 18 years of age, this would mean that they would have to send the attribute "age", which reveals more information than necessary. Fortunately, this can be addressed in a very simple way by combining the anonymous credential protocol with *zero-knowledge* proofs adapted to the needs of the case of use. In our example, to prove that a user is over 18 without revealing their age, it would be enough to consider age as a hidden attribute and to use a *zero-knowledge* proof that they belong to an interval ("age $\in [18, a]$" would then be proved for a relevant interval a), such as those described in Canard et al. (2013). Any other property can be proved on the attributes in a similar way, from the moment that a suitable *zero-knowledge* protocol exists and has secrets intervening as exponents in the verification equation.

8.3.2. *Group signatures*

It is difficult today to talk of anonymous authentication without mentioning group signatures, since this primitive has become so central within this domain. Introduced by Chaum and van Heyst (1991) in 1991, this mechanism allows *users* to join a group managed by a *group manager* using an enrollment procedure. Once this has been achieved, users become full members of the group and can then produce signatures in the name of the group. More precisely, any entity is able to check, with the help of the group's public key, that these signatures were indeed produced by a member of the group but it is not possible to identify the member who did this. If we were to stop there, it would not be very difficult to construct the group signatures. It would suffice in fact for the group manager to create a pair of keys (sk, pk) for any digital signature scheme and then to distribute sk to all the new members of the group. Thus, only the group members would be able to produce valid signatures and anonymity would be perfect and irrevocable.

Unfortunately, irrevocable anonymity is likely to favor some deviations that could taint the whole group's reputation, disrupt its functioning or even engage the responsibility of all its members. It is therefore more sensible in practice to implement safeguards that consist of the case of group signatures of an opening process, in the hands of a dedicated authority, called *the opening authority*. This procedure makes it possible to remove the anonymity of any signature and so to identify the member responsible for possible deviations. Of course, this process should not be undertaken lightly and in practice it is advised to share opening authority capacities between multiple entities, using very traditional threshold cryptographic techniques (see Chapter 4 or Camenisch et al. (2020)). Whatever the case, this need for responsible anonymity has the effect of invalidating the basic solution of sharing the same key that we outlined above.

Chaum's and van Heyst's original article justified the introduction of this new primitive through the use case of a printer on a business network. Thanks to the group signatures, each member of the group (in this case, the group of employees in the business) can authenticate themselves on the printer anonymously. If the printer is over-used, the director can find the employee(s) who have not respected the rules in order to take the appropriate measures. With regards to this use case, it can be difficult to understand the enthusiasm of the cryptography community for group signatures. It would be sensible however to specify two things.

On the one hand, it is fairly easy to transpose this example to more universal problems. For example, if we consider, within a city, all the users of a transport network as a group, we can quite easily see how to integrate existing actors into a group signature mechanism to create an anonymous transport card. More generally, this ability to reconcile the opposing needs of different protagonists (user anonymity, authentication for the service provider, ability to lift anonymity to meet legal constraints) makes group signatures a solution that may be suitable in multiple usage cases.

On the other hand, techniques developed to meet these properties can be recycled in other contexts. The progress made in the domain of group signatures, as much on the basis of security (e.g. Bellare et al. (2003, 2005)) as on the constructions themselves (e.g. Delerablée and Pointcheval (2006) and Bichsel et al. (2010)), have moreover often had repercussions on connected primitives. This central position has thus, logically, led the cryptography community to focus on it and so makes group signatures an emblem of anonymous authentication protocols.

Conceptually, it is possible to see membership of a group as an attribute, which brings us to the anonymous credentials cited above. The fact of being able to identify the author of a group signature by means of the opening process means that each member has their own key signature. As each member remains responsible for the signatures they send, it is necessary for this key to be generated from a secret known only to them. We thus return precisely to the situation of anonymous credentials that had led to each user being sent a certificate on a secret attribute. Thus, a group signature can therefore be constructed around the following principle. During enrollment, each new member obtains from the group manager a certificate on a secret value. As we have explained, it is very simple to obtain such a certificate if we use the advanced signature mechanisms described in the first section of this chapter. Because of this certificate, and to adapted *zero-knowledge* proofs, each member can then prove that they are really a member of the group.

Up until now we have found ourselves therefore with an anonymous credentials protocol. It remains however to add this capacity to lift anonymity, which did not exist before. There are multiple solutions for doing this, the most commonly used is certainly the one that consists of encrypting data linked to the user's identity and proving, still with the help of *zero-knowledge* proofs, that these data are really linked to a valid certificate delivered by the group administrator.

There again, the need of combining certificates and *zero-knowledge* proofs leads quite naturally to significant recourse to advanced signature mechanisms. As an example, we describe below a simplified version of the group signature scheme proposed by Delerablée and Pointcheval (2006) in 2006 based on the Boneh–Boyen signatures described above.

8.3.2.1. *Delerablée–Pointcheval group signatures*

– IssuerKeygen: This algorithm generates pair of keys (isk, ipk) for the Boneh and Boyen signature scheme. The secret key isk $= x \in \mathbb{Z}_p$ is conserved by the group administrator, whereas ipk, containing $\widetilde{g}^x$, is made public.

– OpenerKeygen: This algorithm generates a pair of keys (osk, opk) for a IND-CCA2 encryption system created by applying the Naor–Yung transform (Naor and Yung 1990) to ElGamal encryption (ElGamal 1984). The secret key osk is kept by the opening authority, whereas opk is made public.

– Join: This protocol is initiated by the new member who essentially sends h^b to the group manager, where b is a random element of $\mathbb{Z}_p$ and $h \in \mathbb{G}_1$ is an element provided in the group's public key. The group manager then generates another random scalar $a \in \mathbb{Z}_p$ and calculates an $A \in \mathbb{G}_1$ element such as $A^{x+a} = g \cdot h^b$. The triplet (A, a, b) thus constitutes the new member's signature key.

– Sign: To sign a message m, the group member generates a ciphertext C from the element A using the key opk and produces *zero-knowledge* proof that the element A constitutes along with a and b a valid Boneh–Boyen signature, that is, they verify the equation together

$$e(A, \widetilde{g}^x \cdot \widetilde{g}^a) = e(g, \widetilde{g}) \cdot e(h, \widetilde{g})^b.$$

The proof thus obtained is then transformed into a signature of knowledge π on m using the Fiat–Shamir technique (Fiat and Shamir 1987). The group signature is then formed by C and π.

– Verify: Verification of a group signature (C, π) consists simply of verifying the validity of π on m.

– Open: To lift the anonymity of a signature, the opening authority uses the decryption key osk to decrypt C and find the element A that it contains. With the help of the group manager (who has generated A during the enrollment phase), he/she can then identify the signer.

We can note that the Boneh–Boyen signature used here is not exactly the one described in section 8.2.1. This is effectively a variant making it possible to sign committed messages (b in this case), in the same vein as the variant of Pointcheval–Sanders signatures that we presented for anonymous credentials. Because of this, b is known only by the member of the group who is then the only one able to produce a signature with the help of the corresponding certificate A. Whatever the case, this variant conserves all the properties expected of advanced signatures, and especially their compatibility with Schnorr proofs, since the "message" b thus signed still appears in the form of an exponent in the verification equation:

$$e(A, \widetilde{g}^x \cdot \widetilde{g}^a) = e(g, \widetilde{g}) \cdot e(h, \widetilde{g})^b.$$

A slight subtlety of group signatures appears through the use of an IND-CCA2 encryption. It is explained by the need in security proofs, to be able to respond to requests to lift anonymity coming from the adversary. Without this, anonymity could only be guaranteed on condition that the adversary never has access to the results of a procedure to lift anonymity, which seems relatively unrealistic.

From a security perspective, the informal guarantees mentioned above have been formalized by Bellare et al. (2003, 2005) into three properties: *anonymity, traceability* and *non-frameability* (i.e. immunity to false accusations). Anonymity guarantees that it is impossible (except for the opening authority of course) to link a signature to a group member, even though the latter's signature key has just been revealed. The last two properties are complementary. Traceability guarantees that any valid group signature can be linked to a member of the group. Non-frameability guarantees that the member thus designated is indeed at the origin of this signature.

In the Delerablée–Pointcheval scheme, anonymity is fairly simple to prove since the signature is formed of a ciphertext and a *zero-knowledge* proof. Any attack would therefore essentially amount to breaking the IND-CCA2 security of the encryption used. As for traceability, it relies on the following principle. Given that the opening of a signature consists of finding the A element encrypted by the group member, the only solution for an adversary who does not want to be identified would be to use a A' value different to those delivered by the group administrator during enrollments. However, the proof contained in the group signature then guarantees that this value A' satisfies the equation $e(A', \widetilde{g}^x \cdot \widetilde{g}^{a'}) = e(g, \widetilde{g}) \cdot e(h, \widetilde{g})^{b'}$ for the values a' and b', which can be extracted from the proof. The triplet (A', a', b') therefore constitutes a (new) valid Boneh-Boyen signature that has not been generated by the group manager. It is therefore a forgery that contradicts the security of Boneh–Boyen signatures. To finish, it is not possible to accuse a member of the group that by producing a group signature involving the A element that he/she has received during his/her enrollment. As this element can only be used with the corresponding secret b, such a group signature induces production of a proof of knowledge of b and so the implication of the member in question.

8.3.3. *Direct anonymous attestations*

The strength of the group signatures mentioned previously is this ability to counterbalance strong anonymity (guaranteed even in cases where the user's secret key is leaked) through a procedure to lift anonymity, which threatens to identify any author of abuse. However, this supposes the existence of at least one opening authority that would accept this regulatory role and which would benefit from the confidence of all members of the group.

In practice, it is not clear that this hypothesis is always verified and it is therefore useful to reflect on alternative tracing mechanisms that are a little more decentralized. The most popular example today is probably that of direct anonymous attestations (Brickell et al. 2004), which we will denote DAA, and their variant known by the name of EPID (enhanced privacy ID) (Brickell and Li 2007). Today, both these mechanisms are deployed in billions of chips (TCG 2015; Intel 2017), mainly to allow secure enclaves to be authenticated anonymously.

Intuitively, a DAA is essentially a group signature because it allows an entity to be authenticated anonymously as a member of a particular group after enrollment by a group manager $\mathcal{I}$. The novelty is that there is no longer an opening process but only a controlled tracing mechanism that operates as follows. During an authentication, the signer is able to generate a tag T deterministically dependent[2] on the secret key and a particular string bsn. Thus, all the signatures produced by a single member with the same string bsn will contain the same tag T, which allows them to be linked immediately. The idea is, for example, to allow a service provider to trace users (or their contacts) over a certain period of time. In the case of a transport card, this can in

---

2 it is not in fact necessary for this tag to be deterministic, but this simplifies the tracing process considerably.

particular make it possible to implement anti-*passback* mechanisms preventing several individuals from using the same card.

Quite evidently, it makes sense in practice to find a satisfactory compromise between service needs and anonymity. Use of the same bsn over a system's lifetime would, for example, render the use of a DAA completely absurd since members would be constantly traceable. In the instance of transport cited above, we can imagine the use of a single bsn over a window of 10 minutes. A dishonest user could no longer simply pass their card to an accomplice after having passed the access gates at least until a particular timeframe has passed. In the same timeframe, honest users would be certain that their different validations would not be traceable after these 10 minutes, which seems very reasonable in practice. In all cases, the important point is that users know, at the moment of their authentication, whether they are traceable and under what conditions.

From a concrete perspective, the choice made by DAAs has two consequences. On the one hand, it is no longer necessary to encrypt identifying data and to include it in the DAA because there is no longer any opening process. This makes it possible to reduce noticeably the complexity of the DAA compared to a group signature, above all when advanced signatures can be randomized, as we will see below. On the other hand, it is necessary to construct a tracing tag that guarantees the properties sketched above, that is, that the signatures of a single member can be linked, but only if they are linked to a single string bsn.

8.3.3.1. *Generating the tag*

Most classical DAA systems (i.e. not post-quantum ones) generate their tags in almost identical manner. The signer begins by hashing the string bsn to obtain a group element $H(bsn) \in \mathbb{G}$ using a hash function H adapted to the group $\mathbb{G}$. He/she then uses a s element contained in the secret key to generate the tag $T = H(bsn)^s$.

Aside from its simplicity, this tag presents several advantages. First, it is deterministic since use of a single string bsn and a single secret key necessarily lead to the same tag. Second, it guarantees the untraceability of the tag generated with two different strings bsn and bsn'. In fact, in the random oracle model, linking $H(bsn)^s$ and $H(bsn')^s$ is equivalent to solving the DDH problem in $\mathbb{G}$. Third, it involves the secret s as an exponent, which makes it possible to prove knowledge of it. It is in fact vital to check that the signer has really used the right secret value s, which induces use of *zero-knowledge* proofs. In other words, the signer could use different s values at each authentication to evade the tracing mechanism.

It is fairly easy to combine this system of tags with the ideas of the previous primitives to construct a DAA system. To demonstrate membership of the group, it is enough in fact to prove knowledge of a certificate sent by $\mathcal{I}$ on the secret s, which can be done very simply with advanced signatures such as those that we have seen in the first section of this chapter. Using the Pointcheval–Sanders signature scheme that we will call Σ, this leads to the following protocol, which is a simplified version of the DAA scheme proposed by Barki et al. (2017).

8.3.3.2. *Barki et al.'s (2017) DAA*

– IssuerKeygen: This algorithm generates a pair of keys $(\text{isk}, \text{ipk}) = ((x, y), (\widetilde{g}, \widetilde{X}, \widetilde{Y})) \leftarrow \Sigma.\text{Keygen}$ for $\mathcal{I}$ and defines a hash function $H : \{0,1\} \rightarrow \mathbb{G}_1$.

– Join: This protocol is initiated by the new member who sends g^s and a proof of knowledge of s to $\mathcal{I}$. He/she then receives a Pointcheval–Sanders σ signature generated with isk using the protocol described in section 8.3.1 for committed messages.

– Sign: To sign a message m with the string bsn, the group member generates a randomized version σ' of the signature σ as well as the tag $T = H(bsn)^s$. He/she then produces a proof of knowledge of s for which $\sigma' = (\sigma'_1, \sigma'_2)$ (respectively, T) is a valid certificate (respectively, tag), so that:

$$H(bsn)^s = T;$$

$$e(\sigma'_1, \widetilde{Y})^s = e(\sigma'_2, \widetilde{g}) \cdot e((\sigma'_1)^{-1}, \widetilde{X}).$$

This proof is then transformed into a signature of knowledge π on m with the help of the Fiat–Shamir technique. The concatenation of π, σ' and T then constitutes the DAA on m for the string bsn.

– Verify: Verifying a DAA (π, σ, T) on (m, bsn) consists simply of verifying the validity of π.

– Link: To test whether two DAAs (π_1, σ_1, T_1) and (π_2, σ_2, T_2) linked to the same string bsn have been generated by the same member, it is enough to test whether $T_1 = T_2$.

The protocol thus obtained is remarkably effective because a DAA contains only three elements of the group $\mathbb{G}_1$ and two scalars (for the signature of knowledge). This is due essentially to the fact that the proof contained in a DAA is perfectly compatible with Schnorr proofs through the tag's construction but above all through the use of advanced signatures designed to this effect. Barki et al.'s article describes several improvements that make it possible to lower the complexity of calculations for the signer as well as to rely on weaker computational assumptions but the resulting construction is still based on the same idea as the version described above. It is moreover quite easy to translate this construction with other advanced signatures, as illustrated by Chen's DAA (Chen 2009), based on Boneh–Boyen signatures, or the DAA by Chen et al. (2010), based on Camenisch–Lysyanskaya signatures.

Whatever the case, the security of this construction follows on very simply from previous security analyses and the properties of the tracing tag.

8.3.3.3. *EPID*

DAAs offer an interesting compromise between the irrevocable anonymity of anonymous credentials and the completely revocable anonymity of group signatures. It is not suitable however for all situations, in particular those where it is necessary to revoke the rights of some users. We consider, for example, the case of a service provider who has observed abuses by a user and who consequently wishes to forbid him/her from accessing the service. The absence of an opening process prevents the provider from identifying this user. The only element known to the provider is the DAA that this dishonest user has produced to access the service and commit these abuses. In these conditions, how do we guarantee that this user will no longer be able to access the service in future?

With a classical DAA, the only solution would be to divert the tracing mechanism. If the DAA produced by the user is linked to a string bsn (and therefore contains a particular tag T), the service provider can require the use of this string for any future authentication (whoever the member). Thus, he/she could identify the dishonest user, whose DAAs will all contain T. Unfortunately, this solution would have consequences for other users of the service who could all be traced. More generally, as we mentioned previously, use of a constant string bsn means that the DAA loses all benefit.

This problem led Brickell and Li (2007) to propose a variant of DAAs, called EPID, which removes the tracing system based on the string bsn in favor of a system of revocation by signature. Concretely, the signature process already takes as input a list of revoked signatures rather than a string bsn. The signer should then not only prove that they are really a member of the group, as before, but also prove that they are not responsible for the revoked signatures. The service provider, who plays the role of signature checker, therefore has the guarantee that the member who is authenticated is not the one they wish to exclude, without endangering the anonymity of honest users of the system.

The idea of Brickell and Li, taken up by the constructions that followed, is to recycle the tag from the DAAs by generating this time in the form $T = H(rnd)^s$ for a particular random string rnd. The signer can then rely on the $T_i = H(rnd_i)^{s_i}$ tag of the revoked signatures to prove that their own was generated by means of a s key different to s_i. This can be done in a modular (and very efficient) fashion using the *zero-knowledge* proof protocol of the inequality of discreet logarithms proposed by Camenisch and Shoup (2003). Concretely, the signer uses this protocol to demonstrate that $\log_{H(rnd)}(T) \neq \log_{H(rnd_i)}(T_i)$ for all the tags T_i. The interest of the Camenisch and Shoup protocol in our case is that it transforms the inequality relationship to prove, in a single proof, knowledge of discrete logarithms that can be implemented with the help of the Schnorr protocol and that therefore matches very well with other elements of the signature. Moreover, these latter consist essentially of a proof of knowledge of a certificate on s and are therefore identical to the previous construction.

8.4. References

Abe, M., Fuchsbauer, G., Groth, J., Haralambiev, K., Ohkubo, M. (2010). Structure-preserving signatures and commitments to group elements. In *CRYPTO 2010*, vol. 6223 of *LNCS*, Rabin, T. (ed.). Springer, Heidelberg.

Abe, M., Groth, J., Haralambiev, K., Ohkubo, M. (2011). Optimal structure-preserving signatures in asymmetric bilinear groups. In *CRYPTO 2011*, vol. 6841 of *LNCS*, Rogaway, P. (ed.). Springer, Heidelberg.

Au, M.H., Susilo, W., Mu, Y. (2006). Constant-size dynamic k-TAA. In *SCN 06*, vol. 4116 of *LNCS*, Prisco, R.D., Yung, M. (eds). Springer, Heidelberg.

Barki, A., Desmoulins, N., Gharout, S., Traoré, J. (2017). Anonymous attestations made practical. In *Proceedings of the 10th ACM Conference on Security and Privacy in Wireless and Mobile Networks, WiSec 2017*, Noubir, G., Conti, M., Kasera, S.K. (eds). ACM Press.

Bellare, M., Micciancio, D., Warinschi, B. (2003). Foundations of group signatures: Formal definitions, simplified requirements, and a construction based on general assumptions. In *EUROCRYPT 2003*, vol. 2656 of *LNCS*, Biham, E. (ed.). Springer, Heidelberg.

Bellare, M., Shi, H., Zhang, C. (2005). Foundations of group signatures: The case of dynamic groups. In *CT-RSA 2005*, vol. 3376 of *LNCS*, Menezes, A. (ed.). Springer, Heidelberg.

Bichsel, P., Camenisch, J., Neven, G., Smart, N.P., Warinschi, B. (2010). Get shorty via group signatures without encryption. In *SCN 10*, vol. 6280 of *LNCS*, Garay, J.A., Prisco, R.D. (eds). Springer, Heidelberg.

Boneh, D. and Boyen, X. (2008). Short signatures without random oracles and the SDH assumption in bilinear groups. *Journal of Cryptology*, 21(2), 149–177.

Brands, S. (2000). *Rethinking Public Key Infrastructures and Digital Certificates: Building in Privacy*. MIT Press, Cambridge.

Brickell, E.F. and Li, J. (2007). Enhanced privacy id: A direct anonymous attestation scheme with enhanced revocation capabilities. In *WPES 2007*, ACM Press.

Brickell, E.F., Camenisch, J., Chen, L. (2004). Direct anonymous attestation. In *ACM CCS 2004*, Atluri, V., Pfitzmann, B., McDaniel, P. (eds). ACM Press.

Camenisch, J. and Lysyanskaya, A. (2003). A signature scheme with efficient protocols. In *SCN 02*, vol. 2576 of *LNCS*, Cimato, S., Galdi, C., Persiano, G. (eds). Springer, Heidelberg.

Camenisch, J. and Lysyanskaya, A. (2004). Signature schemes and anonymous credentials from bilinear maps. In *CRYPTO 2004*, vol. 3152 of *LNCS*, Franklin, M. (ed.). Springer, Heidelberg.

Camenisch, J. and Shoup, V. (2003). Practical verifiable encryption and decryption of discrete logarithms. In *CRYPTO 2003*, vol. 2729 of *LNCS*, Boneh, D. (ed.). Springer, Heidelberg.

Camenisch, J., Dubovitskaya, M., Haralambiev, K., Kohlweiss, M. (2015). Composable and modular anonymous credentials: Definitions and practical constructions. In *ASIACRYPT 2015, Part II*, vol. 9453 of *LNCS*, Iwata, T., Cheon, J.H. (eds). Springer, Heidelberg.

Camenisch, J., Drijvers, M., Lehmann, A., Neven, G., Towa, P. (2020). Short threshold dynamic group signatures. In *SCN 20*, vol. 12238 of *LNCS*, Galdi, C., Kolesnikov, V. (eds). Springer, Heidelberg.

Canard, S., Coisel, I., Jambert, A., Traoré, J. (2013). New results for the practical use of range proofs. In *Public Key Infrastructures, Services and Applications – 10th European Workshop, EuroPKI 2013*, vol. 8341 of *LNCS*, Katsikas, S.K., Agudo, I. (eds). Springer, Heidelberg.

Canetti, R., Goldreich, O., Halevi, S. (1998). The random oracle methodology, revisited (preliminary version). In *30th ACM STOC*. ACM Press.

Canetti, R., Goldreich, O., Halevi, S. (2004). On the random-oracle methodology as applied to length-restricted signature schemes. In *TCC 2004*, vol. 2951 of *LNCS*, Naor, M. (ed.). Springer, Heidelberg.

Chaum, D. and van Heyst, E. (1991). Group signatures. In *EUROCRYPT'91*, vol. 547 of *LNCS*, Davies, D.W. (ed.). Springer, Heidelberg.

Chen, L. (2009). A DAA scheme requiring less TPM resources. In *Information Security and Cryptology – 5th International Conference, Inscrypt 2009*, vol. 6151 of *LNCS*, Bao, F., Yung, M., Lin, D., Jing, J. (eds). Springer, Heidelberg.

Chen, L., Page, D., Smart, N.P. (2010). On the design and implementation of an efficient DAA scheme. In *Smart Card Research and Advanced Application, 9th IFIP WG 8.8/11.2 International Conference, CARDIS 2010*, vol. 6035 of *LNCS*, Gollmann, D., Lanet, J., Iguchi-Cartigny, J. (eds). Springer, Heidelberg.

Delerablée, C. and Pointcheval, D. (2006). Dynamic fully anonymous short group signatures. In *Progress in Cryptology – VIETCRYPT 06*, vol. 4341 of *LNCS*, Nguyen, P.Q. (ed.). Springer, Heidelberg.

Diffie, W. and Hellman, M.E. (1976). New directions in cryptography. *IEEE Transactions on Information Theory*, 22(6), 644–654.

ElGamal, T. (1984). A public key cryptosystem and a signature scheme based on discrete logarithms. In *CRYPTO'84*, vol. 196 of *LNCS*, Blakley, G.R., Chaum, D. (eds). Springer, Heidelberg.

Fiat, A. and Shamir, A. (1987). How to prove yourself: Practical solutions to identification and signature problems. In *CRYPTO'86*, vol. 263 of *LNCS*, Odlyzko, A.M. (ed.). Springer, Heidelberg.

Fuchsbauer, G., Hanser, C., Slamanig, D. (2015). Practical round-optimal blind signatures in the standard model. In *CRYPTO 2015, Part II*, vol. 9216 of *LNCS*, Gennaro, R., Robshaw, M.J.B. (eds). Springer, Heidelberg.

Fuchsbauer, G., Hanser, C., Slamanig, D. (2019). Structure-preserving signatures on equivalence classes and constant-size anonymous credentials. *Journal of Cryptology*, 32(2), 498–546.

Groth, J. and Sahai, A. (2008). Efficient non-interactive proof systems for bilinear groups. In *EUROCRYPT 2008*, vol. 4965 of *LNCS*, Smart, N.P. (ed.). Springer, Heidelberg.

Intel (2017). Enhanced privacy id (epid) security technology [Online]. Available at: software. intel.com/content/www/us/en/develop/articles/intel-enhanced-privacy-id-epid-security-technology.html.

Naor, M. and Yung, M. (1990). Public-key cryptosystems provably secure against chosen ciphertext attacks. In *22nd ACM STOC*. ACM Press.

Petit, J., Schaub, F., Feiri, M., Kargl, F. (2015). Pseudonym schemes in vehicular networks: A survey. *IEEE Communications Surveys & Tutorials*, 17(1), 228–255.

Pointcheval, D. and Sanders, O. (2016). Short randomizable signatures. In *CT-RSA 2016*, vol. 9610 of *LNCS*, Sako, K. (ed.). Springer, Heidelberg.

Pointcheval, D. and Stern, J. (2000). Security arguments for digital signatures and blind signatures. *Journal of Cryptology*, 13(3), 361–396.

Sanders, O. (2020). Efficient redactable signature and application to anonymous credentials. In *PKC 2020, Part II*, vol. 12111 of *LNCS*, Kiayias, A., Kohlweiss, M., Wallden, P., Zikas, V. (eds). Springer, Heidelberg.

Schnorr, C.-P. (1990). Efficient identification and signatures for smart cards. In *CRYPTO'89*, vol. 435 of *LNCS*, Brassard, G. (ed.). Springer, Heidelberg.

Trusted Computing Group (2015). Trusted Platform Module (TPM): Built-in Authentication [Online]. Available at: trustedcomputinggroup.org/authentication/.

9

Key Exchange

Colin BOYD

NTNU, Trondheim, Norway

Key exchange refers to the process of setting up a cryptographic shared key between two or more parties. Typically, this process involves a cryptographic protocol run between the parties who are going to share the output key, usually called a *session key*. There are several other terms in the literature used more or less synonymously with the term "key exchange", including *key establishment* and *key distribution*. There are also several different kinds of key exchange protocol characterized by different protocol features.

In this chapter, we will first consider the elements of key exchange, specifically the steps in a key exchange protocol, the parties that are involved and the messages which may be sent. After that, we look in more detail at key exchange security models and protocols, considering first the simpler case of unauthenticated key exchange before turning to authenticated protocols.

9.1. Key exchange fundamentals

What is a key exchange protocol? At a high level, we can identify four stages that are used in most protocols, although we will see that there are some exceptions which do not include all stages.

– *Setup*: This stage defines the system parameters used by all protocol participants for the duration of the protocol lifetime. These may typically include definitions of suitable groups and generators as well as shared algorithms such as hash functions, encryption and signatures schemes.

Asymmetric Cryptography,
coordinated by David POINTCHEVAL. © ISTE Ltd. 2022.

– *Key generation*: This stage defines setting up the initial keys used by the protocol participants. These may typically be long-term public–private key pairs, but there are other possibilities too as will be discussed later.

– *Message exchange*: The messages passed between protocol participants are defined in this stage. This is often regarded as the core of the protocol.

– *Key derivation*: The outcome of the previous stage, the message exchange, is some shared secret known to the protocol participants. The key derivation stage applies a key derivation function (KDF) to compute a suitable session key.

9.1.1. *Key exchange parties*

A key exchange protocol involves two or more parties who wish to cooperate to set up the new session key. The simplest two-party case is familiar in many contexts, such as a session between a client and a server or between two entities wishing to share information. Multi-party key exchange, often called *group key exchange*, involves any number of parties and can be applied in group messaging and conference communications.

In some protocols, the new session key, or the shared secret it is derived from, is generated by one party and communicated confidentially (e.g. encrypted) to the other party, or parties, of the protocol. In such cases, the mode of the protocol is called *key transport*. In other cases, the new session key is a function of inputs from multiple parties (typically all parties, or both parties in the case of a two-party protocol) and the mode of the protocol is called *key agreement*.

An authenticated key exchange protocol must allow parties to use existing keys in order to authenticate peer parties. These keys are often called *long-term* keys and may be shared symmetric keys or public keys. Long-term symmetric keys are often called *pre-shared keys* (PSK), which includes the case of shared passwords (see Chapter 10 for detail on this case). We often assume that long-term keys are static for the lifetime of the system, but it is also possible for keys to evolve. We usually ignore the problem of setting up long-term keys when we analyze key exchange protocols. Keys which are generated and used in a single protocol instance are often called *ephemeral keys*.

In addition to the participants intended to obtain the new session key, some protocols rely on other parties, often called *trusted third parties* (TTP), who may be trusted to carry out their functions. These functions can include generation and distribution of session keys or shared secrets and certification of public keys. In some cases, the TTP may share long-term symmetric keys with protocol participants, such as in the Kerberos protocol (Needham and Schroeder 1978; Neuman and Ts'o 1994). In this chapter, we focus on key exchange using asymmetric cryptography.

9.1.2. *Key exchange messages*

A protocol consists of messages passed between the parties. In addition to cryptographic components, protocol messages typically include fixed strings such as identifiers of parties or protocol structures and random values, sometimes known as *nonces*. Messages may also be processed by cryptographic algorithms such as encryption or signatures.

From a practical viewpoint, the number and length of the messages is an important factor. A message sent by one party may depend on a message previously received from a different party, so that these two messages must be sent sequentially rather than in parallel. We say that a set of messages which can be sent simultaneously constitute one protocol *round*. In some applications, reducing the number of rounds may be important. A group key exchange protocol may have many messages but few rounds. Note that the number of rounds and messages in a protocol is not necessarily fixed; for example, it is common to be able to transform a protocol with three messages and three rounds into one with four messages and two rounds (Gong 1995).

Since long-term keys are usually assumed to be available to parties via channels outside the protocol itself, it is possible to have a meaningful protocol with zero messages and rounds. Such protocols are said to provide *non-interactive key exchange* (NIKE, see section 9.3.1). Although NIKE has been used as a building block for other protocols, it can only provide static keys; we normally want a key exchange protocol to set up a new or *fresh* session key. Therefore, at least one message is needed. On the assumption that key exchange is followed by a communications session protected by the session key, delay from communication can be minimized by reducing *round trip* communication. A round trip is a back and forth communication between two protocol parties. A key exchange protocol is said to be zero round-trip, denoted 0-RTT, if the session key can be used without waiting for any response from the peer party.

9.1.3. *Key derivation functions*

After the initial processing of the protocol messages, the protocol parties will compute a shared secret value Z. In many protocols, the value Z will have high entropy but will not be uniformly random or have the correct length to use directly in a symmetric key algorithm. For example, Z may be a group element. It is the purpose of a KDF to convert Z into a pseudo-random bit string of suitable size. Following usual terminology, we call the output of the KDF a *session key* which we denote K. This terminology reflects the traditional usage of key exchange as a protocol to secure a communications session. The inputs to the KDF include the shared secret Z and other public values as shown below.

In addition to ensuring that the session key is pseudorandom, another purpose of the KDF is to bind certain protocol components to the session key. Thus, the inputs to a KDF may include a *context string*, c, with components such as a protocol and version identifier; the identities of participants in the protocol and the protocol messages themselves. Such inputs can ensure that certain types of attacks, where an adversary tries to fool participants about the correct protocol details, are avoided.

A formal definition of KDFs was first provided by Krawczyk (2010). In addition to the elements Z and c, Krawczyk's definition includes an optional *salt* input, s, from some set S, whose purpose is to add public randomness. This element is often omitted in key exchange but can be useful in other contexts.

DEFINITION 9.1 (Krawczyk (2010)).– *A KDF of output length l is a function:*

$$\text{KDF} : \mathbf{Z} \times S \times C \to \{0, 1\}^l$$

where $\mathbf{Z}$ *is the source of input secret values, S is the set of salt values and C is a set of context strings.*

In order to define the security of a KDF, Krawczyk defines a security game outlined in Figure 9.1. The adversary, **Adv**, can query the KDF adaptively up to q times and has to distinguish whether an output on a chosen context value is random or the real KDF output.

1) A sample z is chosen from the input source and given to **Adv** along with the protocol messages from which this sample was derived.

2) A salt value s is chosen randomly from S.

3) **Adv** can call $\text{KDF}(z, s, c_i)$ up to q times for c_i values of its choice.

4) **Adv** chooses a value c_0 which is different from all c_i values used in the previous step and is given either $\text{KDF}(z, s, c_0)$ or a random string of length l.

5) **Adv** can call $\text{KDF}(z, s, c_i)$ for $c_i \neq c_0$ as long as it does not exceed q queries in total.

6) **Adv** returns its decision on whether the value given in Step 4 was the KDF output or random, and wins if its choice is correct.

Figure 9.1. *Security game for KDF security*

In practice, there are two main choices for KDFs, both of which are recommended by the US NIST (Barker et al. 2020). The first is a *one-step* process where Z and other parameters are entered directly into a hash function or a MAC. The second is a *two-step* process where the first step is *extraction* of entropy from Z and the second step is *expansion* of the entropy into one or more keys. A prominent example of the two-step process is HKDF, defined by Krawczyk (2010) and based on HMAC (Bellare et al. 1996). Given key material Z, a constant (possibly null) salt string s and optional context information c, the function computes one or more keys K_i as:

$$HKDF(Z, s, c) = K_1 \parallel K_2 \parallel \ldots \parallel K_t$$

where $K_{i+1} = HMAC(PRK, K_i \parallel c \parallel i)$, $K_1 = HMAC(PRK, c \parallel 0)$ and $PRK = HMAC(s, Z)$. If s is empty, then it is interpreted as a string of zero bits of length equal to an HMAC key.

HKDF has been subsequently standardized (Krawczyk and Eronen 2010; ISO 2016; Barker et al. 2020) and is required in prominent key exchange protocols such as TLS 1.3. Krawczyk (2010) gives a security proof for HKDF (see the security game from Figure 9.1). This proof assumes that the compression function h, used in the underlying iterative hash function defined in HMAC, is a random oracle. Krawczyk remarks that this assumption is reasonable as long as h is sufficiently independent of the randomness source Z.

9.2. Unauthenticated key exchange

This section is concerned with key exchange protocols designed to be secure against a passive adversary. Such an adversary observes messages passed between protocol parties but does not change them or fabricate new messages. Unauthenticated protocols may be used as building blocks for authenticated key exchange protocols, which we examine in section 9.3.

9.2.1. *Formal definitions and security models*

We may consider key exchange protocols as message-driven protocols (Canetti and Krawczyk 2001). A n-party key exchange protocol consists of a **Setup**() algorithm, which generates shared parameters for the protocol, and a specification for n parties $U_1, U_2, \ldots, U_n$. The parties accept messages (or an initial call with an empty message) as inputs and output messages in response (or return a final accepting output with an empty message). Later we will see that for authenticated key exchange we define parties by their long-term key material and then there may be multiple protocol instances at each such party. However, since we are now considering parties without long-term key material, we can consider each party instance as distinct.

Any useful protocol has a well-defined sequence of activation of the protocol parties so that when each party outputs a message it can be used as input to one or more other parties. Each party eventually accepts with the same session key K from a key space **K**. A protocol execution is such an activation of the parties and the sequence of messages sent between the parties is called a *transcript*.

DEFINITION 9.2.– *An adversary* **Adv** *against an (unauthenticated) key exchange protocol has advantage* ϵ *if* **Adv** *can distinguish the output of a protocol execution from a key chosen uniformly randomly from* **K** *with probability* $(1/2 + \epsilon)$. *More precisely,* **Adv** *is given the protocol parameters and the transcript of a successful execution. Then a bit* b *is chosen randomly and if* $b = 0$, *then* **Adv** *is given the agreed session key or, if* $b = 1$, **Adv** *is given a random value from* **K**. **Adv** *wins if it successfully computes* b.

Since it is essential to keep session keys confidential from an adversary, we may expect public key encryption to play an important role in key exchange protocols. However, a more flexible primitive is a key encapsulation mechanism (KEM). Although a public key encryption scheme and a public key KEM are formally equivalent; using a KEM avoids encrypting a chosen input value and can therefore be more efficient.

DEFINITION 9.3.– *A KEM consists of four algorithms, the first three of which take as input an implicit security parameter* λ, *and are randomized, while the fourth is deterministic.*

- **KEMSetup**()*: It outputs a set of common parameters* cp.

- **KEMKeyGen**$(\mathbb{G}, g)$*: It takes as input parameters* cp *and outputs a public and private key pair* (pk, sk).

- **Encap**(pk)*: Given a public key* pk *outputs both a key* k *and an encapsulated key (ciphertext)* c.

- **Decap**(sk, c)*: Given a private key* sk *and encapsulated key* c *outputs a key* k.

Correctness should mean that for any properly generated key pair (pk, sk), if $(k, c) \leftarrow$ **Encap**(pk), then $k \leftarrow$ **Decap**(sk, c). Sometimes correctness is not guaranteed and then we may want to associate a probability to it.

9.2.2. *Constructions and examples*

Figure 9.2 shows how to construct a passively secure key exchange protocol from a KEM. There is a straightforward reduction which transforms an adversary against the protocol in Figure 9.2 into one against a CPA-secure KEM. Therefore, we can conclude the following security result.

THEOREM 9.1.– *If the KEM used in the construction shown in Figure 9.2 is CPA-secure, then the protocol shown is a secure unauthenticated key exchange protocol in the sense of definition 9.2.*

9.2.2.1. *Diffie–Hellman key exchange*

The most well-known example of a KEM used as a key exchange protocol is the Diffie–Hellman protocol (Diffie and Hellman 1976).

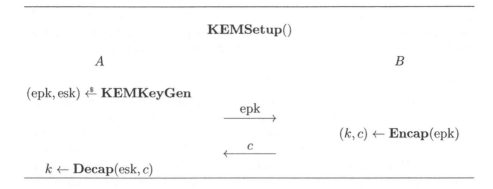

Figure 9.2. *Generic key exchange from key encapsulation*

DEFINITION 9.4 (Diffie–Hellman KEM).– *With notation from definition 9.3, the steps are as follows:*

– **KEMSetup**()*: Generate a suitable multiplicative group* $\mathbb{G}$ *with element* g *of order,* s.

– **KEMKeyGen**($\mathbb{G}, g$)*: Choose random* sk $\xleftarrow{\$} \mathbb{Z}_s$ *and set* pk $\leftarrow g^{\mathsf{sk}}$.

– **Encap**(pk)*: Choose random* $r \xleftarrow{\$} \mathbb{Z}_s$ *and output* $k = \mathsf{pk}^r$ *and* $c = g^r$.

– **Decap**(sk, c)*: Set* $k = c^{\mathsf{sk}}$.

Diffie–Hellman is widely used as a building block for authenticated key exchange where $\mathbb{G}$ is a sub-group of $\mathbb{Z}_p^*$ (the non-zero integers modulo a prime p) or one of various elliptic curve groups. For such groups, the derived unauthenticated key exchange protocol construction in Figure 9.2 is believed to be secure. However, it has been known for many years that the protocol will be broken efficiently by quantum computers since Shor's algorithm can find discrete logarithms in both $\mathbb{Z}_p^*$ and elliptic curve groups. This has led to a huge research effort to find KEMs, which are believed secure against an adversary with quantum computational power. Today, there are several promising candidates in the lattice-based setting (such as Saber (D'Anvers et al. 2018)) or in the isogeny-based setting (such as SIKE (Jao et al. 2020)).

The Diffie–Hellman protocol is not usually defined as a KEM and indeed it has a special property not shared by general KEMs, namely that the ciphertext c generated in the **Encap** algorithm is independent of pk. This leads to the interesting property of the Diffie–Hellman protocol that it can be run in one round so that both parties can compute their respective message before receiving the other party's message. This property is not shared by many of the KEMs proposed as Diffie–Hellman replacements for post-quantum security. This does not obstruct the generic construction in Figure 9.2 but it does mean that the protocol must now run in two rounds since B needs to receive the message from A before responding.

9.2.2.2. *Unauthenticated group key exchange*

For constructing group key exchange, we would like to have a version of the Diffie–Hellman protocol for more than two parties. A three-party version was constructed by Joux (2004) from a bilinear pairing $\hat{e} : \mathbb{G} \times \mathbb{G} \to \mathbb{G}_T$ so that each of three parties can choose a random input a, b and c and broadcast g^a, g^b and g^c (see Chapter 5). Then knowledge of one input is sufficient to compute the shared secret value $\hat{e}(g, g)^{abc} = \hat{e}(g^a, g^b)^c = \hat{e}(g^a, g^c)^b = \hat{e}(g^b, g^c)^a$. Extending this idea to any number of parties would be possible with suitable multilinear maps (Boneh and Silverberg 2002) but despite this attractive idea no suitable maps are currently known.

Several protocols are known which generalize Diffie–Hellman to the group setting, but they all need to balance increased computation or communications. An elegant construction of Burmester and Desmedt (1995) allows a group of parties to compute a shared secret Z in only two rounds with almost a fixed computation per party. Katz and Yung (2003) provide a security proof for the protocol of Burmester and Desmedt against a passive adversary based on the decisional DH assumption. A more recent example of such a generalized Diffie–Hellman protocol is TreeKEM (Alwen et al. 2020), which is designed to facilitate addition and deletion of group members, and also has the flexibility of being based on any KEM.

9.3. Authenticated key exchange

The protocols considered in section 9.2 can be secure only against passive attackers because there we ignored authentication. Consequently, an active attacker can always participate in protocol runs and the honest parties will not know which peer party shares a session key. In order to provide security against active attackers, parties must hold *long-term keys* that can be used by other parties to authenticate them. Key exchange protocols that allow parties to verify the identity of other participating parties are called *authenticated key exchange* (AKE) protocols.

Long-term keys may typically be public keys certified by some authority trusted by all protocol parties. In many academic protocols, it is implicitly assumed that public keys are available to the parties whenever they need them. This is not always the case in practice and can have a major influence on protocol efficiency. It is also possible to model the security of certificates as part of the protocol (Boyd et al. 2013) but this complicates the analysis and is usually avoided in academic papers.

9.3.1. *Non-interactive key exchange*

The simplest kind of AKE protocol is arguably one which makes use of only long-term keys, without any ephemeral keys. If we suppose that protocol participants can obtain long-term keys from some directory, for example, a directory of certified public keys, then we can obtain protocols without a single message, in other words non-interactive protocols.

DEFINITION 9.5.– *A non-interactive key exchange (NIKE) protocol consists of three algorithms, the first two of which take as input an implicit security parameter λ, and are randomized, while the third is deterministic.*

– **NIKESetup**()*: It outputs a set of common parameters cp.*

– **NIKEKeyGen**(cp, ID)*: It takes as input the parameters cp and identity* ID *and outputs a public and private key pair* $(\mathsf{pk}, \mathsf{sk})$.

– **NIKEkey**$(\mathsf{ID}_1, \mathsf{pk}_1, \mathsf{ID}_2, \mathsf{sk}_2)$*: Given a public key* pk_1 *and private key* sk_2, *it outputs a shared key* K *or a failure symbol.*

Correctness of the NIKE protocol demands that:

$$\mathbf{NIKEkey}(\mathsf{ID}_1, \mathsf{pk}_1, \mathsf{ID}_2, \mathsf{sk}_2) = \mathbf{NIKEkey}(\mathsf{ID}_2, \mathsf{pk}_2, \mathsf{ID}_1, \mathsf{sk}_1).$$

Although we may think of a NIKE protocol as one with no messages using long-term keys, we can also think of it as an unauthenticated protocol where two parties A and B each generate an ephemeral key pair, send the public key to the peer party and then compute a shared key. In this way the Diffie–Hellman protocol, introduced in definition 9.4, can be recast as a NIKE protocol. The **NIKESetup**() algorithm is the same as **KEMSetup** in definition 9.4; the **NIKEKeyGen**(cp, U_i) algorithm generates a private and public key pair $(\mathsf{sk}_i, g^{\mathsf{sk}_i})$ for a party U_i and **NIKEkey**$(U_1, \mathsf{pk}_1, U_2, \mathsf{sk}_2)$ is $g^{\mathsf{sk}_1\mathsf{sk}_2}$. Other NIKE protocols can be built (Freire et al. 2013) based on problems such as factorization and elliptic curve pairings.

Freire et al. (2013) give a formal analysis of a generic conversion from any NIKE to a KEM. Such a mapping uses **NIKEKeyGen**(cp, ID) to generate a new key for **Encap**(pk) independent of pk. Generally, we cannot go in the other direction and use a KEM directly as a NIKE protocol since the encapsulated key generated by **Encap**(pk) may depend on pk. However, in cases where the encapsulation is independent of the recipient public key, such as with the Diffie–Hellman KEM, a NIKE and KEM can be interchanged.

Freire et al. (2013) provide a hierarchy of security models for NIKE security. In all models, the adversary's goal is to distinguish from random a secret shared by an uncorrupted pair of parties chosen by the adversary. Stronger models allow the adversary to register and/or corrupt public and private keys, or to have more attempts at guessing. Some of the previous studies (Freire et al. 2014) have also proposed a security functionality in the UC model.

Recall that the goal of key exchange is to establish a key to protect a communications session. Security models for key exchange therefore usually allow the adversary to obtain session keys from independent protocol runs, including those run between the same parties. Thus, NIKE protocols are insufficient as a general AKE construction because they define a static key between any two parties. They can, however, be used as building blocks for key exchange as we see in section 9.3.3.1.

9.3.2. *AKE security models*

There exist today many different cryptographic security models for authenticated key exchange. Although there has been a tendency, over the course of many years, for models to demand an increasing level of security, it remains the case that many models are not comparable and there is no strict hierarchy of model strength.

9.3.2.1. *Game-based models for AKE*

The history of game-based security models goes back to a 1993 paper of Bellare and Rogaway, formally published in 1994 (Bellare and Rogaway 1994). This model, which we refer to as the BR93 model, defined a separate security goal for entity authentication, which guarantees that an accepting party in a protocol run has a specific, unique peer that engaged in that run. In practice, many AKE protocols do not provide such a property and many later models, including a 1995 follow-up paper of Bellare and Rogaway (1995), remove the requirement for explicit authentication. Instead, such models require only *implicit authentication*, which requires that when a party accepts a session key, a known peer party is the only party who may also have computed the same session key.

Game-based definitions for AKE security can be differentiated by a number of factors, but perhaps the most obvious is the set of capabilities (oracles) afforded the adversary. We allow the adversary, **Adv**, to completely control the network so that nothing happens in the security game until the adversary requests it. These models therefore always include an adversarial query, usually called Send, which allows **Adv** to send an input (possible empty) to a protocol session at a party and observe the response when that session runs its current protocol step. The Send query thus allows **Adv** to act as a passive adversary observing benign protocol runs, or as an active adversary sending any messages that it can compute. Security is usually defined using a Test query through which the adversary selects a *target session* to attack, and receive either the session key accepted in that session or a random key; **Adv** wins the security game if it can distinguish between these two possibilities.

Query	Purpose	Model
Send	Send message to protocol session and observe response	Bellare and Rogaway (1994)
Reveal	Return any accepted session key	Bellare and Rogaway (1994)
Corrupt	Return the long-term private key of a party	Bellare and Rogaway (1995)
StateReveal	Return session temporary state	Canetti and Krawczyk (2001)
EphemeralReveal	Returns session private ephemeral keys	LaMacchia et al. (2007)
Test	Returns either session key or random key	Bellare and Rogaway (1994)

Table 9.1. *Common adversarial queries in AKE security models*

In addition to the Send query, Table 9.1 lists several other adversarial queries commonly used in AKE security models. Not all models include all of these queries and in any case it is not reasonable to allow an adversary unrestricted access to all of these queries. It is normal to allow **Adv** access to session keys from sessions other than the target session being attacked, through the Reveal query. We also expect **Adv** to have access to long-term keys of parties not involved in the target session through the Corrupt query.

Earlier key exchange models were typically designed to capture the kinds of attacks that were known against existing protocols. Thus, the following attacks can be modeled when the adversary is given specific powers.

– *Known-key security*: **Adv** is allowed to obtain session keys from other protocol runs, as captured through the Reveal query.

– *Unknown key-share*: **Adv** is allowed to send messages to unintended parties, as captured through the Send query, to make parties accept keys with different parties than intended.

– *Forward secrecy*: **Adv** is allowed to obtain long terms keys, through the Corrupt query, after the target session has completed.

– *Key compromise impersonation*: **Adv** is allowed access to the long-term keys of the intended partner of the target session (at any time) allowing an impersonation attack, but may still not be able to win the security game.

– *Post-compromise security*: **Adv** is allowed access to an evolving party-specific key before the target session, but may still not be able to win the security game if a re-synchronising step has occurred (Cohn-Gordon et al. 2016).

Starting with the model of LaMacchia et al. (2007) efforts have been made to define *maximal security*, in other words, to find the strongest adversary against which we can still guarantee security. Their eCK model (an extension to the Canetti and

Krawczyk (CK) model (Canetti and Krawczyk 2001)) added a query allowing **Adv** to obtain ephemeral session secrets, such as ephemeral Diffie–Hellman secret keys. **Adv** is allowed to obtain ephemeral or long-term keys of parties, even those in the target session, as long as this does not lead to a trivial win of the security game. Unfortunately, the quest to find a strongest security model, or even a partial order on models, has not yet succeeded. Cremers (2011) showed that the CK model (in two versions) and the eCK model cannot be compared in the sense that a protocol can be secure in any one and insecure in another.

In addition to the adversarial queries, a critical element of any AKE security model is to specify when, and in what combinations, the queries can be made. For example, it may be disallowed to ask both EphemeralReveal to the target session and a Corrupt query to the owner of the target session. A generalized formulation of this notion is the *freshness predicate* introduced by Cremers and Feltz (2012). They give a generalized model for AKE security as follows, where **Q** is some set of queries (such as those described in Table 9.1) and **F** is the freshness predicate that specifies which queries are valid at any specific point in the security game.

1) Generate the system parameters;

2) **Adv** has access to queries in **Q** as long as **F** holds;

3) **Adv** specifies a target session via a Test query;

4) **Adv** again has access to queries in **Q** as long as **F** continues to hold;

5) **Adv** outputs its guess for whether it was given a real or a random key in Step 3 and wins if its guess is correct.

This formulation can be used to specify most of the known game-based security models.

9.3.2.2. *Flavors of forward secrecy*

Forward secrecy is the property that any session key should remain secure if a party is corrupted, as long as the session key was accepted prior to the corruption occurring. The strongest definition would allow **Adv** to corrupt all parties after the session key is accepted, but some protocols may only tolerate limited corruption. One important situation is identity-based protocols where a key generation center (KGC) can find the private keys of all users. Identity-based AKE protocols may provide *KGC forward secrecy* (Chen et al. 2007) even when the KGC is corrupted.

An important flavor is *weak forward secrecy* in which **Adv** is not permitted to be active during the run of the target session. Many well-known two-message protocols achieve only this weaker flavor of forward secrecy (we will see examples later in this chapter), which has led to an unfortunate misunderstanding that no two-message protocol can achieve full forward secrecy. In fact, there are many two-message protocols which do achieve full forward secrecy, typically by providing explicit authentication of the parties through signatures or MACs. Arguably weak forward secrecy is sufficient in many scenarios since a protocol with weak forward secrecy can be converted to one with full forward secrecy by adding extra messages confirming that both parties are able to compute the session key. This is because a protocol, which is secure with weak forward secrecy would, not allow an active adversary to show knowledge of the session key before the session key is accepted.

9.3.2.3. *ACCE models*

One of the consequences of the game-based security definitions for AKE is that the adversary is never allowed to see the real session key in use, since that would likely be usable as an oracle to distinguish the session key from a random key. This does not cause a problem when key exchange is completed before a separate session using the agreed key, but unfortunately this does not always occur in real world protocols, and may be impossible to achieve when *early data* are allowed in 0-RTT protocols. This mismatch between formal security goals and reality for a long time prevented a security proof for the most widely used practical key exchange protocol, TLS.

In 2012, Jager et al. (2012, 2017) introduced the Authenticated and Confidential Channel Establishment (ACCE) model, specifically in order to prove the security of the TLS 1.2 handshake protocol. The ACCE model considers the combination of key exchange with usage of the session key for authenticated encryption of exchanged application data, reflecting actual usage in protocols such as TLS. Later work developed the model further to account for other constraints. Dowling et al. (2020) proposed the *flexible ACCE* (fACCE) model and used it to analyze the flexible suite of protocols known as the *Noise Framework*.

9.3.2.4. *Privacy properties*

Although not usually considered a primary goal of key exchange, there has been significant work on enhanced privacy provisions. Two specific goals are *deniability*, which is concerned with allowing protocol parties to plausibly deny that they participated in a certain protocol run, and *anonymity*, which is concerned with hiding the identities of those parties which did participate. Both of these properties are easy to achieve, in an informal sense, if the adversary is not a participant in the protocol run of concern. For example, there are many protocols where the messages exchanged are random values (once the protocol parameters are chosen) so that it is impossible to connect any identity from the messages alone.

Achieving privacy when the adversary is a party in the protocol is difficult. There are a few different definitions for what deniability should mean in this situation (Di Raimondo et al. 2006; Yao and Zhao 2010) and corresponding protocol constructions. Similarly, with anonymity, different definitions are possible. In a client–server scenario, it may only be meaningful to provide anonymity of the client so a general strategy can be for the client to hide its identity by encrypting all of its messages with a server public key such as is done in the IKE protocol of IPsec (Kaufman 2005). Specific protocols have also been proposed by Goldberg et al. (2013) to use with the anonymity network Tor.

9.3.2.5. *Multi-stage security and continuous key exchange*

Traditional key exchange security models apply to protocols where each successful run results in one session key agreed between the participating parties. Some practical protocols are more complex than this and may output different keys at different stages. One example of this is the TLS protocol which, depending on the protocol version, allows session resumption or session renegotiation where a previous session key can be used to help set up a new session key. TLS 1.3 also allows an initial key to be agreed and used to protect early data and then replaced by a stronger key to protect subsequent data.

In order to model such protocols, the notion of *multi-stage security* was introduced by Fischlin and Günther (2014), who used it to analyze the QUIC protocol. It has subsequently been used to analyze other protocols, including TLS 1.3 (Dowling et al. 2021). Extending the idea of updating keys to the limit, there are also protocols which change the session key for every message sent. This can use a process known as *ratcheting* of keys, which refers to updating keys in a one-way fashion so that it is only possible to go forwards, not backwards. A prime example of this is the messaging protocol Signal, which has also been analyzed using the multi-stage security model (Cohn-Gordon et al. 2017).

9.3.2.6. *Universal composability*

Although game-based definitions have been more common in the research literature, there has also been considerable work on models based on simulatability between ideal and real world views, particularly in the universal composability (UC) model (Canetti and Krawczyk 2002). In such models, an ideal functionality is defined for protocol behavior and security is defined by showing that adversarial interaction with the functionality in the real world is indistinguishable from the ideal world. Such models have been prominent in the area of PAKE protocols (see Chapter 10).

9.3.3. *Constructions and examples*

Examples of AKE protocols abound in both the academic literature and in practice, attesting to the importance of this primitive. In this chapter, we cannot comprehensively cover the literature, but in the subsequent sections we show some generic constructions and some prominent examples.

9.3.3.1. *AKE from NIKE*

As mentioned above, a NIKE protocol (see definition 9.5) is flexible as to whether it uses long-term or ephemeral keys. Bergsma et al. (2015) showed how to use a generic secure NIKE mixing both long-term and ephemeral keys, together with a deterministic signature scheme, to construct an AKE protocol as shown in Figure 9.3. We will refer to this protocol as the BJS protocol.

Long-term keys: $(\mathsf{pk}_A, \mathsf{sk}_A); (\mathsf{pk}_B, \mathsf{sk}_B) \xleftarrow{\$} \textbf{NIKEKeyGen}$; signing keys for A and B.

Shared information: Long-term public keys; NIKE shared parameters; pseudo-random function F.

$$A \qquad\qquad\qquad\qquad\qquad\qquad\qquad\qquad\qquad B$$

$(\mathrm{epk}_A, \mathrm{esk}_A) \xleftarrow{\$} \textbf{NIKEKeyGen}$

$$\xrightarrow{\quad \mathrm{epk}_A, \mathsf{Sig}_A(\mathrm{epk}_A) \quad}$$

$$(\mathrm{epk}_B, \mathrm{esk}_B) \xleftarrow{\$} \textbf{NIKEKeyGen}$$

$$\xleftarrow{\quad \mathrm{epk}_B, \mathsf{Sig}_B(\mathrm{epk}_B) \quad}$$

$$Z_1 = \textbf{NIKEkey}(\mathsf{ID}_B, \mathsf{pk}_B, \mathsf{ID}_A, \mathsf{sk}_A) = \textbf{NIKEkey}(\mathsf{ID}_A, \mathsf{pk}_A, \mathsf{ID}_B, \mathsf{sk}_B)$$
$$Z_2 = \textbf{NIKEkey}(\mathsf{ID}_B, \mathrm{epk}_B, \mathsf{ID}_A, \mathsf{sk}_A) = \textbf{NIKEkey}(\mathsf{ID}_A, \mathsf{pk}_A, \mathsf{ID}_B, \mathrm{esk}_B)$$
$$Z_3 = \textbf{NIKEkey}(\mathsf{ID}_B, \mathsf{pk}_B, \mathsf{ID}_A, \mathrm{esk}_A) = \textbf{NIKEkey}(\mathsf{ID}_A, \mathrm{epk}_A, \mathsf{ID}_B, \mathsf{sk}_B)$$
$$Z_4 = \textbf{NIKEkey}(\mathsf{ID}_B, \mathrm{epk}_B, \mathsf{ID}_A, \mathrm{esk}_A) = \textbf{NIKEkey}(\mathsf{ID}_A, \mathrm{epk}_A, \mathsf{ID}_B, \mathrm{esk}_B)$$

$$T = \mathrm{epk}_A, \mathrm{epk}_B$$

$$\mathsf{K} = F_{Z_1}(T) \oplus F_{Z_2}(T) \oplus F_{Z_3}(T) \oplus F_{Z_4}(T)$$

Figure 9.3. *Bergsma–Jager–Schwenk (BJS) generic protocol from NIKE (Bergsma et al. 2015)*

The BJS protocol makes use of the NIKE protocol four times, using the shared **NIKEkey** to combine keys of A and B in the four possible combinations of long-term and ephemeral keys. The protocol also makes use of a PRF F and a deterministic signature scheme, with $\mathsf{Sig}_X(M)$ denoting signature of party X on message M. Bergsma et al. (2015) proved that their protocol is secure in a strong AKE security model as long as the NIKE, PRF and signature scheme are secure in a commonly used sense. The flexibility of using a generic NIKE allows for different instantiations – when the NIKE has a security proof in the standard model, then so does the BJS protocol. NIKEs with proofs in the random oracle model are known (Freire et al. 2013), including the Diffie–Hellman instantiation, and tend to be more efficient than those with standard model proofs.

In common with most AKE protocols in the literature, the security proof that comes with the BJS protocol is not tight, incurring a security loss that is quadratic in both the number of protocol parties and the number of sessions at each party. More recently, there have been protocols with similar designs (Gjøsteen and Jager 2018; Cohn-Gordon et al. 2019; Pan et al. 2021), instantiated with Diffie–Hellman, that have much tighter security proofs at a modest cost in performance and assuming random oracles.

Flexibility and strong security are two significant benefits of the BJS protocol. One price to pay for these benefits is that the protocol is less efficient than other known protocols. For example, when instantiated with Diffie–Hellman each party must compute five exponentiations in each protocol run. Another limitation is that, at the time of writing, there is a lack of NIKE protocols believed to be secure in the post-quantum setting, and this is one motivation for using KEMs as the basis for AKE instead of NIKE-based protocols.

9.3.3.2. AKE from KEMs

As discussed in section 9.2, a KEM can be used as an unauthenticated key exchange protocol. There are several known methods for adding authentication to a passively secure key exchange protocol in order to convert to an AKE protocol. Perhaps the simplest way is to add signatures to the messages of the protocol in Figure 9.2. Generic conversion of unauthenticated protocols to AKE protocols can be achieved via *authenticators* proposed by Bellare et al. (1998) and Canetti and Krawczyk (2001). Applying their signature-based authenticator to the protocol in Figure 9.2 leads to a protocol construction shown in Figure 9.4. Both parties provide signatures on the exchanged messages from the original unauthenticated protocol. The generic theorems of Canetti and Krawczyk (2001) guarantee security in their model.

Although the protocol in Figure 9.4 is attractive in its simplicity and flexibility, such protocols derived from generic authenticators have their limitations. One is that an additional message flow is required so that two-message protocols with mutual authentication cannot be achieved. A second limitation is that protocols which apply authentication independently do not reach the highest level of security because they are necessarily insecure against adversaries who can obtain ephemeral keys. (Note, however, that this approach does always achieve forward secrecy since the long-term keys are used only for authentication.)

An alternative approach to obtaining AKE from KEMs is not to use signatures at all, but to authenticate in another way. An attractive option is to use KEMs with long-term keys in addition to KEMs with ephemeral keys. Fujioka et al. (2012) provided a generic AKE construction following this approach as shown in Figure 9.5. We will refer to this protocol as the FSXY protocol. In this description, the randomness used in the KEM encapsulation is shown explicitly and is chosen in a special way for the FSXY protocol as discussed below.

Long-term keys: Signing keys for A and B.

Shared information: Long-term signature verification keys.

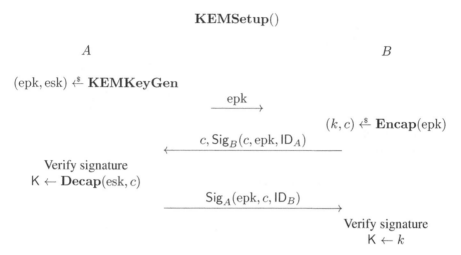

$$\textbf{KEMSetup}()$$

A $\qquad\qquad\qquad\qquad\qquad\qquad\qquad\qquad\qquad\qquad\qquad$ B

$(\mathrm{epk},\mathrm{esk}) \xleftarrow{\$} \textbf{KEMKeyGen}$

$\xrightarrow{\quad\mathrm{epk}\quad}$

$(k,c) \xleftarrow{\$} \textbf{Encap}(\mathrm{epk})$

$\xleftarrow{\quad c, \mathsf{Sig}_B(c,\mathrm{epk},\mathsf{ID}_A) \quad}$

Verify signature
$\mathsf{K} \leftarrow \textbf{Decap}(\mathrm{esk}, c)$

$\xrightarrow{\quad \mathsf{Sig}_A(\mathrm{epk}, c, \mathsf{ID}_B) \quad}$

Verify signature
$\mathsf{K} \leftarrow k$

Figure 9.4. *Generic authenticated key exchange from signed KEMs*

The advantage of this generic approach is that different concrete KEM constructions can be applied, including those designed for post-quantum security. The two KEMs used in the FSXY protocol are shown with the same notation in Figure 9.5, but could be the same or different. The choice of KEM will of course influence both the security and efficiency of the protocol. Fujioka et al. (2012) provide a security proof in a strong security model (Krawczyk 2005) assuming that the KEM used with long-term keys is CCA secure, and that the KEM used with ephemeral keys is CPA secure. They give concrete instantiations based on factoring, codes and lattices. Hülsing et al. (2021) have used the FSXY protocol as the basis of a post-quantum version of the WireGuard protocol.

9.3.3.3. *NAXOS and Twisted-PRF tricks*

The randomness input values r_A and r_B used in the FSXY protocol can be computed in different ways, including being chosen simply randomly as in a standard usage of the KEM. An alternative choice is to compute these values by combining long-term and ephemeral secrets, an idea that arises from the study of LaMacchia et al. (2007), who used it in the design of their NAXOS protocol. The reason for doing this is to provide security against an adversary who can obtain the ephemeral secret or the long-term secret (but not both). This idea has been re-used in several subsequent protocol designs, usually in one of two different forms.

Long-term keys: $(\mathsf{pk}_A, \mathsf{sk}_A); (\mathsf{pk}_B, \mathsf{sk}_B) \overset{\$}{\leftarrow} \mathbf{KEMKeyGen}$

A $\qquad\qquad\qquad\qquad\qquad\qquad\qquad\qquad\qquad B$

Generate r_A
$(k_A, c_A) \leftarrow \mathbf{Encap}(\mathsf{pk}_B; r_A)$
$(\mathsf{epk}, \mathsf{esk}) \overset{\$}{\leftarrow} \mathbf{KEMKeyGen}$

$$\xrightarrow{\quad c_A, \mathsf{epk} \quad}$$

$k_A \overset{\$}{\leftarrow} \mathbf{Decap}(\mathsf{sk}_B, c_A)$
Generate r_B
$(k_B, c_B) \leftarrow \mathbf{Encap}(\mathsf{pk}_A; r_B)$
$(k_e, c_e) \overset{\$}{\leftarrow} \mathbf{Encap}(\mathsf{epk})$

$k_B = \mathbf{Decap}(\mathsf{sk}_A, c_B)$ $\qquad\xleftarrow{\quad c_B, c_e \quad}$
$k_e = \mathbf{Decap}(\mathsf{esk}, c_e)$

Shared secret: $Z \leftarrow k_A \parallel k_B \parallel k_e$

Figure 9.5. *Simplified protocol of Fujioka et al. (2012)*

– *NAXOS trick*: The randomness value is computed as $H(e, l)$ where e is an ephemeral secret, l is a long-term secret and H is a hash function. In the NAXOS protocol (LaMacchia et al. 2007), H is modeled as a random oracle and $H(e, l)$ is used as a Diffie–Hellman ephemeral input.

– *Twisted PRF trick*: The randomness value is computed as $F_{e_1}(l_1) \oplus F_{l_2}(e_2)$ where e_1 and e_2 are ephemeral secrets, l_1 and l_2 are long-term secrets, and F is a PRF. This idea was first used by Okamoto (2007) with the same motivation as the NAXOS trick but avoiding the random oracle model in order to obtain security in the standard model. This is how the values r_A and r_B used in the FSXY protocol are calculated.

9.3.3.4. *HMQV: a very efficient AKE protocol*

Generic protocol constructions tend to be less efficient than custom constructions. One of the most efficient AKE protocols known was originally proposed in 1995 by Menezes, Qu and Vanstone in a conference without formal proceedings. Their protocol was later adapted in 2005 by Krawczyk (2005) into a version, known as HMQV, with a reductionist security proof. The main, two message, version of the HMQV protocol is shown in Figure 9.6 using the notation from the Diffie–Hellman KEM (definition 9.4). Alternative versions, with one and with three messages, are also proposed by Krawczyk.

Shared information: $g, \mathbb{G} \leftarrow$ **KEMSetup**(). Hash functions H, H'.

Long-term keys: $(\mathsf{pk}_A, \mathsf{sk}_A); (\mathsf{pk}_B, \mathsf{sk}_B) \xleftarrow{\$}$ **KEMKeyGen**

A B

$\mathsf{esk}_A \xleftarrow{\$} \mathbb{Z}_q$

$\mathsf{epk}_A \leftarrow g^{\mathsf{esk}_A}$ $\xrightarrow{\quad \mathsf{epk}_A \quad}$ $\mathsf{esk}_B \xleftarrow{\$} \mathbb{Z}_q$

                                      $\mathsf{epk}_B \leftarrow g^{\mathsf{esk}_B}$

                $\xleftarrow{\quad \mathsf{epk}_B \quad}$

$d \leftarrow H(\mathsf{epk}_A, \mathsf{ID}_B)$ $d \leftarrow H(\mathsf{epk}_A, \mathsf{ID}_B)$

$e \leftarrow H(\mathsf{epk}_B, \mathsf{ID}_A)$ $e \leftarrow H(\mathsf{epk}_B, \mathsf{ID}_A)$

$S_A \leftarrow \mathsf{esk}_A + d \cdot \mathsf{sk}_A \bmod q$ $S_B \leftarrow \mathsf{esk}_B + e \cdot \mathsf{sk}_B \bmod q$

$\mathsf{Z} \leftarrow (\mathsf{epk}_B \cdot \mathsf{pk}_B^e)^{S_A}$ $\mathsf{Z} \leftarrow (\mathsf{epk}_A \cdot \mathsf{pk}_A^d)^{S_B}$

$\mathsf{K} \leftarrow H'(\mathsf{Z})$

Figure 9.6. *HMQV protocol*

The HMQV protocol messages are the same as ephemeral Diffie–Hellman, but the session key computation uses a function of both the long-term and ephemeral keys to compute a shared secret $\mathsf{Z} = g^{(\mathsf{esk}_A + d \cdot \mathsf{sk}_A)(\mathsf{esk}_B + e \cdot \mathsf{sk}_B)}$. The temporary values d and e are computed using a hash function H whose output size is only half the length of the exponent size used for the Diffie–Hellman computations. This results in a protocol where we may say that each party uses approximately 2.5 exponentiations to achieve authenticated key exchange, in contrast to the two exponentiations used in the plain unauthenticated Diffie–Hellman key exchange. Krawczyk provides a security proof in a model similar to the CK model (Canetti and Krawczyk 2001), assuming that the hash function H acts as a random oracle. Note that HMQV achieves only weak forward secrecy since an active adversary is free to choose a valid input for, say, esk_A and, after B accepts, corrupt A to obtain sk_A and compute S_A and then K in the same way as A does.

The HMQV protocol was the subject of controversy when first published, particularly regarding whether the security proof was sound. Much of this revolved around the question of whether *key validation* was required, which is a check that the received ephemeral keys, epk_A and epk_B, and possibly also the long-term public keys, pk_A and pk_B, are in the correct Diffie–Hellman group. Depending on the algebraic setting, the cost of key validation can be as much as an additional exponentiation. Whether or not key validation is required depends on what level of security is needed, but to reach the higher security levels it may be necessary (Menezes and Ustaoglu 2006). The preface of the full version of the HMQV paper (Krawczyk 2005b) discusses the situation.

It is not obvious how to generalize the HMQV protocol into other algebraic settings. A protocol of Zhang et al. (2015) uses HMQV as a basis for an AKE protocol in the lattice setting, aimed at achieving post-quantum security. However, they do not claim to achieve the same level of security, specifically disallowing the adversary from obtaining session state. Moreover, the one message variant of their protocol has been the subject of attacks (Gong and Zhao 2017).

9.3.3.5. *Authenticated group key exchange*

Security of group key exchange is more complex than for two-party key exchange. In addition to the threats from an external adversary, there are also opportunities for an adversary to act as an insider in protocol runs and deceive other participants regarding the active group members. Another complication that does not apply to the two-party case is that group key exchange protocols can be *dynamic*, providing the opportunity to add to, or remove, current group members. Particularly for large groups, there are potentially significant efficiency gains from using dynamic operations rather than having to run the whole protocol again when the group membership changes.

Poettering et al. (2021) have conducted a survey of the many group key exchange security models and concluded that a new model is needed to capture all of the desirable properties. Just as in the two-party case, there are generic tools to convert unauthenticated protocols into group AKE in the group key exchange case; the compiler of Katz and Yung (2003) is a well-known example that adds signatures from each party and can be used, for example, to convert the protocol of Desmedt and Burmester (see section 9.2.2.2) into a secure group AKE. A lattice-based version of both the compiler and the unauthenticated group protocol has also been proposed (Apon et al. 2019). Unfortunately, the generic construction of Katz and Yung, like several other security models, does not support dynamic groups. There are, however, models and constructions that do so (Bresson et al. 2002). Advanced properties such as post-compromise security are desirable in the group setting too. There is ongoing work in developing a standard for key exchange in group messaging, which can support strong security and provide efficient solutions.

9.4. Conclusion

Key exchange has a long history and a vast literature, yet remains a very active research area with significant practical impact. It is inevitable that as new computational assumptions emerge as the basis for cryptographic security, so will their use in key exchange be relevant. At the same time, we often see new requirements for key exchange protocols that demand new designs. Some of the important future research challenges for key exchange are likely to be as follows:

– *Post-quantum security*: Advances in post-quantum key exchange in the recent literature have focused mainly on KEMs rather than on authenticated key exchange, and it remains unclear how best to provide post-quantum secure AKE in different application scenarios. Currently, there is no trusted post-quantum NIKE available as a drop-in replacement for the Diffie–Hellman protocol, although CSIDH (Castryck et al. 2018) is a promising candidate.

– *Efficiency*: No matter how fast processors become, there always remains demand for more efficient processing and communication. New applications such as the Internet of Things will deploy lightweight devices with limited computational, storage and communication capabilities, which may not be able to support public key infrastructure.

– *Stateful protocols*: New security requirements such as post-compromise security have led to techniques of ratcheting, which move away from the traditional security model accommodating fixed long-term keys and ephemeral keys. Keys with intermediate lifetimes, and protocols producing streams of keys, need new security models and innovative design methods.

9.5. References

Alwen, J., Coretti, S., Dodis, Y., Tselekounis, Y. (2020). Security analysis and improvements for the IETF MLS standard for group messaging. In *CRYPTO 2020, Part I*, vol. 12170 of *LNCS*, Micciancio, D., Ristenpart, T. (eds). Springer, Heidelberg.

Apon, D., Dachman-Soled, D., Gong, H., Katz, J. (2019). Constant-round group key exchange from the ring-LWE assumption. In *Post-Quantum Cryptography – 10th International Conference, PQCrypto 2019*, Ding, J., Steinwandt, R. (eds). Springer, Heidelberg.

Barker, E., Chen, L., Davis, R. (2020). Recommendation for key-derivation methods in key-establishment schemes. NIST Special Publication 800-56C, National Institute of Standards and Technology.

Bellare, M. and Rogaway, P. (1994). Entity authentication and key distribution. In *CRYPTO'93*, vol. 773 of *LNCS*, Stinson, D.R. (ed.). Springer, Heidelberg.

Bellare, M. and Rogaway, P. (1995). Provably secure session key distribution: The three party case. In *27th ACM STOC*. ACM Press.

Bellare, M., Canetti, R., Krawczyk, H. (1996). Keying hash functions for message authentication. In *CRYPTO'96*, vol. 1109 of *LNCS*, Koblitz, N. (ed.). Springer, Heidelberg.

Bellare, M., Canetti, R., Krawczyk, H. (1998). A modular approach to the design and analysis of authentication and key exchange protocols (extended abstract). In *30th ACM STOC*. ACM Press.

Bergsma, F., Jager, T., Schwenk, J. (2015). One-round key exchange with strong security: An efficient and generic construction in the standard model. In *PKC 2015*, vol. 9020 of *LNCS*, Katz, J. (ed.). Springer, Heidelberg.

Boneh, D. and Silverberg, A. (2002). Applications of multilinear forms to cryptography. Cryptology ePrint Archive, Report 2002/080 [Online]. Available at: https://eprint.iacr.org/2002/080.

Boyd, C., Cremers, C., Feltz, M., Paterson, K.G., Poettering, B., Stebila, D. (2013). ASICS: Authenticated key exchange security incorporating certification systems. In *ESORICS 2013*, vol. 8134 of *LNCS*, Crampton, J., Jajodia, S., Mayes, K. (eds). Springer, Heidelberg.

Bresson, E., Chevassut, O., Pointcheval, D. (2002). Dynamic group Diffie–Hellman key exchange under standard assumptions. In *EUROCRYPT 2002*, vol. 2332 of *LNCS*, Knudsen, L.R. (ed.). Springer, Heidelberg.

Burmester, M. and Desmedt, Y. (1995). A secure and efficient conference key distribution system (extended abstract). In *EUROCRYPT'94*, vol. 950 of *LNCS*, Santis, A.D. (ed.). Springer, Heidelberg.

Canetti, R. and Krawczyk, H. (2001). Analysis of key-exchange protocols and their use for building secure channels. In *EUROCRYPT 2001*, vol. 2045 of *LNCS*, Pfitzmann, B. (ed.). Springer, Heidelberg.

Canetti, R. and Krawczyk, H. (2002). Security analysis of IKE's signature-based key-exchange protocol. In *CRYPTO 2002*, vol. 2442 of *LNCS*, Yung, M. (ed.). Springer, Heidelberg [Online]. Available at: https://eprint.iacr.org/2002/120/.

Castryck, W., Lange, T., Martindale, C., Panny, L., Renes, J. (2018). CSIDH: An efficient post-quantum commutative group action. In *ASIACRYPT 2018, Part III*, vol. 11274 of *LNCS*, Peyrin, T., Galbraith, S. (eds). Springer, Heidelberg.

Chen, L., Cheng, Z., Smart, N.P. (2007). Identity-based key agreement protocols from pairings. *International Journal of Information Security*, 6(4), 213–241.

Cohn-Gordon, K., Cremers, C.J.F., Garratt, L. (2016). On post-compromise security. In *CSF 2016 Computer Security Foundations Symposium*, Hicks, M., Köpf, B. (eds). IEEE Computer Society Press.

Cohn-Gordon, K., Cremers, C.J.F., Dowling, B., Garratt, L., Stebila, D. (2017). A formal security analysis of the Signal messaging protocol. In *2017 IEEE European Symposium on Security and Privacy*, 26–28 April.

Cohn-Gordon, K., Cremers, C., Gjøsteen, K., Jacobsen, H., Jager, T. (2019). Highly efficient key exchange protocols with optimal tightness. In *CRYPTO 2019, Part III*, vol. 11694 of *LNCS*, Boldyreva, A., Micciancio, D. (eds). Springer, Heidelberg.

Cremers, C. (2011). Examining indistinguishability-based security models for key exchange protocols: The case of CK, CK-HMQV, and eCK. In *ASIACCS 11*, Cheung, B.S.N., Hui, L.C.K., Sandhu, R.S., Wong, D.S. (eds). ACM Press.

Cremers, C.J.F. and Feltz, M. (2012). Beyond eCK: Perfect forward secrecy under actor compromise and ephemeral-key reveal. In *ESORICS 2012*, vol. 7459 of *LNCS*, Foresti, S., Yung, M., Martinelli, F. (eds). Springer, Heidelberg.

D'Anvers, J.-P., Karmakar, A., Roy, S.S., Vercauteren, F. (2018). Saber: Module-LWR based key exchange, CPA-secure encryption and CCA-secure KEM. In *AFRICACRYPT 18*, vol. 10831 of *LNCS*, Joux, A., Nitaj, A., Rachidi, T. (eds). Springer, Heidelberg.

Di Raimondo, M., Gennaro, R., Krawczyk, H. (2006). Deniable authentication and key exchange. In *ACM CCS 2006*, Juels, A., Wright, R.N., De Capitani di Vimercati, S. (eds). ACM Press.

Diffie, W. and Hellman, M.E. (1976). New directions in cryptography. *IEEE Transactions on Information Theory*, 22(6), 644–654.

Dowling, B., Rösler, P., Schwenk, J. (2020). Flexible authenticated and confidential channel establishment (fACCE): Analyzing the noise protocol framework. In *PKC 2020, Part I*, vol. 12110 of *LNCS*, Kiayias, A., Kohlweiss, M., Wallden, P., Zikas, V. (eds). Springer, Heidelberg.

Dowling, B., Fischlin, M., Günther, F., Stebila, D. (2021). A cryptographic analysis of the TLS 1.3 handshake protocol. *Journal of Cryptology*, 34(4), 37.

Fischlin, M. and Günther, F. (2014). Multi-stage key exchange and the case of Google's QUIC protocol. In *ACM CCS 2014*, Ahn, G.-J., Yung, M., Li, N. (eds). ACM Press.

Freire, E.S.V., Hofheinz, D., Kiltz, E., Paterson, K.G. (2013). Non-interactive key exchange. In *PKC 2013*, vol. 7778 of *LNCS*, Kurosawa, K., Hanaoka, G. (eds). Springer, Heidelberg.

Freire, E.S.V., Hesse, J., Hofheinz, D. (2014). Universally composable non-interactive key exchange. In *SCN 14*, vol. 8642 of *LNCS*, Abdalla, M., Prisco, R.D. (eds). Springer, Heidelberg.

Fujioka, A., Suzuki, K., Xagawa, K., Yoneyama, K. (2012). Strongly secure authenticated key exchange from factoring, codes, and lattices. In *PKC 2012*, vol. 7293 of *LNCS*, Fischlin, M., Buchmann, J., Manulis, M. (eds). Springer, Heidelberg.

Gjøsteen, K. and Jager, T. (2018). Practical and tightly-secure digital signatures and authenticated key exchange. In *CRYPTO 2018, Part II*, vol. 10992 of *LNCS*, Shacham, H., Boldyreva, A. (eds). Springer, Heidelberg.

Goldberg, I., Stebila, D., Ustaoglu, B. (2013). Anonymity and one-way authentication in key exchange protocols. *Designs, Codes and Cryptography*, 67(2), 245–269.

Gong, L. (1995). Efficient network authentication protocols: Lower bounds and optimal implementations. *Distributed Computing*, 9(3), 131–145.

Gong, B. and Zhao, Y. (2017). Cryptanalysis of RLWE-based one-pass authenticated key exchange. In *Post-Quantum Cryptography – 8th International Workshop, PQCrypto 2017*, Lange, T., Takagi, T. (eds). Springer, Heidelberg.

Hülsing, A., Ning, K.-C., Schwabe, P., Weber, F., Zimmermann, P.R. (2021). Post-quantum wireguard. In *42nd IEEE Symposium on Security and Privacy*, May 24–27.

ISO (2016). Information technology – security techniques – key management – part 6: Key derivation ISO/IEC 11770-6. International Standard, International Organization for Standardization.

Jager, T., Kohlar, F., Schäge, S., Schwenk, J. (2012). On the security of TLS-DHE in the standard model. In *CRYPTO 2012*, vol. 7417 of *LNCS*, Safavi-Naini, R., Canetti, R. (eds). Springer, Heidelberg.

Jager, T., Kohlar, F., Schäge, S., Schwenk, J. (2017). Authenticated confidential channel establishment and the security of TLS-DHE. *Journal of Cryptology*, 30(4), 1276–1324.

Jao, D., Azarderakhsh, R., Campagna, M., Costello, C., De Feo, L., Hess, B., Jalali, A., Koziel, B., LaMacchia, B., Longa, P. et al. (2020). SIKE. Technical report, National Institute of Standards and Technology [Online]. Available at: https://csrc.nist.gov/projects/post-quantum-cryptography/round-3-submissions.

Joux, A. (2004). A one round protocol for tripartite Diffie–Hellman. *Journal of Cryptology*, 17(4), 263–276.

Katz, J. and Yung, M. (2003). Scalable protocols for authenticated group key exchange. In *CRYPTO 2003*, vol. 2729 of *LNCS*, Boneh, D. (ed.). Springer, Heidelberg.

Kaufman, C. (2005). Internet Key Exchange (IKEv2) protocol. IETF RFC 4306 (Proposed Standard).

Krawczyk, H. (2005a). HMQV: A high-performance secure Diffie–Hellman protocol. In *CRYPTO 2005*, vol. 3621 of *LNCS*, Shoup, V. (ed.). Springer, Heidelberg.

Krawczyk, H. (2005b). HMQV: A high-performance secure Diffie–Hellman protocol. Cryptology ePrint Archive, Report 2005/176 [Online]. Available at: https://eprint.iacr.org/2005/176.

Krawczyk, H. (2010). Cryptographic extraction and key derivation: The HKDF scheme. In *CRYPTO 2010*, vol. 6223 of *LNCS*, Rabin, T. (ed.). Springer, Heidelberg.

Krawczyk, H. and Eronen, P. (2010). HMAC-based extract-and-expand key derivation function (HKDF). *RFC*, 5869, 1–14.

LaMacchia, B.A., Lauter, K., Mityagin, A. (2007). Stronger security of authenticated key exchange. In *ProvSec 2007*, vol. 4784 of *LNCS*, Susilo, W., Liu, J.K., Mu, Y. (eds). Springer, Heidelberg.

Menezes, A.J. and Ustaoglu, B. (2006). On the importance of public-key validation in the MQV and HMQV key agreement protocols. In *INDOCRYPT 2006*, vol. 4329 of *LNCS*, Barua, R., Lange, T. (eds). Springer, Heidelberg.

Menezes, A.J., Qu, M., Vanstone, S.A. (1995). Some new key agreement protocols providing implicit authentication. In *Workshop on Selected Areas in Cryptography (SAC'95)*.

Needham, R.M. and Schroeder, M.D. (1978). Using encryption for authentication in large networks of computers. *Communications of the Association for Computing Machinery*, 21(21), 993–999.

Neuman, B.C. and Ts'o, T. (1994). Kerberos: An authentication service for computer networks. *IEEE Communications Magazine*, 32(9), 33–38.

Okamoto, T. (2007). Authenticated key exchange and key encapsulation in the standard model (invited talk). In *ASIACRYPT 2007*, vol. 4833 of *LNCS*, Kurosawa, K. (ed.). Springer, Heidelberg.

Pan, J., Qian, C., Ringerud, M. (2021). Signed Diffie–Hellman key exchange with tight security. In *CT-RSA 2021*, vol. 12704 of *LNCS*, Paterson, K.G. (ed.). Springer, Heidelberg.

Poettering, B., Rösler, P., Schwenk, J., Stebila, D. (2021). SoK: Game-based security models for group key exchange. In *CT-RSA 2021*, vol. 12704 of *LNCS*, Paterson, K.G. (ed.). Springer, Heidelberg.

Yao, A.C.-C. and Zhao, Y. (2010). Deniable Internet key exchange. In *ACNS 10*, vol. 6123 of *LNCS*, Zhou, J., Yung, M. (eds). Springer, Heidelberg.

Zhang, J., Zhang, Z., Ding, J., Snook, M., Dagdelen, Ö. (2015). Authenticated key exchange from ideal lattices. In *EUROCRYPT 2015, Part II*, vol. 9057 of *LNCS*, Oswald, E., Fischlin, M. (eds). Springer, Heidelberg.

10

Password Authenticated Key Exchange: Protocols and Security Models

Stanislaw JARECKI
University of California, Irvine, United States

10.1. Introduction

Protocols for *password authenticated key exchange* (PAKE) allow two parties who share only a low-entropy password to agree on a cryptographically strong key by communicating over an insecure network. PAKE protocols have been studied extensively in the cryptographic literature, starting from the seminal paper of Bellovin and Merritt (1992). PAKE protocols have attracted much attention because passwords have been and still are commonly used for authentication of users on the Internet. Password authentication has many vulnerabilities in practice: Some users pick passwords with low entropy so attackers can guess them. Many re-use their passwords so password leakage at one Internet service allows the attacker to compromise that user's account with other services. Users also forget their passwords, which necessitates fallback on some other and usually less secure means of authentication. This list can be continued and yet despite these weaknesses, the trade-off between security and usability offered by passwords is sufficiently attractive to make passwords a dominant authentication technique.

Focus on PAKE security definitions: This chapter overviews cryptographic literature on PAKE, but it discusses in depth PAKE security models, and in that

Asymmetric Cryptography,
coordinated by David POINTCHEVAL. © ISTE Ltd. 2022.

aspect it is more a tutorial and reassessment than a survey. Once the differences between definitions are clear, we survey various PAKE solutions, dividing them between the standard computational model and the random oracle model (ROM). Finally, we survey two important variants of the PAKE problem: the client-server, also known as asymmetric PAKE, and multi-server, a.k.a. threshold PAKE. There are many PAKE-related areas which we have not included in this survey, for example, three-party PAKEs, group PAKEs, or extensions to multi-factor or biometric authentication. We also have not included lattice-based and post-quantum PAKEs, an area that grows in importance but might fit better in a survey of lattice-based cryptosystems.

Key exchange: PAKE is a specialization of key exchange (KE), a.k.a. key agreement. A KE protocol allows two parties communicating over an insecure network to create a shared symmetric key k, which is secure against an eavesdropper, a.k.a. a passive attacker. For example, no efficient algorithm, given a KE transcript, can distinguish between session key sk output by either party in this KE instance, and an independent random key sk'. By the result of Impagliazzo and Rudich (1989), we know that KE is unlikely to exist based only on symmetric key cryptography. In particular, it is easy to see the equivalence between two-round KE and a key encapsulation mechanism (KEM), a variant of public key encryption (PKE) used for encrypting random keys rather than arbitrary messages (see Chapter 9).

Adding password authentication to KE: A KE protocol by itself is insecure against an active attacker, which can interact with either party and just follow the KE protocol. The question asked by PAKE is how to add password authentication to the KE: If parties A and B share a password pw, can they use this pre-agreed password to protect their session key from an active attacker? And what does it mean to share a password? Note that if A and B choose their shared password with high entropy, then one could use an extractor (Trevisan 2001) to extract a cryptographic key from it, and then use a PRF to derive from it any number of fresh pseudorandom session keys. However, if pw is chosen with only a constant entropy then an adversary would have a constant probability of finding keys derived in this way. The question PAKE asks is as follows: If A and B choose the shared password pw with min-entropy t, that is, the probability of guessing pw is 2^{-t}, then is there a protocol that allows them to establish a shared key sk such that

1) key sk should be as secure as unauthenticated KE against a passive attacker, regardless of the entropy in password pw;

2) if the attacker is active, then it must have at most 2^{-t} probability of learning any information about key sk output by the attacked party;

3) the protocol remains secure even if run repeatedly on the same password pw.

Requirement (1) asks that PAKE is no worse than KE; for example, even if the attacker knows the password, the PAKE protocol transcript must leak no information about the established key. Regarding requirement (2), note that an active attacker can follow the prescribed PAKE protocol on any password guess pw', and if this guess is correct, that is, if $pw' = pw$, then the attacker will compute the same key sk as the party it interacts with. By the assumption on the entropy in the choice of pw, this strategy has 2^{-t} probability of success, and requirement (2) asks that there are no other (or at least no better) attacks against the PAKE protocol than this unavoidable "on-line password test" attack. Finally, requirement (3) asks that A and B can re-use the same password in multiple instances of PAKE. Specifically, in every instance which the adversary observes passively the resulting keys must be as secure as in KE, and if an adversary actively attacks any protocol instance, then its best strategy is to make different password guesses and test each guess against an attacked session instance. In particular, a PAKE protocol must not be vulnerable to "off-line password tests", that is, the protocol transcript must not allow the adversary to off-line test any (further) password guesses. An online attack against a protocol instance must be the only way to test passwords, and each instance must allow an attacker to test only one guess.

Outline: In section 10.2, we sketch PAKE challenges using the *encrypted key exchange* (EKE) (Bellovin and Merritt 1992) as a flagship protocol example. We then go into depth reviewing the three security models proposed for PAKEs: the game-based BPR model (Bellare et al. 2000) in section 10.3, the simulation-based BMP model (Boyko et al. 2000) in section 10.4 and the UC PAKE model (Canetti et al. 2005) in section 10.5. Next, we survey results on PAKEs, dividing them into the standard model solutions in section 10.6 and the ROM or the ideal cipher (IC) model solutions in section 10.7. We end by surveying results on asymmetric or client-server PAKEs in section 10.8 and threshold PAKEs in section 10.9.

10.2. First PAKE: EKE

The first password-authenticated KE was the EKE scheme of Bellovin and Merritt (1992). In this section, we go over the EKE protocol in detail to illustrate the challenges of PAKE security analysis in spite of an apparent simplicity of a protocol proposal. This initial foray into PAKE territory will also highlight several recurring themes of PAKE research, for example, security against off-line attacks and the need for protocol messages to form a commitment to a password.

EKE compiler: The EKE protocol is a compiler that constructs a PAKE from two ingredients: an unauthenticated KE and a symmetric key encryption (SKE) scheme (E, D) designed for the KE. In EKE protocol, Alice and Bob run the underlying KE protocol, but whenever Alice generates the next KE protocol message m_A, she authenticates it using her password pw_A by sending it to Bob encrypted as $c_A = E(pw_A, m_A)$. If Bob uses his password pw_B to decrypt her message as $m'_A = D(pw_B, c_A)$, then $m'_A = m_A$ if $pw_B = pw_A$. Indeed, if the parties password-encrypt every KE protocol message in this way, they will compute the same keys if their passwords match. On the other hand, if their passwords differ, then there are natural KE and SKE schemes that assure that the two parties output uncorrelated keys.

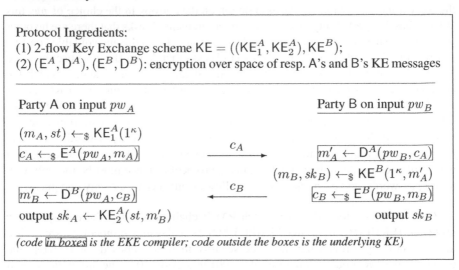

Protocol Ingredients:
(1) 2-flow Key Exchange scheme $\mathsf{KE} = ((\mathsf{KE}_1^A, \mathsf{KE}_2^A), \mathsf{KE}^B)$;
(2) $(\mathsf{E}^A, \mathsf{D}^A)$, $(\mathsf{E}^B, \mathsf{D}^B)$: encryption over space of resp. A's and B's KE messages

Party A on input pw_A		Party B on input pw_B
$(m_A, st) \leftarrow_\$ \mathsf{KE}_1^A(1^\kappa)$		
$\boxed{c_A \leftarrow_\$ \mathsf{E}^A(pw_A, m_A)}$	$\xrightarrow{\;c_A\;}$	$\boxed{m_A' \leftarrow \mathsf{D}^A(pw_B, c_A)}$
		$(m_B, sk_B) \leftarrow_\$ \mathsf{KE}^B(1^\kappa, m_A')$
$\boxed{m_B' \leftarrow \mathsf{D}^B(pw_A, c_B)}$	$\xleftarrow{\;c_B\;}$	$\boxed{c_B \leftarrow_\$ \mathsf{E}^B(pw_B, m_B)}$
output $sk_A \leftarrow \mathsf{KE}_2^A(st, m_B')$		output sk_B

(code in boxes is the EKE compiler; code outside the boxes is the underlying KE)

Figure 10.1. *Encrypted key exchange (EKE)*
(Bellovin and Merritt 1992) (without key confirmation)

In Figure 10.1, we show the EKE protocol instantiated for KE scheme with two message flows, as would be the case, for example, for KE built from KEM. In the original presentation of EKE (Bellovin and Merritt 1992), this protocol is followed by *key confirmation* messages used to confirm if the two parties compute the same key. We will come back to the key confirmation step below. In Figure 10.1, we denote KE scheme as an algorithm tuple $\mathsf{KE} = ((\mathsf{KE}_1^A, \mathsf{KE}_2^A), \mathsf{KE}^B)$, where KE_1^A on security parameter κ samples Alice's message m_A, KE^B given message m_A computes Bob's response m_B and session key sk_B, and KE_2^A computes Alice's session key sk_A given m_B and state st output by KE_1^A. If KE is built from KEM, then KE_1^A is the key generation algorithm, m_A is a public key, st is a private key, KE^B is an encryption algorithm, m_B is a ciphertext, KE_2^A is a decryption algorithm and $sk_A = sk_B$ is the one-time key encrypted in ciphertext m_B under public key m_A. For example, using a hashed Diffie–Hellman KEM, we would have $m_A = g^x$, $m_B = g^y$ and $sk_A = sk_B = \mathsf{H}(g^{xy})$.

EKE requirements on KE and symmetric encryption: An immediate objection to EKE is that it uses passwords as keys, and since passwords are not full-entropy strings, and encodings of plausible passwords could occupy only a negligible fraction of the key space, standard security properties of encryption might not imply anything about using E on keys derived from passwords. Indeed, the EKE compiler works only if the key agreement and encryption have several special properties. The first is that ciphertexts sent by either party do not allow off-line testing of passwords used to encrypt them. For any password guess pw^*, decryption $m^* = D(pw^*, c)$ of ciphertext $c = E(pw, m)$ must look like a plausible KE message computed for that round. This would be assured under the following conditions. First, the KE must have *random transcripts* in the sense that in each round there is a message space M such that for all messages sent in prior rounds, the message generated by an honest party is indistinguishable from a random value in M. (If KE is built from KEM, this requires KEM *key privacy*, that is, that a ciphertext is unlinkable to a public key (Bellare et al. 2001).) Second, for any two keys k, k', decryption $\{m' = D_{k'}(E_k(m))\}_{m \leftarrow_\$ M}$ must also be pseudorandom in M, which implies that the SKE must satisfy the following *uniform ciphertexts* property:

DEFINITION 10.1.– *Symmetric key encryption scheme* (E, D) *has* uniform ciphertexts *on message space M if for any pair of keys k_0, k_1, distributions $\{E_{k_0}(m)\}_{m \leftarrow_\$ M}$ and $\{E_{k_1}(m)\}_{m \leftarrow_\$ M}$ are computationally indistinguishable.*

Uniform ciphertext property is implied if E_k is a permutation on M for every k. For example, $E_k(m) = G(k) \oplus m$ where G is a PRG with range M. If M is a set of fixed-length bitstrings, then G can be implemented using a standard cipher. However, messages in DH KE are random group elements, which requires either a surjective encoding of group elements as bitstrings or an encryption which is natively a permutation on a group. Employing RSA KEM would be even trickier because we would need an encryption with uniform ciphertexts on a space of RSA public keys.

The second property that EKE must satisfy is that the SKE ciphertexts must commit their senders to the passwords used as encryption keys. For example, if Alice found two passwords pw, pw' such that $c = E_{pw}(m) = E_{pw'}(m')$ where m, m' are first-round messages output by two KE instances, then she could send such ciphertext as her message, and by decrypting Bob's response under pw and pw' she could complete the KE instance if Bob's password was *either* pw or pw'. This would be an attack against PAKE since Alice would test two password guesses in a single interaction. We can make symmetric encryption *key-committing* (Abdalla et al. 2010; Canetti et al. 2010; Farshim et al. 2017), for example, using a MAC, which is a collision-resistant hash on the key (Krawczyk 2010). However, this would make EKE insecure against off-line password tests. Indeed, the uniform ciphertexts property of E seems to preclude any notion of key-commitment because it requires that every ciphertext decrypts to a plausible message under any key. It thus seems that EKE imposes two contradictory requirements on SKE, because a ciphertext must look like a plausible encryption for every password, and yet it must commit its sender to a single password. Bellovin and Merritt (1992) did not pin down the KE and SKE properties that suffice for EKE to be a secure PAKE. Indeed, this was only possible after establishing a security model in which one could prove such conditions sufficient.

10.3. Game-based model of PAKE security

The EKE protocol is beautiful in its simplicity, but this simplicity belies subtle implementation and security analysis challenges. The difficulty of finding a convincing security argument (and a convincingly secure implementation) for EKE, and the need to create secure password authentication protocols, inspired much follow-up work (Bellovin and Merritt 1993; Gong et al. 1993; Gong 1995; Steiner et al. 1995; Jablon 1996; Lucks 1998; Jablon 1997; Patel 1997; Wu 1998; MacKenzie et al. 2000; Buhler et al. 2000; Kaufman and Perlman 2001). In the process, it became increasingly clear that putting PAKE research on a firm footing requires capturing PAKE security objectives in a well-defined security model. This call was concurrently answered by Bellare–Pointcheval–Rogaway (BPR) (Bellare et al. 2000) and Boyko–MacKenzie–Patel (BMP) (Boyko et al. 2000), who proposed two independent PAKE security models.[1] Both papers showed that their respective PAKE definitions can be satisfied by variants of an EKE protocol. With the PAKE security models proposed in these two papers, the research on PAKE entered a new phase of provable security. However, the two models were quite different, and it was not clear whether they were comparable. Here, we overview the *game-based* PAKE security model of Bellare et al. (2000), and we recall their result on EKE. In section 10.4, we do the same for the *simulation-based* PAKE security model of Boyko et al. (2000), and we compare the two.

10.3.1. *The BPR security model*

The PAKE security model proposed by Bellare et al. (2000) follows a *game-based* paradigm: (1) it considers a security game which is an interaction of an adversary $\mathcal{A}$ with honest parties running polynomially many instances of the PAKE protocol, (2) it defines certain event as a "break" of this protocol and (3) it defines PAKE security as the requirement that for all efficient adversaries this break happens with the probability at most negligibly higher than what is inevitable, that is, what would have to happen in every PAKE scheme because of its prescribed functionality. Since PAKE can be seen

---

1 Prior to the work of Bellare et al. (2000), Boyko et al. (2000), Halevi and Krawczyk (1998) and Boyarsky (1999) extended the authenticated key exchange (AKE) model of Bellare and Rogaway (1994) to the "half-PKI" case where in addition to a password one party has a public key which its counterparty can authenticate. We note also that Goldreich and Lindell (2001) concurrently proposed another PAKE model, but it can be seen as a weakening of the BPR model, allowing only sequential executions of each party, and relaxing bound $q_{ses}/|D|$ in definition 10.2 to $O(q_{ses})/|D|$.

as a specialization of AKE, the BPR security game is based on the Bellare–Rogaway model for AKE (Bellare and Rogaway 1994). Namely, $\mathcal{A}$ interacts with protocol instance oracles that implement PAKE protocol actions on behalf of honest players. $\mathcal{A}$ can play a man-in-the-middle adversary between these instances, but it can also choose to "connect" two instances by forwarding their messages back and forth, which models passive adversarial behavior on a session. A protocol session which $\mathcal{A}$ interacts with can either terminate with no outputs (e.g. because the session rejects its counterparty) or it can output a session key sk. Security is modeled as in KE, that is, the protocol must guarantee that honest parties' session keys are indistinguishable from random strings. Technically, in the BPR security game at some point $\mathcal{A}$ chooses the session it wants to *test*, and a random challenge bit b determines if $\mathcal{A}$ receives the *real key* sk output by that session or an independent *random key* sk'. $\mathcal{A}$'s goal is to distinguish these two cases. Namely, after an arbitrary number of further interactions, $\mathcal{A}$ outputs bit b' and its advantage is defined as $\mathsf{Adv}_{\mathcal{A}}^{\mathrm{pake}} = (\Pr\,[b' = b] - 1/2)$, which measures how much better $\mathcal{A}$ distinguishes between real and random key compared to a random guess.

The first requirement is that regardless of the password a session uses, that is, even if the adversary chose its password, PAKE must be no worse than unauthenticated KE against a passive attacker. Therefore, if an adversary passively *connects* two sessions, then its advantage against them should be at most negligible. However, if the adversary is active on some PAKE session, that is, it sends to it the messages of its own choice, then just by running the PAKE protocol on password guess pw^*, the adversary would compute the same session key as the attacked session if that session runs on password pw^*. Thus, the baseline advantage $\mathsf{Adv}_{\mathcal{A}}^{\mathrm{pake}}$ of an active adversary against any PAKE scheme depends on the distribution from which attacked sessions sample their passwords. The BPR security game has each pair of honest parties pick a password uniformly from a fixed set D, called *password dictionary*, which leads to the following security notion:

DEFINITION 10.2.– *We call a PAKE protocol secure in the BPR model (Bellare et al. 2000) if for all sets D and all efficient algorithms $\mathcal{A}$,*

$$\mathsf{Adv}_{\mathcal{A}}^{\mathrm{pake}} \leq \frac{q_{\mathrm{ses}}}{|D|} + \mathsf{negl}(\kappa) \qquad\qquad [10.1]$$

where q_{ses} is the number of sessions on which $\mathcal{A}$ is active, $\mathsf{Adv}_{\mathcal{A}}^{\mathrm{pake}}$ is defined as above, and negl is a negligible function.

Which session keys can be leaked to the adversary? In the security game mentioned above, $\mathcal{A}$ fully controls the network but it gets no information about the internal output of honest sessions except for the single chosen session it tests. Such notion of KE security would be insufficient because it would render secure even schemes in which an attacker can make two honest sessions of the same party output the same session key. If one such key was used by a higher level application in a way that reveals the key (classic examples are using a key for one-time pad encryption or as a one-time authenticator), this would render the other session insecure. The BPR security game incorporates the requirement that each sk output is fresh by adding a *reveal* interface, which $\mathcal{A}$ can use to see sk output of every honest session (if a session terminates with rejection, then $sk = \bot$) except for the session it tests.

However, adding reveal queries complicates things, because if the adversary can reveal the keys of all sessions except the tested one, then what about the session which is "connected" to the tested session? Note that PAKE must allow two sessions to output the same key if their messages are exchanged and if they run on the same input pw. Hence, the PAKE security model must bar the adversary from revealing the key not only on the tested session but also on a session connected to the tested one. BPR defined session partnering by assuming additional inputs and outputs for each PAKE session. The additional inputs were (1) the party's *own identifier*, a unique string publicly recognized as this party's identity, and (2) *bit* role that determines whether the party is an initiator or a responder in a protocol. The additional outputs were (1) a *session identifier* sid, a nonce which would uniquely identify a single session between two honest parties (without loss of generality, sid can be set to the protocol transcript), and (2) a *partner identifier* pid, the identifier of the counterparty with whom the party (apparently) establishes a session key. The BPR model then defined two sessions P_i and P'_j as *partnered* if and only if $(\mathsf{sid}_i, P, \mathsf{pid}_i, pw_i) = (\mathsf{sid}_j, \mathsf{pid}_j, P', pw_j)$ and $\mathsf{role}_i \neq \mathsf{role}_j$, and relaxed correctness by requiring two sessions to establish the same session key only if they are partnered. Finally, the security game allows $\mathcal{A}$ to reveal every session except the tested session and a session partnered with it.

Leaking passwords and session state (PFS and adaptive security): When an adversary interacts with a PAKE session, it can learn more than the messages it sends and its outputs. First, the adversary could at some point learn an honest party's password, or some partial information about it. Second, it could learn an ephemeral state of a session. If $\mathcal{A}$ learns P's password pw, then PAKE scheme can still protect P's passively observed sessions and sessions on which the attacker was active *before* it learned pw. Since passwords are long-term secrets, security of past PAKE sessions against future password-leakage is referred to as *perfect forward secrecy (PFS)*. (Restricting PFS to the security of only passively observed KE sessions given long-term secret leakage is called *weak PFS*, e.g. Krawczyk (2005).) Leaking session state to $\mathcal{A}$ is called *adaptive compromise* (or *corruption*), and security in the presence of adaptive compromise is called *adaptive security*. Note that adaptive security implies PFS, because session state includes a password (indeed PFS was defined as adaptive security in Bellare et al. (2000)), and since session state reveals session output, $\mathcal{A}$ cannot test a compromised session nor a session which is partnered with a tested session.

10.3.2. Implicit versus explicit authentication

So far we assumed that PAKE's goal is for sessions P_i and P'_j to output fresh keys sk_i, sk_j such that $sk_k = sk_j$ if these sessions run on matching passwords, that is, if $pw_i = pw_j$. (Generally, if P_i and P'_j are partnered, which requires equality of session and entity identifiers as well, see above.) However, this does not pose any restriction on P_i's outputs in case it *does not* interact with a matching counterparty. In particular, such session can also output a fresh session key sk_i. However, a PAKE protocol must imply an *implicit authentication* property: Session P_i does not know if its counterparty can compute the same key sk_i, but *if* it can, then it must have known P_i's password pw_i and it must have used it when interacting with P_i. (One of the limitations of the BPR model is that it is not clear if it formally implies the above statement, in contrast to the BMP model; see section 10.4.)

A stronger notion would be PAKE-EA, that is, PAKE with *explicit authentication* or *entity authentication*, where P_i outputs $sk_i \neq \perp$ only if it verifies that such counterparty indeed must exist. If P_i's counterparty did not follow the protocol on the same password as P_i, then P_i should output a special rejection symbol $sk_i = \perp$ rather than a "dangling" session key, which is not shared with any other party. Bellare et al. (2000) treated PAKE-EA somewhat informally, but they argued that the implicitly authenticated PAKE is a more fundamental notion. In particular, a simple compiler (see Figure 10.2) can convert any (implicitly authenticated) PAKE into PAKE-EA. Values τ and γ in Figure 10.2 are called *key confirmation* messages, or *authenticators*, where τ proves to B that A computed the same key $sk_A = sk_B$, and γ proves the corresponding statement to A. (For simplicity of notation, we omit handling of identifiers sid_i, pid_i, but these can be passed from the PAKE outputs to the outputs of PAKE-EA.)

In Figure 10.2, values sk', τ, γ are derived from PAKE's session key sk using any PRF function with κ-bit keys and outputs. In KE literature, this usage of PRF is called a *key derivation function* (KDF) (see Dodis et al. (2004); Krawczyk (2010)). Note that since the PRF is evaluated only on domain $\{0, 1, 2\}$, it can be implemented as $(sk'||\tau||\gamma) \leftarrow PRG(sk)$. KDF implementation used in Bellare et al. (2000) was $PRF(k, c) = H(k, c)$ where H is modeled as RO.

10.3.3. Limitations of the BPR model

In the BPR model, each pair of parties chooses a password with a uniform distribution over the same set D, which seems far from what the real-world behavior where parties pick their passwords from different distributions, depending on their language. Definition 10.2 can be adjusted to handle arbitrary password distributions by replacing the base-line advantage $\frac{q_{ses}}{|D|}$ with the sum of q_{ses} highest probabilities in the distribution. However, the BPR model has other limitations, which seem difficult to overcome.

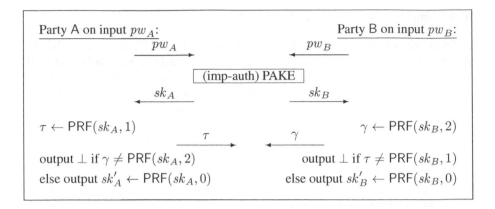

Figure 10.2. *Compiler from implicitly-authenticated PAKE to PAKE-EA*

No support for correlated password distributions and dynamic information leakage: It appears difficult to generalize the BPR security game to the common real-world case of *correlated password distributions*, where a computer user picks a new password that depends on a password she previously established, perhaps with a different counterparty. One commonly quoted application of this is password mistyping: An honest user might run the protocol on a password very closely related to the correct one, and the BPR notion does not imply that executing the protocol on such related passwords is secure. Another aspect which is hard to capture within BPR notion is *dynamic leakage* of password information, for example, an effect of revealing some password information to the adversary in the middle of the security game.

Other non-adaptive aspects of the BPR model: When discussing PFS security, in section 10.3.1, we noted that the BPR security model allows adaptive session state compromise. However, there are some definitional choices in the BPR model which have subtle non-adaptive aspects. One such aspect is that *the adversary must a priori decide between a passive or an active attack*, that is, the adversary separately invokes an oracle that allows passive observation of sessions, and separately an oracle that allows the attacker to interact with active sessions. Only the second queries count toward the $q_{ses}/|D|$ bound on the adversary's advantage, but can an adversary first see the messages a session sends and only then decide whether to actively attack it or not? Further, if the adversary can test only one session, then it is not clear what this implies about simultaneous security of many sessions, because a standard hybrid argument implies only a suboptimal bound of $(q_{ses})^2/|D|$ on the adversary's advantage if the challenge bit decides on the real-or-random status of q_{ses} tested sessions instead of one. This latter issue was resolved by Abdalla et al. (2005b), who extended the BPR model so the adversary can test arbitrary number of sessions. The former issue can be resolved as well, but it would further complicate the model.

10.3.4. *EKE instantiated with Diffie–Hellman KE*

Bellare et al. (2000) tested the BPR security model on the EKE protocol (see Figure 10.1), instantiated with the DH KE, as shown in Figure 10.3. This instantiation of EKE was named "EKE2" in Bellare et al. (2000), where it was shown in a sequential form, but it appears that the security proof should go through if either party sends its message first.

Party A on input pw_A			Party B on input pw_B
$x \leftarrow_\$ \mathbb{Z}_q, c_A \leftarrow \mathsf{E}(pw_A, g^x)$			$y \leftarrow_\$ \mathbb{Z}_q, c_B \leftarrow \mathsf{E}(pw_B, g^y)$
	$\xrightarrow{A, c_A}$	$\xleftarrow{B, c_B}$	
$Y \leftarrow \mathsf{D}(pw_A, c_B)$			$X \leftarrow \mathsf{D}(pw_B, c_A)$
$sk_A \leftarrow \mathsf{H}(A, B, g^x, Y, Y^x)$			$sk_B \leftarrow \mathsf{H}(A, B, X, g^y, X^y)$
$\mathsf{sid}_A \leftarrow \mathsf{H}(A, c_A, B, c_B)$			$\mathsf{sid}_B \leftarrow \mathsf{H}(A, c_A, B, c_B)$
$\mathsf{pid}_A \leftarrow B$			$\mathsf{pid}_B \leftarrow A$
output $(sk_A, \mathsf{sid}_A, \mathsf{pid}_A)$			output $(sk_b, \mathsf{sid}_B, \mathsf{pid}_B)$

g generates group $\langle g \rangle$ of order q; (E, D): an ideal cipher on $\langle g \rangle$; H: RO hash

Figure 10.3. *Protocol EKE2: Instantiation of EKE with DH KE analyzed in Bellare et al. (2000)*

As we discussed in section 10.2, the encryption scheme (E, D) used in EKE must have uniform ciphertexts on the space of KE messages (see definition 10.1), which in the case of EKE2 is group $\langle g \rangle$ used in DH KE. In the analysis of Bellare et al. (2000), this encryption is assumed to be an *IC*, that is, it is a collection $\{E_k\}$ of random bijections between message space $M = \langle g \rangle$ and ciphertext space $\mathcal{C}$. Bellare et al. made the following security claim:

THEOREM 10.1.– *Bellare et al. (2000): If* (E, D) *is an IC and* H *is a random oracle, then the EKE2 scheme shown in Figure 10.3 is a secure PAKE in the BPR model (with adaptive corruptions) under the computational Diffie–Hellman assumption on group* $\langle g \rangle$.

Disclaimers: Since a random oracle is easy to implement using an IC, for example, $\mathsf{H}(x) = \mathsf{E}(0^\kappa, x)$, the above implies EKE2 security in the *IC model* only. In Bellare et al. (2000), this bound is claimed only for a "weak corruption model", but it appears that this model corresponds to the adaptive security notion described above.

10.3.5. *Implementing ideal cipher on arbitrary groups*

The security analysis of EKE2 of Bellare et al. (2000) assumes an IC E on group $\langle g \rangle$ used in DH KE. One can implement a *randomized* IC E on $\langle g \rangle$ as $E(k, m) = E'(k, \xi(m))$, where E' is an IC on $\{0, 1\}^n$ and $\xi : \langle g \rangle \to \{0, 1\}^n$ is a randomized invertible encoding, which is *uniform* in the sense that $\{\xi(m)\}_{m \leftarrow_\$ \langle g \rangle}$ is statistically close to a uniform n-bit string. Such randomized IC on $\langle g \rangle$ would suffice in the proof of theorem 10.1: A simulator that extracts (k, m') from ciphertext c such that $m' = D'(k, c)$ can compute $m = \xi^{-1}(m')$ which satisfies $m = D(k, c)$, and it can embed $m \in \langle g \rangle$ into $D(k, c)$ by embedding $\xi(m)$ into $D'(k, c)$. Thus, the existence of uniform randomized invertible encoding on $\langle g \rangle$ implies security in ROM, because an IC on *bitstrings* can be constructed from a random oracle using Feistel (Holenstein et al. 2011; Dachman-Soled et al. 2016; Dai and Steinberger 2016). In the special case when $\langle g \rangle = \mathbb{Z}_p^*$ for prime p, that is, $\langle g \rangle$ is an integer interval $[1, ..., p-1]$, such encoding is easy to construct for $n \geq |p| + \kappa$: $\xi(m)$ picks $r \leftarrow_\$ [2^n/p]$ and outputs $m' = m + rp$ (over integers), and $\xi^{-1}(m')$ outputs $m = (m' \mod p)$. However, for elliptic curve groups such encodings are not immediate.

Before such elliptic curve encodings appeared, Black and Rogaway (2002) showed an expected constant-time implementation of an IC E' on any group $\mathbb{G}$, which is *dense* over $\{0, 1\}^n$, that is, if elements of $\mathbb{G}$ can be encoded as n-bit strings such that $|\mathbb{G}|/2^n$ is a constant, given an IC E on n-bit strings. In that construction, $E'(k, m)$ for $m \in \mathbb{G}$ defines $c_0 = E(k, m)$ and $c_{i+1} = E(k, c_i)$ for all $i \geq 0$, and sets $E'(k, m) = c_i$ for i such that c_i is the first element of $\mathbb{G}$ in the sequence $c_1, ..., c_i$. The decryption implements the same process in reverse, that is, it recurses on $D(k, \cdot)$ until it finds an element in $\mathbb{G}$. One weakness of this method is that timing information would reveal the number of $E(k, \cdot)$ or $D(k, \cdot)$ applications the encryptor/decryptor applied, and if $k = pw$ then this would reveal information about the password, because for any password guess pw^* the adversary can see how many $D(pw^*, \cdot)$ operations are needed to get from a given ciphertext c to an element in $\mathbb{G}$.

Bernstein et al. (2013) constructed a uniform encoding for a class of elliptic curve groups, called *Elligator2*, which works for half the elements in the group. Specifically, Elligator2 maps $\xi : \mathbb{G}' \to [0, ..., (q-1)/2]$ for a subdomain $\mathbb{G}'$ of an elliptic curve group $\mathbb{G}$ of order q such that $|\mathbb{G}'| = (q+1)/2$. (Since $[0, ..., (q-1)/2]$ is an integer interval, Elligator2 would be composed with the integer interval encoding shown above.) However, since Elligator2 works only on half the domain, each party would have to re-sample its DH KE contribution until it finds an element in $\mathbb{G}'$, which is suboptimal because it would take expected 2 iterations. Tibouchi (2014); Kim and Tibouchi (2015) showed a uniform encoding for a larger class of elliptic curve groups, called *Elligator-squared*, which works on the full domain $\langle g \rangle$. Its decoding ξ^{-1} has similar costs as Elligator2 decoding, but encoding ξ requires sampling and testing preimage points, and appears to be about three times more expensive (depending on a curve). Furthermore, Elligator-squared encodes an EC point as a pair of field elements so it uses 2x more bandwidth than Elligator2. Alternatively, one can apply results of Holenstein et al. (2011); Dachman-Soled et al. (2016); Dai and Steinberger (2016) to construct a randomized IC on group $\langle g \rangle$ using a "mixed" Feistel, where one wire holds group elements, XOR on that wire is replaced with a group operation, and round hash functions onto that wire are an RO-indifferentiable hash onto $\langle g \rangle$. (The proofs of these Feistel results appear to generalize to this case.) Using 8-round Feistel of Dachman-Soled et al. (2016), this would incur four hash-onto-group operations in both encryption and decryption, but McQuoid et al. (2020) optimized this design significantly, by showing that a two-round mixed Feistel, hence a single hash-onto-group, realizes a form of "one-time" IC that suffices for EKE2.

10.4. Simulation-based model of PAKE security

The Boyko–MacKenzie–Patel (BMP) model for PAKE security (Boyko et al. 2000) appeared in the same year as the Bellare–Pointcheval–Rogaway (BPR) model (Bellare et al. 2000) overviewed in section 10.3. Here, we explain the BMP model and we contrast it with the BPR model.

10.4.1. *The BMP security model*

The BMP security model for PAKE takes inspiration from the Bellare–Canetti–Krawczyk model for AKE protocols (Bellare et al. 1998), and its refinement by Shoup (1999). These models follow a *simulation-based* security definition paradigm, which was used before to model secure multi-party computation (MPC) (e.g. Beaver 1991; Micali and Rogaway 1992; Canetti 2000; see Chapter 4). The simulation-based paradigm considers two security games, involving two types of adversaries. The first game, called the *real-world* game, is an interaction of adversary $\mathcal{A}$ with honest parties running protocol Π. The second game, called the *ideal-world* game, is an interaction of an algorithm $\mathcal{A}^*$, called the *ideal-world adversary*, with the idealized system, denoted $\mathcal{F}$ for a *functionality*, which by definition leaks no information to the adversary except what is necessary by the functionality of the scheme. The scheme is then defined as secure if for all efficient real-world adversaries $\mathcal{A}$ there exists an efficient ideal-world adversary $\mathcal{A}^*$, also called a *simulator*, such that the two games produce indistinguishable views, where the "view" is in each case defined as a joint distribution of an adversary's output (which without loss of generality includes its entire transcript) and the outputs of all honest parties. This notion captures security of scheme Π because it implies that everything that an adversary $\mathcal{A}$ can do when interacting with honest parties running Π (and this "doing" includes both everything $\mathcal{A}$ learns, that is, its transcript, and everything $\mathcal{A}$ causes the honest parties to do, that is, their outputs) could also be done, and this is the role played by the simulator $\mathcal{A}^*$, when interacting with an ideal system $\mathcal{F}$.[2] The BMP model adapts this general paradigm to the case of PAKE protocols, where it implies that no one (i.e. no efficient $\mathcal{A}$) can do anything more against the real-world PAKE protocol Π than what can be done (by efficient $\mathcal{A}^*$) against an "ideal" PAKE scheme, as captured by $\mathcal{F}$. The essence of the security notion is therefore the specification of the idealized scheme $\mathcal{F}$. Following the MPC paradigm, functionality $\mathcal{F}$ must (1) let the adversary know that P_i runs the protocol but leak no information about P_i's inputs, which in the case of PAKE is P_i's password, (2) for every such instance $\mathcal{F}$ should accept a *single* well-defined input which $\mathcal{A}^*$ can contribute to this instance, which in the case of PAKE would be a unique password pw^* on which an active attacker can run the real-world PAKE protocol interacting with P_i, and (3) $\mathcal{F}$ should pick P_i's output in a perfect way, which in the case of PAKE means that if $pw^* \neq pw$ then P_i outputs a random session key, and if $pw^* = pw$, then P_i outputs a key which should be decided by the adversary. This captures the essence of the MPC-style definition of PAKE security given by Boyko et al. (2000), but there are subtle issues that need accounting for, as we explain below.

The real-world game: Let us first describe the real-world game in the BMP model, which captures an interaction of $\mathcal{A}$ with honest parties $(P_1, \ldots, P_n)$ running polynomially many instances of the PAKE protocol. This interaction is similar to the BPR security game, and just like there the adversary $\mathcal{A}$ is assumed to fully control the network between all honest parties. However, unlike in the BPR security game, there is no event that defines a "break" of this protocol, or a challenge bit b which the adversary has to predict.[3] Instead, all the messages which $\mathcal{A}$ sends and receives in this interaction are logged as part of the *adversarial view*, denoted $\text{view}_{\mathcal{A}}$, and all the honest parties' outputs, that is, session keys as well as accept/reject bits, form the *honest parties' view*, denoted $\text{view}_{(P_1, \ldots, P_n)}$. The two views together form a transcript of the real-world game, denoted $\text{transcript}^{\text{real}}[\mathcal{A}, \Pi]$, where each part of $\text{view}_{\mathcal{A}}$, that is, each message sent or received by $\mathcal{A}$, and each part of $\text{view}_{(P_1, \ldots, P_n)}$, that is, each P_i's input and output, are appended to $\text{transcript}^{\text{real}}[\mathcal{A}, \Pi]$ in the order they are created.

---

2 Here and further down in this section the terminology we use differs from the one used by Boyko et al. (2000), who in particular did not use the term "functionality" to describe the ideal-world game. However, this is how the BMP definition can be interpreted using the UC framework of Canetti (2001), and how it was subsequently re-cast in the UC PAKE model of Canetti et al. (2005) (see section 10.5).

3 The game-based BPR security definition can be re-stated in terms of $\mathcal{A}$'s distinguishing advantage between two games: the real-world game with real session key(s), and the real-world game with random session key(s). In the BMP notion, the second game is not a real-world game with some modified values, but a *simulated* game, in which messages are created by algorithm $\mathcal{A}^*$ interacting with an idealized PAKE functionality $\mathcal{F}$ that defines what $\mathcal{A}^*$ learns about P_i's inputs and how $\mathcal{A}^*$ can influence P_i's outputs.

The sharpest contrast with the BPR security game is who decides the password inputs of honest P_i's. In the BMP model, the honest parties' inputs are decided by a special entity called the *ring master*, but without loss of generality the ring master can follow the directions of the adversary $\mathcal{A}$. Hence, somewhat counterintuitively, it is the adversary $\mathcal{A}$ who decides all passwords. This is in a strong contrast to the BPR security game where P_i's passwords are chosen at random from some dictionary by the game challenger, not by the adversary. However, as we will see shortly, this seemingly counterintuitive choice not only makes sense, but it implies security for arbitrary password distributions, and helps overcome several other limitations of the BPR model (see section 10.3.3). As in the BPR model, $\mathcal{A}$ can reveal the session keys of any honest party, but since there are no longer any sessions which the adversary "tests", without loss of generality $\mathcal{A}$ can get the session keys output by of all P_i's.

The ideal-world game: We reverse the presentation used in Boyko et al. (2000) by starting with the *implicitly authenticated* PAKE case, which serves as the base case of the BPR definition, and which subsequently became the standard notion of PAKE. We will explain an extension to *explicit authentication* (PAKE-EA) in section 10.4.4. The ideal-world game in the BMP model is an interaction between a simulator algorithm $\mathcal{A}^*$ and the ideal functionality of a PAKE scheme, denoted $\mathcal{F}_{\mathsf{PAKE}}$, which proceeds as follows:

1) When an honest party P_i is invoked on some password $pw[P_i]$ by the ring master, $\mathcal{F}_{\mathsf{PAKE}}$ sends $(\mathsf{NewSession}, P, i)$ to $\mathcal{A}^*$ and creates an internal state for this session, marking it fresh. Therefore, the ideal-world adversary knows if some P_i runs a protocol but it does not know their password inputs. The ring master starts P_i on a signal from $\mathcal{A}^*$, also setting P_i's role bit and its intended counterparty identifier pid.

2) For any session P_i adversary $\mathcal{A}^*$ can send message $(\mathsf{TestPwd}, P, i, pw^*)$ to $\mathcal{F}_{\mathsf{PAKE}}$, which models an active attack in which a real-world adversary follows a PAKE scheme on password guess pw^* when interacting with P_i. If $pw^* = pw[P_i]$, then $\mathcal{F}_{\mathsf{PAKE}}$ marks P_i's session as compromised, otherwise it marks it as interrupted. (These markings will determine how $\mathcal{F}_{\mathsf{PAKE}}$ acts in response to NewKey queries; see below.) In addition, $\mathcal{F}_{\mathsf{PAKE}}$ reveals this marking to $\mathcal{A}^*$, which implies that a real-world PAKE protocol can reveal whether an active attack is successful. Crucially, $\mathcal{A}^*$ can send *at most one* TestPwd query per each P_i session, which enforces the requirement that an adversary can test at most one password guess on an attacked session. This query can be made on either a fresh session or on a dangling terminated session; see NewKey processing below. Indeed, the ability of $\mathcal{A}^*$ to make *post-termination* password tests (which remains even for PAKE-EA, see section 10.4.4) is a crucial difference between the simulation-based BMP model and the UC PAKE model of Canetti et al. (2005) (see section 10.5).

3) For any session P_i adversary $\mathcal{A}^*$ can send $(\mathsf{NewKey}, P, i, P', j, sk^*)$ to $\mathcal{F}_{\mathsf{PAKE}}$, which models P_i receiving the last protocol message (supposedly from P'_j) and

terminating with some output. In response, $\mathcal{F}_{\text{PAKE}}$ terminates this session and decides on its output sk_i as follows:[4]

a) If P_i session is compromised, then set $sk_i \leftarrow sk^*$.

b) If P_i and P'_j are both fresh, $pw[P_i] = pw[P'_j]$, $\text{pid}[P_i] = P'$ and $\text{pid}[P'_j] = P$, the role bits of P'_j and P_i define them as the first and the last to complete, and P'_j outputted sk_j, then $sk_i \leftarrow sk_j$.

c) Else set $sk_i \leftarrow_\$ \{0,1\}^\kappa$, and if $\mathcal{A}^*$ requests so, mark P_i as dangling.

4) $\mathcal{A}^*$ can also ask for output sk_i of any terminated session P_i (hence without loss of generality one can assume that all sk_i outputs are sent to $\mathcal{A}^*$), and terminate any running session P_i to output $\perp$ (which models a denial-of-service attack on P_i in the real world).

5) The inputs pw_i and outputs sk_i of each P_i are recorded in the ideal-world interaction transcript $\text{transcript}^{\text{ideal}}[\mathcal{A}^*, \mathcal{F}_{\text{PAKE}}]$, and $\mathcal{A}^*$ can also add any message to the transcript at any moment, emulating the messages which $\mathcal{A}$ would receive and send in the real-world protocol.

The BMP security definition: Given the above rules of the real-world and the ideal world games, the BMP notion of PAKE security is as follows:

DEFINITION 10.3.– *We call a PAKE scheme Π secure in the BMP model (Boyko et al. 2000) if for all efficient algorithms $\mathcal{A}$ there exists an efficient algorithm $\mathcal{A}^*$ such that*

$$\text{transcript}^{\text{real}}[\mathcal{A}, \Pi] \stackrel{(c)}{\approx} \text{transcript}^{\text{ideal}}[\mathcal{A}^*, \mathcal{F}_{\text{PAKE}}]$$

that is, the real-world game transcript defined by $\mathcal{A}$ and Π and the ideal-world game transcript defined by $\mathcal{A}^*$ and $\mathcal{F}_{\text{PAKE}}$, are computationally indistinguishable.

Since the proof has to exhibit an algorithm $\mathcal{A}^*$ that works for any $\mathcal{A}$, a natural construction of $\mathcal{A}^*$ uses $\mathcal{A}$ as an *oracle*. Since $\mathcal{A}$ expects to interact with real-world P_i's running protocol Π, $\mathcal{A}^*$ needs to *simulate* these Π instances to $\mathcal{A}$, that is, it needs to create messages which are indistinguishable from P_i's messages in protocol Π.

---

4 *Explanations*: Case (a) says that if $\mathcal{A}^*$ attacks P_i with a *correct* password then $\mathcal{A}^*$ determines P_i's output sk_i; case (b) says that if $\mathcal{A}^*$ connects P_i and P'_j, they use the same passwords, they are intended counterparties, and P'_j is the first-to-complete, then P_i gets the same session key as P_j; case (c) covers the case of $\mathcal{A}^*$ attacking P_i with an *incorrect* password, and the case of P_i which is fresh, that is, not actively attacked, but it is either first-to-complete, or it is "connected" to a wrong counterparty. The dangling state corresponds to a "last minute active attack" by the adversary: If the session is so marked, then it is no longer fresh so $\mathcal{F}_{\text{PAKE}}$ will not copy its output to any other honest session, as in case (b), but a session so marked is open to a *future* TestPwd queries, see item (2) above.

The challenge of the security proof is that $\mathcal{A}^*$ must do so given only the information supplied by $\mathcal{F}_{PAKE}$, which, for example, does not contain P_i's inputs pw. However, if $\mathcal{A}^*$ succeeds in such simulation, then $\mathcal{A}$ must reply to these simulated messages as it would in the real-world game (except for negligible probability of distinguishing the simulated messages of $\mathcal{A}^*$ from the real messages of P_i's), and the ideal-world transcript can be indistinguishable from the real-world transcript if $\mathcal{A}^*$ places in transcript$^{\text{ideal}}[\mathcal{A}^*, \mathcal{F}_{PAKE}]$ all the messages it sends to and receives from oracle $\mathcal{A}$.

10.4.2. *Advantages of BMP definition: arbitrary passwords, tight security*

One advantage of the simulation-based definition over the game-based one is that the former accommodates *arbitrary password distributions*, including correlated passwords, and arbitrary password information leakage. One way to see this is to split the BMP-model adversary $\mathcal{A}$ into two parts, call them $\mathcal{A}_{real}$ and $\mathcal{A}_{rm}$. Let $\mathcal{A}_{real}$ be the part of $\mathcal{A}$ which models the "real adversary", that is, the network attacker who observes and/or interferes with honest parties' PAKE instances, and let $\mathcal{A}_{rm}$ be the part of $\mathcal{A}$ which plays the role of the "ring master", and which models arbitrary human and application-driven behavior of honest parties that run these instances, by adaptively deciding the password (as well as pid, role inputs) for any session P_i. Since the BMP model combines these two entities, it means that $\mathcal{A}_{real}$ and $\mathcal{A}_{rm}$ can communicate arbitrarily. Jumping ahead, this split of the BMP-model adversary into the ring master $\mathcal{A}_{rm}$ and the real-world adversary $\mathcal{A}$, reflects the universal composability (UC) framework of Canetti (2001) (see section 10.5), where $\mathcal{A}_{rm}$ is what the UC framework calls *environment $\mathcal{Z}$*, and $\mathcal{A}_{real}$ is what the UC framework calls *adversary $\mathcal{A}$*.

In particular, $\mathcal{A}_{rm}$ can choose each P_i's password from some dictionary D, as in the BPR-security model, and it can reveal that password to $\mathcal{A}_{real}$ at any point afterwards, which implies *PFS security*. (This suggests that BMP-security implies BPR-security in principle, that is, after eliminating surface-level technicalities, and this was essentially shown by Abdalla et al. (2020).) However, $\mathcal{A}_{rm}$ can also choose passwords with arbitrary correlations, and it can leak arbitrary partial information about them to $\mathcal{A}_{real}$. Further, since the communication between $\mathcal{A}_{rm}$ and $\mathcal{A}_{real}$ can go in both directions, the way some PAKE instance chooses a password can be influenced by what the real-world adversary $\mathcal{A}_{real}$ observes in interaction with previous PAKE protocols.

The simulation-based security notion eliminates other non-adaptive aspects of BPR-security mentioned in section 10.3.3. First, $\mathcal{A}_{real}$ can adaptively decide whether to actively attack any session by playing a man-in-the-middle between some two sessions or to "connect" two sessions by routing their messages without modifications. Second, in the simulation-based notion there is no difference between the sessions which the adversary *reveals* and the sessions which it *tests*, because without loss of generality $\mathcal{A}_{rm}$ can pass to $\mathcal{A}_{real}$ all session keys. Both aspects suggest that if a PAKE scheme realizes the BMP notion with a *tight* relation to some assumption, then this is a stronger statement than a corresponding one with regard to the BPR notion.

Static versus adaptive security: The BMP security model (Boyko et al. 2000) was formulated only for *static security*, where honest parties P_i are never compromised. However, provision for adaptive session compromise could be added to the BMP model. Indeed, the UC PAKE model (see section 10.5), which supersedes the BMP model, allows for such compromises. The BMP model corresponds to the *static* variant of UC security, where all honest parties P_i stay uncompromised, and the adversary controls the network and the a priori corrupt entities on this network. The *adaptive* variant of UC security corresponds to the BMP-model adversary that can adaptively request the ephemeral session state of any honest P_i, as was done in the BPR model. Note that to simulate such corruptions, $\mathcal{A}^*$ must be able to request P_i's password input, via command $(\mathsf{Compromise}, \mathsf{P}, i)$, because an ephemeral PAKE session state in particular reveals the password input on which it executes.

10.4.3. *EKE using RO-derived one-time pad encryption*

Boyko et al. (2000) provide three PAKE protocols: (1) an implicitly authenticated PAKE protocol, shown in Figure 10.4; (2) a PAKE-EA protocol, discussed below; and (3) an *asymmetric* PAKE protocol (see section 10.8), which is also a variant of PPK.

Protocol PPK was not presented in Boyko et al. (2000) in this way, but it is an instance of EKE, see Figure 10.1, with encryption E implemented as a one-time pad in group $\langle g \rangle$, with the one-time pad derived via an RO hash onto the group, that is, $\mathsf{E}(pw, m) = \mathsf{H}(pw) \cdot m$. (In Boyko et al. (2000), H inputs include also identifiers A, B, because the BMP model enforces an agreement of entity identifiers, but the protocol probably realizes the same functionality when A, B are omitted in H inputs, because they are also included in the inputs to H'.)

Intuition for the security argument: One-time pad encryption is not an ideal cipher. In particular, ciphertext c_A (and likewise c_B) does not by itself commit party A to the choice of password. However, if H is an RO, then under DH assumption on group $\langle g \rangle$, an adversary who sends any c_A on behalf of party A can then compute function $\mathsf{DH}_{X[pw]}(\cdot)$ defined as $\mathsf{DH}_{g^x}(Y) = y^x$ for at most one pw, where $X[pw] = c_A \cdot (\mathsf{H}(pw))^{-1}$. Specifically, if an attacker can hash H' on inputs including $\mathsf{DH}_X(Y)$ for $Y = c_B \cdot (\mathsf{H}(pw))^{-1}$ for two different values $X = X[pw_1]$ and $X = X[pw_2]$, then a reduction can solve CDH. (This reduction must be done carefully because $\mathsf{H}(pw)$ affects DH challenges Y and X in a different way.) Note that simulator $\mathcal{A}^*$ can learn password pw used by the real-world adversary $\mathcal{A}$ only from $\mathcal{A}$'s query to H'. Since $\mathcal{A}$ can make this query after the attacked session P_i terminates, the BMP model must allow $\mathcal{A}^*$ to send $(\mathsf{TestPwd}, \mathsf{P}, i, pw)$ to $\mathcal{F}_{PAKE}$ after P_i terminates.

Party A on input pw_A Party B on input pw_B

$x \leftarrow_\$ \mathbb{Z}_q, c_A \leftarrow g^x \cdot \mathsf{H}(pw_A)$ $y \leftarrow_\$ \mathbb{Z}_q, c_B \leftarrow g^y \cdot \mathsf{H}(pw_B)$

$\qquad\qquad\qquad\xrightarrow{A, c_A}\qquad\xleftarrow{B, c_B}$

$Y \leftarrow c_B \cdot (\mathsf{H}(pw_A))^{-1}$ $X \leftarrow c_A \cdot (\mathsf{H}(pw_B))^{-1}$

$sk_A \leftarrow \mathsf{H}'(A, B, c_A, c_B, Y^x, pw_A)$ $sk_B \leftarrow \mathsf{H}'(A, B, c_A, c_B, X^y, pw_B)$

g generates group $\langle g \rangle$ of order q;   H, H': RO hash onto resp. $\langle g \rangle$ and $\{0,1\}^\kappa$

Figure 10.4. *Protocol PPK: PAKE of Bellare et al. (2000)*
(simplified and adapted to arbitrary groups)

Boyko et al. (2000) state the security of PPK under the decisional DH assumption, although this seems to be done for better exact security of the reduction, and PPK should remain secure under the computational DH assumption as well:

THEOREM 10.2.– *Boyko et al. (2000) If* H, H' *are ROs, then protocol PPK, Figure 10.4, is a secure PAKE in the BMP model under the decisional Diffie–Hellman assumption on* $\langle g \rangle$.

10.4.4. *BMP model for PAKE with explicit authentication (PAKE-EA)*

The BMP security model discussed in section 10.4.1 corresponds to PAKE with implicit authentication. However, Boyko et al. (2000) also defined a variant of their simulation-based model that corresponds to PAKE-EA, that is, PAKE with explicit authentication. This is handled by two changes in the code of functionality $\mathcal{F}_{\mathsf{PAKE}}$ which defines the idealized scheme. The first change is in the handling of $(\mathsf{NewKey}, \mathsf{P}, i, \mathsf{P}', j, sk^*)$ queries; see item (3) in the ideal-world game of section 10.4.1. First, $\mathcal{A}^*$ can no longer request P_i to terminate in the dangling state. Second, case 3 of NewKey processing is replaced by the following cases:

3a) If P_i is marked fresh, it is the first to complete, $pw[\mathsf{P}_i] = pw[\mathsf{P}'_j]$, $\mathsf{pid}[\mathsf{P}_i] = \mathsf{P}'$, and no other session has outputted $sk \neq \perp$ in response to NewKey specifying the same counterparty P'_j, then set $sk_i \leftarrow_\$ \{0,1\}^\kappa$.

3b) In every other case, set $sk_i \leftarrow \perp$.

In other words, the only way P_i can output $sk_i \neq \perp$ is via case 1, that is, if it is actively attacked using the correct password, or via cases 2 and 3a, that is, if NewKey requests pertain to two sessions which are *partnered* because they run on the same password and their roles and intended counterparty identifiers match. The second change is in the $\mathcal{F}_{\mathsf{PAKE}}$ rules that determine whether $\mathcal{A}^*$ can send TestPwd for session P_i, see item (2) in the ideal-world game. Since the PAKE-EA model eliminates "dangling" sessions, a TestPwd query can be made for fresh sessions *and* for sessions that are terminated with an abort output $sk = \perp$.

PAKE-EA protocol of Boyko et al. (2000): One-sided EKE with key confirmation: The PAKE-EA protocol of Boyko et al. (2000); MacKenzie (2002), called PAK, works like the generic PAKE-to-PAKE-EA compiler (Figure 10.2) instantiated with PPK, except for the following optimization: If the PPK is used sequentially and the responder's key confirmation message is piggybacked to its KE message, then the responder can send its KE message g^y in the clear, that is, it does not have to password-encrypt it. This is because the key confirmation message serves as a sufficient commitment to the password used by the responder in decryption of the initiator's EKE message.

10.5. Universally composable model of PAKE security

Neither the game-based model of Bellare–Pointcheval–Rogaway (BPR) (Bellare et al. 2000) nor the simulation-based model of Boyko–MacKenzie–Patel (BMP) (Boyko et al. 2000) appeared to be fully satisfactory. The BPR model has several weaknesses (see section 10.3.3), while the main weakness of the BMP model seems to be that it was non-standard, and that writing and understanding BMP-model proofs required understanding a special-purpose model whose consequences were difficult to assess. However, 5 years later, Canetti et al. proposed a *universally composable* (UC) model for PAKE security (Canetti et al. 2005), which effectively casts the BMP model into the general UC framework of Canetti (2001). Since the BPR model became a more widely used point of reference than the BMP model, Canetti et al. (2005) show that the UC PAKE model is at least as strong as the BPR model, that is, that every PAKE which is UC-secure is also BPR-secure (after the BPR model is adjusted so session and party identifiers work as in UC PAKE model). It appears that a much stronger statement can be shown for the BMP model, namely that after two adjustments discussed below, the BMP and UC PAKE models are equivalent. Nevertheless, by refining the BMP model and by casting it into the general framework, Canetti et al. (2005) gave a simulation-based model for PAKE that is easier to use than the BMP model. The learning curve is still there, as one must understand the UC framework to understand UC PAKE proofs, but it is no longer a special-purpose framework used only for PAKE protocols, as was the case in Boyko et al. (2000).

Universal composability framework: The UC framework of Canetti (2001) allows for specifying security of a cryptographic scheme using the simulation-based paradigm, similarly as in the BMP model described in section 10.4. Indeed, the latter can be thought of as a specialization of this framework to PAKEs, but the two came out almost concurrently as both took inspiration in the simulation-based definition of MPC security. As in the BMP security model, the UC framework defines security as indistinguishability, for any efficient distinguishing environment $\mathcal{Z}$ and any efficient adversarial algorithm $\mathcal{A}$, between a *real-world* game, where the real-world adversary $\mathcal{A}$ interacts with honest parties executing the real-world scheme Π, and the *ideal-world* game, where an efficient ideal-world adversary, a.k.a. a *simulator*, $\mathcal{A}^*$ interacts with *functionality* $\mathcal{F}$ which defines an idealized model for this cryptographic scheme. Following this paradigm, Canetti et al. (2005) specified an ideal PAKE functionality $\mathcal{F}_{\mathsf{PAKE}}$ (adopting some conventions proposed for UC AKE in Canetti and Krawczyk (2002)), thus defining UC PAKE as a protocol Π for which there exists an efficient simulator $\mathcal{A}^*$ that ensures indistinguishability between the above real-world and ideal-world games.

As in the BMP model, the UC PAKE model assures security under arbitrary password distribution and arbitrary password information leakage (implying security for correlated passwords, and security of execution on mistyped passwords) and security of concurrent protocol executions, including arbitrary information leaked about protocol outputs. However, by fitting into the general UC framework, the UC PAKE model has the advantage of ensuring security under arbitrary protocol composition: If a PAKE protocol Π is shown to be UC secure, then any protocol Π' which uses Π as a subroutine can be analyzed in a simplified setting when Π is replaced by functionality $\mathcal{F}_{\mathsf{PAKE}}$, that is, by an "ideal" PAKE scheme. PAKE protocols can indeed be used in such a way because they realize an *equality-testing functionality*, which is a very natural building block in secure protocol design. To give one example, (symmetric) UC PAKE protocol has been used as a sub-protocol in several black-box constructions of asymmetric PAKE (e.g. Gentry et al. 2006; Hwang et al. 2018; Jarecki et al. 2018; see section 10.8).

Requirements of UC security for PAKEs: The UC PAKE protocol shown in Canetti et al. (2005) is a modification of the PAKE of Katz–Ostrovsky–Yung (KOY) protocol (Katz et al. 2001), which is the first standard-model PAKE protocol that was shown BPR-secure (see section 10.6). The UC secure version of KOY proposed by Canetti et al. (2005) adds to A's last message a second ciphertext c'_A which encrypts the same password pw_A, and a simulation-sound zero-knowledge proof that ciphertexts c'_A and c_A encrypt the same value (see the KOY protocol in Figure 10.5). The import of this additional flow appears at first unclear. However, UC-secure PAKEs tend to be more expensive than BPR-secure PAKEs, for the following two main reasons: (I) *Input extraction*: In a UC PAKE proof, simulator $\mathcal{A}^*$ needs to (straight-line) extract from attacker's messages a unique password pw^*, which the attacker tests on that session. (This follows from the general UC security framework, where any action of the real-world attacker $\mathcal{A}$ must be translated by $\mathcal{A}^*$ into a unique input to an ideal functionality.) In the BPR model, there is no such requirement, and many BPR-model secure PAKEs do not seem to allow for such extraction. (II) *Simulating "successfully attacked" parties*: In a UC PAKE proof simulator, $\mathcal{A}^*$ must correctly emulate the real-world view in all cases, including when the attacker's password guess pw^* matches an honest session password pw. In the BPR model such an event would end the security game, hence, it does not matter if an efficient simulator can compute a session key which an attacked party outputs. Indeed, the benefit of the mysterious "password re-encryption + NIZK" step added by Canetti et al. (2005) to the KOY protocol is that it allows for efficient simulation precisely in that case, where a simulated session has been attacked and the simulator has to compute the session key which the attacked real-world party would output.

In the standard computation model, there is an efficiency/assumptions gap between the best known UC PAKEs and BPR-model PAKEs (see section 10.6), while in the ROM these efficiency differences are bridged (Abdalla et al. 2020; McQuoid et al. 2020) (see section 10.7). We should note, however, that UC-secure PAKEs, as any non-trivial UC functionality, can exist only in a common reference string (CRS) model (Canetti 2001), whereas BPR-secure PAKEs were constructed without any common trust assumptions (Goldreich and Lindell 2001; Nguyen and Vadhan 2004; Barak et al. 2005; Goyal et al. 2010), albeit at much higher concrete costs (see section 10.6).

Differences from the BMP model: The BMP security model can be thought of as a specialization of the above paradigm to the case of PAKE protocols (see section 10.4.2). However, Canetti et al. (2005) made some definitional choices which differentiate between their UC PAKE notion and the BMP model of Boyko et al. (2000). These differences can be captured as follows (for comparison, see the "ideal-world game" paragraph in section 10.4.1):

– Parties are started by command $(\mathsf{NewSession}, \mathsf{sid}, \mathsf{P}, \mathsf{P}', pw, \mathsf{role})$ where $\mathsf{P}, \mathsf{P}', pw, \mathsf{role}$ are as in BMP model, that is, party's identity, intended counterparty identity, password and the initiator/responder role a party plays in the protocol. However, in the UC PAKE model there is a new input element, a *session identifier* sid, which is assumed to be *globally unique*, except for two parties who intend to run PAKE with each other. As in BMP, all inputs except pw are assumed non-secret, hence $\mathcal{F}_{\mathsf{PAKE}}$ sends them to $\mathcal{A}^*$.

– The ideal-world adversary can send the TestPwd command only for a fresh session, in particular not for a session which terminates in a dangling state.

– The NewKey rules are the same as in BMP, except that two sessions $\mathsf{P}_{\mathsf{sid}}$ and $\mathsf{P}'_{\mathsf{sid}'}$ establish the same key only if in addition to satisfying the BMP-model criteria, that is, that both sessions are fresh, $pw[\mathsf{P}_{\mathsf{sid}}] = pw[\mathsf{P}'_{\mathsf{sid}'}]$, $\mathsf{pid}[\mathsf{P}_{\mathsf{sid}}] = \mathsf{P}'$, $\mathsf{pid}[\mathsf{P}'_{\mathsf{sid}'}] = \mathsf{P}$ and $\mathsf{role}[\mathsf{P}_{\mathsf{sid}}] \neq \mathsf{role}[\mathsf{P}'_{\mathsf{sid}'}]$, it also holds that $\mathsf{sid} = \mathsf{sid}'$.

As in the BMP model the adversary can set input pw and receive output sk for each session, but this is now implied by the general UC framework, where the environment $\mathcal{Z}$ determines inputs and observes outputs for each party, and since UC security implies indistinguishability of the real-world and ideal-world games for any environment $\mathcal{Z}$ and adversary $\mathcal{A}$, all these values can be without loss of generality passed to and from $\mathcal{A}$. Indeed, without loss of generality one can consider $\mathcal{A}$ to be a sub-procedure of $\mathcal{Z}$, hence in the security proof one can think of them as the same entity, as in the BMP model.

Relaxation of UC PAKE model: The above modeling decisions created two separate differences from the BMP model: First, the parties running PAKE must first establish a matching globally unique identifier sid. Second, a password test in an active attack must be completed before the attacked session terminates. The first requirement is satisfied if each PAKE interaction is preceded by an exchange of random nonces, which defines sid as a concatenation of these nonces. However, this adds one extra flow to the protocol (the second nonce can be piggybacked on the first PAKE flow). The second requirement implies that simulator $\mathcal{A}^*$ must extract password guess pw^* effectively used by an active attacker $\mathcal{A}$ against session $\mathsf{P}_{\mathsf{sid}}$ before this session terminates, which precludes protocols like PPK of Boyko et al. (2000) (see Figure 10.4), whose protocol messages are distributed independently of the password and where $\mathcal{A}^*$ can extract password pw^* used by adversary from adversarial hash queries to H', which can be made after party $\mathsf{P}_{\mathsf{sid}}$ terminates.

Both modeling could be relaxed to admit protocols with fewer rounds and better efficiency. Although UC framework (Canetti 2001) requires a locally unambiguous pointer to each protocol instance, there is no need for such pointers to be the same for two communicating parties, and PAKE functionality $\mathcal{F}_{\mathsf{PAKE}}$ could be relaxed as an "opportunistic dating" functionality, which allows the adversary to connect any two sessions with matching party identifiers and opposed roles. Indeed, one can go further and remove also the requirement that UC PAKE parties pre-specify their counterparty identifiers, and set both party and sessions identifiers as PAKE outputs.

Post-termination password tests of Boyko et al. (2000) were reintroduced to the UC framework by Abdalla et al. (2020) as a *lazy-extraction* UC PAKE. Apart from the matching-sid requirement (Abdalla et al. 2020), which is copied from Canetti et al. (2005), the lazy-extraction UC PAKE model of Abdalla et al. (2020) appears equivalent to the BMP model. Consequently, PPK in Figure 10.4 is probably a secure lazy-extraction UC PAKE after simple adjustments to enforce the UC PAKE matching-sid requirement.

UC variant of PAKE-EA: The *explicit authentication* PAKE was formalized within the UC framework first for the case of client-to-server authentication by Abdalla et al. (2008), and then by Groce and Katz (2010) for the case of mutual authentication. Technically, UC PAKE-EA is defined in Abdalla et al. (2008) and Groce and Katz (2010) via a functionality that strengthened the PAKE-EA variant of the simulation-based BMP (see section 10.4.4) by eliminating post-termination passwords tests, and creating stricter rules for when two partnered sessions can establish a key, in particular ensuring that if an honest party outputs $sk \neq \bot$, then its partnered counterparty can only output $sk' = sk$ or $\bot$.

10.6. PAKE protocols in the standard model

The two versions of EKE discussed in sections 10.3 and 10.4, that is, EKE2 in Figure 10.3 and PPK in Figure 10.4, were shown secured only in the idealized ROM, where some deterministic hash function is treated as a random oracle. (EKE2 in addition assumes an IC on a group, but as we explain in section 10.3.5 this can be reduced to a random oracle for most groups of interest.) Given that the random oracle methodology is merely a heuristic (Bellare and Rogaway 1993), which can lead to insecure protocols if the random oracle is instantiated (Canetti et al. 1998), a natural question emerges whether PAKEs can be shown secure in the standard computational model, that is, without assuming idealized un-instantiable black boxes like a random oracle.

The KOY protocol: The first such solution was given by Goldreich and Lindell (2001), but their standard model PAKE was not practical and it was shown secure only in a limited sense (see footnote 1). Katz et al. (2001) constructed the first practical PAKE secure in the BPR model under DDH assumption, assuming a CRS. The idea of the KOY protocol is inspired by the concept of SPHF introduced by Cramer and Shoup (2002). If each party P sends a commitment c_P to its password pw_P, then we would be done if party A can (1) prove to party B that its commitment c_A commits to B's password pw_B, and (2) this proof could be tied to a KE so that A and B establish a shared key iff the two proven statements are correct. Unfortunately, it is not clear how to use zero-knowledge proofs to accomplish task (1) without enabling off-line attacks, because the statement x that A needs to prove to B in ZK is that "c_A commits to pw_B" (prover A would use pw_A in place of pw_B), hence a password is not a witness, which ZK proof hides, but a part of a statement, which ZK proof can reveal. (In particular, using any NIZK would enable off-line attacks because the verifier can verify the NIZK proof under statement x completed with any password guess pw^*.) However, replacing ZK proof with an SPHF of Cramer and Shoup (2002) solves the problem. An SPHF for language $\mathcal{L}$ allows the verifier to *hash* a statement x into a random value sk together with creating a *projection key* hp such that (1) if the prover knows the witness w for $x \in \mathcal{L}$, then it can recompute the same hash value sk given (hp, w), but (2) if $x \notin \mathcal{L}$, then the hash value sk is (statistically) random given the projection key hp. (Technically, the SPHF must have a property that hp does not reveal the statement x on which it was computed, but that is the case for the SPHFs used in the KOY protocol.) Doing this in both directions creates a PAKE, except for several subtleties which come from man-in-the-middle attacks. First, the commitment must be non-malleable (this requirement was reduced in subsequent work, e.g. Abdalla et al. (2015b)), for example, Katz et al. (2001) implemented it by CCA encryption, specifically Cramer–Shoup encryption (Cramer and Shoup 1998). Second, since SPHF's are malleable, man-in-the-middle attacks ensue (and/or black-box security arguments fail) unless the SPHFs are better "tied" to the c_A, c_B values. This was accomplished in KOY using a one-time signature (OTS) scheme: (1) The initiator A picks an OTS public key and uses it as a label in its ciphertext c_A, hence c_A hides pw_A even if the attacker re-uses c_A with another OTS key, (2) B uses its projection key hp_B as a label in ciphertext c_B, hence c_B hides pw_B even if the attacker re-uses c_B with another projection key, (3) in its last message A signs its projection key hp_A together the label used in B's encryption (that move is somewhat non-black-box and in Gennaro and Lindell (2003) it is replaced by simply signing the whole transcript).

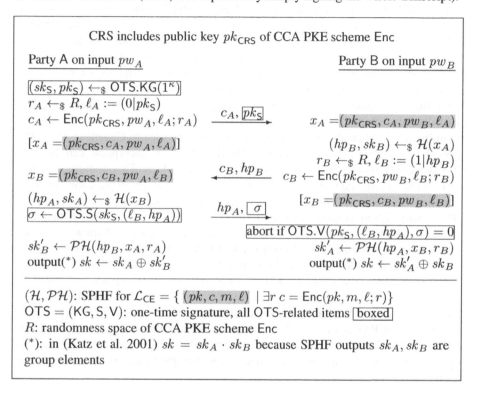

Figure 10.5. *Protocol KOY: PAKE of Katz et al. (2001)*
in generic form given by Gennaro and Lindell (2003)

We present the KOY protocol in Figure 10.5 in a generic form, as in Gennaro-Lindell (GL) (Gennaro and Lindell 2003), but without the latter modifications. In the figure OTS $=$ (KG, S, V) is a one-time signature, Enc is a labeled CCA PKE, and $(\mathcal{H}, \mathcal{PH})$ is a Smooth Projective Hash Function (SPHF) system (Cramer and Shoup 2002) for the language $\mathcal{L}_{CE}$ of tuples (pk, c, m, ℓ) such that $c = \text{Enc}(pk, m, \ell; r)$ for some r. We use a simplified SPHF syntax where $\mathcal{H}(x)$ samples (hp, sk) and $\mathcal{PH}(hp, x, w)$ outputs sk' such that (1) if w is a witness that $x \in \mathcal{L}$, then $sk' = sk$, and (2) if $x \notin \mathcal{L}$, then sk is random given hp. The KOY protocol in Katz et al. (2001) instantiates the generic protocol in

Figure 10.5 with Cramer–Shoup encryption (Cramer and Shoup 1998), where Enc takes 6 fixed-base (fb) exps, $\mathcal{H}$ takes 5 fb and $\mathcal{PH}$ takes one (multi-base) variable-base (vb) exp, leading to a PAKE with 11 fb and 1 vb per party. Assuming 1 vb $\approx$ 6 fb the total cost is about 3x larger than either EKE2 or PPK, which were proven secure only in ROM.

Other PAKEs in the standard model: Nguyen and Vadhan (2004), Barak et al. (2005) and Goyal et al. (2010) improved on the Goldreich-Lindell plain-model PAKE (Goldreich and Lindell 2001), but none of these plain-model constructions are practical. Regarding the CRS model, Gennaro and Lindell (2003) generalized the KOY protocol, allowing for other instantiations of SPHF-friendly Cramer-Shoup encryption, for example, under the quadratic residuosity assumption or the N-residuosity assumption used in Paillier encryption (Paillier 1999). The same paper also observed that CCA-secure encryption can be relaxed to non-malleable commitment. Katz et al. (2005) observed, re-using the idea in Canetti et al. (2005) applied therein in the context of UC PAKE, that B's encryption can be only CPA-secure. Gennaro (2008) showed that one can replace A's one-time signature with a MAC. Jiang and Gong (2004) showed an even stronger simplification of KOY (which also achieves a 3-flow PAKE-EA, see section 10.4.4): A's encryption can be CPA-secure with associated SPHF, and B can use CCA-secure encryption that does not need SPHF. Instead, in a way reminiscent of Fujisaki–Okamoto compiler (Fujisaki and Okamoto 1999) from CPA to CCA PKE (however, the compiler of Fujisaki and Okamoto (1999) works in ROM while the PAKE of Jiang and Gong (2004) works in the standard model), B's randomness in encryption c_B is derived from its SPHF key sk_B, hence it can be re-computed (and thus verified) by A. Abdalla et al. (2015b) showed also a BPR-secure version of KOY where B's encryption is CPA-secure and A's encryption is PCA-secure, that is, it is secure against only plaintext-checking attack (intuitively, a decryption oracle can be replaced by an oracle that only recognizes if an encrypted value is a fixed challenge password).

Minimal-round PAKEs: Katz and Vaikuntanathan (2011) showed that the KOY protocol can be made *non-interactive*, that is, each party can independently pick an SPHF hash key with its projection, encrypt its password, send the encryption, projection pair to the counterparty and then each can locally hash its statement using the received projection key and the counterparty's statement using its own hash key. This would be possible if CCA PKE has an SPHF where the projection key can be computed without the (full) statement. (Such SPHFs were from then on called *KV-SPHF*). Katz and Vaikuntanathan (2011) did it in a standard group using Naor-Yung CCA PKE (Naor and Yung 1990) formed by two ElGamal ciphertexts and a simulation-sound NIZK (of plaintext equality) of Sahai (1999), and in a bilinear map group using the decision linear (DLIN) assumption using Groth-Sahai NIZK (Groth and Sahai 2008), with the resulting PAKE using 70 group elements per party. This was reduced to 32 elements by Libert and Yung (2012), and then Jutla and

Roy (2012) showed a relaxation in simulation-sound NIZKs, resulting in non-interactive BPR-model PAKE with 20 group elements per party, under the Symmetric-eXternal Diffie–Hellman (SXDH) assumption on a bilinear map curve. Benhamouda et al. (2013) then showed an efficient KV-SPHF for Cramer-Shoup CCA PKE, resulting in non-interactive BPR-model PAKE using standard groups, secure under DDH, with just six group elements per party.

UC PAKEs in the standard model: Canetti et al. (2005) showed the first UC PAKE by adding password re-encryption and a simulation-sound NIZK to the final flow of the KOY protocol (see section 10.5). Groce and Katz (2010) generalized the BPR-model PAKE scheme of Jiang and Gong (2004) and showed its UC-secure version formalized as UC PAKE-EA. The UC PAKE-EA of Groce and Katz (2010) adds an additional encryption flow and a simulation-sound NIZK of plaintext equality to the PAKE-EA of Jiang and Gong (2004), essentially the same overhead as the UC PAKE of Canetti et al. (2005) added to the BPR-model PAKE of KOY protocol (Katz et al. 2001).

Katz and Vaikuntanathan (2011) extended their non-interactive BPR-model PAKE to a non-interactive UC PAKE, by building a trapdoor into an SPHF (they encrypt the hash key under the CRS and add a simulation-sound NIZK that the encrypted hash key corresponds to the projection key) so the simulator can compute SPHF hash values even on *incorrect* statements (recall that the simulator does not know honest parties' passwords). Their non-interactive UC PAKE was secure under DLIN on standard group but it was a feasibility result ((Jutla and Roy 2015) estimate that it requires more than 65 group elements per party). Benhamouda et al. (2013) formalized this type of SPHF as *Trapdoor SPHF* (TSPHF) and showed a more efficient TSPHF construction under SXDH which resulted in an non-interactive UC PAKE with 11 group elements.

Adaptive UC PAKEs: Abdalla et al. (2009) used extractable and equivocable (E^2) commitments to upgrade UC PAKE of Canetti et al. (2005) to the *adaptive adversary* setting (assuming reliable erasures) but their construction used $\Omega(\kappa^2)$ group elements. This was improved by Abdalla et al. (2013) using SPHF-friendly E^2 commitment so the resulting adaptive UC PAKE (with erasures) was non-interactive and used $\Omega(\kappa)$ elements on the SXDH curve. Jutla and Roy (2015) then showed a version of Katz-Vaikuntanathan non-interactive PAKE which remains secure using a *dual-system* simulation-sound NIZK they introduced, resulting in adaptive UC PAKE (with erasures) using only four group elements in the same SXDH setting. With regard to adaptive security without erasures, we are aware only of an OT-based PAKE by Canetti et al. (2012), which uses $\Theta(\kappa)$ UC OT instances.

10.7. PAKE efficiency optimizations

The two versions of EKE discussed in sections 10.3 and 10.4, that is, protocol EKE2 of Bellare et al. (2000) and protocol PPK of Boyko et al. (2000), were proven secure under CDH and/or DDH assuming idealized models, IC and ROM. (Recall that IC stands here for an IC on *group* elements; see section 10.3.5.) In section 10.6, we discussed PAKEs in a standard model, but PAKEs that assume idealized models are not limited to the results of Bellare et al. (2000) and Boyko et al. (2000). The biggest issue with the EKE2 version of EKE (Figure 10.3) was that it used an IC on a group, and with PPK version (Figure 10.4) it used a hash onto a group. Moreover, the full proofs of either version took some time to appear and/or were developed by subsequent works.

Bresson et al. (2003) gave a BPR-model security proof under CDH in the IC+ROM model for the *AuthA* protocol of Bellare and Rogaway (2000), which was considered for the IEEE P1363.2 public-key cryptography standard. Protocol AuthA is like EKE2 (Figure 10.3) except that A goes first and sends g^x without password-encrypting it, but there is a third protocol flow where A sends a key confirmation message, for example, value τ from Figure 10.2. Crucially, B cannot attach its authenticator γ to the second flow, otherwise there would be an off-line attack, so AuthA implies mutual PAKE-EA in four rounds, in contrast to the three-round PAKE-EA version *PAK* of EKE of Boyko et al. (2000); MacKenzie (2001b, 2002) (see section 10.4.4), which also saves one side of password-encryption but from the responder B. Bresson et al. (2004) also showed BPR-model security under CDH in ROM for a variant of PAKE-EA of Boyko et al. (2000), which cuts off the last A-to-B key confirmation flow, resulting in two-flow PAKE with server-to-client authentication.

Abdalla and Pointcheval (2005) showed BPR-security under CDH in ROM of a minimum-round version of EKE called SPAKE2, which goes like protocol PPK of Figure 10.4 except the CRS is amended by two random group elements M, N and $H(pw_A)$ and $H(pw_B)$ are replaced resp. by group elements M^{pwd_A} and N^{pw_B}. (Passwords are assumed to be hashed onto $\mathbb{Z}_q$, and symmetry must be broken somehow because A and B cannot use the same CRS element.)[5] The SPAKE2 protocol provided the first BPR-secure EKE version which did not need either IC or an RO hash onto a group, at the (moderate) cost of adding 2 fixed-base exp's per each party to the 1fb+1vb exp's baseline cost of DH KE ("vb" = variable-base).

Protocol SPEKE of Jablon (1996) and Hao and Shahandashti (2014) proposed the following twist on EKE: In EKE instantiated with DH KE, instead of encrypting g^x and g^y under a password, the two parties can run DH KE using DH base g set as $g = H(pw)$ where H is an RO hash onto the group. A specific elliptic-curve

---

5 Kobara-Imai (Kobara and Imai 2002) claimed almost the same protocol BPR-secure in the standard model except in their version $M = N$, the protocol is followed by a key confirmation round, see Figure 10.2, and the session key and the key confirmation messages τ, γ are derived by PRF/MAC applied directly to the DH secret g^{xy} instead of sk derived from g^{xy} by an RO hash. However, Kobara and Imai (2002) relied on a strong and non-standard notion of MAC security which seems hard to implement in the standard model.

instantiation of SPEKE was proposed by Haase and Labrique (2019) as CPace, and it was recommended for adoption by the IETF CFRG competition in symmetric PAKE category (Smyshlyaev 2020). MacKenzie (2001a) showed that SPEKE is BMP-model secure (if the simulator gets *two* test password queries for each attacked session) under an *Inverted-Additive DDH* assumption, that is, that tuples $(g^{1/x}, g^{1/y}, g^{1/(x+y)})$ are indistinguishable from a random group element triple. Note that in addition to a non-standard security assumption, SPEKE requires a hash onto a group while SPAKE2 does not, and SPEKE costs 2vb exp/party while SPAKE2 costs 3fb+1vb, so SPEKE is less expensive only in space-constrained cases which cannot use precomputation to speed-up fixed-base exponentiations. However, Pointcheval and Wang (2017) showed a SPEKE variant, called TBPEKE, which addresses both issues by setting $\mathsf{H}(pw) = \bar{g} \cdot \bar{h}^{pw}$ where $\bar{g}, \bar{h}$ are two (random) group elements in CRS.

PAKE protocol, which is *not* an EKE variant but which gained traction in practice, was J-PAKE (Hao and Ryan 2010), which is included in the OpenSSL library. Abdalla et al. (2015a) showed BPR-security of J-PAKE under a variant of DDH in ROM, but J-PAKE seems to have no advantages over SPAKE2 or TBPEKE, as it requires more rounds and a factor of about 6x more bandwidth and computation.

PAKEs based on RSA: Basing PAKE on EKE instantiated with RSA-based KEM seemed like an attractive option because it could create a PAKE with imbalanced costs: If the client sends $c_A \leftarrow \mathsf{E}(pw, (r^e \bmod N))$ for random key r and the server recovers the KEM key as $r \leftarrow [\mathsf{D}(pw, c_A)]^d \bmod N$, then such PAKE would support weak clients *if* exponent e can be short. However, the server party could cheat if (e, N) is tweaked so that $r^e \bmod N$ is not a random integer mod N. Indeed, several RSA-based EKE versions (Bellovin and Merritt 1992; Lucks 1998) were subsequently broken (Patel 1997; MacKenzie et al. 2000; Zhang 2004a). Secure versions (in the BPR model under RSA assumption in ROM) were given by MacKenzie et al. (2000), Zhang (2004b) and Park et al. (2007), secure for e's of decreasing length but even (Park et al. 2007) requires $|e| = \Omega(\kappa)$ and the client must test e's primality. RSA-based PAKE proposals include some provioud studies (Zhu et al. 2002; Wong et al. 2003; Catalano et al. 2004; Zhang 2004c; Gentry et al. 2005) but they all have either high client costs or require more rounds and bandwidth than PAKEs using prime-order groups. Creating PAKEs for weak clients is still an unsolved puzzle, but the interest in RSA-based solutions seems to have waned, possibly because any client-side cost savings would come at the cost of inherently higher bandwidth.

UC PAKEs in RO or IC models: Abdalla et al. (2008) showed that the three-round EKE variant AuthA (Bellare and Rogaway 2000; Bresson et al. 2003) (see above) realizes UC PAKE functionality of Canetti et al. (2005) even against *adaptive adversaries* and without erasures, under CDH in the IC+RO model. Bradley et al. (2019a) showed two two-round variants of EKE that realize UC PAKE, one minimum-cost but in the IC+RO model and one in RO but with additional exponentiations. Abdalla et al. (2020) proposed a "lazy extraction" relaxation of the UC PAKE functionality (see section 10.5) and showed that several efficient minimum-round EKE versions, including SPAKE2, SPEKE, CPace and TBPEKE, realize the lazy-extraction UC PAKE model under gap versions of the assumptions used in the corresponding BPR-model proofs, all in ROM. McQuoid et al. (2020) showed that EKE2 with encryption implemented using a specific two-round Feistel construction (see section 10.3.5) realizes the UC PAKE notion of Canetti et al. (2005) under CDH in ROM. Thus, the currently most efficient and minimum-round EKE versions, EKE2 and SPAKE2, realize UC PAKE and lazy-extraction UC PAKE, under CDH and GapDH, and they cost 1fb+1vb plus 2 RO hashes onto a group per party for EKE2 implemented as in McQuoid et al. (2020), and 3fb+1vb per party for SPAKE2.

10.8. Asymmetric PAKE: PAKE for the client-server setting

Bellovin and Merritt (1993) proposed an *augmented* PAKE (aPAKE) for the client-server setting, where the server holds a password *hash* $hpw = f(pw)$ instead of the password itself, and the protocol checks that C and S hold, respectively, pw_C and hpw_S such that $f(pwd_C) = (pw_S)$, instead of pw_C and pw_S such that $pw_C = pw_S$. If f is a *tight* one-way function (OWF) (Benhamouda and Pointcheval 2013), that is, if for any domain D it takes $\Omega(\epsilon|D|)$ effort to find x with probability at least ϵ given $y = f(x)$ for $x \leftarrow_\$ D$, then an attacker who compromises hpw held by S can recover password pw only with $\Omega(2^d)$ effort where d is the password entropy. This is optimal since an attacker given hpw can off-line test any pw^* by emulating aPAKE execution on, respectively, inputs pw^* and hpw. In ROM, one can set $f(x) = H(x)$, but then an aPAKE protocol would depend on the circuit complexity of H. However, setting $f(x) = g^{H(x)}$ still gives a tight OWF in the generic group model and ROM (Benhamouda and Pointcheval 2013), and it allows for efficient aPAKE that checks if C-held $hpw_C = H(pw_C)$ is a discrete logarithm of S-held hpw_S. This can be done using either a Diffie–Hellman KEM, or a ZK proof of knowledge of DL, where in either option this DL-relation verification must be protected against off-line attacks.

Solution to aPAKE developed along these lines, called variously *augmented*, *extended*, *verifier-based*, or *asymmetric* PAKE, were shown in Bellovin and Merritt (1993); Jablon (1997); Wu (1998); Boyko et al. (2000); MacKenzie et al. (2000); MacKenzie (2001b); Kwon (2001); Cash et al. (2008); Abdalla et al. (2015a), either without proofs or with proofs under DH assumption variants in ROM in an augmented BPR model. Gentry et al. (2006) formalized UC notion of aPAKE as an extension of the UC PAKE model of Canetti et al. (2005), and showed an Ω-method, a generic compiler which converts UC PAKE to UC aPAKE using any signature in ROM, at the cost two additional flows (or 1 if the last PAKE flow is server-to-client) and a signature generation (for C) and verification (for S). Using a signature scheme where the secret key is a random element of some field (or group) F, the server's hpw includes signature public key pk and one-time authenticated encryption $(\mathsf{H}_1(pw) \cdot sk, \mathsf{H}_2(sk))$ of the secret key sk, which S sends to C on a PAKE-authenticated channel. (Here H_1 is a hash onto field F.) Other PAKE-to-aPAKE compilers were given by Hwang et al. (2018), using either DH KEM or ZKPK of DL, removing the server-to-client flow in the Ω-method. Shoup (2020) showed that SPAKE2+ (Cash et al. 2008), a KEM-based augmentation of SPAKE2 (Abdalla and Pointcheval 2005), realizes UC aPAKE (relaxed akin to Abdalla et al. (2020); see section 10.5) under CDH in ROM. Both SPAKE2+ and the generic compilers (Gentry et al. 2006; Hwang et al. 2018) instantiated with SPAKE2 (see section 10.7), give 3-flow UC aPAKEs with two variable-based (vb) exp per party, or 1 for C and 2 for S.

Recently, Gu et al. (2021) showed a compiler that creates UC aPAKE from public-key based KE (AKE) with a key-hiding property (which is akin to the EKE compiler (Bellovin and Merritt 1992) that creates UC PAKE from a random-transcript KE), resulting in a 4-flow UC aPAKE with 1 vb exp per party under GapDH in ROM, that is, essentially matching the cost (but not the round complexity) of symmetric UC PAKE and plain KE. In other results, Benhamouda and Pointcheval (2013) showed a minimal-round aPAKE with 3 vb exp per party, relying on ROM for the tight OWF but not in the protocol itself, secure under DDH in the augmented BPR model. Jutla and Roy (2018) showed a minimal-round UC aPAKE using type-3 curve, secure in ROM under SXDH.

An aPAKE has stronger security than the "password-over-TLS" authentication used on the web, because the latter relies on PKI to authenticate server S to client C. However, password-over-TLS supports (privately) salted password hashes, that is, S can hold (s, hpw) where $hpw = f(s|pw)$ where s is a random value, and this accomplishes two objectives: First, an adversary who learns hpw by compromising S has to perform $\Omega(D)$ work per each user account. Second, this workload cannot be eased by precomputation. (An aPAKE protocol can generically support salted passwords using an extra S-to-C flow which sends the S-held salt s to C, but this support *public* salt, and accomplishes objective #1 but not #2.) Boyen (2009b) showed the first *privately salted* aPAKE, analyzed in an augmented BPR model, combining the *password-strengthening* protocol of Ford and Kaliski Jr. (2000), conceptualized as a *hidden credential retrieval* (Boyen 2009a), with an AKE scheme. Jarecki et al. (2018) defined privately salted aPAKE in UC framework as UC *strong* aPAKE (saPAKE), and showed that it is realized by essentially the same protocol as Boyen's but recast as a composition of UC Oblivious PRF (OPRF) (Freedman et al. 2005; Jarecki et al. 2014) and AKE. A specific instantiation called *OPAQUE*, secure under *One More* GapDH assumption (OM-GapDH) in ROM, which takes three flows and 2 or 3 vb exp/party (later reduced to 2 vb exp/party in Jarecki et al. (2021)), was chosen in the IETF CFRG competition in asymmetric PAKE category (Smyshlyaev

2020). Another UC saPAKE was shown by Bradley et al. (2019b), with two flows and 1 or 2 vb exp per party, but with more fixed-base exponentiations.

10.9. Threshold PAKE

In addition to asymmetric PAKEs (see section 10.8), server-held data can be protected by implementing the server using a (t, n)-*threshold cryptosystem* (Desmedt 1993), where the server's data are secret-shared among servers $S_1, ..., S_n$, compromise of any t of the S_i's leaks no information, and $t + 1$ servers suffice to emulate the server in a single-server PAKE scheme. In principle, any PAKE can be implemented this way using multi-party computation (MPC) (Goldreich et al. 1987; Ben-Or et al. 1988; Beaver 1991), but in practice we need a PAKE with an *MPC friendly* server code.

First, T-PAKE proposals were shown by Ford and Kaliski Jr. (2000) and Jablon (2001), but with informal security arguments. MacKenzie et al. (2002) gave the first efficient (t, n)-threshold PAKE (T-PAKE), secure in a multi-server extension of the BPR model in ROM, with three rounds of server-to-server communication, but assuming PKI for S_i-to-C authentication. Di Raimondo and Gennaro (2003) showed an MPC version of the KOY protocol (see section 10.6), resulting in the first T-PAKE in the password-only setting, for $t < n/3$, with security in the standard model, but with $\Omega(\kappa^3)$ communication complexity and at least 12 rounds of communication. Abdalla et al. (2005a) showed a password-only T-PAKE (with a dedicated server getting a session key) for $t < n/2$, secure under a DH assumption variant in ROM, with five rounds of server-to-server communication (including three rounds of reliable broadcast).

Bagherzandi et al. (2011) gave a game-based definition of a password-protected secret-sharing (PPSS) scheme, which allows for a password-authenticated recovery of a secret-shared secret. The same notion was then defined in the UC framework as threshold password-authenticated secret-sharing (TPASS) by Camenisch et al. (2014), building on the two-server variant defined earlier in Camenisch et al. (2012). (Abdalla et al. (2016) also investigated robustness of minimum-round PPSS.) PPSS/TPASS implies T-PAKE with a minimal overhead since the recovered secret can include key credentials that let C run an AKE with each server (Jarecki et al. 2014, 2016). The PPSS (Bagherzandi et al. 2011), secure under DDH in ROM, is in the PKI model, but it takes two rounds of C-to-S_i communication, resulting in round improvement for PKI-model T-PAKE. The UC TPASS of Camenisch et al. (2014) is in the password-only setting (with CRS), and instantiated under DDH in ROM it has five rounds of C-to-S_i communication, which implies T-PAKE of comparable costs to Abdalla et al. (2005a). Yi et al. (2015) showed a UC TPASS (hence also T-PAKE) secure under DDH in the standard model, that is, not ROM, with four rounds of server-to-server communication (including two broadcasts), thus improving on Abdalla et al. (2005a) in both assumptions and round complexity. In a chain of papers on PPSS, Jarecki et al. (2014, 2016, 2017) proposed a UC PPSS notion which relaxed UC TPASS of Camenisch et al. (2014), and showed password-only PPSS with a *single round* of C-to-S_i communication, implying a two-round T-PAKE, with costs as low as 2 exps (for any n) for C and 1 exp for S, secure in ROM under (generalized) OM-GapDH assumption.

Two-server PAKE (2-PAKE): T-PAKE for the particular case of $(t, n) = (1, 2)$ is known as two-server PAKE or *2-PAKE*. In the PKI model, testing equality between a registered secret-shared password and the secret-shared password submitted by C is equivalent to equality-testing of secret-shared data. This gave rise to the PKI-model 2-PAKEs of Brainard et al. (2003) and Szydlo and Kaliski Jr. (2005), which both use only three messages exchanged by the two servers. Katz et al. (2005) gave an efficient 2-PAKE in the password-only setting (with CRS) with only 5 message flows, secure under DDH in the standard model, that is, not ROM. (A generalization of 2-PAKE of Katz et al. (2005) was given by Kiefer and Manulis (2014).) Camenisch et al. (2012) showed a two-server TPASS in the password-only setting, which implies a 2-PAKE, but their protocol had 6 message flows under DDH in ROM. Camenisch et al. (2015a) showed two-server TPASS with *proactive security*, that is, security against transient faults (Ostrovsky and Yung 1991; Herzberg et al. 1995), implying the same level of security for 2-PAKE. Other 2-PAKEs were given by Yang et al. (2006) and Jin et al. (2008) with slightly reduced message count compared to Katz et al. (2005) but with security under DDH argued only somewhat informally. The notion of 2-PAKE was also formalized in the UC setting in Zhang et al. (2016) and Kiefer and Manulis (2016).

Distributed password verification: Camenisch et al. (2015b) gave a UC definition of a *distributed password verification* (DPV) protocol. A DPV protocol is like a T-PAKE in the PKI model but where one designated server, for example, S_1, gets the client's password at login in the clear, and the DPV protocol allows S_1 and the rest of S_i's to confirm if this password corresponds to the password (or a salted password hash, see section 10.8) which was secret-shared during password registration. The DPV protocol is thus customized to allow servers that authenticate clients using the password-over-TLS method (see section 10.8) to secret-share users' password data, and yet be able to efficiently authenticate them. The DPV protocol of Camenisch et al. (2015b) supports only the $t = n - 1$ case, it uses only 3 exps for S_1 and 1 exp for each other S_i, it supports proactive update, and it is secure under OM-DH assumption in ROM,

Everspaugh et al. (2015) built a DPV in the general (t, n) threshold case using a threshold implementation of a *partially oblivious PRF* (POPRF). The idea is similar to Ford-Kaliski password-strengthening (Ford and Kaliski Jr. 2000), but unlike the saPAKEs of Boyen (2009a) and Jarecki et al. (2018), the role of the POPRF client is played by server S_1 and not a remote user. Their computational costs are slightly higher than (Camenisch et al. 2015b) because their scheme use a bilinear map group, and they give only a game-based security analysis, under OM-DH assumption in ROM. Other DPV schemes were given by Schneider et al. (2016) and Lai et al. (2017) for the specific case of $n = 2$ servers, but they extend the DPV functionality by including a proactive update that updates only the keys stored by each server, and thus has $O(1)$ bandwidth, and then only server S_1 locally performs $O(m)$ work to update the (encrypted) password data of m users.

10.10. References

Abdalla, M. and Pointcheval, D. (2005). Simple password-based encrypted key exchange protocols, In *CT-RSA 2005*, vol. 3376 of *LNCS*, Menezes, A. (ed.). Springer, Heidelberg.

Abdalla, M., Chevassut, O., Fouque, P.-A., Pointcheval, D. (2005a). A simple threshold authenticated key exchange from short secrets. In *ASIACRYPT 2005*, vol. 3788 of *LNCS*, Roy, B.K. (ed.). Springer, Heidelberg.

Abdalla, M., Fouque, P.-A., Pointcheval, D. (2005b). Password-based authenticated key exchange in the three-party setting. In *PKC 2005*, vol. 3386 of *LNCS*, Vaudenay, S. (ed.). Springer, Heidelberg.

Abdalla, M., Catalano, D., Chevalier, C., Pointcheval, D. (2008). Efficient two-party password-based key exchange protocols in the UC framework. In *CT-RSA 2008*, vol. 4964 of *LNCS*, Malkin, T. (ed.). Springer, Heidelberg.

Abdalla, M., Chevalier, C., Pointcheval, D. (2009). Smooth projective hashing for conditionally extractable commitments. In *CRYPTO 2009*, vol. 5677 of *LNCS*, Halevi, S. (ed.). Springer, Heidelberg.

Abdalla, M., Bellare, M., Neven, G. (2010). Robust encryption. In *TCC 2010*, vol. 5978 of *LNCS*, Micciancio, D. (ed.). Springer, Heidelberg.

Abdalla, M., Benhamouda, F., Blazy, O., Chevalier, C., Pointcheval, D. (2013). SPHF-friendly non-interactive commitments. In *ASIACRYPT 2013, Part I*, vol. 8269 of *LNCS*, Sako, K., Sarkar, P. (eds). Springer, Heidelberg.

Abdalla, M., Benhamouda, F., MacKenzie, P.D. (2015a). Security of the J-PAKE password-authenticated key exchange protocol. In *2015 IEEE Symposium on Security and Privacy*. IEEE Computer Society Press.

Abdalla, M., Benhamouda, F., Pointcheval, D. (2015b). Public-key encryption indistinguishable under plaintext-checkable attacks. In *PKC 2015*, vol. 9020 of *LNCS*, Katz, J. (ed.). Springer, Heidelberg.

Abdalla, M., Cornejo, M., Nitulescu, A., Pointcheval, D. (2016). Robust password-protected secret sharing. In *ESORICS 2016, Part II*, vol. 9879 of *LNCS*, Askoxylakis, I.G., Ioannidis, S., Katsikas, S.K., Meadows, C.A. (eds). Springer, Heidelberg.

Abdalla, M., Barbosa, M., Bradley, T., Jarecki, S., Katz, J., Xu, J. (2020). Universally composable relaxed password authenticated key exchange. In *CRYPTO 2020, Part I*, vol. 12170 of *LNCS*., Micciancio, D., Ristenpart, T. (eds). Springer, Heidelberg.

Bagherzandi, A., Jarecki, S., Saxena, N., Lu, Y. (2011). Password-protected secret sharing. In *ACM CCS 2011*, Chen, Y., Danezis, G., Shmatikov, V. (eds). ACM Press.

Barak, B., Canetti, R., Lindell, Y., Pass, R., Rabin, T. (2005). Secure computation without authentication. In *CRYPTO 2005*, vol. 3621 of *LNCS*, Shoup, V. (ed.). Springer, Heidelberg.

Beaver, D. (1991). Secure multiparty protocols and zero-knowledge proof systems tolerating a faulty minority. *Journal of Cryptology*, 4(2), 75–122.

Bellare, M. and Rogaway, P. (1993). Random oracles are practical: A paradigm for designing efficient protocols. In *ACM CCS 93*, Denning, D.E., Pyle, R., Ganesan, R., Sandhu, R.S., Ashby, V. (eds), ACM Press.

Bellare, M. and Rogaway, P. (1994). Entity authentication and key distribution. In *CRYPTO'93*, vol. 773 of *LNCS*, Stinson, D.R. (ed.). Springer, Heidelberg.

Bellare, M. and Rogaway, P. (2000). The AuthA protocol for password-based authenticated key exchange. IEEE P1363, 14 March.

Bellare, M., Canetti, R., Krawczyk, H. (1998). A modular approach to the design and analysis of authentication and key exchange protocols (extended abstract). In *30th ACM STOC*. ACM Press.

Bellare, M., Pointcheval, D., Rogaway, P. (2000). Authenticated key exchange secure against dictionary attacks. In *EUROCRYPT 2000*, vol. 1807 of *LNCS*, Preneel, B. (ed.). Springer, Heidelberg.

Bellare, M., Boldyreva, A., Desai, A., Pointcheval, D. (2001). Key-privacy in public-key encryption. In *ASIACRYPT 2001*, vol. 2248 of *LNCS*, Boyd, C. (ed.). Springer, Heidelberg.

Bellovin, S.M. and Merritt, M. (1992). Encrypted key exchange: Password-based protocols secure against dictionary attacks. In *1992 IEEE Symposium on Research in Security and Privacy*, May.

Bellovin, S.M. and Merritt, M. (1993). Augmented encrypted key exchange: A password-based protocol secure against dictionary attacks and password file compromise. In *ACM CCS 93*, Denning, D.E., Pyle, R., Ganesan, R., Sandhu, R.S., Ashby, V. (eds). ACM Press.

Ben-Or, M., Goldwasser, S., Wigderson, A. (1988). Completeness theorems for non-cryptographic fault-tolerant distributed computation (extended abstract). In *20th ACM STOC*. ACM Press.

Benhamouda, F. and Pointcheval, D. (2013). Verifier-based password-authenticated key exchange: New models and constructions. Cryptology ePrint Archive, Report 2013/833 [Online]. Available at: https://eprint.iacr.org/2013/833.

Benhamouda, F., Blazy, O., Chevalier, C., Pointcheval, D., Vergnaud, D. (2013). New techniques for SPHFs and efficient one-round PAKE protocols. In *CRYPTO 2013, Part I*, vol. 8042 of *LNCS*, Canetti, R., Garay, J.A. (eds). Springer, Heidelberg.

Bernstein, D.J., Hamburg, M., Krasnova, A., Lange, T. (2013). Elligator: Elliptic-curve points indistinguishable from uniform random strings. In *ACM CCS 2013*, Sadeghi, A.-R., Gligor, V.D., Yung, M. (eds). ACM Press.

Black, J. and Rogaway, P. (2002). Ciphers with arbitrary finite domains. In *CT-RSA 2002*, vol. 2271 of *LNCS*, Preneel, B. (ed.). Springer, Heidelberg.

Boyarsky, M.K. (1999). Public-key cryptography and password protocols: The multi-user case. In *ACM CCS 99*, Motiwalla, J., Tsudik, G. (eds). ACM Press.

Boyen, X. (2009a). Hidden credential retrieval from a reusable password. In *ASIACCS 09*, Li, W., Susilo, W., Tupakula, U.K., Safavi-Naini, R., Varadharajan, V. (eds). ACM Press.

Boyen, X. (2009b). HPAKE: Password authentication secure against cross-site user impersonation. In *CANS 09*, vol. 5888 of *LNCS*, Garay, J.A., Miyaji, A., Otsuka, A. (eds). Springer, Heidelberg.

Boyko, V., MacKenzie, P.D., Patel, S. (2000). Provably secure password-authenticated key exchange using Diffie–Hellman. In *EUROCRYPT 2000*, vol. 1807 of *LNCS*, Preneel, B. (ed.). Springer, Heidelberg.

Bradley, T., Camenisch, J., Jarecki, S., Lehmann, A., Neven, G., Xu, J. (2019a). Password-authenticated public-key encryption. In *ACNS 19*, vol. 11464 of *LNCS*, Deng, R.H., Gauthier-Umaña, V., Ochoa, M., Yung, M. (eds). Springer, Heidelberg.

Bradley, T., Jarecki, S., Xu, J. (2019b). Strong asymmetric PAKE based on trapdoor CKEM. In *CRYPTO 2019, Part III*, vol. 11694 of *LNCS*, Boldyreva, A., Micciancio, D. (eds). Springer, Heidelberg.

Brainard, J.G., Juels, A., Kaliski, B., Szydlo, M. (2003). A new two-server approach for authentication with short secrets. In *USENIX Security 2003*. USENIX Association.

Bresson, E., Chevassut, O., Pointcheval, D. (2003). Security proofs for an efficient password-based key exchange. In *ACM CCS 2003*, Jajodia, S., Atluri, V., Jaeger, T. (eds). ACM Press.

Bresson, E., Chevassut, O., Pointcheval, D. (2004). New security results on encrypted key exchange. In *PKC 2004*, vol. 2947 of *LNCS*, Bao, F., Deng, R., Zhou, J. (eds). Springer, Heidelberg.

Buhler, P., Eirich, T., Waidner, M., Steiner, M. (2000). Secure password-based cipher suite for TLS. In *NDSS 2000*. The Internet Society.

Camenisch, J., Lysyanskaya, A., Neven, G. (2012). Practical yet universally composable two-server password-authenticated secret sharing. In *ACM CCS 2012*, Yu, T., Danezis, G., Gligor, V.D. (eds). ACM Press.

Camenisch, J., Lehmann, A., Lysyanskaya, A., Neven, G. (2014). Memento: How to reconstruct your secrets from a single password in a hostile environment. In *CRYPTO 2014, Part II*, vol. 8617 of *LNCS*, Garay, J.A., Gennaro, R. (eds). Springer, Heidelberg.

Camenisch, J., Enderlein, R.R., Neven, G. (2015a). Two-server password-authenticated secret sharing UC-secure against transient corruptions. In *PKC 2015*, vol. 9020 of *LNCS*, Katz, J. (ed.). Springer, Heidelberg.

Camenisch, J., Lehmann, A., Neven, G. (2015b). Optimal distributed password verification. In *ACM CCS 2015*, Ray, I., Li, N., Kruegel, C. (eds). ACM Press.

Canetti, R. (2000). Security and composition of multiparty cryptographic protocols. *Journal of Cryptology*, 13(1), 143–202.

Canetti, R. (2001). Universally composable security: A new paradigm for cryptographic protocols. In *42nd FOCS*. IEEE Computer Society Press.

Canetti, R. and Krawczyk, H. (2002). Universally composable notions of key exchange and secure channels. In *EUROCRYPT 2002*, vol. 2332 of *LNCS*, Knudsen, L.R. (ed.). Springer, Heidelberg.

Canetti, R., Goldreich, O., Halevi, S. (1998). The random oracle methodology, revisited (preliminary version). In *30th ACM STOC*. ACM Press.

Canetti, R., Halevi, S., Katz, J., Lindell, Y., MacKenzie, P.D. (2005). Universally composable password-based key exchange. In *EUROCRYPT 2005*, vol. 3494 of *LNCS*, Cramer, R. (ed.). Springer, Heidelberg.

Canetti, R., Kalai, Y.T., Varia, M., Wichs, D. (2010). On symmetric encryption and point obfuscation. In *TCC 2010*, vol. 5978 of *LNCS*, Micciancio, D. (ed.). Springer, Heidelberg.

Canetti, R., Dachman-Soled, D., Vaikuntanathan, V., Wee, H. (2012). Efficient password authenticated key exchange via oblivious transfer. In *PKC 2012*, vol. 7293 of *LNCS*, Fischlin, M., Buchmann, J., Manulis, M. (eds). Springer, Heidelberg.

Cash, D., Kiltz, E., Shoup, V. (2008). The twin Diffie–Hellman problem and applications. In *EUROCRYPT 2008*, vol. 4965 of *LNCS*, Smart, N.P. (ed.). Springer, Heidelberg.

Catalano, D., Pointcheval, D., Pornin, T. (2004). IPAKE: Isomorphisms for password-based authenticated key exchange. In *CRYPTO 2004*, vol. 3152 of *LNCS*, Franklin, M. (ed.). Springer, Heidelberg.

Cramer, R. and Shoup, V. (1998). A practical public key cryptosystem provably secure against adaptive chosen ciphertext attack. In *CRYPTO'98*, vol. 1462 of *LNCS*, Krawczyk, H. (ed.). Springer, Heidelberg.

Cramer, R. and Shoup, V. (2002). Universal hash proofs and a paradigm for adaptive chosen ciphertext secure public-key encryption. In *EUROCRYPT 2002*, vol. 2332 of *LNCS*, Knudsen, L.R. (ed.). Springer, Heidelberg.

Dachman-Soled, D., Katz, J., Thiruvengadam, A. (2016). 10-Round Feistel is indifferentiable from an ideal cipher. In *EUROCRYPT 2016, Part II*, vol. 9666 of *LNCS*, Fischlin, M., Coron, J.-S. (eds). Springer, Heidelberg.

Dai, Y. and Steinberger, J.P. (2016). Indifferentiability of 8-round Feistel networks. In *CRYPTO 2016, Part I*, vol. 9814 of *LNCS*, Robshaw, M., Katz, J. (eds). Springer, Heidelberg.

Desmedt, Y. (1993). Treshold cryptosystems (invited talk). In *AUSCRYPT'92*, Seberry, J., vol. 718 of *LNCS*, Zheng, Y. (eds). Springer, Heidelberg.

Di Raimondo, M. and Gennaro, R. (2003). Provably secure threshold password-authenticated key exchange. In *EUROCRYPT 2003*, vol. 2656 of *LNCS*, Biham, E. (ed.). Springer, Heidelberg.

Dodis, Y., Gennaro, R., Håstad, J., Krawczyk, H., Rabin, T. (2004). Randomness extraction and key derivation using the CBC, cascade and HMAC modes. In *CRYPTO 2004*, vol. 3152 of *LNCS*, Franklin, M. (ed.). Springer, Heidelberg.

Everspaugh, A., Chatterjee, R., Scott, S., Juels, A., Ristenpart, T. (2015). The pythia PRF service. In *USENIX Security 2015*, Jung, J., Holz, T. (eds). USENIX Association.

Farshim, P., Orlandi, C., Rosie, R. (2017). Security of symmetric primitives under incorrect usage of keys. *IACR Transactions on Symmetric Cryptology*, 2017(1), 449–473.

Ford, W. and Kaliski Jr., B.S. (2000). Server-assisted generation of a strong secret from a password. In *9th IEEE International Workshops on Enabling Technologies: Infrastructure for Collaborative Enterprises (WETICE 2000)*, Gaithersburg, MD.

Freedman, M.J., Ishai, Y., Pinkas, B., Reingold, O. (2005). Keyword search and oblivious pseudorandom functions. In *TCC 2005*, vol. 3378 of *LNCS*, Kilian, J. (ed.). Springer, Heidelberg.

Fujisaki, E. and Okamoto, T. (1999). How to enhance the security of public-key encryption at minimum cost. In *PKC'99*, vol. 1560 of *LNCS*, Imai, H., Zheng, Y. (eds). Springer, Heidelberg.

Gennaro, R. (2008). Faster and shorter password-authenticated key exchange. In *TCC 2008*, vol. 4948 of *LNCS*, Canetti, R. (ed.). Springer, Heidelberg.

Gennaro, R. and Lindell, Y. (2003). A framework for password-based authenticated key exchange. In *EUROCRYPT 2003*, vol. 2656 of *LNCS*, Biham, E. (ed.). Springer, Heidelberg [Online]. Available at: https://eprint.iacr.org/2003/032.ps.gz.

Gentry, C., Mackenzie, P.D., Ramzan, Z. (2005). Password authenticated key exchange using hidden smooth subgroups. In *ACM CCS 2005*, Atluri, V., Meadows, C., Juels, A. (eds). ACM Press.

Gentry, C., MacKenzie, P.D., Ramzan, Z. (2006). A method for making password-based key exchange resilient to server compromise. In *CRYPTO 2006*, vol. 4117 of *LNCS*, Dwork, C. (ed.). Springer, Heidelberg.

Goldreich, O. and Lindell, Y. (2001). Session-key generation using human passwords only. In *CRYPTO 2001*, vol. 2139 of *LNCS*, Kilian, J. (ed.). Springer, Heidelberg.

Goldreich, O., Micali, S., Wigderson, A. (1987). How to play any mental game or A completeness theorem for protocols with honest majority. In *19th ACM STOC*, Aho, A. (ed.). ACM Press.

Gong, L. (1995). Optimal authentication protocols resistant to password guessing attacks. In *CSFW'95: The 8th IEEE Computer Security Foundation Workshop*, Kenmare, County Kerry.

Gong, L., Lomas, T.M.A., Needham, R.M., Saltzer, J.H. (1993). Protecting poorly chosen secrets from guessing attacks. *IEEE JSAC*, 11(5), 648–656.

Goyal, V., Jain, A., Ostrovsky, R. (2010). Password-authenticated session-key generation on the Internet in the plain model. In *CRYPTO 2010*, vol. 6223 of *LNCS*, Rabin, T. (ed.). Springer, Heidelberg.

Groce, A. and Katz, J. (2010). A new framework for efficient password-based authenticated key exchange. In *ACM CCS 2010*, Al-Shaer, E., Keromytis, A.D., Shmatikov, V. (eds). ACM Press.

Groth, J. and Sahai, A. (2008). Efficient non-interactive proof systems for bilinear groups. In *EUROCRYPT 2008*, vol. 4965 of *LNCS*, Smart, N.P. (ed.). Springer, Heidelberg.

Gu, Y., Jarecki, S., Krawczyk, H. (2021). KHAPE: Asymmetric PAKE from key-hiding key exchange. In *CRYPTO 2021, Part IV*, vol. 12828 of *LNCS*, Malkin, T., Peikert, C. (eds). Springer, Heidelberg.

Haase, B. and Labrique, B. (2019). AuCPace: Efficient verifier-based PAKE protocol tailored for the IIoT. *IACR TCHES*, 2019(2), 1–48.

Halevi, S. and Krawczyk, H. (1998). Public-key cryptography and password protocols. In *ACM CCS 98*, Gong, L., Reiter, M.K. (eds). ACM Press.

Hao, F. and Ryan, P. (2010). J-PAKE: Authenticated key exchange without PKI. Cryptology ePrint Archive, Report 2010/190 [Online]. Available at: https://eprint.iacr.org/2010/190.

Hao, F. and Shahandashti, S.F. (2014). The SPEKE protocol revisited. Cryptology ePrint Archive, Report 2014/585 [Online]. Available at: https://eprint.iacr.org/2014/585.

Herzberg, A., Jarecki, S., Krawczyk, H., Yung, M. (1995). Proactive secret sharing or: How to cope with perpetual leakage. In *CRYPTO'95*, vol. 963 of *LNCS*, Coppersmith, D. (ed.). Springer, Heidelberg.

Holenstein, T., Künzler, R., Tessaro, S. (2011). The equivalence of the random oracle model and the ideal cipher model, revisited. In *43rd ACM STOC*, Fortnow, L., Vadhan, S.P. (eds). ACM Press.

Hwang, J.Y., Jarecki, S., Kwon, T., Lee, J., Shin, J.S., Xu, J. (2018). Round-reduced modular construction of asymmetric password-authenticated key exchange. In *SCN 18*, vol. 11035 of *LNCS*, Catalano, D., De Prisco, R. (eds). Springer, Heidelberg.

Impagliazzo, R. and Rudich, S. (1989). Limits on the provable consequences of one-way permutations. In *21st ACM STOC*. ACM Press.

Jablon, D.P. (1996). Strong password-only authenticated key exchange. *Computer Communication Review*, 26(5), 5–26.

Jablon, D.P. (1997). Extended password key exchange protocols immune to dictionary attacks. In *6th IEEE International Workshops on Enabling Technologies: Infrastructure for Collaborative Enterprises (WETICE 1997)*, Cambridge, MA.

Jablon, D.P. (2001). Password authentication using multiple servers. In *CT-RSA 2001*, vol. 2020 of *LNCS*, Naccache, D. (ed.). Springer, Heidelberg.

Jarecki, S., Kiayias, A., Krawczyk, H. (2014). Round-optimal password-protected secret sharing and T-PAKE in the password-only model. In *ASIACRYPT 2014, Part II*, vol. 8874 of *LNCS*, Sarkar, P., Iwata, T. (eds). Springer, Heidelberg.

Jarecki, S., Kiayias, A., Krawczyk, H., Xu, J. (2016). Highly-efficient and composable password-protected secret sharing (or: How to protect your bitcoin wallet online). In *IEEE European Symposium on Security and Privacy, EuroS&P 2016*, Saarbrücken, March 21–24.

Jarecki, S., Kiayias, A., Krawczyk, H., Xu, J. (2017). TOPPSS: Cost-minimal password-protected secret sharing based on threshold OPRF. In *ACNS 17*, vol. 10355 of *LNCS*, Gollmann, D., Miyaji, A., Kikuchi, H. (eds). Springer, Heidelberg.

Jarecki, S., Krawczyk, H., Xu, J. (2018). OPAQUE: An asymmetric PAKE protocol secure against pre-computation attacks. In *EUROCRYPT 2018, Part III*, vol. 10822 of *LNCS*, Nielsen, J.B., Rijmen, V. (eds). Springer, Heidelberg.

Jarecki, S., Krawczyk, H., Xu, J. (2021). On the (in)security of the Diffie–Hellman oblivious PRF with multiplicative blinding. In *PKC 2021, Part II*, vol. 12711 of *LNCS*, Garay, J. (ed.). Springer, Heidelberg.

Jiang, S. and Gong, G. (2004). Password based key exchange with mutual authentication. In *SAC 2004*, vol. 3357 of *LNCS*, Handschuh, H., Hasan, A. (eds). Springer, Heidelberg.

Jin, H., Wong, D.S., Xu, Y. (2008). An efficient password-only two-server authenticated key exchange system. In *ICICS 07*, vol. 4861 of *LNCS*, Qing, S., Imai, H., Wang, G. (eds). Springer, Heidelberg.

Jutla, C.S. and Roy, A. (2012). Relatively-sound NIZKs and password-based key-exchange. In *PKC 2012*, vol. 7293 of *LNCS*, Fischlin, M., Buchmann, J., Manulis, M. (eds). Springer, Heidelberg.

Jutla, C.S. and Roy, A. (2015). Dual-system simulation-soundness with applications to UC-PAKE and more. In *ASIACRYPT 2015, Part I*, vol. 9452 of *LNCS*, Iwata, T., Cheon, J.H. (eds). Springer, Heidelberg.

Jutla, C.S. and Roy, A. (2018). Smooth NIZK arguments. In *TCC 2018, Part I*, vol. 11239 of *LNCS*, Beimel, A., Dziembowski, S. (eds). Springer, Heidelberg.

Katz, J., Ostrovsky, R., Yung, M. (2001). Efficient password-authenticated key exchange using human-memorable passwords. In *EUROCRYPT 2001*, vol. 2045 of *LNCS*, Pfitzmann, B. (ed.). Springer, Heidelberg.

Katz, J., MacKenzie, P.D., Taban, G., Gligor, V.D. (2005). Two-server password-only authenticated key exchange. In *ACNS 05*, vol. 3531 of *LNCS*, Ioannidis, J., Keromytis, A., Yung, M. (eds). Springer, Heidelberg.

Katz, J. and Vaikuntanathan, V. (2011). Round-optimal password-based authenticated key exchange. In *TCC 2011*, vol. 6597 of *LNCS*, Ishai, Y. (ed.). Springer, Heidelberg.

Kaufman, C. and Perlman, R.J. (2001). PDM: A new strong password-based protocol. In *USENIX Security 2001*, Wallach, D.S. (ed.). USENIX Association.

Kiefer, F. and Manulis, M. (2014). Distributed smooth projective hashing and its application to two-server password authenticated key exchange. In *ACNS 14*, vol. 8479 of *LNCS*, Boureanu, I., Owesarski, P., Vaudenay, S. (eds). Springer, Heidelberg.

Kiefer, F. and Manulis, M. (2016). Universally composable two-server PAKE. In *ISC 2016*, vol. 9866 of *LNCS*, Bishop, M., Nascimento, A.C.A. (eds). Springer, Heidelberg.

Kim, T. and Tibouchi, M. (2015). Invalid curve attacks in a GLS setting. In *IWSEC 15*, vol. 9241 of *LNCS*, Tanaka, K., Suga, Y. (eds). Springer, Heidelberg.

Kobara, K. and Imai, H. (2002). Pretty-simple password-authenticated key-exchange under standard assumptions. *IEICE Transactions*, E85-A(10), 2229–2237.

Krawczyk, H. (2005). HMQV: A high-performance secure Diffie–Hellman protocol. In *CRYPTO 2005*, vol. 3621 of *LNCS*, Shoup, V. (ed.). Springer, Heidelberg.

Krawczyk, H. (2010). Cryptographic extraction and key derivation: The HKDF scheme. In *CRYPTO 2010*, vol. 6223 of *LNCS*, Rabin, T. (ed.). Springer, Heidelberg.

Kwon, T. (2001). Authentication and key agreement via memorable passwords. In *NDSS 2001*. The Internet Society, 8–9 February.

Lai, R.W.F., Egger, C., Schröder, D., Chow, S.S.M. (2017). Phoenix: Rebirth of a cryptographic password-hardening service. In *USENIX Security 2017*, Kirda, E., Ristenpart, T. (eds). USENIX Association.

Libert, B. and Yung, M. (2012). Non-interactive CCA-secure threshold cryptosystems with adaptive security: New framework and constructions. In *TCC 2012*, vol. 7194 of *LNCS*, Cramer, R. (ed.). Springer, Heidelberg.

Lucks, S. (1998). Open key exchange: How to defeat dictionary attacks without encrypting public keys. In *Security Protocols: 5th International Workshop, Paris, France, April 7–9, 1997, Proceedings*, Christianson, B., Crispo, B., Lomas, M., Roe, M. (eds). Springer, Berlin, Heidelberg.

MacKenzie, P.D. (2001a). On the security of the SPEKE password-authenticated key exchange protocol. Cryptology ePrint Archive, Report 2001/057 [Online]. Available at: https://eprint.iacr.org/2001/057.

MacKenzie, P.D. (2001b). More efficient password-authenticated key exchange. In *CT-RSA 2001*, vol. 2020 of *LNCS*, Naccache, D. (ed.). Springer, Heidelberg.

MacKenzie, P.D. (2002). The PAK suite: Protocols for password-authenticated key exchange. DIMACS technical report, IEEE P1363.2.

MacKenzie, P.D., Patel, S., Swaminathan, R. (2000). Password-authenticated key exchange based on RSA. In *ASIACRYPT 2000*, vol. 1976 of *LNCS*, Okamoto, T. (ed.). Springer, Heidelberg.

MacKenzie, P.D., Shrimpton, T., Jakobsson, M. (2002). Threshold password-authenticated key exchange. In *CRYPTO 2002*, vol. 2442 of *LNCS*, Yung, M. (ed.). Springer, Heidelberg.

McQuoid, I., Rosulek, M., Roy, L. (2020). Minimal symmetric PAKE and 1-out-of-N OT from programmable-once public functions. In *ACM CCS 2020*, Ligatti, J., Ou, X., Katz, J., Vigna, G. (eds). ACM Press.

Micali, S. and Rogaway, P. (1992). Secure computation (abstract). In *CRYPTO'91*, vol. 576 of *LNCS*, Feigenbaum, J. (ed.). Springer, Heidelberg.

Naor, M. and Yung, M. (1990). Public-key cryptosystems provably secure against chosen ciphertext attacks. In *22nd ACM STOC*, Ortiz, H. (ed.). ACM Press.

Nguyen, M.-H. and Vadhan, S.P. (2004). Simpler session-key generation from short random passwords. In *TCC 2004*, vol. 2951 of *LNCS*, Naor, M. (ed.). Springer, Heidelberg.

Ostrovsky, R. and Yung, M. (1991). How to withstand mobile virus attacks (extended abstract). In *10th ACM PODC*, Logrippo, L. (ed.). ACM Press.

Paillier, P. (1999). Public-key cryptosystems based on composite degree residuosity classes. In *EUROCRYPT'99*, vol. 1592 of *LNCS*, Stern, J. (ed.). Springer, Heidelberg.

Park, S., Nam, J., Kim, S., Won, D. (2007). Efficient password-authenticated key exchange based on RSA. In *CT-RSA 2007*, vol. 4377 of *LNCS*, Abe, M. (ed.). Springer, Heidelberg.

Patel, S. (1997). Number theoretic attacks on secure password schemes. In *1997 IEEE Symposium on Security and Privacy*. IEEE Computer Society Press, 4–7 May.

Pointcheval, D. and Wang, G. (2017). VTBPEKE: Verifier-based two-basis password exponential key exchange. In *ASIACCS 17*, Karri, R., Sinanoglu, O., Sadeghi, A.-R., Yi, X. (eds). ACM Press.

Sahai, A. (1999). Non-malleable non-interactive zero knowledge and adaptive chosen-ciphertext security. In *40th FOCS*. IEEE Computer Society Press, 17–19 October.

Schneider, J., Fleischhacker, N., Schröder, D., Backes, M. (2016). Efficient cryptographic password hardening services from partially oblivious commitments. In *ACM CCS 2016*, Weippl, E.R., Katzenbeisser, S., Kruegel, C., Myers, A.C., Halevi, S. (eds). ACM Press.

Shoup, V. (1999). On formal models for secure key exchange. Cryptology ePrint Archive, Report 1999/012 [Online]. Available at: https://eprint.iacr.org/1999/012.

Shoup, V. (2020). Security analysis of SPAKE2+. In *TCC 2020, Part III*, vol. 12552 of *LNCS*, Pass, R., Pietrzak, K. (eds). Springer, Heidelberg.

Smyshlyaev, S.V. (2020). [cfrg] results of the pake selection process [Online]. Available at: https://mailarchive.ietf.org/arch/msg/cfrg/LKbwodpa5yXo6VuNDU66vtAca8/.

Steiner, M., Tsudik, G., Waidner, M. (1995). Refinement and extension of encrypted key exchange. *ACM SIGOPS Operating Systems Review*, 29(3), 22–30.

Szydlo, M. and Kaliski Jr., B.S. (2005). Proofs for two-server password authentication. In *CT-RSA 2005*, vol. 3376 of *LNCS*, Menezes, A. (ed.). Springer, Heidelberg.

Tibouchi, M. (2014). Elligator squared: Uniform points on elliptic curves of prime order as uniform random strings. In *FC 2014*, vol. 8437 of *LNCS*, Christin, N., Safavi-Naini, R. (eds). Springer, Heidelberg.

Trevisan, L. (2001). Extractors and pseudorandom generators. *J. ACM*, 48(4), 860–879.

Wong, D.S., Chan, A.H., Zhu, F. (2003). More efficient password authenticated key exchange based on RSA. In *INDOCRYPT 2003*, vol. 2904 of *LNCS*, Johansson, T., Maitra, S. (eds). Springer, Heidelberg.

Wu, T.D. (1998). The secure remote password protocol. In *NDSS'98*, Kent, S.T. (ed.). The Internet Society.

Yang, Y., Deng, R., Bao, F. (2006). A practical password-based two-server authentication and key exchange system. *IEEE Transactions on Dependable and Secure Computing*, 3, 105–114.

Yi, X., Hao, F., Chen, L., Liu, J.K. (2015). Practical threshold password-authenticated secret sharing protocol. In *ESORICS 2015, Part I*, vol. 9326 of *LNCS*, Pernul, G., Ryan, P.Y.A., Weippl, E.R. (eds). Springer, Heidelberg.

Zhang, M. (2004a). Further analysis of password authenticated key exchange protocol based on RSA for imbalanced wireless networks. In *ISC 2004*, vol. 3225 of *LNCS*, Zhang, K., Zheng, Y. (eds). Springer, Heidelberg.

Zhang, M. (2004b). New approaches to password authenticated key exchange based on RSA. In *ASIACRYPT 2004*, vol. 3329 of *LNCS*, Lee, P.J. (ed.). Springer, Heidelberg.

Zhang, M. (2004c). Password authenticated key exchange using quadratic residues. In *ACNS 04*, vol. 3089 of *LNCS*, Jakobsson, M., Yung, M., Zhou, J. (eds). Springer, Heidelberg.

Zhang, L., Zhang, Z., Hu, X. (2016). UC-secure two-server password-based authentication protocol and its applications. In *ASIACCS 16*, Chen, X., Wang, X., Huang, X. (eds). ACM Press.

Zhu, F., Wong, D.S., Chan, A.H., Ye, R. (2002). Password authenticated key exchange based on RSA for imbalanced wireless networks. In *ISC 2002*, vol. 2433 of *LNCS*, Chan, A.H., Gligor, V.D. (eds). Springer, Heidelberg.

11

Verifiable Computation and Succinct Arguments for NP

Dario FIORE
IMDEA Software Institute, Madrid, Spain

11.1. Introduction

Verifiable computation (VC) is a cryptographic notion that enables a client to delegate a computation to an untrusted server in a *secure* and *efficient* way.

In this context, "security" means that the client can be assured that the result received from the untrusted machine is correct; "efficiency" means that the computational resources needed by the client to run this protocol (including being convinced of the result's correctness) are significantly lower than those needed to execute the computation. In other words, efficiency ensures that delegating the computation using VC is cost effective for the client. In fact, if the efficiency requirement is dropped, then it is trivial to design a secure VC protocol: the client checks the result by simply re-executing the computation locally.

The simultaneous achievement of security and efficiency makes VC an intriguing notion that attracts interest from both the theory and the practice sides of computer science.

From a practical perspective, VC is particularly attractive for the potential of bringing security to Cloud computing, a paradigm in which clients rent computing resources from powerful external entities and that is widely adopted in the modern IT

Asymmetric Cryptography,
coordinated by David POINTCHEVAL. © ISTE Ltd. 2022.

infrastructures. From a theoretical perspective, VC goes hand in hand with the notions of interactive (and non-interactive) proofs and arguments (see Chapter 3), which are fundamental in theoretical computer science.

The goal of this chapter is to present the definition of VC, and to describe a construction of VC for computations expressible as polynomial-size arithmetic circuits.

Before turning to the details of VC, in the next section we provide background on VC and related notions, as well as a brief overview of the milestones in the literature about this notion.

11.1.1. *Background*

Interactive proofs (Goldwasser et al. 1985) are protocols in which a powerful prover can convince (in a probabilistic way) a weak verifier that a statement is true. In traditional interactive proofs (e.g. proving that *IP=PSPACE* (Lund et al. 1990; Shamir 1990)), this unbalance of computational resources considers superpolynomial-time provers and polynomial-time verifiers, which can be unsuitable in real-world scenarios where provers are supposed to be real machines that should run in polynomial time. Goldwasser et al. (2008) proposed an interactive proof (known as GKR in the literature) that works for polynomial-time provers and polylogarithmic verifiers, but that achieves this complexity only for specific classes of computations (e.g. those computable by a log-space-uniform *NC* boolean circuit).

Probabilistically checkable proofs (PCPs) (Arora and Safra 1992) are an evolution of interactive proofs in which a polynomial-time prover can produce a polynomial-size proof string that the verifier can check in only a few positions in order to be (probabilistically) convinced. However, PCPs do not, by themselves, constitute a VC protocol, as the verifier must receive the proof string, which may be too long to keep the verifier low cost.

To address this problem, Kilian proposed a protocol to turn PCPs into *succinct interactive arguments* that are secure against polynomial-time provers (Kilian 1992). The idea of Kilian's protocol is that the prover first sends a commitment of the PCP string using a Merkle tree (or, more generally, using a vector commitment (Catalano and Fiore 2013; Lai and Malavolta 2019)) and then opens only the positions of the proof selected by the verifier and proves (by giving Merkle tree authentication paths) that they are indeed the values at the requested positions in the committed string. This approach can also be made non-interactive in the random oracle model by using Micali's computationally sound (CS) proofs (Micali 1994).

A completely different approach to VC was proposed by Gennaro et al. (2010) who defined the notion of *non-interactive VC* and proposed a construction based on fully homomorphic encryption (Gentry 2009) and garbled circuits (Yao 1982). Notably, the scheme of Gennaro et al. can also ensure the confidentiality of the computation's inputs against the server and, in contrast to CS proofs and the GKR protocol, is non-interactive without the need of random oracles. The VC of Gennaro et al. (2010) works in a model where the client who delegates and verifies computations uses a secret key. Parno et al. (2012) introduced a model where, after a trusted preprocessing, everyone can delegate and verify using only public information. This notion is called *public VC*, and Parno et al. (2012) proposed a construction of it based on attribute-based encryption.

Finally, another approach to (non-interactive) VC is that based on succinct non-interactive arguments (SNARGs) for NP (e.g. Parno et al. 2013). SNARGs for NP are essentially VC protocols for non-deterministic computation, that is, to prove that $\exists w : C(x, w) = y$, and basically further formalize the notion of CS proofs proposed by Micali. However, while Micali's construction was specifically relying on the random oracle heuristic by using the Fiat–Shamir transform, SNARGs may be secure in the standard model, albeit under strong cryptographic assumptions. Indeed, in a celebrated work, Gentry and Wichs (2011) proved that SNARGs are likely to require non-falsifiable assumptions, namely assumptions in which it may not be efficient to decide whether an adversary won or not.

Constructing SNARGs is a prolific research area that has produced many protocols whose efficiency was significantly advanced. Notably, some of these protocols have been implemented and deployed in real-world systems (e.g. Zcash[1]). It is not the goal of this chapter to present an exhaustive survey of the state of the art of SNARGs. We rather focus on presenting a construction of VC based on SNARGs and in particular on the quadratic arithmetic programs (QAPs) techniques of Gennaro et al. (2013).

11.2. Preliminaries

NOTATION. We denote by $\lambda \in \mathbb{N}$ the security parameter, and by $\mathsf{poly}(\lambda)$ and $\mathsf{negl}(\lambda)$ the set of polynomial and negligible functions, respectively. A function $\varepsilon(\lambda)$ is said to be *negligible*, denoted $\varepsilon(\lambda) = \mathsf{negl}(\lambda)$, if $\varepsilon(\lambda)$ vanishes faster than the inverse of any polynomial in λ. An algorithm is called PPT if it can be modeled as a Turing machine running in probabilistic polynomial time.

For a positive integer $n \in \mathbb{N}$, we denote by $[n]$ the set $\{1, \ldots, n\}$. For a set S, $|S|$ denotes its cardinality, and $x \leftarrow_\$ S$ denotes the process of selecting x uniformly at random over S. We write matrices in boldface font, for example, $\mathbf{V}$. So for a set S, $\vec{v} \in S^n$ is a short-hand for the tuple $(v_1, \ldots, v_n)$. Given two vectors $\vec{u}$ and $\vec{v}$, we denote by $\vec{u} \circ \vec{v}$ their entry-wise (also known as Hadamard) product.

---

1 Available at: https://z.cash.

We denote by $\mathbb{F}$ a finite field and by $\mathbb{F}[X_1, \ldots, X_\mu]$ the ring of μ-variate polynomials in variables $\vec{X} = X_1, \ldots, X_\mu$.

11.3. Verifiable computation

The goal of this section is to present a formal definition of a non-interactive VC scheme. In brief, a VC scheme consists of a collection of algorithms because of which a client can outsource the computation of a function f to an untrusted machine, in such a way that the client can verify the correctness of the result returned by this machine. To make the outsourcing profitable, it is a crucial requirement that the cost of verification must be for the client cheaper than computing the function by itself. As introduced in the original formalization of Gennaro et al. (2010), it can be enough that such efficiency requirement holds in an amortized sense. Namely, the client may perform a one-time preprocessing whose cost is proportional to that of running the function, but afterwards delegating the computation on a specific input and verifying the result must be considerably cheaper than running the function locally. It is worth noting that in VC the verifier must know the computation that it wants to check and, at least, must read its description. In some models of computation, such as circuits, reading the description can be as costly as performing the computation. Hence, in this case the adoption of the amortized preprocessing model can also be necessary to make VC meaningful.

Gennaro et al. (2010) formalized VC in a model where the client who delegates and verifies computations uses a secret key. Parno et al. (2012) introduced a model where, after a trusted preprocessing, everyone can delegate and verify using only public information. This model, called *public verifiable computation*, is the one that we adopt in this work. For simplicity, in the rest of this chapter, when we refer to VC we mean public VC.

We present below the formal definition.

DEFINITION 11.1 (VC).– *Let $\mathcal{F}$ be a family of functions. A public VC scheme VC for $\mathcal{F}$ is defined by the following algorithms:*

– $\mathsf{KGen}(1^\lambda, f) \rightarrow (pk_f, ek_f)$: *On input the security parameter λ and a function $f \in \mathcal{F}$, it produces a public key pk_f to be used for input delegation and for verification, and a public evaluation key ek_f which is handed to the server to delegate the computation of f.*

– $\mathsf{ProbGen}(pk_f, x) \rightarrow (\sigma_x, vk_x)$: *Given an input x, the problem generation algorithm is run by the delegator to produce an encoding σ_x of x, together with a public verification key vk_x.*

– $\mathsf{Compute}(ek_f, \sigma_x) \rightarrow \sigma_y$: *Given the evaluation key ek_f and an encoded input σ_x, this algorithm is run by the server to compute an encoded output σ_y for $y = f(x)$.*

– $\mathsf{Verify}(pk_f, vk_x, \sigma_y) \to y \cup \perp$: *On input of the public key* pk_f, *the verification key* vk_x *and an encoded output* σ_y, *this algorithm returns a value* y *or an error* $\perp$.

A VC scheme is required to satisfy the properties of correctness, security *and* outsourceability *that are defined below.*

CORRECTNESS. *Informally, a VC scheme* VC *is* correct *if the values generated by the problem generation algorithm allow a honest server to output values that will verify correctly. More formally, for any* $f \in \mathcal{F}$, *any* $(\mathsf{pk}_f, \mathsf{ek}_f) \leftarrow_\$ \mathsf{KGen}(1^\lambda, f)$, *any* $x \in \mathsf{Dom}(f)$, *if* $(\sigma_x, \mathsf{vk}_x) \leftarrow_\$ \mathsf{ProbGen}(\mathsf{pk}_f, x)$ *and* $\sigma_y \leftarrow \mathsf{Compute}(\mathsf{ek}_f, \sigma_x)$, *then* $f(x) \leftarrow \mathsf{Verify}(\mathsf{pk}_f, \mathsf{vk}_x, \sigma_y)$ *holds with all but negligible probability.*

SECURITY. *A public VC scheme* VC *is* secure *for* $\mathcal{F}$ *if for any* $f \in \mathcal{F}$, *and any PPT* $\mathcal{A}$ *it holds that* $\Pr[\mathbf{Exp}_{\mathsf{VC},\mathcal{A}}^{VC\text{-}sec}(\lambda, f) = 1] = \mathsf{negl}(\lambda)$. *where the experiment* $\mathbf{Exp}_{\mathsf{VC},\mathcal{A}}^{VC\text{-}sec}(\lambda, f)$ *is defined below.*

$\mathbf{Exp}_{\mathsf{VC},\mathcal{A}}^{VC\text{-}sec}(\lambda, f)$

$(\mathsf{pk}_f, \mathsf{ek}_f) \leftarrow_\$ \mathsf{KGen}(1^\lambda, f)$

$(x^*, \mathsf{st}) \leftarrow \mathcal{A}(\mathsf{pk}_f, \mathsf{ek}_f)$

$(\sigma_x^*, \mathsf{vk}_x^*) \leftarrow \mathsf{ProbGen}(\mathsf{pk}_f, x^*)$

$\sigma_y^* \leftarrow \mathcal{A}(\mathsf{st}, \sigma_x^*, \mathsf{vk}_x^*)$

$y^* \leftarrow \mathsf{Verify}(\mathsf{pk}_f, \mathsf{vk}_x^*, \sigma_y^*)$

if $y^* \neq \perp \wedge y^* \neq f(x^*)$ **return** 1

else return 0

OUTSOURCEABILITY. VC *is* outsourceable *if the time needed to run* ProbGen *and* Verify *is (asymptotically) sub-linear in the time needed to compute* $f(x)$.

11.4. Constructing VC

After having defined the notion of VC, the rest of this chapter focuses on showing how to construct a VC scheme for an important class of computations that are arithmetic circuits of polynomial size.

In the next section, we provide an overview of our construction approach, which is obtained by combining three main steps in a modular way.

11.4.1. *VC for circuits in three steps*

Among the multiple existing approaches to construct VC schemes, in this work we choose to present the one based on SNARGs for NP, a notion that is rather close to (but much stronger and more powerful[2] than) that of VC. In fact, a SNARG can be seen as a VC for non-deterministic computations, that is, to prove that, for a public function f, input x and output y, there exists w such that $y = f(x, w)$. It is clear that constructing a VC from a SNARG is straightforward. It is instead more interesting to see how to build a SNARG, and our chapter is mostly devoted to this task.

Our choice to present a SNARG-based VC construction is due to the efficiency of this approach and the popularity of the techniques that in the past years have given rise to rich lines of work.

We show how to obtain a VC for circuits in three main steps; a summary of this approach is shown in Figure 11.1.

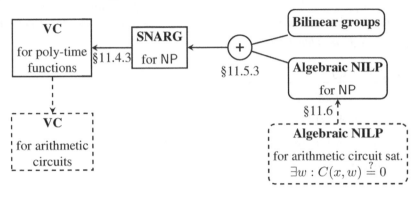

Figure 11.1. *Modular approach to construct VC for arithmetic circuits*

First, we present the notion of SNARGs and show how any SNARG for NP can be used to build a VC for polynomial time functions (*see* section 11.4.3).

Second, we show how to construct a SNARG for NP by compiling, using bilinear groups, an information theoretic primitive called *algebraic non-interactive linear proofs* (NILP). We show the security of this compiler in the algebraic group model (AGM) (Fuchsbauer et al. 2018) under a q-type generalization of the discrete logarithm assumption. This compiler is a small revisitation of a generic modular construction by Bitansky et al. (2013).

Third, we present a construction of an algebraic NILP for the NP-complete language of arithmetic circuit satisfiability. This step is based on abstracting away the

---

2 As shown by Gentry and Wichs (2011), SNARGs are likely to require strong non-falsifiable assumptions, whereas VC can be built from rather standard assumptions, see e.g. Gennaro et al. (2010); Parno et al. (2012).

Pinocchio SNARG (Parno et al. 2013), which in turn relies on the celebrated QAPs of Gennaro et al. (2013).

By combining together these three steps, we obtain a VC scheme for arithmetic circuits that is secure under a strengthening of the discrete logarithm assumption in the AGM.

11.4.2. Succinct non-interactive arguments for non-deterministic computation

To define SNARGs, we begin by recalling the notion of NP relation.

DEFINITION 11.2 (NP Relations).– *Let* $R : \{0,1\}^* \times \{0,1\}^* \to \{\text{true}, \text{false}\}$ *and let* $\mathcal{L}_R := \{x : \exists w \, R(x,w) = \text{true}\}$ *be the language associated with* R. *We say that* R *is an* NP *relation, and thus* $\mathcal{L}_R \in$ NP, *if* R *is computable in deterministic polynomial time.*

A succinct non-interactive argument is defined as follows.

DEFINITION 11.3 (SNARGs).– *Let* $\mathcal{R}$ *be a family of relations. A succinct non-interactive argument (SNARG)* Π *for* $\mathcal{R}$ *is a triple of algorithms* (Setup, P, V) *such that:*

– Setup$(1^\lambda, R) \to$ crs: *It is a probabilistic algorithm that, on input the security parameter and a relation* $R \in \mathcal{R}$, *generates a common reference string* crs.

– P(crs, R, x, w) → π: *The probabilistic prover algorithm, on input a common reference string and a triple* (R, x, w) *such that* R(x, w) = true, *generates a proof* π.

– V(crs, x, π) → $b \in \{0,1\}$: *The deterministic verification algorithm takes as input a common reference string, a statement x and a proof π, and returns a bit $b \in \{0,1\}$ such that $b = 1$ indicates "accept" and $b = 0$ indicates "reject".*

Π = (Setup, P, V) *is a SNARG if it satisfies the correctness, soundness and succinctness properties defined below.*

CORRECTNESS. Π *is* correct *if for any* $R \in \mathcal{R}$ *and any* (x, w) *such that* R(x, w) = true *it holds*

$$\Pr\left[V(\text{crs}, x, \pi) = 1 \;\middle|\; \begin{array}{l} \text{crs} \leftarrow \text{Setup}(1^\lambda, R) \\ \pi \leftarrow P(\text{crs}, x, w) \end{array}\right] = 1$$

SOUNDNESS. Π *is* sound *if for any* $R \in \mathcal{R}$ *and any PPT* $\mathcal{A}$ *it holds that*

$$\Pr\left[\begin{array}{l} V(\text{crs}, x, \pi) = 1 \\ \wedge x \notin \mathcal{L}_R \end{array} \;\middle|\; \begin{array}{l} \text{crs} \leftarrow \text{Setup}(1^\lambda, R) \\ (x, \pi) \leftarrow \mathcal{A}(\text{crs}) \end{array}\right] = \text{negl}(\lambda)$$

SUCCINCTNESS. Π *is succinct if there exists a fixed polynomial* $p(\lambda) = \text{poly}(\lambda)$ *such that the running time of* V *is bounded by* $p(\lambda + |x| + \log|w|)$ *and the size of* π *is bounded by* $p(\lambda + \log|w|)$.

Precisely, the definition given above is that of a *preprocessing* SNARG. A "regular", non-preprocessing, SNARG is one where Setup must run in time $\text{poly}(\lambda + \log T)$ where T is a bound on the time needed to evaluate the relation R.

11.4.3. *Verifiable computation from SNARG*

Given a SNARG for an NP-complete language one can immediately build a VC scheme. The construction is based on the idea that, given any function f computable in polynomial time, one can define an NP relation R_f that on input (x, y) outputs true iff $y = f(x)$. Then, the VC can be obtained by letting the Compute algorithm generate a SNARG proof for the NP statement $y = f(x)$.

For completeness, we give the formal construction in Figure 11.2 and state its properties in the following theorem.

THEOREM 11.1.– *If* Π *is a SNARG for* NP *(see definition 11.3), then the VC scheme described in Figure 11.2 is a VC for polynomial-time computations (see definition 11.1).*

We leave the proof of this theorem as an exercise. In brief, the completeness, security and outsourceability of the VC follow from, respectively, the completeness, soundness and succinctness of the SNARG.

11.5. A modular construction of SNARGs

Our next goal is showing how to build SNARGs. We find it instructive to present a construction that follows a modular approach based on combining two objects: (1) an information theoretic proof system working in an ideal abstract model and (2) a cryptographic component that turns the information-theoretic proof into an efficient computationally sound argument.

This modular approach has been adopted in several works. Here, we use specifically the one formalized by Bitansky et al. (2013) in which the information-theoretic proof is a *linear probabilistically checkable proof* (LPCP) and the cryptographic component is a linear-only encoding.

In a nutshell, an LPCP is a variant of classical PCPs in which the verifier's queries are linear functions of the proof, rather than queries that inspect a few symbols of the proof. In section 11.5.1, we define a special case of the LPCP notion, called non-interactive linear proofs (NILP), that is sufficient to build SNARGs.

$\mathsf{KGen}(1^\lambda, f)$

    $\mathsf{crs} \leftarrow \mathsf{Setup}(1^\lambda, \mathsf{R}_f)$

    $\mathbf{return}\ (\mathsf{pk}_f := \mathsf{crs}, \mathsf{ek}_f := \mathsf{crs}, f)$

$\mathsf{Compute}(\mathsf{ek}_f, \sigma_x)$

    $y \leftarrow f(x)$

    $\pi \leftarrow \mathsf{P}(\mathsf{crs}, (x, y), \emptyset)$

    $\mathbf{return}\ \sigma_y := (y, \pi)$

$\mathsf{ProbGen}(\mathsf{pk}_f, x)$

    $\mathbf{return}\ (\sigma_x := x, \mathsf{vk}_x := x)$

$\mathsf{Verify}(\mathsf{pk}_f, \mathsf{vk}_x, \sigma_y)$

    $b \leftarrow \mathsf{V}(\mathsf{crs}, (x, y), \pi)$

    $\mathbf{if}\ b = 1\ \mathbf{return}\ y$

    $\mathbf{else\ return}\ \bot$

Figure 11.2. *VC from SNARG*

A linear-only encoding Enc is instead a scheme that maps elements m of a finite ring into encodings E that are linearly-homomorphic – $E_1 + E_2 \in Enc(m_1 + m_2)$ – and no more than that. Namely, it is computationally hard to compute, say, multiplications of encoded elements, for example, to obtain $E \in Enc(m_1 \cdot m_2)$. At the same time, this encoding must allow one to test quadratic equations over encoded elements (e.g. if the messages m_1, m_2, m_3 encoded in E_1, E_2, E_3 are such that $m_1 \cdot m_2 = m_3$).

A popular instantiation of this linear-only encoding notion are bilinear groups: given a generator g, $Enc(m)$ is g^m and the quadratic test can be implemented using the pairing function. The security assumption that this encoding is linear-only can be reduced to specific computational assumptions in bilinear groups, or in general to hardness in the generic group model (Shoup 1997). Another instantiation can be obtained by using linearly homomorphic encryption and making some conjectures on the hardness of computing more than linear functions over its ciphertexts. This idea of using encoding that are linear-only-homomorphic was first suggested by Gennaro et al. (2013) and later fully characterized by Bitansky et al. (2013). In this work, we present directly the instantiation based on bilinear groups.

11.5.1. *Algebraic non-interactive linear proofs*

A *non-interactive linear proof* (NILP) is an information-theoretic proof system in which the prover generates a proof which is a matrix $\boldsymbol{\Pi}$; the verifier can "query" the proof by sending a vector $\vec{q}$ and obtaining the answer $\vec{\alpha} = \boldsymbol{\Pi} \cdot \vec{q}$ (see Figure 11.3).

Additionally, an NILP is called a (d_Q, d_D)-*algebraic NILP* if the verifier's query and decision algorithms can be computed with arithmetic circuits of degree d_Q and d_D, respectively.

We stress that an NILP works in an ideal abstract model in which, even in the soundness experiment, the answer is honestly computed from the matrix $\mathbf{\Pi}$. In the soundness game, however, $\mathbf{\Pi}$ may be generated by a dishonest prover.

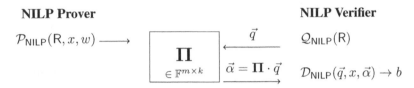

NILP Prover   **NILP Verifier**

$\mathcal{P}_{\mathsf{NILP}}(\mathsf{R}, x, w) \longrightarrow$ $\overset{\vec{q}}{\longleftarrow}$ $\mathcal{Q}_{\mathsf{NILP}}(\mathsf{R})$

$\mathbf{\Pi}$ $\vec{\alpha} = \mathbf{\Pi} \cdot \vec{q}$ $\mathcal{D}_{\mathsf{NILP}}(\vec{q}, x, \vec{\alpha}) \to b$

$\in \mathbb{F}^{m \times k}$ $\overset{\vec{\alpha} = \mathbf{\Pi} \cdot \vec{q}}{\longrightarrow}$

Figure 11.3. *Algebraic NILPs*

DEFINITION 11.4 (Algebraic NILPs).– *Let $\mathcal{R} = \{\mathsf{R}_i\}_i$ be a family of relations and $\mathbb{F}$ be a finite field. A (d_Q, d_D)-algebraic NILP for $\mathcal{R}$ over $\mathbb{F}$ consists of three algorithms working as follows:*

– *$\mathcal{P}_{\mathsf{NILP}}(\mathsf{R}, x, w) \to \mathbf{\Pi}$: The probabilistic prover algorithm, on input a relation $\mathsf{R} \in \mathcal{R}$ and a pair (x, w) such that $\mathsf{R}(x, w) = $ true, outputs a proof consisting of a matrix $\mathbf{\Pi} \in \mathbb{F}^{k \times m}$.*

– *$\mathcal{Q}_{\mathsf{NILP}}(\mathsf{R}) \to \vec{q}$: The probabilistic query algorithm takes as input a relation $\mathsf{R} \in \mathcal{R}$ and consists of two steps:*

1) generate (deterministically) a vector $\vec{p}(\vec{X}) \leftarrow \mathcal{Q}_{\mathsf{NILP}}^{poly}(\mathsf{R})$ of m μ-variate polynomials $\vec{p}(\vec{X}) \in \mathbb{F}[\vec{X}]^m$ of degree $\leq d_Q$;

2) sample a random point $\vec{s} \leftarrow_\$ \mathbb{F}^\mu$, compute $\vec{q} \leftarrow \vec{p}(\vec{s})$ and return $\vec{q}$. For simplicity, we assume that $\vec{q}$ always contains an entry 1; this way we do not have to distinguish between affine and linear (adversarial) prover strategies. The query answers are computed as $\vec{\alpha} = \mathbf{\Pi} \cdot \vec{q}$.

– *$\mathcal{D}_{\mathsf{NILP}}(\vec{q}, x, \vec{\alpha}) \to 0, 1$: The deterministic decision algorithm outputs 1 (accept) or 0 (reject) and consists of two steps:*

1) Run $t_1(\vec{Z}), \ldots, t_\eta(\vec{Z}) \leftarrow \mathsf{Test}(\mathsf{R}, x)$ to obtain η polynomials $\{t_i : \mathbb{F}^{m+k} \to \mathbb{F}\}_i$ of degree $\leq d_D$;

2) Return 1 if and only if $\forall i \in [\eta] : t_i(\vec{q}, \vec{\alpha}) = 0$.

COMPLETENESS. *An algebraic NILP for a family $\mathcal{R}$ is perfectly* complete *if for every $\mathsf{R} \in \mathcal{R}$, $(x, w) \in \mathsf{R}$, all $\vec{q} \leftarrow \mathcal{Q}_{\mathsf{NILP}}(\mathsf{R})$, $\mathbf{\Pi} \leftarrow \mathcal{P}_{\mathsf{NILP}}(\mathsf{R}, x, w)$, we have $\mathcal{D}_{\mathsf{NILP}}(\vec{q}, x, \mathbf{\Pi} \cdot \vec{q}) = 1$.*

SOUNDNESS. *An algebraic NILP is* sound *if for every relation* $R \in \mathcal{R}$, *any* $x \notin \mathcal{L}_R$ *and any proof matrix* $\Pi^* \in \mathbb{F}^{k \times m}$, *we have that for* $\vec{p}(\vec{X}) \leftarrow \mathcal{Q}_{\mathsf{NILP}}^{poly}(R)$ *and* $t_1, \ldots, t_\eta \leftarrow$ $\mathsf{Test}(R, x)$ *there is at least an index* $i \in [\eta]$ *such that* $t_i(\vec{p}(\vec{X}), \Pi^* \cdot \vec{p}(\vec{X}))$ *is non-zero over* $\mathbb{F}[\vec{X}]$.

The above notion of soundness is defined to hold perfectly for the deterministic version of the algebraic query of the verifier. Using the commonly known Schwartz (1980) and Zippel (1979), the notion above implies $(d_Q \cdot d_D / |\mathbb{F}|)$-statistical soundness for the full probabilistic version of the verifier's query. Namely, it guarantees that, over the random coins of $\mathcal{Q}_{\mathsf{NILP}}$ (i.e. over the choice of $\vec{s} \leftarrow_\$ \mathbb{F}^\mu$), for any $x \notin \mathcal{L}_R$ and any proof matrix $\Pi^* \in \mathbb{F}^{k \times m}$ it holds $\Pr[\mathcal{D}_{\mathsf{NILP}}(\vec{p}(\vec{s}), x, \Pi^* \cdot \vec{p}(\vec{s})) = 1] \leq (d_Q \cdot d_D) / |\mathbb{F}|$.

The notion of algebraic NILP presented above is quite similar to the notion of algebraic, input-oblivious, two-message linear interactive proofs introduced by Bitansky et al. (2013). The main difference in the syntax is that in the LIP notion the proof is supposed to be a single linear function, that is, a vector $\vec{\pi}$, and the verifier makes more linear queries, that is, the query is a matrix.

11.5.2. *Bilinear groups*

A general introduction to pairings has been presented in Chapter 5; we briefly precise here our notations. A *bilinear group generator* $\mathcal{BG}(1^\lambda)$ outputs $(p, \mathbb{G}_1, \mathbb{G}_2, \mathbb{G}_T, e)$, where $\mathbb{G}_1$, $\mathbb{G}_2$, $\mathbb{G}_T$ are additive groups of prime order q, and $e : \mathbb{G}_1 \times \mathbb{G}_2 \to \mathbb{G}_T$ is an efficiently computable, non-degenerate, bilinear map. We use the bracket notation of Escala et al. (2013), that is, for $s \in \{1, 2, T\}$ and $a \in \mathbb{Z}_q$, we write $[a]_s$ to denote $a \cdot g_s \in \mathbb{G}_s$, where g_s is a fixed generator of $\mathbb{G}_s$. From an element $[a]_s \in \mathbb{G}_s$ and a scalar b, it is possible to efficiently compute $[ab] \in \mathbb{G}_s$. Also, given elements $[a]_1 \in \mathbb{G}_1$ and $[b]_2 \in \mathbb{G}_2$, one can efficiently compute $[a \cdot b]_T$ by using the pairing $e([a]_1, [b]_2)$, that we compactly denote with $[a]_1 \cdot [b]_2$. Using these properties, we observe that it is possible to evaluate a quadratic polynomial f over two vectors of elements $([\vec{a}]_1, [\vec{b}]_2)$ and obtain its result in the target group, that is, $[f(\vec{a}, \vec{b})]_T$ – by abusing notation we denote this operation by $f([\vec{a}]_1, [\vec{b}]_2)$. Although it may not be efficient to extract the result $f(\vec{a}, \vec{b})$ from the encoding $[f(\vec{a}, \vec{b})]_T$, one can efficiently check if the result is 0. In our compiler, we make use of the latter property. In addition, for simplicity of presentation, in this work we use Type-1, also known as symmetric, pairings where $\mathbb{G}_1 = \mathbb{G}_2$, denoted with $\mathbb{G}$.

In the next sections, we explain the AGM of Fuchsbauer et al. (2018), which formalizes the notion of algebraic adversaries in security reductions, and then we state the computational assumptions needed for our SNARG construction.

11.5.2.1. *Algebraic group model*

Consider a group $\mathbb{G}$ of prime order p. An *algebraic security game* is an experiment where one distinguishes between elements of the group $\mathbb{G}$ and all other elements which do not depend on the group elements. An *algebraic algorithm* that is executed in an algebraic game is an algorithm that, for any group element $h \in \mathbb{G}$ that it outputs, it also returns an "algebraic explanation" of h relative to all the previously received elements. Namely, if $\mathcal{A}$ is executed in an algebraic game where it receives as input a vector of group elements $[\vec{v}]$ and outputs h, then $\mathcal{A}$ additionally outputs a vector $\vec{z}_h \in \mathbb{Z}_p$ such that $h = \vec{z}_h^{\top} \cdot [\vec{v}]$.

Proving that a cryptographic scheme reduces to a certain assumption in the algebraic group model means that any algebraic adversary against the security of the scheme can be transformed into an algebraic adversary against the assumption with a polynomially related running time and success probability.

11.5.2.2. *Computational assumptions*

We define a stronger variant of the discrete logarithm assumption in bilinear groups. The standard discrete logarithm problem, for a fixed generator $g = [1]$, asks to extract s from $[s]$. The power discrete logarithm problem, first formalized by Lipmaa (2012), is a generalization in which the adversary additionally receives $[s^2, \ldots, s^d]$ for some $d = \mathrm{poly}(\lambda)$.

DEFINITION 11.5 (*d*-PDL Assumption).– *Let* $\mathcal{BG}$ *be a bilinear group generator and let* $d \in \mathbb{N}$ *be a positive integer. We say that the* d-power discrete logarithm assumption (*d*-PDL) *holds in* $\mathcal{BG}$ *if for every PPT* $\mathcal{A}$

$$\Pr\left[s^* = s \;\middle|\; \begin{array}{l} \mathsf{bgp} := (p, \mathbb{G}, \mathbb{G}_T, e) \leftarrow \mathcal{BG}(1^\lambda), \; s \leftarrow_{\!\$} \mathbb{Z}_p \\ s^* \leftarrow \mathcal{A}(\mathsf{bgp}, [1, s, s^2, \ldots, s^d]) \end{array} \right] = \mathsf{negl}(\lambda)$$

More precisely, we prove security of our SNARG under the following assumption, which Bitansky et al. (2013) showed to reduce to the PDL assumption above.[3]

DEFINITION 11.6 ((d, μ)-MPDL Assumption).– *Let* $\mathcal{BG}$ *be a bilinear group generator and let* $d \in \mathbb{N}$ *be a positive integer, and let* $p_1(\vec{X}), \ldots, p_n(\vec{X}) \in \mathbb{Z}_p[\vec{X}]$ *be* μ-variate polynomials of total degree at most d. We say that the (d, μ)-multivariate power discrete logarithm assumption ((d, μ)-MPDL) holds for $\mathcal{BG}$ if for every PPT $\mathcal{A}$

$$\Pr\left[\begin{array}{l} p^*(\vec{X}) \neq 0 \\ \wedge \; p^*(\vec{s}) = 0 \end{array} \;\middle|\; \begin{array}{l} \mathsf{bgp} := (p, \mathbb{G}, \mathbb{G}_T, e) \leftarrow \mathcal{BG}(1^\lambda), \; \vec{s} \leftarrow_{\!\$} \mathbb{Z}_p^\mu \\ p^* \leftarrow \mathcal{A}(\mathsf{bgp}, [p_1(\vec{s}), \ldots, p_n(\vec{s})]) \end{array} \right] = \mathsf{negl}(\lambda)$$

LEMMA 11.1 (Bitansky et al. 2013, Proposition 5.15).– *If the d-PDL assumption holds for* $\mathcal{BG}$, *then so does the* (d, μ)-MPDL *assumption for any* $\mu = \mathrm{poly}(\lambda)$.

---

3 Bitansky et al. state these assumptions for the more general notion of linear-only encodings, of which the bilinear group setting presented here is a special case instantiation.

Setup(1^λ, R)	P(crs, R, x, w)	V(crs, x, π)
$(p, \mathbb{G}, \mathbb{G}_T, e) \leftarrow \mathcal{BG}(1^\lambda)$	$\mathbf{\Pi} \leftarrow \mathcal{P}_{\mathsf{NILP}}(\mathsf{R}, x, w)$	$t_1, \ldots, t_\eta \leftarrow \mathsf{Test}(\mathsf{R}, x)$
$\mathbb{F} \leftarrow \mathbb{Z}_p$	$[\vec{\alpha}] := \mathbf{\Pi} \cdot [\vec{q}]$	$\mathbf{return}\ 1\ \text{iff}\ \forall i \in [\eta]:$
$\vec{q} \leftarrow_{\$} \mathcal{Q}_{\mathsf{NILP}}(\mathsf{R})$	$\mathbf{return}\ \pi := [\vec{\alpha}]$	$t_i([\vec{q}], [\vec{\alpha}]) = [0]_T$
$\mathbf{return}\ \mathsf{crs} := [\vec{q}]$		

Figure 11.4. *Generic SNARG in symmetric bilinear groups from a degree-2 NILP.*

11.5.3. *SNARGs from algebraic NILPs with degree-2 verifiers using bilinear groups*

In this section, we present how to convert a $(d_Q, 2)$-algebraic NILP for a family of relations $\mathcal{R}$ into a SNARG for $\mathcal{R}$. The construction uses bilinear groups.

Let $\mathcal{BG}$ be a generator for bilinear groups of prime order p, and let $(\mathcal{P}_{\mathsf{NILP}}, \mathcal{Q}_{\mathsf{NILP}}, \mathcal{D}_{\mathsf{NILP}})$ be a $(d_Q, 2)$-algebraic NILP for a family of relations $\mathcal{R}$ over the finite field $\mathbb{F} := \mathbb{Z}_p$.

We present the construction of a SNARG for $\mathcal{R}$ in Figure 11.4. For simplicity, we give the construction using symmetric pairings.

The correctness of the SNARG construction follows immediately from that of the NILP, using the fact that the bilinear groups have order p and that the pairing allows one to compute a quadratic polynomial over the discrete logarithms of group elements, and to test if it evaluates to 0.

11.5.3.1. *Efficiency analysis*

We briefly mention how some efficiency measures of the NILP translate into the efficiency of the SNARG. The CRS size corresponds to the size of the NILP query: for a NILP with a query vector of length m we obtain a SNARG where the CRS has m elements of $\mathbb{G}$. The prover complexity is at most $m \cdot k$ group multiplications. The proof size is k elements of $\mathbb{G}$, where k are the number of rows of the NILP proof matrix. The complexity of the verifier depends on the sparsity of the t_i polynomials generated by the NILP algorithm $\mathsf{Test}(\mathsf{R}, x)$. Indeed, a dense t_i would need to touch many elements of $\vec{q}$. Hence, in order for the SNARG to be *succinct* the NILP must be such that k, η and the number of nonzero monomials in all the t_i polynomials are at most polylogarithmic in the size of the witnesses for R.

This analysis suggests that in order to improve the efficiency of SNARG constructions one may focus on improving specific efficiency aspects of algebraic NILPs.

11.5.3.2. *Proof of soundness*

THEOREM 11.2.– *Let* $(\mathcal{P}_{\text{NILP}}, \mathcal{Q}_{\text{NILP}}, \mathcal{D}_{\text{NILP}})$ *be a* $(d_Q, 2)$-*Algebraic NILP. If* $\mathcal{BG}$ *is a bilinear group generators where the* (d_Q, μ)-*MPDL assumption holds, then the SNARG of Figure 11.4 is sound in the algebraic group model.*

Proof. We show how to convert an algebraic adversary $\mathcal{A}$ against the soundness of the SNARG into an algebraic adversary $\mathcal{B}$ against the MPDL assumption.

Let $R \in \mathcal{R}$ be the relation for which $\mathcal{A}$ is supposed to break soundness, and let $(p_1(\vec{X}), \ldots, p_m(\vec{X}) \leftarrow \mathcal{Q}_{\text{NILP}}^{poly}(R)$ be the m polynomials obtained through the deterministic $\mathcal{Q}_{\text{NILP}}^{poly}$ algorithm. We consider an instantiation of the MPDL assumption where $p_1(\vec{X}), \ldots, p_m(\vec{X})$ are the m polynomials in μ variables and total degree d_Q.

So, our adversary $\mathcal{B}$ runs on input $(p_1(\vec{s}), \ldots, p_m(\vec{s})) \in \mathbb{G}^n$ for a random $\vec{s} \leftarrow_\$ \mathbb{F}^\mu$ and proceeds as follows.

It sets $\text{crs} := [\vec{q}] = [\vec{p}(\vec{s})]$ and then runs the SNARG adversary $(x, [\vec{\alpha}]) \leftarrow \mathcal{A}(\text{crs})$. By the AGM assumption, $\mathcal{A}$ is algebraic and thus it also returns a matrix $\mathbf{\Pi}^*$ such that $[\vec{\alpha}] = \mathbf{\Pi}^* \cdot [\vec{q}]$.

Next $\mathcal{B}$ generates $t_1, \ldots, t_\eta \leftarrow \text{Test}(R, x)$, looks for an index $i \in [\eta]$ such that

$$\tau_i(\vec{X}) := t_i(\vec{p}(\vec{X}), \mathbf{\Pi}^* \cdot \vec{p}(\vec{X})) \neq 0$$

and returns $\tau_i(\vec{X})$.

We show that if $\mathcal{A}$ breaks soundness with probability ϵ, then $\mathcal{B}$ breaks the MPDL assumption with the same probability.

If $\mathcal{A}$ breaks soundness, then $(x, [\vec{\alpha}])$ is such that $x \notin \mathcal{L}_R$ and $V(\text{crs}, x, [\alpha]) = 1$. By the soundness notion of the algebraic NILP , if $x \notin \mathcal{L}_R$, then for any prover strategy $\mathbf{\Pi}^*$ there is an index $i \in [\eta]$ such that $t_i(\vec{p}(\vec{X}), \mathbf{\Pi}^* \cdot \vec{p}(\vec{X}))$ is non-zero.

On the other hand, since the proof verifies we have that for all $i \in [\eta] : t_i([\vec{q}], [\vec{\alpha}]) = [0]_T$, and thus $\tau_i(\vec{s}) = 0$.

Therefore, $\mathcal{B}$ has found a non-zero polynomial $\tau_i(\vec{X})$ such that $\tau_i(\vec{s}) = 0$, that is, a solution to the MPDL assumption. $\qquad\square$

11.6. Constructing algebraic NILPs for arithmetic circuits

In this section, we present the last step that allows us to instantiate our generic construction of SNARGs (and thus of VC). Our goal is to obtain argument systems for proving the correct computation of arithmetic circuits. A bit more precisely, we consider non-deterministic computations, namely the prover wants to convince the verifier that there exists a value w, called the witness, such that $C(x, w) = y$

Following our modular approach, we show the construction of an algebraic NILP for arithmetic circuit satisfiability, which can be used to instantiate the generic SNARG construction of the previous section.

11.6.1. *Arithmetic circuits*

An arithmetic circuit over a field $\mathbb{F}$ and a set of variables $X_1, \ldots, X_n$ is a directed acyclic graph with the following properties. Each node is called a *gate*; gates with in-degree 0 are either *input* gates labeled with some variable X_i, or *constant* gates labeled with a field value $c \in \mathbb{F}$; gates with out-degree 0 are called *output* gates; gates with in-degree and out-degree greater than 0 are called *internal* gates. Without loss of generality, we consider arithmetic circuits with in-degree 2. There are two types of internal gates: *addition* and *multiplication* gates, which compute the sum and the product, respectively, of the two inputs.

DEFINITION 11.7 (Arithmetic Circuit Satisfiability).– *Let $\mathbb{F}$ be a finite field and C : $\mathbb{F}^{\ell_{in}} \times \mathbb{F}^{\ell_{wit}} \to \mathbb{F}^{\ell_{out}}$ be an arithmetic circuit. The arithmetic circuit satisfiability relation $R_C : (\mathbb{F}^{\ell_{in}} \times \mathbb{F}^{\ell_{out}}) \times \mathbb{F}^{\ell_{wit}} \to \{\text{true}, \text{false}\}$ is the relation that on input a tuple $((\vec{x}, \vec{y}), \vec{w})$ returns* true *if $C(\vec{x}, \vec{w}) = \vec{y}$ and* false *otherwise.*

11.6.2. *Quadratic arithmetic programs*

We present the notion of QAPs introduced by Gennaro et al. (2013).

DEFINITION 11.8 (QAP (Gennaro et al. 2013)).– *A QAP is a tuple $(\mathbb{F}, n, m, \ell, v(X), \vec{a}(X), \vec{b}(X), \vec{c}(X))$, where $\mathbb{F}$ is a finite field, $n, m, \ell \in \mathbb{N}$ are positive integers, $v(X)$ is a degree-n polynomial and $\vec{a}(X), \vec{b}(X), \vec{c}(X)$ are three vectors of m polynomials of degree $< n$. The QAP relation $R_{QAP} : \mathbb{F}^{\ell} \times \mathbb{F}^{m-\ell-1} \to \{\text{true}, \text{false}\}$ is the binary relation that on input $(\vec{x}, \vec{w})$ returns* true *if and only if*

$$\left(\sum_{j \in [m]} z_j \cdot a_j(X) \right) \cdot \left(\sum_{j \in [m]} z_j \cdot b_j(X) \right) = \left(\sum_{j \in [m]} z_j \cdot c_j(X) \right) \mod v(X)$$

where $\vec{z} := (1, \vec{x}, \vec{w})$.

Gennaro et al. (2013) proved how to encode arithmetic circuit satisfiability with a QAP. In what follows, we state and prove their result, which we believe is a nice example of how to arithmetize the checks of a circuit.

THEOREM 11.3.– *Let* $C : \mathbb{F}^{\ell_{in}} \times \mathbb{F}^{\ell_{wit}} \to \mathbb{F}^{\ell_{out}}$ *be an arithmetic circuit with* N *multiplication gates, and let* R_C *be the associated arithmetic circuit satisfiability relation. Then, there exists a QAP relation* $\mathsf{R}_{QAP} := (\mathbb{F}, n, m, \ell, v(X), \vec{a}(X),$ $\vec{b}(X), \vec{c}(X))$ *with* $n = \ell_{out} + N$, $m = \ell_{in} + \ell_{out} + N + 1$ *and* $\ell = \ell_{in} + \ell_{out}$, *such that:*

$$(\vec{x}, \vec{y}) \in \mathcal{L}_{\mathsf{R}_C} \text{ if and only if } \vec{x}' = (\vec{x}, \vec{y}) \in \mathcal{L}_{\mathsf{R}_{QAP}}.$$

Proof. In the proof, we show how to construct a QAP starting from the circuit C. By its construction, it can be seen that the QAP relation expresses the same language as R_C, that is, it accepts the same set of $(\vec{x}, \vec{y}) \in \mathbb{F}^{\ell_{in}} \times \mathbb{F}^{\ell_{out}}$ as the circuit C.

The idea is that the satisfiability of the circuit can be checked by verifying that there is an assignment of values for all the input, output and multiplication gates that is consistent with the circuit. More precisely, since inputs and outputs are public we need to show that there is a valid assignment of the internal gates. Let $\vec{w}' \in \mathbb{F}^N$ be the vector with such assignments and define $\vec{z} := (1, \vec{x}, \vec{y}, \vec{w}') \in \mathbb{F}^m$ as the vector that contains the values of the inputs, outputs and internal gates, in addition to the constant 1.

Let us fix $m = \ell_{in} + \ell_{out} + N + 1$ and $\ell = \ell_{in} + \ell_{out} + 1$ as in the theorem's statement, and let us partition the set $[m]$ into three sets: $I_{in} = \{2, \ldots, \ell_{in} + 1\}$, $I_{out} = \{\ell_{in} + 2, \ldots, \ell\}$ and $I_{mid} = \{\ell + 1, \ldots, m\}$.

Intuitively, we use the integers in I_{mid} to label all the N multiplication gates of the circuit C, and the integers in I_{in} (respectively, I_{out}) to label the ℓ_{in} (respectively, ℓ_{out}) input (respectively, output) gates.

Then, the consistency of all multiplication gates can be checked as:

$$\forall j \in I_{mid} : (\vec{A}_j^\top \cdot \vec{z}) \cdot (\vec{B}_j^\top \cdot \vec{z}) = z_j$$

where, for every $j \in I_{mid}$, $\vec{A}_j, \vec{B}_j$ are appropriate vectors that express the linear subcircuits for the left and input wires of the jth multiplication gate.

Next, we add constraints for the public outputs:

$$\forall j \in I_{out} : (\vec{A}_j^\top \cdot \vec{z}) \cdot (\vec{B}_j^\top \cdot \vec{z}) = z_j$$

where every $\vec{B}_j^\top = (1, 0, \ldots, 0)$. Since $z_1 = 1$, these constraints are checking that $\vec{A}_j^\top \cdot \vec{z} = z_j$, which ensures that each public output z_j is correctly obtained after computing a linear subcircuits, expressed by the vector $\vec{A}_j$, on outputs of multiplication gates. We note that this set of constraints could be avoided for circuits where every output gate is a multiplication gate.

At this point, we can put together all the constraints above in the form of three matrices $\mathbf{A}, \mathbf{B}, \mathbf{C} \in \mathbb{F}^{n \times m}$ that are defined as follows:

$$
\mathbf{A} = \begin{pmatrix} \vec{A}_{\ell_{in}+2}^\top \\ \vdots \\ \vec{A}_m^\top \end{pmatrix}, \quad \mathbf{B} = \begin{pmatrix} \vec{B}_{\ell_{in}+2}^\top \\ \vdots \\ \vec{B}_m^\top \end{pmatrix}, \quad \mathbf{C} = \begin{pmatrix} \vec{I}_{\ell_{in}+2} \\ \vdots \\ \vec{I}_m \end{pmatrix}
$$

where $\vec{I}_j \in \mathbb{F}^{1 \times m}$ is the jth row of the $m \times m$ identity matrix.

It can be seen that $C(\vec{x}, \vec{w}) = \vec{y}$ if and only if

$$
(\mathbf{A} \cdot \vec{z}) \circ (\mathbf{B} \cdot \vec{z}) = \mathbf{C} \cdot \vec{z}
$$

where the vector $\vec{z}$ is defined as above, that is, $(1, \vec{x}, \vec{w})$. The above equation is what in the literature is called a rank-1 constraint system (R1CS).

To finalize the proof of the theorem, we show how to convert the quadratic systems of the equation above in polynomial form by using interpolation.

– choose n distinct points of $\mathbb{F}$ to build a subset $\mathbb{H} := \{h_1, \ldots, h_n\} \subset \mathbb{F}$;

– compute $v(X) := \prod_{i \in [n]} (X - h_i)$, which is the degree-$n$ polynomial that vanishes on $\mathbb{H}$, that is, $\forall h \in \mathbb{H} : v(h) = 0$;

– for any $j \in [m]$, build $a_j(X)$ (respectively, $b_j(X), c_j(X)$) as the unique degree-$(n-1)$ polynomial such that $\forall i \in [n], a_j(h_i) = A_{i,j}$ (respectively, $b_j(h_i) = B_{i,j}, c_j(h_i) = C_{i,j}$).

We leave it as an exercise to verify that, with this construction of the polynomials $\{a_j(X), b_j(X), c_j(X)\}_{j=1}^m$ and $v(X)$, we have

$$
(\mathbf{A} \cdot \vec{z}) \circ (\mathbf{B} \cdot \vec{z}) = \mathbf{C} \cdot \vec{z}
$$

if and only if

$$\left(\sum_{j\in[m]} z_j \cdot a_j(X)\right) \cdot \left(\sum_{j\in[m]} z_j \cdot b_j(X)\right) = \left(\sum_{j\in[m]} z_j \cdot c_j(X)\right) \bmod v(X)$$

$\square$

11.6.3. *Algebraic NILP for QAPs*

Let $R_{QAP} := (\mathbb{F}, n, m, \ell, v(X), \vec{a}(X), \vec{b}(X), \vec{c}(X))$ be a QAP relation as in definition 11.8. Below we describe a $(n, 2)$-algebraic NILP for R_{QAP} over $\mathbb{F}$.

This NILP abstracts away the Pinocchio SNARG construction of Parno et al. (2013). This is not by now the most efficient NILP (and SNARG); for instance, the celebrated Groth16 scheme (Groth 2016) is much more optimized and nearly optimal in proof size. Nevertheless, the techniques behind Parno et al. (2013) lead to a NILP which has more intuition, and we therefore prefer this construction for presentation reasons.

We give first a full description of the algebraic NILP, and then an intuitive explanation of it.

– $\mathcal{Q}_{\mathsf{NILP}}(R_{QAP}) \to \vec{q}$: The algorithm $\mathcal{Q}_{\mathsf{NILP}}^{poly}(R_{QAP})$ generates the following vector $\vec{p}(X, T_a, T_b, T_a', T_b', T_c', U, Y)$ of 8-variate polynomials:

$$\left|(a_j(X)T_a)_{j=1}^m\left|(b_j(X)T_b)_{j=1}^m\left|(c_j(X)T_aT_b)_{j=1}^m\right|\cdots\right.\right.$$

$$\cdots\left|(a_j(X)T_aT_a')_{j=\ell+1}^m\left|(b_j(X)T_bT_b')_{j=\ell+1}^m\left|(c_j(X)T_aT_bT_c')_{j=\ell+1}^m\right|\cdots\right.\right.$$

$$\cdots\left|(U(a_j(X)T_a + b_j(X)T_b + c_j(X)T_aT_b))_{j=\ell+1}^m\left|(X^i)_{i=0}^{n-2}\right|\cdots\right.$$

$$\cdots\left|v(X)T_aT_b\left|T_a'\right|T_b'\left|T_c'\right|Y\left|UY\right.\right.$$

Second, sample $s, t_a, t_b, t_a', t_b', t_c', u, y \leftarrow_\$ \mathbb{F}$ and return the query vector $\vec{q} = \vec{p}(s, t_a, t_b, t_a', t_b', t_c', u, y)$.

– $\mathcal{P}_{\mathsf{NILP}}(R_{QAP}, \vec{x}, \vec{w}) \to \mathbf{\Pi}$: Set $\vec{z} := (1, \vec{x}^\top, \vec{w}^\top) \in \mathbb{F}^{1\times m}$ and compute

$$h(X) := \sum_{i=0}^{n-2} h_i \cdot X^i := \frac{\left(\vec{z}^\top \cdot \vec{a}(X)\right) \cdot \left(\vec{z}^\top \cdot \vec{b}(X)\right) - \left(\vec{z}^\top \cdot \vec{c}(X)\right)}{v(X)}$$

By letting $\vec{h}$ be the coefficients vector $(h_i)_{i=0}^{n-2}$ of $h(X)$, the proof matrix $\mathbf{\Pi} \in \mathbb{F}^{8 \times (7m+n-4\ell+1)}$ is built as follows:

$$
\mathbf{\Pi} = \begin{pmatrix}
(\vec{0}_{\ell+1}^{\mathsf{T}}, \vec{w}^{\mathsf{T}}) & & & & & & & \\
 & (\vec{0}_{\ell+1}^{\mathsf{T}}, \vec{w}^{\mathsf{T}}) & & & (0,0)\mathbf{0} & & & \\
 & & (\vec{0}_{\ell+1}^{\mathsf{T}}, \vec{w}^{\mathsf{T}}) & & & & & \\
 & & & \vec{w}^{\mathsf{T}} & & & & \\
 & (0,0)\mathbf{0} & & & \vec{w}^{\mathsf{T}} & & & \\
 & & & & & \vec{w}^{\mathsf{T}} & & \\
 & & & & & & \vec{w}^{\mathsf{T}} & \\
 & & & & & & & (\vec{h}^{\mathsf{T}}, \vec{0}_6^{\mathsf{T}})
\end{pmatrix}
$$

$- \mathcal{D}_{\mathsf{NILP}}(\vec{q}, \vec{x}, \vec{\pi}) \rightarrow 0, 1$: We define the algorithm Test that outputs five quadratic polynomials $t_1, \ldots, t_5$. By defining $\vec{x}' = (1, \vec{x})$ and parsing $\vec{\pi} := (\alpha, \beta, \gamma, \alpha', \beta', \gamma', \delta, \eta)$, the polynomials $t_1, \ldots, t_5$ are such that:

$$
t_1(\vec{q}, \vec{\pi}) = \left(\sum_{j=1}^{\ell} x_j' \cdot a_j(s) t_a + \alpha\right) \cdot \left(\sum_{j=1}^{\ell} x_j' \cdot b_j(s) t_b + \beta\right) -
$$

$$
\left(\sum_{j=1}^{\ell} x_j' \cdot c_j(s) t_a t_b + \gamma\right) - \eta \cdot v(s) t_a t_b
$$

$$
t_2(\vec{q}, \vec{\pi}) = \alpha \cdot t_a' - \alpha'
$$

$$
t_3(\vec{q}, \vec{\pi}) = \beta \cdot t_b' - \beta'
$$

$$
t_4(\vec{q}, \vec{\pi}) = \gamma \cdot t_c' - \gamma'
$$

$$
t_5(\vec{q}, \vec{\pi}) = (\alpha + \beta + \gamma) \cdot (u \cdot y) - \delta \cdot y
$$

INTUITION. By the construction of the query polynomials $\vec{p}(\vec{X})$ and the proof matrix $\mathbf{\Pi}$, we have that a honest proof answer $\vec{\pi} := (\alpha, \beta, \gamma, \alpha', \beta', \gamma', \delta, \eta)$ is such that

$$
\alpha = \sum_{j=\ell+1}^{m} z_j a_j(s) t_a, \quad \beta = \sum_{j=\ell+1}^{m} z_j b_j(s) t_b, \quad \gamma = \sum_{j=\ell+1}^{m} z_j c_j(s) t_a t_b
$$

$$
\alpha' = \sum_{j=\ell+1}^{m} z_j a_j(s) t_a t_a', \quad \beta' = \sum_{j=\ell+1}^{m} z_j b_j(s) t_b t_b', \quad \gamma' = \sum_{j=\ell+1}^{m} z_j c_j(s) t_a t_b t_c'
$$

$$\delta = \sum_{j=\ell+1}^{m} z_j(a_j(s)t_a + b_j(s)t_b + c_j(s)t_at_b)u, \quad \eta = \sum_{i=0} h_i s^i$$

The goal of the five polynomial tests is to ensure that even a proof answer $(\alpha, \beta, \gamma, \alpha', \beta', \gamma', \delta, \eta)$ obtained from an arbitrary linear function of the query vector has exactly the form shown above.

Intuitively, the goal of the polynomials t_2, t_3, t_4 is to ensure that the first three answers (α, β, γ) are in the span of the elements $(a_j(X)T_a)_{j=\ell+1}^m$, $(b_j(X)T_b)_{j=\ell+1}^m$ and $(c_j(X)T_aT_b)_{j=\ell+1}^m$, respectively. This is why the query includes the three sets of polynomials that are defined by multiplying the first three sets of polynomials with fresh indeterminates T'_a, T'_b and T'_c, respectively. More precisely, these fresh indeterminates are applied only to the entries with indices $j = \ell + 1, \ldots, m$; this prevents an adversary from putting non-zero values in the wrong place in the first three rows.

The last polynomial t_5 is used to ensure that (α, β, γ) are obtained by using the same linear combination. For this reason, the query includes the set of polynomials $(U(a_j(X)T_a + b_j(X)T_b + c_j(X)T_aT_b))_{j=\ell+1}^m$.

Finally, the first polynomial t_1 checks the divisibility condition of the QAP. To this end, the verifier first "completes" the prover answers with the linear combinations of the public elements $(1, \vec{x})$. By the conditions enforced by the other four polynomial tests, we have that the QAP divisibility check is indeed applied on $a(X)b(X) - c(X)$ where each polynomial $a(X), b(X), c(X)$ is obtained by applying the *same* linear combination $\vec{z}$ over the corresponding vector of polynomials $\vec{a}(X), \vec{b}(X), \vec{c}(X)$, respectively.

THEOREM 11.4.– *The algebraic NILP described above is complete and sound.*

Proof. Completeness is obvious by construction, so its proof is omitted. To prove soundness, we proceed as follows.

Let us fix a QAP relation $R_{QAP} = (\mathbb{F}, n, m, \ell, v(X), \vec{a}(X), \vec{b}(X), \vec{c}(X))$ and a vector $\vec{x} \notin \mathcal{L}_{R_{QAP}}$, and let the matrix $\mathbf{\Pi}^*$ be any prover strategy. Let $\vec{p}(X, T_a, T_b, T'_a, T'_b, T'_c, U, Y)$ be the vector of polynomials built by $\mathcal{Q}_{NILP}(R_{QAP})$. For compactness, let us denote $\vec{X} := (X, T_a, T_b, T'_a, T'_b, T'_c, U, Y)$.

For convenience, we denote by

$$\vec{\Pi}^*_\alpha, \vec{\Pi}^*_\beta, \vec{\Pi}^*_\gamma, \vec{\Pi}^*_{\alpha'}, \vec{\Pi}^*_{\beta'}, \vec{\Pi}^*_{\gamma'}, \vec{\Pi}^*_\delta, \vec{\Pi}^*_\eta \in \mathbb{F}^{1 \times (7m+n-4\ell+1)}$$

the rows of $\mathbf{\Pi}^*$.

Also, for $\chi = \alpha, \beta, \gamma, \alpha', \beta', \gamma', \eta, \delta$, we parse each row $\vec{\Pi}_{\chi}^{*}$ as the concatenation of the following blocks:

$$(\vec{\Pi}_{\chi,a}^{*}, \vec{\Pi}_{\chi,b}^{*}, \vec{\Pi}_{\chi,c}^{*}, \vec{\Pi}_{\chi,a'}^{*}, \vec{\Pi}_{\chi,b'}^{*}, \vec{\Pi}_{\chi,c'}^{*}, \vec{\Pi}_{\chi,d}^{*}, \vec{\Pi}_{\chi,\eta}^{*}, \Pi_{\chi,v}^{*},$$
$$\Pi_{\chi,T_a'}^{*}, \Pi_{\chi,T_b'}^{*}, \Pi_{\chi,T_c'}^{*}, \Pi_{\chi,Y}^{*}, \Pi_{\chi,UY}^{*})$$

For $i = 1, \ldots, 5$, we define $\tau_i(\vec{X}) := t_i(\vec{p}(\vec{X}), \mathbf{\Pi}^{*} \cdot \vec{p}(X, T_a, T_b, T_c))$. By construction of each t_i, we have:

$$\tau_1(\vec{X}) = \left(\sum_{j=1}^{\ell} x_j' \cdot a_j(X) + \vec{\Pi}_{\alpha}^{*} \cdot \vec{p}(\vec{X}) \right) \cdot \left(\sum_{j=1}^{\ell} x_j' \cdot b_j(X) + \vec{\Pi}_{\beta}^{*} \cdot \vec{p}(\vec{X}) \right)$$

$$- \sum_{j=1}^{\ell} x_j' \cdot c_j(X) + (\vec{\Pi}_{\gamma}^{*} - \vec{\Pi}_{\eta}^{*} \cdot v(X)) \cdot \vec{p}(\vec{X})$$

$$\tau_2(\vec{X}) = (\vec{\Pi}_{\alpha}^{*} \cdot T_a' - \vec{\Pi}_{\alpha'}^{*}) \cdot \vec{p}(\vec{X})$$

$$\tau_3(\vec{X}) = (\vec{\Pi}_{\beta}^{*} \cdot T_a' - \vec{\Pi}_{\beta'}^{*}) \cdot \vec{p}(\vec{X})$$

$$\tau_4(\vec{X}) = (\vec{\Pi}_{\gamma}^{*} \cdot T_a' - \vec{\Pi}_{\gamma'}^{*}) \cdot \vec{p}(\vec{X})$$

$$\tau_5(\vec{X}) = ((\vec{\Pi}_{\alpha}^{*} + \vec{\Pi}_{\beta}^{*} + \vec{\Pi}_{\gamma}^{*}) \cdot UY - \vec{\Pi}_{\delta}^{*} \cdot Y) \cdot \vec{p}(\vec{X})$$

To prove soundness, we need to argue that at least one of $\{\tau_i(\vec{X})\}_{i=1}^{5}$ is a non-zero polynomial.

Let us assume by contradiction that they are all zero. We show how to reach a contradiction, namely that in such a case it must hold $\vec{x} \in \mathcal{L}_{R_{QAP}}$.

First, notice that $\tau_2(\vec{X}) = 0$ means

$$\vec{\Pi}_{\alpha}^{*} \cdot \vec{p}(\vec{X}) \cdot T_a' = \vec{\Pi}_{\alpha'}^{*} \cdot \vec{p}(\vec{X})$$

Since in $\vec{p}(\vec{X})$ the variable T_a' appears only in the terms $(a_j(X)T_a T_a')_{j=\ell+1}^{m}$ and T_a', it must be

$$\vec{\Pi}_{\alpha}^{*} \cdot \vec{p}(\vec{X}) = \vec{\Pi}_{\alpha,a}^{*} \cdot \vec{a}'(X)T_a + \Pi_{\alpha,T_a'}^{*} \cdot T_a'. \qquad [11.1]$$

Namely, all the blocks except $\vec{\Pi}^*_{\chi,a}, \Pi^*_{\chi,T'_a}$ are 0. By an analogous reasoning on $\tau_3(\vec{X}) = 0$ and $\tau_4(\vec{X}) = 0$, we obtain:

$$\vec{\Pi}^*_\beta \cdot \vec{p}(\vec{X}) = \vec{\Pi}^*_{\beta,b} \cdot \vec{b}'(X)T_b + \Pi^*_{\beta,T'_b} \cdot T'_b \qquad [11.2]$$

$$\vec{\Pi}^*_\gamma \cdot \vec{p}(\vec{X}) = \vec{\Pi}^*_{\gamma,c} \cdot \vec{c}'(X)T_aT_b + \Pi^*_{\gamma,T'_c} \cdot T'_c. \qquad [11.3]$$

Second, notice that $\tau_5(\vec{X}) = 0$ means

$$\vec{\Pi}^*_\delta \cdot \vec{p}(\vec{X}) \cdot Y = (\vec{\Pi}^*_\alpha + \vec{\Pi}^*_\beta + \vec{\Pi}^*_\gamma) \cdot \vec{p}(\vec{X}) \cdot UY$$

$$= \vec{\Pi}^*_{\alpha,a} \cdot \vec{a}'(X)T_aUY + \vec{\Pi}^*_{\beta,b} \cdot \vec{b}'(X)T_bUY + \vec{\Pi}^*_{\gamma,c} \cdot \vec{c}'(X)T_aT_bUY$$

$$+ \Pi^*_{\alpha,T'_a} \cdot T'_aUY + \Pi^*_{\beta,T'_b} \cdot T'_bUY + \Pi^*_{\gamma,T'_c} \cdot T'_cUY$$

where the second equation is obtained by applying equations [11.1]–[11.3].

Note that by construction of $\vec{p}(\vec{X})$, $\vec{\Pi}^*_\delta \cdot \vec{p}(\vec{X}) \cdot Y$ has no term with UT'_a (respectively, UT'_b, UT'_c). Therefore, we obtain that $\Pi^*_{\alpha,T'_a}, \Pi^*_{\beta,T'_b}, \Pi^*_{\gamma,T'_c} = 0$.

Next, since on the right-hand-side UY appears in all the terms, we obtain that the vector $\vec{\Pi}^*_\delta$ is zero everywhere except in the block $\vec{\Pi}^*_{\delta,\delta}$. Hence, we have

$$\vec{\Pi}^*_{\delta,\delta} \cdot (\vec{a}'(X)T_a + \vec{b}'(X)T_b + \vec{c}'(X)T_aT_b)UY$$

$$= (\vec{\Pi}^*_{\alpha,a} \cdot \vec{a}'(X)T_a + \vec{\Pi}^*_{\beta,b} \cdot \vec{b}'(X)T_b + \vec{\Pi}^*_{\gamma,c} \cdot \vec{c}'(X)T_aT_b)UY$$

and by the linear independence of T_a, T_b and T_aT_b we get that

$$\vec{\Pi}^*_{\alpha,a} = \vec{\Pi}^*_{\beta,b} = \vec{\Pi}^*_{\gamma,c} = \vec{\Pi}^*_{\delta,\delta}$$

Let us rename $\vec{w}^* := \vec{\Pi}^*_{\delta,\delta}$ and define $\vec{z}^* := (\vec{x}', \vec{w}^*)$.

Finally, $\tau_1(\vec{X}) = 0$ means

$$\left(\sum_{j=1}^\ell x'_j \cdot a_j(X)T_a + \vec{w}^* \cdot \vec{a}'(\vec{X})T_a\right) \cdot \left(\sum_{j=1}^\ell x'_j \cdot b_j(X)T_b + \vec{w}^* \cdot \vec{b}'(\vec{X})T_b\right)$$

$$- \sum_{j=1}^\ell x'_j \cdot c_j(X)T_aT_b + \vec{w}^* \cdot \vec{c}'(X)T_aT_b = \vec{\Pi}^*_\eta \cdot \vec{p}(\vec{X}) \cdot v(X)T_aT_b$$

$$T_aT_b\left((\vec{z}^* \cdot \vec{a}(X)) \cdot (\vec{z}^* \cdot \vec{b}(X)) - \vec{z}^* \cdot \vec{c}(X)\right) = T_aT_b \cdot \vec{\Pi}^*_\eta \cdot \vec{p}(\vec{X}) \cdot v(X)$$

Notice that on the left-hand-side of the equation we have a polynomial in which all terms have $T_a T_b$. From this, we get that the vector $\vec{\Pi}_\eta^*$ is zero everywhere except in the block $\vec{\Pi}_{\eta,\eta}^*$. Namely, $\vec{\Pi}_\eta^* \cdot \vec{p}(\vec{X}) = h^*(X)$ for a polynomial h^* of degree $\leq n - 2$. The existence of such polynomial $h^*(X)$ eventually shows that the QAP relation is satisfied for $\vec{x}$, which is a contradiction. $\square$

11.7. Conclusion

In this chapter, we presented the notion of VC, including its definition and a construction approach based on succinct non-interactive arguments for arithmetic circuit satisfiability. We would like to note that our presentation and construction of SNARGs is limited to the basic properties that are sufficient for its use for VC. We choose to do so to keep the presentation lighter and focused on the main goal: building proofs that are secure and efficient to verify.

In particular, among the properties of SNARGs that we neglected there are two which have theoretical and practical relevance. We briefly mention them.

The first property is *knowledge-soundness*. This is a strengthening of soundness that guarantees that the prover producing an accepting proof must also know a witness, which is more than just asking that the witness exists. SNARGs with knowledge-soundness are called SNARKs. One motivation of knowledge soundness is rather cryptographic: it eases the security analysis of larger cryptographic protocols using SNARKs. Another motivation is practical: in some cases (e.g. showing the preimage of a hash function), the statements may be always true; hence it is not enough proving that a witness exists but one would also ensure that the prover knows it.

The second property is *zero-knowledge* (Goldwasser et al. 1985), which in a nutshell guarantees that proofs reveal no information about the non-deterministic witness. Zero-knowledge is a very powerful property with countless applications, in both the cryptographic realm and directly in practical systems. Zero-knowledge enables applications that may be otherwise impossible, and this often gives a justification to accept the currently high computational costs of SNARK implementations.

11.8. References

Arora, S. and Safra, S. (1992). Probabilistic checking of proofs: A new characterization of NP. In *33rd FOCS*. IEEE Computer Society Press, 24–27 October.

Bitansky, N., Chiesa, A., Ishai, Y., Ostrovsky, R., Paneth, O. (2013). Succinct non-interactive arguments via linear interactive proofs. In *TCC 2013*, vol. 7785 of *LNCS*, Sahai, A. (ed.). Springer, Heidelberg.

Catalano, D. and Fiore, D. (2013). Vector commitments and their applications. In *PKC 2013*, vol. 7778 of *LNCS*, Kurosawa, K., Hanaoka, G. (eds). Springer, Heidelberg.

Escala, A., Herold, G., Kiltz, E., Ràfols, C., Villar, J. (2013). An algebraic framework for Diffie–Hellman assumptions. In *CRYPTO 2013, Part II*, vol. 8043 of *LNCS*, Canetti, R., Garay, J.A. (eds). Springer, Heidelberg.

Fuchsbauer, G., Kiltz, E., Loss, J. (2018). The algebraic group model and its applications. In *CRYPTO 2018, Part II*, vol. 10992 of *LNCS*, Shacham, H., Boldyreva, A. (eds). Springer, Heidelberg.

Gennaro, R., Gentry, C., Parno, B. (2010). Non-interactive verifiable computing: Outsourcing computation to untrusted workers. In *CRYPTO 2010*, vol. 6223 of *LNCS*, Rabin, T. (ed.). Springer, Heidelberg.

Gennaro, R., Gentry, C., Parno, B., Raykova, M. (2013). Quadratic span programs and succinct NIZKs without PCPs. In *EUROCRYPT 2013*, vol. 7881 of *LNCS*, Johansson, T., Nguyen, P.Q. (eds). Springer, Heidelberg.

Gentry, C. (2009). Fully homomorphic encryption using ideal lattices. In *41st ACM STOC*, Mitzenmacher, M. (ed.). ACM Press.

Gentry, C. and Wichs, D. (2011). Separating succinct non-interactive arguments from all falsifiable assumptions. In *43rd ACM STOC*, Fortnow, L., Vadhan, S.P. (eds). ACM Press.

Goldwasser, S., Micali, S., Rackoff, C. (1985). The knowledge complexity of interactive proof-systems (extended abstract). In *17th ACM STOC*, Sedgewick, R. (ed.). ACM Press.

Goldwasser, S., Kalai, Y.T., Rothblum, G.N. (2008). Delegating computation: Interactive proofs for muggles. In *40th ACM STOC*, Ladner, R.E., Dwork, C. (eds). ACM Press.

Groth, J. (2016). On the size of pairing-based non-interactive arguments. In *EUROCRYPT 2016, Part II*, vol. 9666 of *LNCS*, Fischlin, M., Coron, J.-S. (eds). Springer, Heidelberg.

Kilian, J. (1992). A note on efficient zero-knowledge proofs and arguments (extended abstract). In *24th ACM STOC*, Kosaraju, R., Fellows, M., Wigderson, A., Ellis, J. (eds). ACM Press.

Lai, R.W.F. and Malavolta, G. (2019). Subvector commitments with application to succinct arguments. In *CRYPTO 2019, Part I*, vol. 11692 of *LNCS*, Boldyreva, A., Micciancio, D. (eds). Springer, Heidelberg.

Lipmaa, H. (2012). Progression-free sets and sublinear pairing-based non-interactive zero-knowledge arguments. In *TCC 2012*, vol. 7194 of *LNCS*, Cramer, R. (ed.). Springer, Heidelberg.

Lund, C., Fortnow, L., Karloff, H.J., Nisan, N. (1990). Algebraic methods for interactive proof systems. In *31st FOCS*. IEEE Computer Society Press, 22–24 October.

Micali, S. (1994). CS proofs (extended abstracts). In *35th FOCS*. IEEE Computer Society Press, 20–22 November.

Parno, B., Raykova, M., Vaikuntanathan, V. (2012). How to delegate and verify in public: Verifiable computation from attribute-based encryption. In *TCC 2012*, vol. 7194 of *LNCS*, Cramer, R. (ed.). Springer, Heidelberg.

Parno, B., Howell, J., Gentry, C., Raykova, M. (2013). Pinocchio: Nearly practical verifiable computation. In *2013 IEEE Symposium on Security and Privacy.* IEEE Computer Society Press, 19–22 May.

Schwartz, J.T. (1980). Fast probabilistic algorithms for verification of polynomial identities. *Journal of the ACM*, 27, 701–717.

Shamir, A. (1990). IP=PSPACE. In *31st FOCS.* IEEE Computer Society Press, 22–24 October.

Shoup, V. (1997). Lower bounds for discrete logarithms and related problems. In *EUROCRYPT'97*, vol. 1233 of *LNCS*, Fumy, W. (ed.). Springer, Heidelberg.

Yao, A.C.-C. (1982). Protocols for secure computations (extended abstract). In *23rd FOCS.* IEEE Computer Society Press, November.

Zippel, R. (1979). Probabilistic algorithms for sparse polynomials. In *EUROSM '79*, vol. 72 of *Lecture Notes in Computer Science*, Ng, E.W. (ed.). Springer.

List of Authors

Nuttapong ATTRAPADUNG
National Institute of Advanced Industrial
Science and Technology (AIST)
Tokyo
Japan

Olivier BLAZY
Ecole Polytechnique
Palaiseau
France

Colin BOYD
NTNU
Trondheim
Norway

Dario FIORE
IMDEA Software Institute
Madrid
Spain

Marc FISCHLIN
Technische Universität Darmstadt
Germany

Romain GAY
IBM Research Zurich
Switzerland

Duong HIEU PHAN
Telecom Paris –
Institut Polytechnique de
Paris
France

Stanislaw JARECKI
University of California
Irvine
United States

Yehuda LINDELL
Coinbase
San Francisco
United States

Takahiro MATSUDA
National Institute of Advanced Industrial
Science and Technology (AIST)
Tokyo
Japan

David POINTCHEVAL
CNRS, ENS/PSL, Inria
Paris
France

Olivier SANDERS
Orange Labs
Rennes
France

Ivan VISCONTI
University of Salerno
Italy

Index

A

anonymous credentials, 173–175,
177–179, 183
arithmetic circuit, 258, 261, 262, 266,
271, 272
asymmetric PAKE, 214, 233,
242–244
attribute-based encryption (ABE),
151, 156

B

bilinear groups, 108, 113, 115, 262,
265, 267–269
black-box tracing, 124, 126, 127, 137
broadcast encryption, 121–125, 143

C

chosen-ciphertext attacks (CCA), 1,
4, 5
chosen-plaintext attacks (CPA), 2
collusion-secure codes, 127, 132
correctness, 86–89
corruption, 90
Cramer–Shoup, 1, 8, 11, 12, 14, 15, 21

D, E

Diffie–Hellman, 192, 193
direct anonymous attestations (DAA),
180
ECDSA, 49, 50, 55, 58, 59
elliptic curves, 107, 108, 110
encrypted key exchange (EKE), 215,
216
encryption, 1–3, 6–8, 11, 15–19,
21–24, 27–30
EPID (enhanced privacy ID), 180,
183

F, G

fairness, 88, 89, 93
Fiat–Shamir, 76
fingerprinting codes, 134, 135
forward secrecy, 197–199, 205
group signatures, 176–180, 183

H, I

HMQV, 204–206

honest
  -majority, 95, 100
  -verifier, 72
identifiable parent property (IPP), 132
identity-based encryption (IBE), 152,
  154
indistinguishability (IND), 1, 2, 4, 5,
  24, 29, 30

K, M

key
  agreement, 188
  derivation function (KDF), 188,
    189
  exchange (*see also* NIKE), 187
monotone span program, 154, 155
multiparty computation, 85

N

NAXOS, 203, 204
non-interactive key exchange
  (NIKE), 189, 195
non-malleability, 4, 5, 25
NP language, 64, 67, 70, 73

P, R

pairing, 107–111, 113, 115, 116, 151,
  152, 164
password, 213, 214, 216, 217, 221,
  222, 229, 239, 243
perfect forward secrecy (PFS), 220
predicate encodings, 152–154, 158,
  164
privacy, 85–87, 89, 93, 101, 102
private set intersection, 87, 97, 98
proof system, 63–68, 70–72, 75, 76, 79
random oracle model, 4, 16
revocation, 122–127, 129, 132, 137,
  140

S

Schnorr, 50, 51, 54–56, 58
security, 1, 2, 4, 5, 7, 9, 15, 16, 25,
  26, 28, 30
semi-honest, 90, 95, 97, 98
signature, 47–55, 57, 167, 168, 170,
  172, 176, 178, 182, 183
smooth projective hash function
  (SPHF), 237
soundness, 64, 65, 68, 69, 71, 74, 76,
  79, 263, 264, 267, 270, 276, 277
strong unforgeability, 47, 56, 58, 59
structure-preserving, 172
subset-cover, 125, 129
succinct non-interactive arguments
  (SNARG), 259, 263

T, U, V

tate pairing, 111, 112
traitor tracing, 121, 122, 135
unforgeability, 47, 48, 51, 52, 54,
  56–59
universal composability (UC), 229,
  232
verifiable computation (VC), 257,
  260, 264

W, Z

Weil pairing, 110, 111
witness indistinguishability, 73
zero-knowledge, 63, 64, 66–69, 72,
  78, 168–170, 172, 176, 178, 179,
  181, 183

Printed and bound by CPI Group (UK) Ltd, Croydon, CR0 4YY

27/10/2024

14580732-0005